D0197670

San Diego Christian College
2100 Greenfield Drive
El Cajon, CA 92019

POLITICAL VISIONS & ILLUSIONS

A Survey and Christian Critique of Contemporary Ideologies

DAVID T. KOYZIS

InterVarsity Press
Downers Grove, Illinois

InterVarsity Press
P.O. Box 1400, Downers Grove, IL 60515-1426
World Wide Web: www.ivpress.com
E-mail: mail@ivpress.com

InterVarsity Press® is the book-publishing division of InterVarsity Christian Fellowship/USA®, a student movement active on campus at hundreds of universities, colleges and schools of nursing in the United States of America, and a member movement of the International Fellowship of Evangelical Students. For information about local and regional activities, write Public Relations Dept., InterVarsity Christian Fellowship/USA, 6400 Schroeder Rd., P.O. Box 7895, Madison, WI 53707-7895, or visit the IVCF website at <www.ivcf.org>.

Scripture quotations, unless otherwise noted, are from the Revised Standard Version of the Bible, *copyright 1946, 1952, 1971 by the Division of Christian Education of the National Council of the Churches of Christ in the U.S.A., and are used by permission.*

Cover design: Kathleen Lay Burrows
Cover image: Roberta Polfus
ISBN 0-8308-2726-9
Printed in the United States of America ∞

Library of Congress Cataloging-in-Publication Data

Koyzis, David Theodore, 1955-
   Political visions & illusions: a survey and Christian critique of
comtemporary ideologies / David T. Koyzis.
      p. cm.
Includes bibliographical references and index.
   ISBN 0-8308-2726-9 (pbk.: alk. paper)
   1. Christianity and politics. 2. Ideology—Religious
aspects—Christianity. I. Title.
   BR115.P7K655 2003
   261.7—dc21

2002156377

P	19	18	17	16	15	14	13	12	11	10	9	8	7	6	5	4	3	2	1
Y	17	16	15	14	13	12	11	10	09	08	07	06	05	04	03				

CONTENTS

PREFACE

The distance between vision and illusion can sometimes be dishearteningly small. All of us strive to be as clear-seeing as possible, and we may even take pride in our ability to grasp and interpret the world as it really is. However, in our ongoing efforts to make sense of the world around us, we inevitably filter our observations through one or more worldviews. A worldview, or what the Germans call *Weltanschauung*, is not yet a theoretical model capable of being verified or falsified through ordinary methods of demonstration. It is, rather, a pretheoretical vision rooted in a basic religious commitment interacting with ordinary life experience.

But visions are capable of distortion, and when they become distorted we speak of them as illusions. An illusion gives us a false picture of the world, but its falsity is not always immediately obvious to everyone, particularly in the short term. In fact, an illusion may be so compelling as to persuade countless people of its claims to the full truth. Yet even an illusion is never altogether bereft of the truth, because of the givenness of the world that it sees. This suggests that we stand in need of some means, perhaps even a gift of God's grace, to enable us to sort out the complex relationship between these competing visions and illusions on the one hand, and the world to which they point on the other.

If it were simply a matter of testing the claim that, say, a thirty-five-year-old woman and an eight-year-old girl are walking across the street and turning into

a toy store, then all that is apparently needed are ordinary powers of observation. But it is when we try to make further sense of our common experience
that we may find our interpretations clashing. Are we seeing two solitary individuals engaging in a common enterprise through the mutual agreement of
their self-interested wills? Are we viewing two members of the bourgeoisie using the leisure afforded them by their dominant position in the capitalist system
of production to engage in a nonessential commercial transaction? Are we looking at two citizens of a state taking advantage of its protection to cross a busy
thoroughfare safely and enter a limited-liability business enterprise? Or are we
seeing a mother and a daughter bound together in an asymmetrical familial relationship characterized by mutual love and devotion? There is a sense in which
we are seeing perhaps all of these, since each of these interpretations gives us
insight into one facet of a fuller reality.

However, in accepting any one of these as an exhaustive account of reality,
we are not simply assenting to the evidence of our senses; we are in fact filtering
this through a worldview that, though to some extent shaped by our experience, itself shapes the way we interpret this experience. The implications for
politics are enormous: many of the battles in the political realm are shaped, not
simply by a refusal of one side or another to "face facts" or to "be reasonable,"
as one typically hears, but by differing views of reality rooted in alternative par-
adigms. In fact, however, as we shall see in this book, many of these different
views of politics, under whatever ideological label they may fall, find their origins in a single religious worldview that sees the cosmos as an essentially closed
system without reference to a creator/redeemer. In short, for all the apparent
conflict among the several ideologies, all are subspecies of the larger category
of idolatry, as I shall argue in chapter one.

I cannot claim to have originated this thesis. Others have argued for it in the
past, most notably the Dutch Christian economist Bob Goudzwaard in several
of his books, including *Capitalism and Progress* and *Idols of Our Time*.[1] At an early
stage in my own development, I was strongly impressed by Goudzwaard's isolation of the connection between ideology and idolatry. Upon reading *Idols of
Our Time*, I became convinced that this connection needed to be worked out
in greater detail with respect to the several ideologies themselves. Thus
Goudzwaard was and remains a formative influence on my own thought.

I am indebted to two more people who have had no small impact on my

---

[1]Bob Goudzwaard, *Idols of Our Time* (Downers Grove, Ill.: InterVarsity Press, 1984).

thinking. James W. Skillen has long been associated with the Center for Public Justice and its predecessor organization, the Association for Public Justice. Skillen can only be described as someone who has grown in wisdom and insight with each passing year. His writings display an uncommon measure of the very discernment I have striven to realize, if only in a small way, in the present book. From Skillen I have learned much, including, as far as the present book is concerned: the extent to which God remains faithful to his creation, even in the midst of our unbelief; and the degree to which all of the ideologies fall short in understanding the character of the state as a differentiated political institution with its own unique place in God's world. If our following after various ideological visions has distorting effects on our life in this world, it is nevertheless true that our world still belongs to God and, due to his conserving grace, the impact of sin remains limited. It is also true that, even where the adherents of various theoretical constructs attempt to reduce the state to something else, whether a voluntary association no different from the private club, a commercial enterprise similar to a business, or an all-encompassing focal point of a community's loyalty, pretheoretical experience is easily able to tell the difference between the political community and other communal structures such as the family. The state's task of doing justice, even when it is perverted in some fashion, tends inevitably to reassert itself. This again is due to God's conserving grace.

I owe much to my friend and colleague Albert M. Wolters, who, despite his possibly tongue-in-cheek claim to have little interest in politics per se, has helped me to understand the connection between the ideologies and the ancient gnostic heresy which locates the source of evil not in our rebellion against God and his word, but in something structural in his creation. By failing to distinguish creational structure from spiritual direction, the followers of these ideologies tend to assume that salvation is to be found in freeing humanity from some facet of God's creation and in putting one's ultimate trust in some other facet.

Many other people have been influential or have played a more direct role in my thinking. Among those I have found especially insightful are the following: Abraham Kuyper, the Dutch Christian statesman and polymath, whose reflections on politics and society were framed in response to the sweeping secularization of the nineteenth-century Netherlands; Herman Dooyeweerd, longtime professor of legal philosophy at the Free University of Amsterdam, whose Christian philosophy I have found enormously helpful in understanding the nature of politics and the state; Jean Bethke Elshtain of the University of Chicago, whose writings show an uncommon degree of good sense motivated by an effort to steer clear of various ideological agendas; Paul Marshall of Freedom House, Washington, D.C., and Mary Ann Glendon of Harvard University Law School, both of whose writings on human rights have demonstrated the complexities of rights claims in an age when rights are treated as the answer to every political controversy; Roy A. Clouser, whose *The Myth of Religious Neutrality*[2] and other writings have illuminated the character of the various types of religious belief and their respective understandings of God's world; the late Bernard Zylstra, my former mentor from the Institute for Christian Studies, Toronto, who introduced me to the writings of, inter alia, Hannah Arendt, Leo Strauss, George Grant and Eric Voegelin; Jacques Maritain, whose application of a Catholic neo-Thomist perspective across the broad range of human activities is impressive in its scope; Yves R. Simon, whose reflections on authority and its place in a democratic society continue to ring true decades after he first articulated them; David L. Schindler, whose Catholic Augustinian approach to an understanding of the ideologies is breathtakingly close to the vision for which I am arguing here; H. Richard Niebuhr, whose seminal reflections on the relationship between Christianity and culture have had an impact on so many thinkers in the past half century; Hannah Arendt, Sheldon S. Wolin and Bernard Crick, who understand that politics is simply politics, an irreplaceable, if non-utopian, way of permitting different and potentially conflicting interests to coexist peacefully; and George Grant and Christopher Lasch, a Canadian and an American respectively, who understand better than most that the contemporary ideological cleavage is not always what it appears to be and that the popular, bipolar left-right division in the contemporary political debate is simplistic at best and misleading at worst.

I should acknowledge as well the contributions of others who either read and commented on earlier drafts of this book or in other ways aided in its writing. These include, in addition to Skillen and Wolters, John Hiemstra (The King's University College, Edmonton, Alberta), Fred VanGeest (Dordt College, Sioux Center, Iowa), Anthony Wells (Deputy Correspondence Secretary for Rt. Hon. William Hague, former Leader of the Conservative Party of the United Kingdom), John Fawcett (Buswell Memorial Library, Wheaton College, Wheaton, Illinois), William G. Witt (Episcopal Church), Donald Leach (Wellesley College), Edward A. Goerner (University of Notre Dame), Elaine Botha, Robert MacLarkey, Harry Van Dyke, Jacob Ellens, Michael Goheen,

[2]Roy A. Clouser, *The Myth of Religious Neutrality* (Notre Dame, Ind.: University of Notre Dame Press, 1992).

Justin Cooper and other colleagues at Redeemer University College, John Bolt (Calvin Theological Seminary), Paul Brink (Eastern University, St. David's, Pennsylvania), Michael C. Hogeterp (Christian Reformed Church), Gary Miedema (Tyndale College, Toronto) and finally Douglas R. Johnson, a great friend and fellow undergraduate classmate, who introduced me to the writings of Kuyper and Dooyeweerd nearly three decades ago. Thanks are also due to Redeemer University College itself for providing funding to cover some of the incidental costs associated with the preparation of this book. All of these and more have contributed something to this project. Naturally I take full responsibility for any defects.

Finally, I wish to make a twofold dedication. First and foremost, this book is dedicated to the two great loves of my life, Nancy and Theresa, whose own love for their husband and father is greater than I could ever have imagined. When I began writing this book, I was a bachelor. At its completion I am the proverbial family man, an experience that has enriched my understanding of the issues under consideration here. Second, this is dedicated to my students, past, present and future, who have stimulated my thinking, have been unfailingly loyal and have been messengers of God's grace to me over the years.

Soli Deo gloria. To God alone be the glory.

1

INTRODUCTION

—

Ideology, Religion and Idolatry

W_e live in extraordinary times. Not long ago it seemed as if the world was locked in an eschatological standoff between two superpowers and their ideologies. During the forty years of the Cold War, both sides expended much energy in an attempt to win the hearts and minds of the world's peoples for either communism or liberal democracy. Although old-fashioned considerations of national interest were certainly involved in this protracted struggle, especially in its later years, the Cold War was unique in that it was based primarily on a clash of opposing *ideas*. If during this time people defected to the other side, such as Kim Philby or Arkady Shevchenko, they were not so much betraying the home country as demonstrating a belief in the ideas undergirding the other country's political and economic system. In this context the entire notion of loyalty to country took on a rather different color than it had in previous conflicts. To be sure, the Cold War was not the first ideological conflict, but it was probably the longest lasting.

Yet in the post-Cold War era—if that is what we might call it—we are experiencing an unprecedented shakeup in longstanding loyalties to such ideas that we may properly label *ideologies*. The most dramatic of these developments has been the collapse of communism, which occurred with astonishing rapidity in late 1989 in Eastern Europe and finally led to the dismemberment of the Soviet Union itself in late 1991. Although most of us on the outside were startled at this, those on the inside, especially Christians, seemed to understand that the Marxist-Leninist system would not last. Indeed, by the end it is fair to say that the ideology had been dead for some time, at least within the hearts of the people. In 1989 appearances simply caught up to the living realities of what people actually believed.

Scarcely less dramatic was the unexpectedly quick end to apartheid in South Africa orchestrated by F. W. de Klerk and Nelson Mandela. For decades Afrikaners[1] had believed—or had attempted to convince themselves—that the way to solve the problems of a plural society was to separate forcibly the various ethnic groups and to "allow" them to develop along their own lines under separate political institutions. Apartheid was further grounded in an ethnic nationalism that celebrated the greatness of Afrikanerdom, including its history, its language and even its particular brand of Reformed Christianity. By the time apartheid came to an end, even most white South Africans understood that it had been a destructive policy. Nothing less than a kind of nationalist faith had to die before apartheid could finally be abolished.

Somewhat less dramatically perhaps, we in the West are experiencing nagging doubts about our own ideologies, especially liberalism and democracy. Liberalism, as we shall see, is based on a belief in the primacy of the individual, and we seem now to be suffering the consequences of an untrammeled individualism in the form of a variety of intractable social ills. An emphasis on rights without the counteremphasis on responsibilities leaves us with precious little basis for genuine community, as we North Americans are learning to our great regret. Even democracy, which values community more highly than liberalism does, has degenerated into something approaching a pure majoritarianism allowing little genuine space for potentially dissenting communities and distrusting anything that might detract from loyalty to the democratic people. Democracy has become popular again, especially in the former communist countries. But there it is synonymous with the consumer-driven prosperity of such countries as Germany and the United States, and not with the public virtues needed to make a participatory political system work.

In Canada national unity is threatened by the clash of two mutually incom-

---

[1]Afrikaners are South Africans of Dutch, French Huguenot and German descent who trace their origins to the establishment by Jan van Riebeeck in 1652 of a trading post at the Cape of Good Hope for the Dutch East India Company. Their language, Afrikaans, is a derivative of Dutch.

patible ideologies, liberalism and nationalism. In English-speaking Canada the dominant ideology, as in its southern neighbor, is liberalism, with its abstract notion of the equality of all individual citizens. In French-speaking Canada, especially in the province of Quebec, nationalism is the dominant ideology. Under its influence most Québecois believe in the equality of the two founding nations, French and English. Given these two contrasting notions of equality, it is not surprising that recent attempts at constitutional reform have met with failure.

Ideologies, in short, are not about to come to an end in this post-Cold War world, despite occasional predictions to the contrary. After the struggle between communism and liberal democracy faded into history, other ideologies have moved in to fill the vacuum left by the collapse of communism, most notably ethnic nationalism and radical Islamism. Non-Leninist Marxism itself is often said to be in decline, except possibly in Western academia and in Latin America, where it has taken the form of liberation theology. But a cluster of postmodern ideologies have come into being based on similar premises, namely that one's concrete position in life, whether economic class, gender, or race, determines one's overall worldview. This has encouraged what has come to be variously labeled the politics of difference, the politics of recognition or identity politics.[2]

So what is an ideology? At this point I shall tip my hand and indicate that I view ideologies as modern types of that ancient phenomenon idolatry, complete with their own accounts of sin and redemption. From the beginning of its narrative, Scripture inveighs against the worship of idols, false gods that human beings have created. Like these biblical idolatries, every ideology is based on taking something out of creation's totality, raising it above that creation, and making the latter revolve around and serve it. It is further based on the assumption that this idol has the capacity to save us from some real or perceived evil in the world. This is a book about political ideologies; the ideologies we shall discuss here have to do with politics and its place within human life. To be sure, they touch other areas of life as well, but we shall largely limit our discussion to assessing their impact within the *state* or *political community*, which is *that community binding together citizens and their government for purposes of doing and maintaining justice.*

---

[2]See Jean Bethke Elshtain, *Democracy on Trial* (Toronto: Anansi, 1993), pp. 65-90; and Charles Taylor, *Philosophical Arguments* (Cambridge, Mass.: Harvard University Press, 1995), pp. 225-56.

Politics and Ideas

At various times it has become fashionable to claim that ideology is a thing of the past with no real relevance for the contemporary political scene. In 1960 Daniel Bell argued that after the Second World War, ideology had come to an end and had been replaced by a widespread consensus that the principal issues of the day were primarily technical in nature.[3] In a growing postwar economy, issues of distribution that had once fueled socialist movements and had polarized labor and management were being supplanted by the purely administrative concerns of a society increasingly seeing itself as wholly middle class. This supposed consensus was shattered in the United States a few years later by the failure of President Lyndon Johnson's domestic and foreign policies and by the emergence of the New Left.

Nevertheless, a generation later, with the Cold War fading into the past, Francis Fukuyama argued that history itself was ending. The temporal succession of days and years would continue, of course, but history in the Hegelian sense of an ongoing conflict of ideas was drawing to a close. In 1989 liberal democracy had scored an apparently final victory over the forces of Marxism-Leninism, which had once seemed so impregnable but finally collapsed with such remarkable speed and so little violence. With the nearly universal acceptance of "liberal democracy" in the wake of communism's demise, all that was left for humanity to do was to settle into a rather bland bourgeois existence in which sameness would replace diversity and thereby supplant the conflicts engendered by the latter.[4]

Much of this premature heralding of the death of ideology may stem from a certain measure of wishful thinking. It may also, as Bernard Crick correctly points out, flow from a certain hostility to the continuing give and take of politics, which in this present life knows no end.[5] There is some irony in this. The followers of ideologies often wish to impose their own simplistic conception of a monolithic social order on the complexities of a real society. But those ringing the death knell for ideology are themselves in the grip of a worldview through which they filter their perception of the political realm, though they are typically reluctant to label it an ideology as such. Bell and Fukuyama are not really harbingers of a new social order lacking ideological commitments; they are

---

[3]Daniel Bell, *The End of Ideology: On the Exhaustion of Political Ideas in the Fifties* (New York: Free Press, 1960), esp. pp. 393-407.

[4]Francis Fukuyama, *The End of History and the Last Man* (New York: Free Press, 1992).

[5]Bernard Crick, *In Defence of Politics* (Harmondsworth, U.K.: Penguin, 1993).

simply forecasting the triumph of their own pet ideology, which for both is some combination of liberalism and democracy, augmented by the technocratic guidance of social scientists. At the dawn of a new century, however, it should be obvious that ideology per se is not on its way out, though specific ideologies may have lost their attraction.

This underscores the need to define ideology as a concept before we can proceed to explore its particular manifestations. Like politics itself, *reflection* about politics has an ancient pedigree, going back to at least Plato and Aristotle. Often this reflection has taken the form of describing in empirical fashion the actual arrangement of political institutions or the activities of rulers and the ruled. Aristotle is perhaps the first empirical political scientist, and is reputed to have written extensively on the constitutions of one hundred fifty-eight cities and tribes, including Athens. But just as often political theorists have gone beyond the empirical and set forth what they believe to be the ideal or best political system. The most famous example of this is, of course, Plato's *Republic*. What we have come to call ideologies can perhaps be said to follow in the latter tradition.

History and Definitions

Despite ideology's roots in Plato's and Aristotle's philosophies, most accounts trace the origins of the concept itself to Antoine Destutt de Tracy (1754-1836), who coined the term at the beginning of the nineteenth century. For Destutt de Tracy *idéologie* is intended to be a comprehensive science of ideas whereby the scientific method can be applied to gain an understanding of the process of forming ideas. Following John Locke and Étienne Bonnot de Condillac, he believes that a scientific *idéologie* must be based on an analysis of the sensory elements of which ideas are composed. Any knowledge that cannot be immediately grounded in sensory experience must be rejected as having no scientific basis. Destutt de Tracy's *idéologie* is, therefore, intended to be rigorously empirical and excludes such phenomena as religious and mystical experiences, which are not strictly experiences at all because they are not rooted in sensation. Obviously *idéologie* is quite different from our contemporary ideology. But it should perhaps be noted that for Destutt de Tracy, scientific knowledge can be used to improve the conditions in which human beings live. Thus even this early form of ideology can already be said to imply action of some sort.

Others have defined *ideology* to imply inaction, or perhaps counteraction. Karl Marx (1818-1883) and Friedrich Engels (1820-1895) define *ideology* negatively, though some of their successors, notably Lenin, would recover a more positive use of the term. For Marx and Engels the animating force behind the historical process is the class struggle. At any particular historical stage, whether this be feudalism or capitalism, one class rules over another and uses the power at its disposal to keep the lower class under its control. Its ability to do so depends on keeping the latter quiet. In a capitalist society the continued rule of the bourgeoisie hinges on the proletariat being convinced that its oppressive conditions are something other than what they are. If industrial workers are denied the vote (as they generally were up to the end of the nineteenth century) and forced to work long hours under harsh conditions, it is because this is in accordance with the natural order of things. Perhaps it is even the will of God. In other words, the bourgeoisie must create and reinforce a "false consciousness" in the proletariat to prevent in them a true consciousness of the real reasons behind their oppression.

Marx and Engels label this false consciousness *ideology*, a phenomenon including politics, law, morality, religion and metaphysics.[6] Everyone is by now familiar with Marx's oft-quoted dictum that religion is the "opium of the people."[7] This does not mean, as some think, that the bourgeoisie has arbitrarily invented something called religion and imposed it on the proletariat. Rather, it arises out of the real miseries and aspirations of the oppressed. But like a narcotic, religion deadens pain and makes people passive in the face of oppression. It keeps them from taking action to change these conditions, and it even prevents them from recognizing them for what they are. Ideology includes virtually everything that exists in people's consciousness and it has come into being as a byproduct of class struggle. *Ideologists*, then, are guilty of turning the order around—of assuming that ideas have an independent existence and determine the real world of social and economic relations. What began as a positive, scientific enterprise in Destutt de Tracy has thus become in Marx and Engels a negative phenomenon based upon a false view of the real world. Since their time, then, it is not surprising that ideology has more often than not had a derogatory connotation, even for those opposed to Marxism.

A variation of this concept of ideology has been advanced by the German sociologist Karl Mannheim (1893-1947). Deeply influenced by Marx, Max Weber and German historicism, Mannheim distinguishes between ideology, a basically

---

[6]Karl Marx and Friedrich Engels, *The German Ideology* (1845), chaps. 1, 4-5.
[7]Karl Marx, "Introduction," in *Critique of Hegel's Rechtsphilosophie.*

conserving force, and utopia, a force for social change. Working out of what he labels a "sociology of knowledge," he argues that ideology consciously or unconsciously masks the concrete realities of a culture or era, or of an individual's life. In its particular form, ideology consists of "opinions, statements, propositions, and systems of ideas" which are not to be taken at face value but must instead be "interpreted in the light of the life-situation of the one who expresses them."[8] In its total form, ideology describes the Weltanschauung of a "concrete historico-social group" or of a particular historical epoch. In both cases, although ideology is a form of false consciousness, as in Marx, it is not necessarily rooted in class struggle but in a life-situation which includes factors other than economic. Ideology itself, however, is fundamentally psychological in nature and must be analyzed as such. It is usually not simply a pack of deliberate lies, but is a function of the social situation in which people find themselves.[9]

Utopia, by contrast, describes a state of mind that transcends the real world and conduces to behavior that tends to break the bonds of a prevailing order. Mannheim's utopia is not an ideal social arrangement that is unrealizable in an absolute sense, as the term tends to be used in popular discourse. It does not transcend all existing states of affairs; it transcends only a particular state of affairs. In this sense, the social conditions that utopians are striving to realize are relative and not absolute utopias. Like ideologies, utopias too are ways of thinking that are incongruent with a current status quo. But while ideologies do not strive to replace the latter with a new social order, utopias do just that. Ideologies are therefore conservative, while utopias are revolutionary, if only in a relative sense.[10]

For both Marx and Mannheim, then, ideologies are types of false consciousness which are used to justify an existing social order and which their proponents may or may not believe. They are nevertheless put forward as true accounts of reality, while they in fact function so as to hide that reality from the vast majority of people. By preventing them from seeing the world as it is, ideologies are thus deeply conservative and tend to militate against change. If we accept this account of ideology, then perhaps the "Myth of the Metals" in Plato's *Republic* falls into this category since it is a kind of "noble lie" used by the philosopher-kings to secure popular acceptance of their superior fitness to

---

[8]Karl Mannheim, *Ideology and Utopia: An Introduction to the Sociology of Knowledge* (New York: Harcourt, Brace, 1936), p. 56.
[9]Ibid., p. 61.
[10]Ibid., pp. 192-263.

rule. Similarly, in Walter Bagehot's nineteenth-century England, monarchical trappings conceal for most of the populace the fact that the prime minister and cabinet actually run the country. Thus the institution of the monarchy confers a legitimacy on the activities of the government, which the person of a mere practical politician would be unable to do.[11] In the United States it may perhaps be said that American civil religion, with its focus on the liberal ideals of the Declaration of Independence and the Constitution, is also an ideology in Marx's and Mannheim's sense.

But why ascribe to ideology a basically conservative role? Why differentiate between ideology and utopia? Cannot erroneous ways of thinking also be called into the service of new social and political projects? Hannah Arendt (1906-1975), Bernard Crick (1929-) and Václav Havel (1936-) clearly believe they can. According to Arendt, whenever a purely rational construct, conceived within the realm of thought, is imposed upon a community, it threatens to put an end to that action and speech necessary to constitute and maintain the free political realm. Ideologies attempt to offer a total explanation for the world and its history and thus "all ideologies contain totalitarian elements."[12] They read the whole of reality through a single idea and deny the possibility that any genuine knowledge can be attained through experience apart from that idea. In contemporary parlance, they exempt themselves from a "reality check." It is a short step from ideology to totalitarianism, which not only interprets the world through a single idea but also attempts to mold it in accordance with its inexorable logic. Hence ideologies such as Nazism and communism have caused much suffering in their attempt to control the supposedly autonomous historical forces they have ostensibly revealed.

Following Arendt, Crick too believes that ideology threatens the continued existence of politics in his specific sense. Here ideology is once again a force for change, but the change it effects is the extinction of legitimate societal diversity and of the ongoing conciliatory process flowing out of it. Ideological thinking "is an explicit and direct challenge to political thinking."[13] For Crick, as for Arendt, ideology is connected with totalitarianism. The latter is antipolitical because it attempts to eliminate different interests and to mold the people in accordance with a single idea. It tries to simplify the complexity of society into a monolithic vision, often of a utopian character. Politics is limited, while total-

---

[11]Walter Bagehot, *The English Constitution* (1867).
[12]Hannah Arendt, *The Origins of Totalitarianism* (New York: Harcourt Brace Jovanovich, 1973), p. 470.
[13]Crick, *In Defence of Politics,* p. 34.

itarianism is not. Politics is content to make do with the existing state of society and to conciliate whatever interests are currently there. Ideology attempts to remake, not only government, but "education, industry, art, even domesticity and private affections."[14] All of these are accountable to this all-embracing ideology, which, in trying to politicize society, ends up destroying politics altogether.

For Havel, ideology threatens not only politics but also the ordinary aims of life itself, as it continually did in his native Czechoslovakia from 1948 until the collapse of the communist regime in November 1989. "Ideology is a specious way of relating to the world."[15] In what he labels the "post-totalitarian" societies of the former Soviet bloc, ideology claims to offer the people a sense of identity and dignity while in reality stripping them of this. "It is a world of appearances trying to pass for reality."[16] It constructs a world which assimilates all people into a self-contained alternative pseudo-reality in which slavery passes for liberty, censorship for free expression, bureaucracy for democracy, and arbitrary power for legal authority. Under such a regime people are compelled to "live within a lie" in which they are made to deny the real aims of life, with all its humanity and unpredictability. In Havel we find ideology realizing its darkest potential.

Of the thinkers surveyed above, four use ideology in a largely pejorative sense. Marx, Arendt, Crick and Havel see it as something to avoid, though certainly for different reasons. For Marx it is an impediment to the coming of the new socialist society, but it is nevertheless destined to pass away once the latter has finally occurred. Ideology slows the pace of change by blinding people to the need for change. For Arendt, Crick and Havel, by contrast, ideology is a destructive force insofar as it attempts to transform societal diversity in accordance with a false, unitary conception of human life and history. For Mannheim, ideology is neither good nor bad in any ultimate sense; it simply exists. It does, however, play fundamentally the same conservative role it plays for Marx. Only in Destutt de Tracy does ideology take on an unequivocally positive character, but for him it means something other than what it does for later thinkers. Leaving him aside, the other five are united in seeing ideology as involving some sort of erroneous thinking or falsification of reality.

More recent observers have followed Mannheim's example and attempted to articulate a neutral conception of ideology. They have, furthermore, maintained

---

[14]Ibid., p. 40.
[15]Václav Havel, *Living in Truth* (London: Faber & Faber, 1986), p. 42.
[16]Ibid., p. 44.

a kind of agnosticism toward the truth or error of its contents. According to Isaac Kramnick and Frederick M. Watkins, ideologies are "patterns of politics, beliefs that introduce normative visions into political life."[17] Max J. Skidmore similarly sees ideology as "a form of thought that presents a pattern of complex political ideas simply and in a manner that inspires action to achieve certain goals."[18] David E. Ingersoll and Richard K. Matthews agree with this view of ideology as simplifying of reality and action-oriented, but they see it also as justifying both the action taken and the worldview on which such action is based.[19] Mark O. Dickerson and Thomas Flanagan add to these elements the observations that ideology is a social, and not merely personal, belief, and that its tenets are "more or less" logically coherent.[20] These are fairly typical definitions taken from standard textbooks in the field. All have to do with the interrelation between ideas and actions as applied to politics, and all attempt to take a more or less clinical, empirical approach to the concept.

Ideology in Christian Perspective

Christians are, of course, concerned with truth, both in absolute and relative senses. Truth is an attribute of God, and Jesus calls himself the way, the truth and the life (Jn 14:6). He further tells us that "you will know the truth, and the truth will make you free" (Jn 8:32). If Marx, Mannheim, Arendt, Crick and Havel are correct in asserting that ideologies represent fundamentally flawed conceptions of the world, then we Christians are obligated to take them seriously and to try to discern in exactly which ways they go wrong. But there is perhaps a paradox inherent in the present enterprise and its relation to truth. I take it as axiomatic that Christians seek the truth above all. I shall concur with the tradition that sees ideology as a type of false consciousness, and will argue further that it is rooted in the biblical category of idolatry. Nevertheless, I admit that I cannot "prove" the truth of this definition any more than the above figures can do so for theirs. Since I cannot do so, there is perhaps a danger of falling into a nominalism that holds that all definitions are arbitrary, or into a relativism that drains truth of any real meaning.

---

[17] Isaac Kramnick and Frederick M. Watkins, *The Age of Ideology: Political Thought, 1750 to the Present* (Englewood Cliffs, N.J.: Prentice-Hall, 1979), p. 2.

[18] Max J. Skidmore, *Ideologies: Politics in Action* (New York: Harcourt Brace Jovanovich, 1993), p. 7.

[19] David E. Ingersoll and Richard K. Matthews, *The Philosophic Roots of Modern Ideology: Liberalism, Communism, Fascism,* 2nd ed. (Englewood Cliffs, N.J.: Prentice-Hall, 1991), pp. 5-10.

[20] Mark O. Dickerson and Thomas Flanagan, *An Introduction to Government and Politics: A Conceptual Approach*, 6th ed. (Scarborough, Ontario: Nelson Thompson Learning, 2002), p. 128.

There may be no wholly satisfactory way out of this quandary. If not, then I am willing to live with it and hope the reader can do so too. But there may be at least two ways to diminish its significance. In the first place, as we have observed above, the notion of ideology as involving erroneous or distorted thinking has a long history extending at least back to Marx. Even now, labeling someone an "ideologue" is hardly a compliment and is close to being an outright insult. In this respect, my own definition does not radically depart from ordinary usage. In the second place, I believe a case can be made that those phenomena normally classified as ideologies do indeed originate in idolatrous religion. These include liberalism, conservatism, nationalism, ideological democracy and socialism, among others. Since these phenomena are almost universally labeled ideologies, then I believe there is some justification in drawing a connection between idolatry and ideology. To some readers this may seem an outrageous claim, but I ask them to bear with me as the argument of this book unfolds.

Preconditions for the Rise of Ideologies

In defining *ideology,* I shall assume that many, if not most, of the definitions recounted above are in large measure correct. Or at least they have fastened on to significant elements necessary to a full understanding of it. Therefore, my own comments below draw on them to a great extent, though I do hope to put them in a different light. To begin with, we need to ask why the ideologies arose when they did and what are the preconditions for their coming into existence.

First, we must be aware of the long tradition of political theorizing that stands in back of the ideologies, which can be said to recycle much of the material of these ancient theories. For example, it is sometimes thought that liberal individualism is an unprecedented philosophy that would have been unthinkable prior to the Enlightenment or perhaps the Renaissance. In its modern form this is certainly true. Yet if we look back to the post-Aristotelian philosophy of epicureanism, we are struck by the similarities between this philosophy and that of, say, Thomas Hobbes (1588-1679), who lived two millennia later. Individualism, as it turns out, is not so new after all. The modern ideologies have thus received much of their content from these older theories. The writer of Ecclesiastes tells us that there is nothing new under the sun. Not surprisingly, then, the inventors of an ideology rarely create *ex nihilo* its intellectual ingredients; they have simply recycled them from earlier ideologies and political theories.

Is there a difference, then, between political theory and ideology, as I seem to be implying thus far? Again, the distinction may seem arbitrary, but others

too have attempted to distinguish different modes of reflection on politics. Leo
Strauss (1899-1973), for example, distinguishes among several of these, including political philosophy and political theory. For him political philosophy is the
highest form of such reflection because it concerns itself with attaining knowledge of the good political order and of that which is right by nature. It aims to
replace opinion with genuine knowledge. Political theory, by contrast, is more
"praxis" oriented. It aims at translating reflection into policy, but it does not
question the fundamental assumptions underlying such reflection.[21] Insofar as
it wishes to put ideas into practice without necessarily testing their truth, ideology may perhaps be said to fall into the category of political theory in the
Straussian sense. For others, however, political theory, philosophy and ideology
are synonymous. For present purposes, I shall assume that ideology is a kind of
popularized form of normative political theory or philosophy.

The second precondition, somewhat ironically, is the preaching of the Christian gospel, as Bishop Lesslie Newbigin points out. Although the gospel stands
in implacable opposition to the various pseudo-gospels put forward by the ideologies, the announcement of the good news of Jesus Christ paves the way for
the possibility of false messiahs to promise another path to salvation.[22] Why? In
contrast to such religions as Hinduism, with their more static conceptions of reality, Christianity is a historical religion based on a succession of real events leading to humanity's redemption. The Bible is not simply a collection of ethereal
wisdom assisting the soul in its ascent to the divine. It is a record of actual oc-
currences whereby God has intervened in history to save his chosen people,
most notably by rescuing Noah from the deluge, calling Abraham into Canaan,
leading Moses and the Israelites out of Egypt and preserving a remnant through
exile in Babylonia. Finally and most significant, of course, God has revealed
himself in the birth, life, suffering, death, resurrection and ascension of Jesus
Christ for our salvation. We are furthermore assured in the Bible and in the
creeds of the church that Jesus will one day come again to inaugurate his eternal
kingdom and to make all things new. However, given the propensity to sin, once
people have come to expect salvation as a real historical possibility, they soon begin to look for it on other terms. Newbigin makes the intriguing observation
that the only places in India where Marxism has gained a foothold are precisely

---

[21]Leo Strauss, *What Is Political Philosophy? and Other Studies* (New York: Free Press, 1959), pp. 9-53, esp.
pp. 13, 27-40.
[22]Lesslie Newbigin, *The Gospel in a Pluralist Society* (Grand Rapids, Mich.: Eerdmans, 1989), pp. 122-23.
Newbigin (1909-1998) was a long-time missionary to India and bishop in the Church of South India.

those parts, primarily the south, that have been thoroughly evangelized.[23] Similarly, in the development of socialist and nationalist movements in the Middle East, Arabs of Christian origin have played a disproportionately large role.[24]

Thus the third precondition contributing to the rise of ideologies is the secularization of the Christian faith and of the cultures—beginning with the West—which have historically been shaped by this faith. As Western culture has further spread its influence to other parts of the world, its distinctive form of secularization, including the allure of the ideologies, has followed in its path. Secularization does not entail the diminishing authority of the institutional church over nonchurch communities, though it is sometimes taken to mean this. In an increasingly differentiated society, a phenomenon we shall further explore in chapters seven and eight, such "secularization" is normal and even to be expected. In the sense used here, however, secularization means nothing less than the increasing rejection of the Christian faith by society as a whole, even as it continues to work within frameworks owing much to its redemptive-historical teachings. We need not pretend that premodern Europe was wholly and consistently Christian in all its ways to recognize that at the Renaissance and Enlightenment the intellectual trendsetters of Europe turned decisively away from traditional Christianity. This is not to say that every philosopher living during these eras was an overt atheist, though a number certainly were. More typical was adherence to a vague deism conceiving God to be little more than a supreme artificer absenting himself from the world following his initial creative act. The deistic god is simply a watchmaker who winds up his handiwork and thereafter leaves it to run by itself. God may be creator, but he is not sustainer and certainly not redeemer.

Fourth, the ideologies presuppose the possibility of mass political movements. It is no accident that the rise of ideologies has coincided with the advent of democracy and the expansion of political participation. Up until the nineteenth century the word *democracy* was not held in high regard. Given that education was confined to the few and that statesmanship was regarded as a profession whose personal qualifications were as specialized as those of a physician, it was thought irresponsible to leave political decision-making to the passions of an untutored majority. Democracy, to our forebears, was synonymous with mob rule. Consequently, the older political theorists did not address themselves primarily to a

---

[23]Ibid., p. 122.
[24]Philip Jenkins, *The Next Christendom: The Coming of Global Christianity* (New York: Oxford University Press, 2002), p. 21.

popular audience. Debate over political principles was limited to the educated
and no one expected that such principles would gain large followings.

Today, of course, it is otherwise. Throughout the forty years of the Cold War,
the two superpowers justified their own existence in ideological terms and saw
themselves as locked in a battle for the hearts and minds of the world's masses.
One implication of this popularization is that, while the classic political theories
were generally formulated in a careful and systematic manner, the modern ideologies are packaged somewhat eclectically for mass consumption. It is not surprising, then, that such ideologies are often internally inconsistent. For
example, economic and moral libertarianism are usually to be found in different
packages along with other, less harmonious, nonlibertarian elements.[25] In
North America those calling themselves political liberals and conservatives have
simply embraced different sides of the broader liberal agenda with bits of socialism, nationalism and other strains thrown in. This is as true of Ronald Reagan
as of Bill Clinton, of Brian Mulroney as of Pierre Trudeau.

The dissemination of ideologies to a mass market would be impossible if it
were not for the fifth precondition, namely, the dramatic increase in technical
capabilities available to governments, and to political movements and parties. In
the eighteenth and nineteenth centuries technical developments took a further
leap ahead with the industrial revolution. These breakthroughs have accelerated
in the last two centuries, resulting in today's information revolution. Vastly improved means of transportation and communication have facilitated the propa-
gation of ideas to millions of people with a swiftness unavailable to the first
book printers. Carl J. Friedrich and Zbigniew K. Brzezinski have emphasized
the technological factor in the rise of totalitarianism, namely, the availability to
the leaders of such potent means as radio, newspapers, motion pictures and
other more subtle techniques of psychological manipulation.[26] But such means

---

[25]Charles Taylor makes a similar point about the internal inconsistencies of the parties to most current political debates in *The Ethics of Authenticity* (Cambridge, Mass.: Harvard University Press, 1991), p. 95:
"Right-wing American-style conservatives speak as advocates of traditional communities when they attack abortion on demand and pornography; but in their economic policies they advocate an untamed
form of capitalist enterprise, which more than anything else has helped to dissolve historical communities, has fostered atomism, which knows no frontiers or loyalties, and is ready to close down a mining
town or savage a forest habitat at the drop of a balance sheet. On the other side, we find supporters of an
attentive, reverential stance to nature who would go to the wall to defend the forest habitat, demonstrating in favor of abortion on demand, on the grounds that a woman's body belongs exclusively to her." See
also Dale Vree, *From Berkeley to East Berlin and Back* (Nashville: Thomas Nelson, 1985), pp. 137-47.
[26]Carl J. Friedrich and Zbigniew K. Brzezinski, *Totalitarian Dictatorship and Autocracy* (Cambridge, Mass:
Harvard University Press, 1965), pp. 129-47.

have also been serviceable to the popularization of ideologies that are not as overtly totalitarian in nature. Enhanced technical capabilities, coupled with the wider sense of community effected by the nation-state, have thus proved to be serviceable to the rise and proliferation of ideologies.

These recent developments are in large measure positive ones and have had undoubted benefits for much of humanity. It is certainly appropriate that as literacy spreads and people come to take an interest in the affairs of state, they should be acknowledged as active participants in the political community and that the government's authority should be exercised in a consultative fashion. We shall explore this further in our discussion of democracy in chapter five. It is also fitting that technical capacities be developed in accordance with the potentialities God has built into his creation. But just as all positive developments have a negative side, so also has the resulting expanded sense of community created fertile ground for the growth of the ideologies.

Ideology as Religious: Toward a Definition

Given the preconditions articulated above, it is appropriate to proceed to an account of ideology itself and to isolate its peculiar characteristics. I believe ideology can be understood in terms of five basic characteristics.

First and foremost, as hinted thus far, ideologies are inescapably religious. I am tempted at this point to equate completely ideology and religion, though it perhaps might be more accurate to say that an ideology *flows out of* the (idolatrous) religious commitment of a person or community. The use of the word idolatry may seem provocative in contemporary discourse because it implies that one religion is making truth claims exclusive of other religions. Although such claims are regarded by many as offensive in this postmodern age, the fact is that religion by its very nature makes such claims. Any attempt to relativize religion risks making it less than what it claims to be and thus trivializes it, despite the fact that such an effort may have grown out of a sincere desire to make room for it. Consequently, idolatry must still be admitted to be an operative category.[27] Furthermore, as Paul Marshall has observed, idolatry is not simply one more sin, of which pride, envy, lust and so forth are other examples; in fact, "all sin is an expression of the basic sin of idolatry, of putting something else in

---

[27]At the same time, it is probably accurate to observe that even from a Christian point of view, not all non-Christian religions are idolatrous in the sense outlined here. In particular, because Judaism and Islam are theistic religions that arguably worship the same God as Christians, these two, at least, can be said also to oppose idolatry.

the place of God."[28] Idolatry, in other words, is the origin of all other sins, as indicated by its proscription being ranked as the first precept of the Decalogue.

Idolatry takes something within God's creation, attempts to elevate it above the boundary separating Creator from creature, and makes of it a kind of god. Because religion is all-embracing, idolatry further tries to bring the rest of creation into the service of that invented god. The sort of idolatry we know best from Scripture is the obvious variety in which people fashion an imagined personal deity out of wood or stone, build temples, contrive liturgical rites and pay sacrifices to it. The Old Testament prophets tirelessly denounce the worship of false gods to which Israel and Judah constantly fell prey. But idolatry also manifests itself in more subtle ways. Human beings are inevitably worshiping creatures, though not all humans will admit this of themselves. An atheist denies belief in God but may effectively worship rationality, artistic prowess or military might as god. Even nominal believers in God may in fact serve such idols as financial success, social prestige or political power. Because idolatry in this second sense is so oblique and less overtly experienced as such, we often do not recognize it for what it is. It is in this sort of idolatry that ideology is rooted.

The connection between idolatry and ideology is forcefully made by Bob Goudzwaard, who argues that the religious nature of human beings can be understood in terms of "three basic biblical rules": First, everyone serves a god of some sort. Second, everyone is transformed into the image of the god she serves. Third, people structure their society in their own image.[29] Augustine states this in terms of two basic principles: our hearts are restless until they rest in God;[30] and a commonwealth is united by shared objects of love.[31] If the members of a community love God and seek to do his will, then the structures that order their common life will reflect this. If on the other hand, its members love such things as material wealth, individual rights and the all-powerful state, this shared love will work itself out in ways that affect the welfare of the community. If their hearts attempt to find rest in those things that do not really bring rest, this continued restlessness will express itself in social and political institutions. In short, the worship of idols brings practical consequences for the shared life of persons in community.

---

[28] Paul Marshall, with Lela Gilbert, *Heaven Is Not My Home: Learning to Live in the Now of God's Creation* (Nashville: Word, 1998), p. 190.

[29] Bob Goudzwaard, *Aid for the Overdeveloped West* (Toronto: Wedge, 1975), pp. 14-15.

[30] Augustine *Confessions* 1.1.

[31] Augustine *City of God* 19.24.

Second, if ideologies deify something within God's creation, they inevitably view this humanly made god as a source of salvation. Thus each of the ideologies is based on a specific soteriology, that is, on a worked-out theory promising deliverance to human beings from some fundamental evil that is viewed as the source of a broad range of human ills, including tyranny, oppression, anarchy, poverty and so forth. As Goudzwaard puts it, "The mature ideology is a false revelation of creation, fall and redemption."[32] Christianity sees Jesus Christ as the source of salvation; the ideologies see salvation coming to us through, for example, the maximization of individual freedom, the communal ownership of all wealth, the liberation of the nation from foreign rule, the submission of individuals to the general will and so forth. This is not to say that salvation in Jesus Christ necessarily manifests itself apart from ordinary policy alternatives in the political realm. Indeed a redemptive understanding of politics—as opposed to the totalitarian pretense that politics itself redeems—requires the fleshing out of the divine calling to do justice in terms of carefully worked-out concrete programs. Yet even if justice should require greater individual freedom, a certain redistribution of wealth, national independence, or greater consideration of the common good, the single-minded pursuit of such goals is not itself of a salvific character and will likely produce destructive consequences. This is where a Christian understanding differs radically from that of the ideologies.

Of course, salvation is always *from* something deemed evil. For orthodox Christians the creation is good because a good God brought it into being. Sin is not to be located in creation but in the rebellion against God and against his purposes for creation. By contrast—and this is the third characteristic—the ideologies tend to locate the source of this fundamental evil somewhere within the creation. "Identifying its own source of evil," Goudzwaard writes, the ideology furthermore "erects its own antithesis between good and evil."[33] Thus the ideology can be seen to partake of that ancient heresy of gnosticism, for which the physical world is deemed intrinsically sinful, and salvation is viewed as deliverance from its supposed confines. Eric Voegelin (1901-1985) has made much of the connection between the modern mass ideological movements and gnosticism. In Voegelin's estimation, gnostics are dissatisfied with the world, which they deem "intrinsically poorly organized." They believe that salvation from the

---

[32]Bob Goudzwaard, *Idols of Our Time* (Downers Grove, Ill.: InterVarsity Press, 1984), p. 25.
[33]Ibid.

world's evil is possible within the immanent historical process and that this will require a structural change in the "order of being"; finally, they believe that the means of effecting such change necessitates seeking a special knowledge—or *gnosis*—available only to the gnostics themselves.[34] Voegelin's isolation of this relationship between the ideologies and gnosticism is compelling, and his account of the gnostic attitude seems largely correct.

What is lacking from his analysis, however, is an understanding of how gnosticism relates to the Christian understanding of creation, fall and redemption. According to Voegelin's account, Christianity teaches that the fulfillment of human nature is to be found in the "*visio beatifica*, in supernatural perfection through grace in death," and that "Christian life on earth takes its special form from the life to come in the next [world]."[35] Although there is a large measure of truth in his eschatological account of the Christian faith, it suffers from the misconception that the kingdom of God is discontinuous with the historical process and cannot be manifested within it. To be sure, the final consummation of God's kingdom does await the second advent of Jesus Christ and his promise to make all things new. In this respect, creation's ultimate fulfillment comes from outside creation itself and is not simply implicit within it, as a number of the ideologies and some "historicist" Christians teach.[36] Yet this fulfillment is precisely the *fulfillment of creation* and not the attainment by a noncorporeal soul of some intelligible form detached from God's world. Indeed Voegelin's "order of being" appears to owe more to a static Platonic notion of being than to the Christian understanding of creation order, a principal difference being that the latter is distorted by sin yet capable of being redeemed by grace to fulfill its intended purpose. Because Voegelin posits too sharp a division between the present life and the life of the world to come, he is thus unable to see that redemption is, once again, "creation regained."[37] Furthermore, if gnosticism is, in Charles Norris Cochrane's words, based on "an absolute antithesis between matter and spirit" and denies "the unity of the cosmos,"[38] then Voegelin

---

[34]Eric Voegelin, *Science, Politics & Gnosticism* (Chicago: Regnery Gateway, 1968), pp. 86-88. See also his *The New Science of Politics* (Chicago: University of Chicago Press, 1952); and *From Enlightenment to Revolution* (Durham, N.C.: Duke University Press, 1975).

[35]Voegelin, *New Science of Politics*, p. 88.

[36]See, e.g., Oliver O'Donovan's discussion of "eschatology and history" in *Resurrection and Moral Order: An Outline for Evangelical Ethics* (Grand Rapids, Mich.: Eerdmans, 1986), pp. 53-75.

[37]Albert M. Wolters, *Creation Regained* (Grand Rapids, Mich.: Eerdmans, 1985), pp. 42, 50-51.

[38]Charles Norris Cochrane, *Christianity and Classical Culture: A Study of Thought and Action from Augustus to Augustine* (New York: Oxford/Galaxy, 1957), pp. 159, 369.

himself has not entirely succeeded in eluding its grasp.

Yet if we can manage to take Voegelin's central insight into the character of gnosticism, separate it from his heavily platonized account of Christianity, and place it within the biblically informed context of creation, fall and redemption, then there is much to be derived from his analysis of the ideologies. According to Albert M. Wolters, gnosticism tends to depreciate one dimension of God's creation, thus effectively ontologizing evil and salvation, which are identified with something intrinsic to the structure of creation itself.[39] The ideologies do precisely the same thing. Thus liberalism sees community, or any heteronomous authority, as uniquely threatening to the well-being of the autonomous individual and thus a source of evil. Libertarians tend to see government as this source of evil. Conservatives tend to see the dynamic character of creation, that is, change and development, as a source of evil. Collectivist ideologies, for example, socialism and nationalism, tend to distrust individual freedom or other alternative communities, thereby identifying their existence with evil. Along with this gnostic tendency comes a propensity to deny the goodness of creation and a concomitant inability to discern the creation order altogether.

Fourth, given this defective soteriology, it should not be surprising that ideologies have a fundamentally distorted view of the world, and hence of government and politics. This distorted worldview has tremendous consequences for political practice, because people inevitably live out their religious worldviews. Because the followers of ideologies see the world as belonging not to God but to themselves, they misunderstand the character of the world in a rather basic fashion. Perhaps they see it as a chance combination of atoms and molecules capable of being shaped to their liking. Or they may see the state as the source of order in the world and effectively make it totalitarian, as, for example, in Nazism and Marxism-Leninism. Conversely, they may see the state as the principal source of evil in the world, as does the libertarianism of Friedrich von Hayek and Ayn Rand. Inevitably, this distorted view has profound implications for policymaking and for concrete political practice.

Fifth and finally, in the modern ideologies goals supplant principles. As Goudzwaard puts it, the adherent of an ideology is "possessed by an end."[40] Or, to echo the familiar maxim, the end justifies the means. Rather than seeing justice as a norm governing political action from the outset, ideology sees it pri-

---

[39] Albert M. Wolters, "Facing the Perplexing History of Philosophy," *Tydskrif vir Christelike Wetenskap* 17, no. 4 (1981): 10.

[40] Goudzwaard, *Idols of Our Time*, p. 14.

marily as a final goal of such action. (Therefore even pragmatism, so often seen as the opposite of ideology, is itself an ideology, given its goal orientation.) The relevant question thus becomes, not whether the state is acting justly, but *whether it is acting so as eventually to achieve justice.* Under the latter approach, justice is seen as an ideal located somewhere in the future, and whatever one does in the here-and-now is permissible if it serves the ultimate attainment of this goal. One can safely put aside for today the immediate issues of justice, as long as current means are serviceable to a better tomorrow. Future justice can therefore be seen to excuse present *in*justice. Here is where sacrifice inevitably enters the picture. If, as Christians believe, the shed blood of Jesus Christ is the sacrifice for our sins, then the ideologies offer a surrogate source of salvation that may also call for bloody sacrifice. In its own way, as Goudzwaard observes, the ideology "imitates the suffering and death of the Messiah" and can thus be seen as a kind of counterfeit Christianity.[41]

That human beings set goals for themselves and their communities is, of course, nothing new or remarkable. The capacity to project into the future and to formulate plans accordingly is implanted by God and is part of how he has created us. But in the ideologies these goals take on a life of their own. They are in the first place rooted in the predominant secular belief in human autonomy, according to which human beings determine the course of their own lives without reference to God's will. In the second place, these goals themselves become gods to which ordinary flesh-and-blood people may have to be sacrificed. It is by no means incidental that the two unquestionably worst ideologies of the twentieth century, namely, Marxism-Leninism and national socialism, left scores of millions of deaths in their wake. Other ideologies have been less obviously destructive but have nevertheless exacted some sort of human toll, perhaps in broken marriages and families, abuse of workers, unemployment, widespread poverty or environmental degradation.

Earlier I expressed reluctance to see ideology and idolatry as identical. This is because most of the ideologies we shall explore can be said to be rooted in a single human-centered religion, often known as *humanism* or, more commonly, *secularism.* Secularism may be described as an idolatry which, as its name indicates, worships some created thing, or more than one thing, within the *saeculum*—the present age. These ideologies are therefore part of a larger spiritual family and as such share significant assumptions about humanity and their rela-

---

[41]Ibid., p. 25.

tionship to their fellow human beings, the rest of the world and God. Thus we shall see that despite the professed enmity existing between different ideologies, such as liberalism and socialism, their animosity might better be interpreted as a kind of sibling rivalry. Brothers and sisters may constantly quarrel with each other in the same household, and when they grow up they may further drift apart, both emotionally and geographically. Yet they are unlikely to be able to conceal that they are closely related because of similar physical appearances. Blue eyes may run in the family, as may high cheekbones and a roman nose. Thus, even while they are protesting their mutual differences, the evidence of their blood relationship remains for all to see. It is the same with the ideologies.

According to Allan Bloom the whole world is divided between the followers of John Locke and Karl Marx—between liberalism and socialism.[42] While the configuration of human ideological loyalties is surely more complex than this statement suggests, and despite the fact that this ideological cleavage has diminished considerably since 1989, it does point to an important truth about the contemporary political debate, namely, that its very parameters have been determined by this secularist religion, whose principal tenet is a belief in human autonomy. Because of this religion's impact, it is no longer doubted that human beings shape their world autonomously. Rather, the principal controversies revolve around the issue of who is the bearer of that autonomy, the individual or some form of community. Those who question autonomy altogether are effectively left out of the discussion. The fact that the world's principal collectivist ideology is in decline and individualism is (at least for now) in the ascendancy has not fundamentally altered this picture. Nor is it likely to do so in the near future.

I shall not pretend that the foregoing presents an exhaustive account of ideology. Undoubtedly one could add other characteristics to these five, which would enhance our understanding of it, but these seem to me to be the most important. Two points still need to be made, however, before we move to the next section. First, if ideologies flow out of an idolatrous worldview, does this mean that they have no positive features or nothing to teach us? Not at all. In chapter seven I shall explain what I believe to be the best way of assessing the ideologies from a Christian viewpoint. Here I shall say only that if ideologies err by making a god out of something in the creation, and if that created thing nevertheless remains good, then it stands to reason that the ideologies and their followers have uncovered fragments of the truth which perhaps even Christians

---

[42]Allan Bloom, *The Closing of the American Mind* (New York: Simon & Schuster, 1987), p. 217.

have failed to see. In fact one might argue the need to assess the good in an ideology before we can begin to understand its deformations. How else can we explain that otherwise good and decent German citizens succumbed to the attractions of national socialism in the 1930s and 1940s? Or that so many intellectuals in Europe and North America, scandalized by the suffering caused by the Great Depression, would turn to communism for answers?

Second, in the midst of the struggles among the ideologies and of the distortions they impose on individuals and communities, God remains faithful to his creation. This explains in large measure how it is possible for the ideologies to have fragmentary insights into the truth. But it also means that even the most deceptive of ideologies is incapable of altogether misshaping the world, including human society, in its own image. Good marriages and healthy families are still possible in a liberal political order, where the forces of individualism might otherwise tend to erode these basic institutions. As Michael Walzer has observed, a liberalism untempered by other, longstanding restraints and allegiances would be unendurable.[43] Not only unendurable, but indeed virtually impossible. Particular loyalties tend to survive, even in the midst of a totalitarian regime openly discouraging all ties other than to itself. In this respect, while capitalism, as the economic counterpart of liberalism, manifests itself in a variety of ways, it is not appropriate to speak in an unqualified way of "capitalist society," as if capitalism were capable of subjecting the whole of human life and relationships to the market. Certainly it is possible for capitalism to distort, for example, family life, but it cannot remake or undo it entirely, notwithstanding recent warnings in some circles of the family's imminent demise. For this we may rightly thank God, who faithfully upholds his creation order in the midst of our disobedience.

The Classification of Ideologies: Left and Right

There is no generally accepted scheme for classifying political ideologies, and those that exist are not especially helpful. One of the more common and, I would argue, least helpful is to group them along a so-called left-right spectrum. The use of left and right is so widespread, in fact, that it deserves some comment. Many people use these labels as if they had some invariable content well known to virtually everyone since time immemorial. If we label Margaret Thatcher a rightist, what precisely are we saying about her political beliefs and policies? If we label

---

[43]Quoted by Elshtain in "Feminists Against the Family," in *Real Politics at the Center of Everyday Life* (Baltimore, Md.: Johns Hopkins University Press, 1997), p. 151.

the late François Mitterrand a leftist, what do we expect our hearers to assume about him? Often these terms are used in a derisive fashion as a way of discrediting those with whom we disagree. By using them we may inadvertently tell more about ourselves than about our political opponents. Why do we use them then? Do they actually communicate something? Are they worth keeping?

The use of left and right originates in nothing more remarkable than the seating arrangement of deputies to the French National Assembly after 1789. Traditional monarchists were seated to the right of the speaker, while republicans were seated to his left. As monarchism diminished as a significant force and as radicalism and socialism came onto the scene, the configuration of political parties changed and their places in the parliamentary chamber drifted to the speaker's right.[44] At the outset, those on the right favored monarchical sovereignty while those on the left supported popular sovereignty. Thus the basic criterion for locating the parties and their ideologies along the continuum was their respective attitudes toward possession of political power.

Needless to say, this criterion is all but obsolete today. No one would seriously suggest that the basic difference between Mitterrand and Thatcher is that, while Mitterrand was a democrat, Thatcher is a monarchist. Rather, the meaning of left and right has changed over the decades as different clusters of issues have come to supplant earlier issues in importance. At various times in France and elsewhere, the overriding issue has been between clericalism and anticlericalism—between those supporting the prerogatives of the institutional church and those wishing to strip the church of its power. In such a context the clerical parties were seated at the right and the anticlerical parties at the left of the chamber. Perhaps as a consequence of this historical peculiarity, there is an enduring popular tendency to see any Christian involvement in politics, ranging from the European Christian democratic parties to the American Christian Coalition, as a phenomenon of the right. Moreover, many Christians themselves tend to gravitate toward parties that position themselves on the right.

Through most of the twentieth century, however, one's place on the left-right spectrum has been largely determined by one's attitude toward social and economic equality. Social democrats and communists, for all their considerable

---

[44]This drift has taken place so much that in contemporary France, parties named Radical and Social Democratic are now positioned to the right of center as part of the *Union pour la Démocratie Française*, a coalition of moderate conservative parties formed in 1978 to support then-President Valéry Giscard d'Estaing. See J. E. S. Hayward, *Governing France: The One and Indivisible Republic* (New York: W. W. Norton, 1983), p. 82.

differences, aspire to distribute the wealth of society equally among its members. Classical liberals and fascists are miles apart, especially in their regard for individual freedom, yet both believe that human beings are either inherently unequal or at least tend to become unequal through the exercise of different individual potentials. Racists are on the extreme right because they believe not only that some people are superior to others, but that such superiority is biologically fixed. Communists are on the extreme left because they believe that virtually all human differences, and the inequalities rooted in them, are culturally determined and thus capable of being eliminated. (In fact, communist societies have been invariably inegalitarian and have succeeded only in creating what Milovan Djilas labeled a "new class" consisting of members of the bureaucracy and the party.[45] But despite the quite different reality, communism's aspirations remained egalitarian to the end.)

In their last days, however, something quite remarkable occurred in the Soviet Union and those countries that had adopted its political and economic system. With the coming of Gorbachev and his twin policies of perestroika (reform) and glasnost (openness), the range of permissible political debate widened considerably and the left–right spectrum actually reversed itself. In the late 1980s, someone like Boris Yeltsin and the late Andrei Sakharov were considered men of the left, while hard-line Communist official Yegor Ligachev was described as a rightist. Gorbachev began his career as party leader on the left but was quickly outflanked by more radical reformers. By 1990 he was being seen as an embattled centrist, but scarcely a year later, following the failed coup of August 1991, he was being perceived as a rightist, hopelessly attached to a system that was in the process of collapsing. Obviously in this context attitudes toward the distribution of economic goods were not considered the decisive criterion for determining who stood on the left and who on the right.

Thus the terms *left* and *right* are unhelpful for at least three reasons. First, they are relative to the issues of the day and therefore cannot be said to have a universally accepted meaning. This is perhaps not the most important reason for rejecting them, but it should at least make us mindful of the fact that, if we criticize someone for being too far to the left or too far to the right, we are doing so by criteria which are hardly set in stone and are likely to change tomorrow. Furthermore, if we label ourselves centrists, we may inadvertently be accepting the Aristotelian definition of virtue as the mean between two vicious extremes.

---

[45]Milovan Djilas, *The New Class* (New York: Harcourt Brace Jovanovich, 1957).

This is not the only account of virtue possible, and the Christian would do well to assess it in a spiritually discerning manner.

Second, the left-right spectrum is one-dimensional and necessarily fastens onto a single overriding evaluative criterion at the expense of many possible others. Why focus so heavily on distribution of economic resources? Why not analyze ideologies in terms of their respective attitudes toward the scope of governmental power? Or freedom versus authority? Or diversity versus unity? Or democracy versus aristocracy? Conceivably, then, we might have to employ several matrices in a multidimensional model. If we were to choose only two such matrices and position them perpendicular to each other, we might end up with something like figure 1. This is one possible two-dimensional way of organizing political ideologies that is an undoubted improvement over the one-dimensional spectrum.

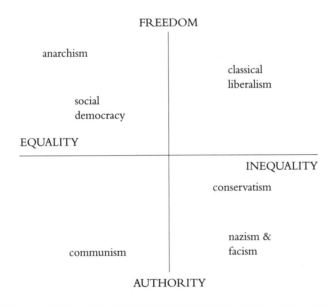

Figure 1. An example of a two-dimensional organization of political ideologies

But there is a third reason for rejecting the left-right spectrum, which even a multidimensional model cannot address. It cannot account for the *religious* differences that may exist among the various ideologies. Most of the modern ideologies are members of the same religious family, as observed already. In some fashion each makes humanity into a god, and thus they have much in common. But they differ on which manifestation of humanity they choose to worship. As we shall see, liberalism idolizes the individual, socialism the economic class, and nationalism the nation-state or ethnic community. Although one might conceivably create a spectrum that places ideologies along a continuum between individual and community, it would be unable to distinguish among varieties of community. Furthermore, there is a cluster of political doctrines that would be difficult to place along any continuum. Such would include European Christian democracy, the radical Islamism of al-Qaeda and Hamas, and the Hindu nationalism of India's Janata Party. The rather basic differences among these historic religions could not be easily captured by a one-, two- or multidimensional model.

For all these reasons, I would prefer to banish right and left from the political discourse altogether. Since this is not likely to happen, however, I ask readers to be aware of the deficiencies inherent in these terms and not to place too much significance in them. However, two other labels have somewhat greater validity, and these are *progressive* and *conservative*, which are often seen as synonymous with left and right respectively. Here I shall do no more than to say that in theory I see progressing and conserving as two mutually compatible and necessary activities that ought not to be played off against each other. A fuller discussion of this will be encountered in chapter three.

Discerning the Spirits in the Ideologies

Now that we have accounted in some measure for ideology as a general phenomenon, we shall turn in chapters two through six to examine the individual ideologies themselves, beginning with liberalism, and moving on in succession to conservatism, nationalism, democracy and socialism. I shall not pretend that everything to be said of the ideologies must necessarily be organized into these five categories. Many readers might wish to see an in-depth analysis of, for example, anarchism or feminism or perhaps even environmentalism. Others might note the conspicuous absence of syndicalism, fascism and Nazism. Still others might wish, in the wake of terrorist attacks in North America, the Middle East and south Asia, to see a treatment of what is now being labeled Islamism. Some might further argue for the existence of an ideology of patriarchalism or even postmodernism. There are at least three reasons why these will not be treated as fully as the ideologies to be discussed in the next five chapters.

First, fascism and Nazism grow out of a kind of nationalism and can be viewed as particularly destructive variants of that ideology. Syndicalism and anarchism are two versions of socialism, as are Marxism and Marxism-Leninism and its permutations. Second, I believe that the five ideologies covered in this book are indeed the most influential in our modern world, notwithstanding the apparent shift, at least in the West, from modernity to postmodernity. To be sure, feminism has been extraordinarily influential in the twentieth century, particularly during its last third. But, as a number of observers have pointed out, there are liberal feminisms, conservative feminisms and radical feminisms akin to Marxist socialism. In short, much of what we shall write concerning the "big five" ideologies could also be said of the several feminisms. Even Islamism bears many of the same features as European nationalism, Marxism-Leninism and fascism, as some observers have pointed out.[46]

Third, in treating as many as five ideologies, I fear I am already spreading myself too thin. This is perhaps a bogus reason for not covering what some might consider significant material, but all books must work within limits. One simply cannot do everything within a few hundred pages.

As for the chapters themselves, we shall not follow a particularly strict pattern in dealing with each ideology in turn. One might, of course, use the same, or at least parallel, internal headings within each chapter to illustrate a certain unity of method applied to the whole. One thinks in this respect of Thomas Aquinas' way of dealing with hundreds of theological and philosophical questions in his magisterial *Summa theologica*: first posing the question, then listing possible objections, citing a relevant authority to the contrary, stating his own response to the question, and finally answering each objection in turn. Such a method certainly makes for consistency, but such consistency comes at the price of readability as well as of a sense of the uniqueness of each issue to be addressed. It would seem better to probe each of the ideologies on its own terms, to explore its unique and unrepeatable contours, and to adjust one's method accordingly. Thus each chapter will look at its subject matter in a somewhat different manner, coming at it from a slightly different angle.

For example, it seems evident that there is a certain familial relationship among liberalism, democracy and socialism, with the first having begotten the second, and the second having generated the third. Thus with these three lineal ideologies we shall devote some space to articulating internal historical developments within the ideology that have led logically to the rise of the succeeding

---

[46]See, e.g., Daniel Pipes, "The Western Mind of Radical Islam," *First Things* 58 (December 1995): 18-23, and *Militant Islam Reaches America* (New York: W. W. Norton, 2002).

ideology. Although not all liberals are destined to become ideological democrats and not all ideological democrats are fated to become socialists, the connections among them are nevertheless as evident as the various physical and psychological characteristics that tie human generations together. Conservatism and nationalism are not as evidently in the same line of descent, although the latter is certainly largely compatible with the presuppositions of ideological democracy. Because conservatism developed as a response to the three lineal ideologies, its familial relationship to them is more like that of a first cousin or first cousin once removed. Nationalism has roots in both conservatism and the three lineal ideologies alike. But less space will be devoted to illustrating nationalism's place in the family tree.

That said, however, six common themes will bring together our discussion of the several ideologies:

- First, what is their creational basis?

- Second, what facets of God's creation have they rightly focused on even as they have effectively deified them?

- Third, what inconsistencies have led to internal tensions within the ideology itself?

- Fourth, what do they see as a source of evil?

- Fifth, where do they locate the source of salvation?

- Sixth and finally, to what extent are they able to account for the distinct place of politics in God's world?

These themes will not necessarily be addressed in the same order in each chapter, but they will be addressed in some fashion.

As readers make their way through these chapters, they should note that the portraits drawn therein represent the ideologies in their pure, unadulterated forms. In the real world the boundaries separating them are hardly airtight, and flesh and blood socialists, for example, often carry within themselves assumptions more properly characteristic of, say, liberalism or nationalism. This apparent eclecticism illustrates two things: first, the interrelatedness of the ideologies themselves and second, the inevitable human tendency to think and to live in ways that are not always fully consistent with the principles one claims to follow. If, as we shall note in chapter seven, Christians often style themselves socialists and liberals without attending sufficiently to the spiritual roots of socialism and liberalism, then it is not surprising that professed liberals should often harbor socialist or conservative ideas or that some people will combine a number of ideological positions in their own unique approaches to the political realm. This does not, however, mean that they are nonideological, as some might claim; it does mean that they are not sufficiently conscious of the ideological underpinnings of their own positions. One of the purposes of this book is to raise the level of general awareness of the ideologies and their powerful influence in the world at large.

Chapters seven through nine represent the heart of the argument of the book, which is that it is possible to transcend the ideologies and to embrace a spirit more compatible with the Christian understanding of creation, fall and redemption. Some might argue for an explicitly Christian ideology, while others would argue for a so-called objective, rational approach. We shall do neither of these here but will argue instead for a biblical—and hence creational and redemptive—understanding of politics and its place in God's world. We shall, in short, offer an alternative vision—one which, it is to be hoped, will take us beyond the reductionisms and idolatries of the ideologies insofar as it offers a truer and fuller account of the world and of politics. Two Christian traditions have proven to be particularly helpful in offering guidance in this direction: the tradition of Roman Catholic social teachings rooted in the neo-Thomist revival of the late nineteenth and early twentieth centuries, and the neo-Calvinist movement arising at the same time in the Netherlands and spreading into the English-speaking world in the late twentieth century. These, we shall argue, continue to have relevance for doing politics at the beginning of the twenty-first century.

2

LIBERALISM

The Sovereignty of the Individual

Given enough time, idolatries tend to make themselves obsolescent, though rarely completely obsolete. Naturally most of Jeremiah's contemporaries did not view him as a true prophet of Yahweh. The king of Judah in particular preferred to listen to his own false prophets, with their rosy forecasts, than to the message of doom announced by Jeremiah. Yet Jerusalem did fall to the Babylonians as Jeremiah had warned. Centuries earlier, and in similar fashion, the Israelite king Ahab and his consort Jezebel chose to patronize the prophets of Baal rather than Elijah. Nevertheless, at the decisive showdown on Mount Carmel, the Canaanite god proved himself to be nothing more than a figment of his followers' imaginations. Yet Baal worship did not come to an end and continued to command the loyalties of many Israelites and Judeans, who either forgot their god's earlier humiliation or possibly decided to reinterpret their false faith.

The same can be said of the ideologies, which are based on taking something out of the creation and making of it a kind of god capable of saving us. During its heyday an ideology often seems invincible and carries a certain illusion of comprehensive veracity that is based on real elements of truth and which untold millions come to accept. But eventually the ideology runs its course and begins to lose support, at least in part because it has failed to deliver on its promises, but also because its contradictions have manifested themselves in such a way as to make it all but untenable. We saw this most dramatically in the collapse of communism at the very end of the 1980s. But even liberalism has endured its crises of faith, which have emerged out of its own inherent tensions. When someone fashions a god out of something the one true God has created, there are real repercussions both for the idolatrous faith and for the believer in that faith. Usually this comes in the form of a series of dialectically related polarities between which believers are forced to choose. These are, as it were, the dogmas of the faith. The changing relationship between these dogmas generates further developments in this faith.

Yet there are also constants in each ideology. However it may change over the decades, liberalism stands and falls on its foundational belief in the sovereignty of the individual. This belief naturally gives rise to subsidiary beliefs with their own incongruities. As the latter work themselves out, they may induce some believers to abandon liberalism outright for another doctrine. But others may try to work with these liberal beliefs, adjusting them here and there and trying as well as they can to make them fit into the larger system. Because this has occurred so frequently in the history of liberalism, professed liberals may look very different today from their ideological forebears of, say, two centuries ago. For example, while eighteenth- and nineteenth-century liberals generally believed the state to be the principal threat to liberty, many twentieth-century liberals came to see the state as the chief promoter of liberty. Yet both varieties of liberals come to their divergent views of the state out of the same commitment to the individual. In this chapter we shall further examine such tensions to try to unmask liberalism's idolatrous character.

In order to gain an understanding of the existing varieties of liberalism, it is necessary to say something about liberalism's history. I shall not, however, attempt an exhaustive historical survey, since there are many already in existence and I would only risk repeating what has been done quite adequately elsewhere. Instead I shall briefly discuss the principal tenets and tensions in liberal ideology, as manifested in several of its key proponents, and the impact they have had on its overall historical shape as it progressed through five major stages. This will demonstrate two things. First, no ideology remains static. All human worldviews and intellectual systems develop and change their shapes over time, in part because the human mind is dynamic by nature. Furthermore, because ideologies are based on certain distorted ways of viewing reality, they contain specific tensions or polarities whose characters are likely to shift over time. For example, the fact that liberalism includes both a belief in the sovereignty of the

individual and a belief in the limited state means that in its historical manifestations liberalism must try to hold onto both but will probably gravitate toward
one or the other at different times.

Second, I hope to show that adherents of the same ideology frequently find
themselves opponents of each other as often as they clash with followers of another ideology. Experience tells us that sibling rivalry is often more intense than
competition among contestants and acquaintances outside the family. The same
can be said of the ideologies. If a George W. Bush and an Al Gore seem to be
implacable foes in the political arena, it is not because they hold to different ideologies. It is because both claim to represent the more authentic legacy of the
same ideology. We shall observe a similar phenomenon among socialists, conservatives, nationalists and others.

The Meanings of Liberalism

Liberalism is the one ideology with which we North Americans are probably
most familiar, even if we are not always conscious of it. Some of our most cherished political convictions concerning, for example, the rights of human beings, the place of freedom and the character and task of the state, owe much to
liberal ways of thinking. There can be little doubt that the enhancement of the
status of the individual over the past several centuries has been a genuinely progressive development. This is where we encounter the truth in liberalism. During the sixteenth century, for example, the notion that an individual subject of
a ruler could claim a right to practice her religion according to her conscience
against the interference of the governing authorities would have been inconceivable. Similarly as late as the nineteenth century in much of Europe, censorship was imposed on those who would publish ideas deemed seditious or
critical of political leaders. John Stuart Mill's (1806-1873) rationale for protecting the right of persons to express even unpopular opinions seems unremark-
able today, but at the time he wrote the point still needed to be argued against
considerable opposition, not the least of which was to be found within the
churches.[1] Today, we Westerners live in a world where it is taken for granted
that people cannot enslave other people, that people can practice their respective faiths without official harassment, and that intellectuals can promote controversial ideas without fear of at least legal if not social reprisals. All of these are
the ripe fruits of liberalism, whose positive side cannot be denied.

---

[1] John Stuart Mill *On Liberty* 2 (1859).

So thoroughly has this liberalism come to suffuse our political culture, especially in the Anglo-Saxon world, that virtually all of us can be said to be liberals in some sense, even if we explicitly repudiate the label. Alasdair MacIntyre believes this liberal monopoly characterizes most modern political systems, where the contemporary debate goes on between "conservative liberals, liberal liberals and radical liberals."[2] In fact, the label itself is confusing in light of contemporary political rhetoric, especially in the United States. Conventional wisdom tells us that Barry Goldwater lost the 1964 presidential election because he was "too conservative," while George McGovern lost his bid for the presidency eight years later because he was "too liberal." *Liberal* and *conservative* are nowadays seen to be polar opposites; to bear the one label means that you cannot bear the other.

Self-styled American conservatives often use the so-called L-word as if it were the ultimate political insult. According to such politicians as Ronald Reagan and the elder George Bush, to be liberal means to be soft on crime, to be lying in the lap of the labor unions, to favor unilateral disarmament (at least prior to the end of the Cold War), to support those unwilling to work at the expense of the industrious middle class, and to favor minimal if any restrictions on the dissemination of, for example, pornography and drugs. Those who claim the liberal label, on the other hand, will assert that they favor protecting the less advantaged in society, maintaining the right of collective bargaining for workers, enhancing equality of opportunity, facilitating the exercise of freedom of individual choice and providing a social safety net for those swept aside by market forces.

What both self-proclaimed liberals and their opponents do not realize, however, is that in the larger historic sense they are all liberals of some stripe and actually share the same fundamental assumptions concerning the nature of man and of political community. In European usage, which is more accurate historically, "liberalism" refers to that body of doctrines found in the writings of John Locke (1632-1704), Adam Smith (1723-1790), Jean Jacques Rousseau (1712-1778)[3] and Immanuel Kant (1724-1804). More recent proponents of liberal ideas include Friedrich von Hayek (1899-1992),[4] Milton

---

[2] Alasdair MacIntyre, *Whose Justice? Which Rationality?* (Notre Dame, Ind.: University of Notre Dame Press, 1988), p. 392.

[3] Rousseau's legacy is more ambiguous and is shared by more than one ideology.

[4] See Friedrich von Hayek, *The Road to Serfdom* (Chicago: University of Chicago Press, 1944); and *The Constitution of Liberty* (London: Routledge & Kegan Paul, 1960).

Friedman (1912-),[5] Robert Nozick (1938-2002)[6] and John Rawls (1921-2002).[7] Liberal ideas contributed to both the American and French Revolutions, and the subsequent European revolutions of 1848. They were the principal influences on the U.S. Declaration of Independence (the first part of which reads like a paraphrase of key sections of Locke's *Second Treatise on Civil Government*) and Constitution (which is also Lockean but owes much to Charles de Montesquieu's [1689-1755] *Ésprit des Lois* as well). Liberal ideas have been so influential on American political culture that even self-styled conservatives there are actually "old-fashioned liberals," in George Grant's words.[8]

In Canada, two of whose political parties are actually labeled Liberal and Conservative, we see once more that the programs of both of these parties largely reflect liberal ideas. But in that country liberal dominance is tempered, on the one hand, by older communitarian "tory" ideas within the Progressive Conservative Party and, on the other, by an active socialist grouping, namely, the New Democratic Party, which at one time or another has governed the provinces of Saskatchewan, Manitoba, British Columbia and Ontario.[9] Nevertheless, like its southern neighbor, Canada too is a largely liberal country. Conservative former Prime Minister Brian Mulroney pursued liberal policies during his nine years in office and is unlikely to be admired by such traditional tories as Grant or Eugene Forsey.[10] The latter would probably like even less the

---

[5]See especially Milton Friedman, *Capitalism and Freedom* (Chicago: University of Chicago Press, 1962); and Milton Friedman and Rose D. Friedman, *Free to Choose: A Personal Statement* (New York: Harcourt Brace Jovanovich, 1980).

[6]See Robert Nozick, *Anarchy, State, and Utopia* (New York: Harper Colophon, 1974).

[7]See John Rawls, *A Theory of Justice* (Cambridge, Mass.: Belknap, 1999); and *Political Liberalism* (New York: Columbia University Press, 1993).

[8]George Grant, *Lament for a Nation* (Toronto: Anansi, 1965), p. 64. Grant (1918-1988) was perhaps the best-known Canadian philosopher of his day. A devout Anglican Christian and a committed Canadian nationalist, he also wrote *English-Speaking Justice* (Sackville, New Brunswick: Mount Allison University Press, 1974), *Technology and Empire* (Toronto: Anansi, 1969), and *Technology and Justice* (Toronto: Anansi, 1986). The influences on his thinking include Jacques Ellul (1912-1994), Leo Strauss and, above all, Simone Weil (1909-1943). He was himself influential on a generation of Canadian nationalists after 1965.

[9]See Gad Horowitz, "Conservatism, Socialism, and Liberalism in Canada; An Interpretation," in *The Canadian Political Tradition: Basic Readings*, ed. R. S. Blair and Jack MacLeod (Toronto: Methuen, 1987), pp. 172-95, for the author's famous interpretation, following that of Louis Hartz, of the relationship among tory conservatism, liberalism and socialism in Canada, in contrast with the United States.

[10]Eugene Forsey (1904-1991) was Canada's foremost constitutional expert and a former senator of the Liberal party in Canada's appointed parliamentary upper chamber. Despite his party label, however, he styled himself a conservative in the tradition of Sir John A. Macdonald, the first prime minister after confederation in 1867. Forsey authored *The Royal Power of Dissolution in the British Commonwealth* (Toronto: Oxford University Press, 1943) and, only months before his death, his autobiography, *A Life on the Fringe* (Toronto: Oxford University Press, 1990).

newer, western-based Canadian Alliance Party, with its more overt espousal of classical liberal economic ideas.

Liberalism's influence in North America is such that the central political debate nowadays is not so much between liberals and their ideological opponents, as between different kinds of liberals, usually styled classical (or traditional) and reform (or revisionist). Even the abortion debate, in which Christians are so deeply involved, is usually framed in terms of the conflicting rights of *individuals*, which is a typically liberal way of approaching the issue. By contrast one could argue either side of the abortion issue on the basis of its impact on the larger society or on such basic human communities as marriage and the family. Such a communitarian approach is not entirely foreign to the North American scene,[11] but individualistic arguments are more accessible and persuasive within our political culture.

Like virtually all of the ideologies treated in this book, then, liberalism is a diverse phenomenon. Different liberals claim to believe in different things, due largely to the contradictions intrinsic to the ideology. Nevertheless, all share a certain core set of common beliefs that mark them as liberals.

The Liberal Creed

To begin with, like the other ideologies we shall explore in this study, liberalism starts with a fundamental belief in human autonomy, which goes well beyond a mere attachment to personal freedom. Autonomy means to be self-directed, to govern oneself in accordance with a law which one has chosen for oneself. Each of the ideologies attaches this autonomy to some manifestation of humanity, be it the individual or some community such as the state or nation. Liberalism assigns this autonomy to the individual. In its Kantian sense, the autonomy of the individual does not mean that she can simply do as she pleases, since this self-chosen law must be capable of being compatible with the choices of other autonomous persons. Thus the first and most basic principle of liberalism runs as follows: Everyone possesses property in their own person and must therefore be free to govern themselves in accordance

---

[11]See, e.g., Christopher Lasch, *The True and Only Heaven* (New York: Norton, 1991), esp. pp. 168-225, in which the author makes the case for what might be labeled republicanism or populism, with its value of community and sense of limits, in the face of the utopianism and individualism of liberalism. Other political theorists call the "other" major political influence in the United States "civic republicanism" and find its origins within the classical Greek and Roman traditions. See, e.g., Thomas L. Pangle, *The Ennobling of Democracy: The Challenge of the Postmodern Age* (Baltimore, Md.: Johns Hopkins University Press, 1992), pp. 105-30.

with their own choices, provided that these choices do not infringe on the equal right of others to do the same. If my proposed actions effectively violate the property another enjoys in her own person, then I have transgressed the primary liberal precept and must thereby be held accountable for what I have done. However, without political authority there is no effective way to enforce this accountability. This is the central dilemma of individual autonomy that the liberal project is called upon to resolve.

If liberalism is a fairly recent phenomenon, its roots are nevertheless ancient. In fact, we can trace it nearly as far into the past as the tradition of political theorizing will allow: to the classical Greek and Roman worlds. Socrates, Plato and Aristotle are remembered as the greatest philosophers of ancient Athens, and each of them took politics into account in his theory. Although the polis was the center of their concern, the focus on the individual could already be seen in their reflections. Plato's Socrates sought to make the case for a standard of human action above and beyond the expectations of the city. Aristotle sought to locate this standard in the nature of the virtuous person himself. Both conceived of the possibility that individual human beings might have direct access to norms for human virtue apart from the conventional standards of the polis. Yet both saw the individual firmly embedded in the life of the polis.

These first political theorists were, of course, living in the last days of the polis, an institution whose decline was hastened by the imperial conquests of Aristotle's pupil Alexander of Macedon. Subsequent political theorizing, lacking the polis as a natural context, would have to fall back on either the individual or the much larger civic community constituted by the empire. One person who took the former route was Epicurus (341-270 B.C.), whose philosophy bears some striking similarities to that of the early liberals, especially Thomas Hobbes. For Epicurus and his followers, human life is a matter of avoiding those things we fear and seeking what gives us pleasure. Good and evil are thus relative to pain and pleasure, as experienced by the sensing individual. Based on his materialist physics, Epicurus affirmed that man is made up of constantly changing patterns of atoms and that there is no life after death. Justice has no essential nature, but is rooted in a mutual contract among human beings not to harm each other. More positively it seeks the mutual advantage of these contracting individuals. Far from being a "political being," as Aristotle had put it, man must avoid being trapped in the "prison" of politics and public affairs, preferring instead the safety of friendships among individuals. Thus we see that Epicurus and his disciples embraced an early form of individualism that, like its much later manifestations, was basically antipolitical.[12]

Liberalism proper arose in the seventeenth and eighteenth centuries, that is, in the intellectual milieu of the scientific revolution and of René Descartes' attempt to construct a unified science on mathematical models. Accordingly, liberalism, in typical Cartesian fashion, reduces society to its component parts and attempts to reconstruct it on a more rational basis. A human community is deemed intangible; we cannot touch it or otherwise perceive it through our senses. The only way to understand it is to subject its component parts to rigorous examination. These components are the individuals who make it up. Individuals are sovereign, and thus it is they who determine the shape of their communities.

According to liberalism, humanity has certain rights that inhere in each person as an individual. The individual is autonomous: that is, she pursues a rational self-interest as she thinks best. This is not to say that the community and its claims lack importance for the liberal. The more thoughtful and nuanced liberal acknowledges that healthy communities are necessary for the well-being of individuals.[13] Nevertheless, the community's claims are subsidiary to the rights of the individual. The individual claims to be able to remake the world and society at large in her own image.

From the time it came into being some three centuries ago, liberalism has also sought to emancipate the individual from the old social hierarchies, such as hereditary class. This in large measure accounts for its enduring appeal. The early liberals were preoccupied with eliminating the remaining vestiges of feudalism, with its ascription of status to persons irrespective of actual merit. Landed nobles and monarchs possessed their privileged positions through inheritance and not by hard work or ingenuity. Liberalism appealed to a real and understandable conviction on the part of many that positions of authority and power ought to be separated from the principle of inheritance and should in-

---

[12]See Epicurus, "Principal Doctrines" and "Fragments," in *The Stoic and Epicurean Philosophers: The Complete Extant Writings of Epicurus, Epictetus, Lecretius, Marcus Aurelius,* ed. Whitney J. Oates (New York: Random House, 1940), pp. 35-52; and J. M. Rist, *Epicurus: An Introduction* (Cambridge: Cambridge University Press, 1972).

[13]See, e.g., Will Kymlicka, *Liberalism, Community and Culture* (Oxford: Clarendon, 1989), in which the author attempts to defend liberalism against its communitarian detractors by arguing for the importance of community within a liberal framework. See also Michael Ignatieff, *The Needs of Strangers: An Essay on Privacy, Solidarity, and the Politics of Being Human* (New York: Elisabeth Sifton Books/Viking, 1984), esp. pp. 135-42. However, in his recent writings Ignatieff has moved more decisively in an individualist direction. See, e.g., his *Human Rights as Politics and Idolatry* (Princeton, N.J.: Princeton University Press, 2001), pp. 66-69, where he argues that human rights can belong only to individuals and not to groups, although he is careful to circumscribe the expansive claims of "rights talk" within a deliberative, democratic framework.

stead be vested in those best qualified to fill them. This would, it was argued, naturally benefit not only those individuals involved, but ultimately the larger society itself.

If individuals are indeed sovereign and if their rights are really prior to the community, then it stands to reason that the individuals themselves exist as such prior to the formation of society and the body politic. Liberals call this presocial or prepolitical condition the *state of nature*, which may or may not have been a historical reality. Prior to the formation of (especially) the political community, the individual lives in a state of nature in which he or she is totally sovereign and is limited only by the restraints of the natural world (that is, by physical laws which govern the world irrespective of whether or not we obey them) and the sovereignty of other individuals. Political theorists have differed on what this state of nature looked like. Locke wrote that "in the beginning all the world was America," by which he meant that before the introduction of the civil commonwealth in Europe, life on that continent resembled the western hemisphere of the seventeenth century with its sparsely settled territory and primitive communities of aboriginal peoples.[14] Other liberal theorists seem to have assumed that the state of nature is simply an abstraction and accordingly made no effort to locate it in prehistory. Rawls's "original position of equality" falls into this latter category.

Whatever this state of nature looked like and whether or not it was to be taken literally, it was nevertheless believed to be characterized by certain difficulties or inconveniences which needed to be overcome for human beings to live secure and productive lives. Thomas Hobbes believed that, because in this prepolitical state everything was licit and anyone could do whatever necessary to secure his own life, the state of nature was invariably a state of general warfare within which life was "solitary, poor, nasty, brutish, and short."[15] Locke was somewhat more inclined to see it as a peaceful state, in which reason was strong enough to assert itself. The law of reason mandates that "no one ought to harm another in his Life, Health, Liberty, or Possessions."[16] Yet even for Locke the state of nature meant that property could not be enjoyed in secure and stable fashion. For this and other reasons human beings deemed it necessary to transcend this state for something more conducive to peace and prosperity. What then replaces the state of nature? The civil commonwealth, answer the liberals. How is the

---

[14]John Locke *Of Civil Government* 2.5.49. Cf. Thomas Hobbes *Leviathan* 1.13.
[15]Hobbes *Leviathan* 1.13.
[16]Locke *Of Civil Government* 2.6.10.

state of nature transcended? By mutual promise or contract. Liberal political theory is often referred to as "social contract" theory. Contract is important for liberals because it flows out of their cherished belief in freedom of choice.

For virtually all liberals, with the possible exception of Hobbes himself,[17]
contract is something to be entered into voluntarily. An obligation not incurred
by means of voluntary contract is not automatically to be spurned, of course. But
there is a strong presumption in liberalism against imposing obligations that have
not been freely assumed by the sovereign individual. If a person has not made a
promise—which, after all, he need not do if he is not so inclined—then he cannot be held to its terms. But if he has indeed promised—if he has entered into
contract—then he is bound by its terms, at least up until that time when its con-
tinuance is no longer in the interest of the contracting parties. This then is the
origin of all obligation, including that within and toward the political community. The state is the product of contract among sovereign individuals. This does
not yet necessarily imply democracy in the modern sense. In fact, the early liberal theorists had little difficulty with constitutional monarchy or with property
qualifications attached to the franchise. Moreover, as we shall see in chapter five,
democracy rests on assumptions that are in significant respects at variance with
liberalism. Nevertheless, this notion of contract does place a premium on the
consent of individuals, without which the body politic loses its legitimacy.

Once the state has come into being, its sole raison d'être is to serve the needs
of individuals. What this entails differs with time and place. The early liberals,
assuming that freedom amounts to the ability of the individual to do as she
pleases unrestrained by the dictates of others, sought to limit the state to a minimal number of functions related to ensuring personal security and the enjoyment of property. This came to be known as the "night watchman" state. Such
a state would limit itself to standing guard, maintaining a stable procedural and
legal framework within which individuals would be free to seek their own respective interests as they themselves understood and determined them. In no in-
stance would the state undertake to coerce subjects for their own good in
paternal fashion, because no one knows better than the individuals themselves
what is most to their own benefit. Yet a small state need not imply a weak state.
In fact, for the early liberals and their more recent followers, the state must be

---

[17]For Hobbes there is no effective difference between a commonwealth by acquisition, i.e., conquest,
and a commonwealth by institution, i.e., voluntary agreement among contracting individuals (*Leviathan* 18). Since a promise not backed by force is void anyway, he is unwilling to play freedom of the
will and external coercion against each other. In this respect he differs from his liberal successors.

strong enough to enforce the "rules of the game" under which individuals seek their own self-chosen ends. By concentrating on these core functions of government, the state actually avoids the inevitable weakness that would ensue were it to spread itself too thin by assuming too many nonessential responsibilities.

The more recent heirs of this classical liberalism believe that this doctrine affords them a powerful safeguard against the omnicompetent, totalitarian state. If it can be shown that a given state does indeed govern best when governing least, that is, if we can place heavy restrictions around governmental responsibilities, then we can prevent it from taking on imperial pretensions and thereby becoming oppressive of its subjects. If we can stop the state from undertaking to provide even fairly minimal services that go beyond the protection of law and order, then we have gone some way toward preventing it from becoming the all-intrusive monolith characteristic of the Soviet Union and the People's Republic of China. This was clearly the belief of Hayek, whose classic *The Road to Serfdom* was written to warn Westerners of the totalitarian tendencies in their own polities as they moved to embrace the welfare state. Such warnings have been echoed by Milton Friedman, Ludwig von Mises and other members of the Chicago and Austrian schools of neoliberal economics.

If the state is indeed a voluntary community, as liberals hold, then the corollary to the social contract establishing it is the concomitant possibility of its abrogation and the withdrawal of consent. To be sure, Hobbes did not believe that the sovereign could be charged with injury by his subjects, because the sovereign himself was not party to the contract that gave him his power.[18] Nevertheless, if the essence of freedom is the individual's right to preserve herself, and if the sovereign fails in some fashion to protect the lives of his subjects, then they might nevertheless decide to take their chances and return to the state of nature rather than to endure the greater possibility of death under a weak or capricious sovereign. Locke, by contrast, believed that the political rulers were indeed bound by the terms of the contract, and thus the contracting individuals retain both a moral and legal right to "appeal to heaven," that is, to take up arms against a government that has failed to live up to its obligations to them. Thus, despite their different views of the moral and legal rights of subjects vis-à-vis their political rulers, Hobbes and Locke both admit the possibility of revolutionary action to overturn their dominion. Nearly a century after Locke wrote his *Two Treatises on Civil Government*, Thomas Jefferson would borrow heavily

---

[18]Hobbes *Leviathan* 2.21.

from Locke's philosophical vocabulary to justify the American revolt against Britain in his Declaration of Independence. It is not surprising, then, that Americans still retain something of the early liberal aversion to overweening government, even as they continue to pursue policies that effectively expand its range of activities.

Late Liberalism and the Expansion of the State

For Hobbes, freedom very simply consists of being able to do those things one wills to do without hindrance. From Hobbes onwards, liberals have gradually expanded the range of freedom to embrace more of what might be said to fall within the range of the individual will. And as they have done so they have expanded—deliberately or inadvertently—the scope of government. This process can be seen to have occurred over the course of several centuries in five stages.

In the *first stage*, corresponding in theory to the hypothetical *Hobbesian commonwealth* and in practice to the early modern absolute monarchies, the primary limits on the state are practical rather than legal or ethical. As noted above, Hobbes believed that the most basic of freedoms is the right to defend one's life. The very purpose of people coming together under the potentially harsh rule of a sovereign is to gain protection against the vicissitudes of life in the state of nature. Hobbes sounds most illiberal in holding that the sovereign, as the origin of all law, justice and indeed morality itself, remains above the law and is thus not subject to it. The state of nature never actually comes to an end between sovereigns and their subjects, who continue to fear them. However, even if rulers should impose excessively harsh taxation or confiscate property or otherwise treat their subjects in ways they dislike, their subjects are still almost certainly better off than they would be in the state of nature. In this respect, fear is never completely banished from the Hobbesian commonwealth; it is merely circumscribed and focused more manageably on the person of the sovereign rather than indiscriminately on all of one's neighbors. As for limits to the state, these are rooted in the self-interest of the sovereign, who refrains from doing anything that might cause his subjects to prefer the state of nature to his own rule. Of course none of this sounds much like liberalism, and perhaps it might better be described as pre-liberal or proto-liberal insofar as it stands at the beginning of its development.

In the *second stage*, corresponding to the *night watchman state*, the focus on the individual right to self-preservation is expanded to cover property, in recognition of the connection between preserving one's life and earning a livelihood. In the years before the industrial revolution, the primary form of productive property was land—a source of food for people and livestock, material for clothing and building materials for shelter. But the position of the small shopkeeper in the larger towns was coming to play an increasingly important role in western Europe and the newly settled territories of North America. For Hobbes, property comes into being only with the advent of the civil commonwealth and the protection of the sovereign. To paraphrase the old saying, possession is *ten*-tenths of the law in the state of nature. Whatever you can take possession of and keep is yours—at least until the next person is able to take it for herself. For Locke, by contrast, property falls within the legitimate range of human liberty, even in the state of nature. With the establishment of civil government, subjects retain control over their own persons and possessions—over their lives, liberty and property, as Locke puts it. But now they are able to enjoy them more securely since the commonwealth's very existence is justified by its provision of this security.

With the emphasis on property, we encounter classical liberalism's pronounced preference for the free market and a concomitant aversion to government intervention in economic transactions. In 1776, the very year of Jefferson's Declaration, the Scottish moral philosopher Adam Smith (1723-1790) published *An Inquiry into the Nature and Causes of the Wealth of Nations*, better known as simply *The Wealth of Nations*. In this book Smith laid out the economic implications of liberalism, initially against the regnant orthodoxies of mercantilism which had encouraged competition among national states for empires and markets as part of an effort to secure as much money as possible for the national coffers. Mercantilism had led to a series of wars between England and France, among others, as they sought to consolidate and defend their empires in North America and elsewhere.

Smith's economic theory, based on individual competition, a division of labor, free domestic markets and unrestricted international trade, seemed better suited to a world in which individual freedom was coming to be valued and was already playing a greater role in political theory. The extension of liberalism from the political into the economic realms seemed the next logical step to take. The American Revolution itself could be seen as an attempt by free-market liberals to escape an outmoded mercantilist British Empire, whose victory over France in the Seven Years War (1763) had only exacerbated colonial grievances and heightened the general desire for freedom. This connection between liberal freedom and the free market has further served to fuel the contemporary revival of classical liberal thought.

Liberalism's economic side has often been labeled *capitalism*, a word that carries much emotional baggage and seems rarely to be used in a simply descriptive manner. Marx describes capitalism as that stage in the ongoing development of human production in which the means of production become concentrated in the hands of the bourgeoisie, whose activities create a new class, the proletariat, whose labor is sold on the market as simply one more commodity.[19] Under capitalism the bourgeoisie stamps its own peculiar character on the society as a whole, using the state and the entire range of social institutions to support its position of supremacy over the proletariat.

Other observers have defined capitalism differently. Max Weber (1864-1920) defines it as a peculiar spirit compelling its adherents to work to multiply their capital and to avoid those enjoyments that might deplete it.[20] R. H. Tawney (1880-1962) regards it as the fruit of the shift to modernity, during which notions of self-adjusting mechanisms, self-interest and efficiency replaced older ethical and ecclesiastical limits on economic activity.[21] Amintore Fanfani (1908-1999) defines the principal characteristic of the capitalist spirit as "the unlimited use of all means of acquiring wealth that are held to be morally lawful and economically useful."[22] In capitalism the precapitalist notion of sufficiency has been replaced by the notion of unlimited accumulation and the instrumentalization of wealth. Goudzwaard similarly defines "modern capitalism" as a social structure in which the broad range of social forces combine to support economic growth and technological development. These factors manifest themselves in the form of market competition "between independent production units organized on the basis of returns on capital." In a capitalist social structure, any "vertical" barriers to economic activity fall away as the orientation toward God and his law is replaced by a "this-worldly" direction.[23] In this foundational spiritual sense, then, it would seem that capitalism can be defined simply as economic endeavor based on human autonomy and severed from its dependence on God's creative

---

[19]Marx's description and analysis of capitalism can be found in a number of his writings. For a compendium of topically organized excerpts dealing with this, see Karl Marx, *Selected Writings in Sociology and Social Philosophy*, ed. T. B. Bottomore and Maximilien Rubel (London: Penguin, 1961), esp. pp. 137-85.

[20]See Max Weber, *The Protestant Ethic and the Spirit of Capitalism* (London: Routledge, 1993), esp. pp. 47-78.

[21]R. H. Tawney, *Religion and the Rise of Capitalism* (Piscataway, N.J.: Transaction, 1998), esp. pp. 11-20.

[22]Amintore Fanfani, *Catholicism, Protestantism and Capitalism* (Notre Dame, Ind.: University of Notre Dame Press, 1984), p. 25.

[23]Bob Goudzwaard, *Capitalism and Progress: A Diagnosis of Western Society* (Grand Rapids, Mich.: Eerdmans, 1979), p. 11. Theologian Harvey Cox goes so far as to argue that devotion to the market is a kind of religion, similar in its functioning to such traditional religions as Christianity. See Cox, "The Market as God: Living in the New Dispensation," *The Atlantic Monthly*, March 1999, pp. 18-23.

and redemptive activity. If this definition is appropriate, then labeling even the former Soviet Union's economic system as "state capitalism" is appropriate.

But this autonomy is usually seen as belonging to the individual, and this is where the connection with liberalism comes in. Capitalism presupposes a rational economic agent who always acts in her own self-interest. She need not be altruistic. Indeed, it is better perhaps if she is not. For in pursuing her own interest, she is led, in Smith's famous expression, by an "invisible hand" to do what is best for the entire society. In this context, the state refrains from interfering in those decisions freely made by the sovereign individual. The state does not try to determine what these decisions will be; rather, it protects the right of individuals to make these decisions and sets only broad procedural rules governing their economic transactions.

Such state protection is extended to all equally. Liberals have long had a strong commitment to equality in some form, though this equality has been subject to different interpretations and has existed in some tension with liberty, their primary focus of loyalty. In the Hobbesian state of nature, all live equally in fear of each other, each having an equal right to preserve himself even at the expense of others, if necessary. In the Hobbesian commonwealth all live equally in fear of the sovereign. In Locke and Smith, however, this equality is expanded beyond the bare right of self-preservation to encompass self-interested economic activity. Here the commonwealth protects people's equal right to amass property for themselves. But of course the results of all this economic activity leave people far from equal, and this led to a crisis of faith in many liberals at the time of the industrial revolution.

In the seventeenth and eighteenth centuries many had come to place their confidence in the unfettered ability of individuals to order their lives as they see fit. This confidence had led to the pursuit of policies that would facilitate this to the greatest extent possible. Agricultural markets that had once been protected to the benefit of the landed gentry were gradually deregulated. Official monopolies, such as the Hudson's Bay Company and the British East India Company, were now subjected to competition from other private concerns. Coming in the wake of the earlier scientific revolution with its tremendous expansion in human knowledge of the physical world, the emancipation of economic activity paved the way for an industrial revolution, initially in England, and then spreading to Europe and the United States. The potential and real benefits were enormous. The invention of the steam engine greatly facilitated transportation over vast distances by land and by sea. With the introduction of the factory system and mass production, goods that had previously been made slowly and laboriously by hand could now be manufactured quickly, in large quantities and at lower cost. This had the potential to ease considerably, and perhaps even put an end to, poverty and want. The invention of the cotton gin even made chattel slavery in North America obsolescent and seemed at last to promise an end to an oppressive social institution. Liberal hopes seemed to be born out by these impressive achievements, which were in part fueled by market-driven economic policies.

But the industrial revolution had a dark side as well. Far from putting an end to poverty, it served only to increase it or perhaps to change its character and distribution. The economy of small independent entrepreneurs so championed by the early liberals gave way to an economic system dominated by a few large firms employing an increasing portion of the population in urban factories for long hours and small wages. Such was the plight of the new working class that Marx and Engels foresaw an increasing immiseration of greater numbers of people causing the collapse of capitalism altogether as a socialist revolution more equally distributed the goods of the community. Marx and Engels abandoned liberalism for a new ideological faith. But not all liberals were willing to do this—even those who were disillusioned by the abuses of industrial capitalism.

There is a paradoxical quality to freedom, given a society of fallen human beings. All people are in theory equally in possession of freedom, yet by virtue of this very freedom, people make themselves unequal, as we have noted. Freedom further makes it possible for some to take freedom away from others and to accumulate for themselves the capacities that accompany it. All this can occur quite legally and without violating the received mores of the community. Many liberals liken the competitive economic struggle to a kind of game, to which government limits itself to setting the rules. In no case should it attempt to determine the outcome. Much as games have winners and losers, so does the economic struggle. In the nineteenth century a number of liberal thinkers such as Herbert Spencer and William Graham Sumner borrowed the evolutionary ideas of Charles Darwin and transplanted them from the biological into the social and economic realms. The principle of natural selection that was believed to apply in the ongoing competition of different species to adapt to their environments was also held to ensure that only the fittest survive in human society. This "social Darwinism" coincided with the "robber baron" era of the industrial revolution, especially in the United States.

But games do not go on forever. They eventually come to an end, and the victorious collect their winnings. In the United States this meant that much of economic activity came to be monopolized by a small group of companies, such as Rockefeller's Standard Oil and Vanderbilt's New York Central. Taking advantage of economies of scale, these large concerns were able to keep their prices low, thereby undercutting and ultimately destroying the competition from smaller, family-owned businesses. This effectively produced a situation not unlike the former mercantile system in which monopolies were protected by the king. Realizing that this hardly conformed to the original vision, liberals who wished to keep their liberal faith had to move in one of two policy directions: either break up the monopolies or heavily regulate them. In 1911 American "trust busters" succeeded in breaking up Standard Oil into smaller, independent producers. On the other hand, the Bell System, or AT&T, was allowed to remain intact for many years as a regulated monopoly, until 1984. At the end of the twentieth century the giant computer software corporation Microsoft was subject to lawsuits under American antitrust laws. If some, though by no means all, liberals favored the breakup strategy, they did so uneasily, recognizing that this new role of government went beyond simply setting the rules of the game and very nearly dictated its outcome.

As a result of these seemingly inherent tensions within liberal faith and practice, many adherents in the nineteenth and twentieth centuries began to move in a different direction from that of their classical forebears, thereby shifting liberalism into its *third stage*, with the arrival of the *regulatory state*. Belatedly coming to understand that possible abridgments of individual freedom could come not only from government but also from private concentrations of power, these "reform" liberals begin to conclude that governmental power might be legitimately brought into the service of freedom. This requires a certain reenvisioning of the place of government in human society. Whereas the early liberals viewed government as the principal threat to individual freedom and sought to restrict it to a minimal number of tasks, later liberals, like their socialist compatriots, concluded that government might actually protect such freedom from the infringements of nonstate centers of power. This would require a considerably larger state apparatus than that envisioned by Locke and Smith.

In the United States this reenvisioning of the state was exemplified by the Sherman and Clayton antitrust acts of 1890 and 1914 respectively, which attempted to prevent business concerns from monopolizing the market and from weakening competition in a particular sector of the economy. Efforts in this direction were championed most famously by President Theodore Roosevelt and his progressive movement just after the beginning of the twentieth century. Believing that control over an "industrial baronage" was necessary to advance real liberty as opposed to a mere nominal liberty, Roosevelt was not afraid to use the power of government in this cause.[24]

But this was not the end of the liberal reenvisioning of the task of the state in a more interventionist direction. Not only are individuals constrained in their freedom by public and private centers of power; they are also limited by such impersonal factors as lack of sufficient economic resources, whatever the origin of this lack might be. Thus liberalism in its *fourth stage* moves beyond the checking of private concentrations of economic power to embrace the *equal opportunity state*. Franklin Delano Roosevelt's famous "four freedoms" included freedom from want, which does not fit into the classical liberal scheme because it takes positive action to achieve. In classical liberalism the government simply steps back and allows individuals the necessary space to pursue their own interests as they see fit. However, children growing up in the south Bronx or the west side of Chicago, for example, lack the sorts of opportunities available to the child raised in suburban New Rochelle or Oak Park. If life is indeed a game, then the contestants have by no means got an equal start. Some have taken off from the starting gate with an extra advantage that will tend to favor their ultimate victory, while others are not only laboring under various handicaps, but may not have reached the gate at all. It is questionable, in other words, whether all are really receiving fair treatment under this arrangement. Liberals understand, of course, that freedom means freedom to fail as well as to succeed. But given their heightened sense of fair play, liberals seem driven to reexamine the rules of the game if some contestants are unjustly handicapped from the outset.

Thus a new generation of liberals in the early twentieth century began to advocate a more concerted effort to control economic contingencies through the use of reason harnessed, once again, to the power of government. John Maynard Keynes announced the "end of laissez-faire" and championed efforts to even out the business cycle and to combat unemployment, thereby giving his name to an entire Keynesian school that dominated Western economic policies from the Great Depression of the 1930s until the first oil shock of 1973.[25] Leonard T. Hobhouse similarly argued the need for the organized action of the community

---

[24]See Theodore Roosevelt, *The Free Citizen: A Summons to Service of the Democratic Ideal*, ed. Hermann Hagedorn (New York: Macmillan, 1956), pp. 159-60.

[25]See John Maynard Keynes, *The End of Laissez-Faire* (London: Hogarth, 1926).

to shape the social forces within which individuals exercise their liberty.[26]

Of course the difficulty arises when we become aware that any attempt to insure individuals an equal start inevitably entails manipulating in some fashion the conditions that have produced such inequality. Fourth-stage liberalism thus champions equality of opportunity as a means of making certain that everyone "gets a fair shake." Equality of opportunity is ostensibly not the same as equality of result, the latter of which smacks of trying to fix the game's outcome. Yet the "game" of life is repeated in every generation, and if one's parents have not fared particularly well in their economic transactions, this will affect one's own ability to enter the game on a fair and equitable footing. It is at this point that the analogy to a game begins to break down, which demonstrates once more a central weakness of liberal individualism: it is not only unable to account for the ontological status of community; it also ignores the connectedness of individuals to previous and succeeding generations. It pretends that the individual is an isolated runner in the race, whose success or failure depends wholly on herself.

When it becomes apparent that this is not the case—that is, when liberals bump up against reality—they are often driven to pursue policies quite at variance with classical liberalism's initial antistatist orientation. Thus late liberals came to embrace the welfare state, a series of government programs which at a minimum would provide a social "safety net" to assist those experiencing the negative effects of the market or, at the maximum would attempt to level the playing field and effect greater economic equality in the society as a whole. It is perhaps one of history's ironies that liberals came to be identified with such programs so thoroughly that in North America the "liberal" label is almost always used to describe someone favoring an expansion of the welfare state to ensure greater economic equality. Elsewhere in the Western world such policies are usually labeled "social democratic," thus indicating a connection with socialism. It must be noted, however, that while socialists might favor the welfare state for distinctly communitarian reasons, liberals favor it for basically individualistic reasons. The welfare state is simply a means to enhance and expand the range of free choices available to the individual, not a weapon of class warfare.

The Right and the Good: Subsidizing Choices

In recent decades the expansion of liberal freedom has moved into yet a *fifth*

---

[26]L. T. Hobhouse, *Liberalism* (New York: Oxford University Press, 1964), especially pp. 74-87.

stage with the rise of what might be called the *choice enhancement state*. Unlike premodern political theories, particularly those rooted in Aristotle or Thomas Aquinas, liberalism denies that there is a substantive good which human beings or their political leaders are obliged by their nature to follow. Beginning with Thomas Hobbes and leading up to John Rawls and Robert Nozick, liberalism assumes that if there are goods, these are sovereignly determined by the individual will and not by any body claiming to speak for an entire community of citizens. There is, in short, no *common* good. As Hobbes puts it:

> For there is no such *finis ultimus*, utmost aim, nor *summum bonum*, greatest good, as is spoken of in the books of the old moral philosophers. Nor can a man any more live, whose desires are at an end, than he, whose senses and imaginations are at a stand. Felicity is a continual progress of the desire, from one object to another; the attaining of the former, being still but the way to the latter.[27]

Goods, then, are not only plural; they are usually in conflict with each other because individuals have varying and conflicting desires that they are constantly struggling to satisfy. The task of liberalism, therefore, is to try to accommodate these desires as much as possible in a reasonably peaceful and stable manner. But in no case should the liberal state attempt to prejudge the choices lying before individuals, since that would be an undue limitation on freedom of choice.

Such accommodation requires to as great an extent as possible what might be called a metaphysically neutral state, or what might better be called a spiritually vacant state.[28] Because the individual citizens are sovereign and because, further, individual preferences differ from one person to the next, the state must refrain from favoring one person's preferences over another's. It must simply establish the broad procedural framework within which individuals are enabled to pursue their chosen goals. In a political community containing Christians, Jews, theosophists, agnostics, golfers and sadomasochists, the state refrains from passing judgment on the goodness of any of these worldviews or proclivities, and acts simply as referee. Michael Sandel describes this approach as "deontological liberalism," whose basic thesis is

---

[27]Hobbes *Leviathan* 2.11.

[28]I prefer the term *spiritual* to *metaphysical* because the former communicates much more clearly the religious character of liberal ideology. Philosophers often seem to use "metaphysical" to avoid having to deal with the foundational *religious* character of a particular theory.

Society, being composed of a plurality of persons, each with his own aims, interests, and conceptions of the good, is best arranged when it is governed by principles that do not themselves presuppose any particular conception of the good; what justifies these regulative principles above all is not that they maximize the social welfare or otherwise promote the good, but rather that they conform to the concept of right, a moral category given prior to the good and independent of it.[29]

This means that what is conventionally called "legislating morality" is not to be admitted in the liberal state. Though not all professed liberals wish to see prostitutes and pornographers allowed to pursue freely their respective trades, there is a pronounced inclination in most to leave such matters to the workings of the market and to refrain from legislating a particular moral conception of, say, proper sexuality. In similar fashion, libertarian economist Friedrich von Hayek objects to a notion such as "social justice" because it assumes that society is a moral agent capable of imposing an overarching purpose on the self-chosen goals of individuals and smaller, purpose-oriented groups.[30]

But at this point fifth-stage liberalism encounters a dilemma. While the liberal state is supposed to refrain from judging the goodness of people's choices and while it claims a benign neutrality toward the various options lying before its citizens, it cannot overlook the unequal consequences following from the exercise of these choices. Canadian Prime Minister Pierre Trudeau famously said that the state has no business in the bedrooms of the nation, meaning that it ought not to set legal norms for human sexual relations which properly belong in the private sphere. During liberalism's earlier stages such a statement might still have been controversial and would likely have raised eyebrows, simply because nonliberal elements in the culture would still have been in place to counteract liberalism's fragmenting influence.

However, in its fifth stage liberal neutrality has come to be extended beyond mere political disagreement and into a much wider range of contingencies. Whether two people decide to marry, to live together in an unofficial and impermanent sexual relationship, or to move promiscuously from one brief sexual encounter to another, the law plays no favorites and refrains from dictating how

---

[29]Michael Sandel, *Liberalism and the Limits of Justice* (Cambridge: Cambridge University Press, 1982), p. 1.

[30]Hayek, *Law, Legislation and Liberty*, vol. 2, *The Mirage of Social Justice* (Chicago: University of Chicago Press, 1976). Hayek is not, of course, a fifth-stage liberal, but his individualistic assumptions are in fundamental continuity with those of his more statist opponents.

consenting partners should behave toward each other in the privacy of their own quarters. Similarly, whereas a previous generation expected as a matter of course that legal divorce would be difficult, if not impossible, to attain; that abortion would be restricted if not entirely prohibited; and that reproductive sex would be officially preferred to nonreproductive sex; contemporary liberals look on such policies as unfair and discriminatory insofar as they infringe on freedom of choice.[31]

However, fifth-stage liberals tend to ignore the fact that if easier divorce helps people to escape from abusive marriages, it also contributes to an increased number of shattered families, with all of their attendant dislocations and dysfunctions, including psychological trauma in children and the increased poverty that inevitably accompanies the financial division of a household.[32] Government may decline to "stigmatize" divorcees or to place legal obstacles in their way, but it cannot proclaim that divorce will have no deleterious effects on the parties involved and on the larger society.[33] It may similarly abstain from adversely judging nonmarital intercourse, but it cannot decree that unwanted pregnancies or sexually transmitted diseases will not proliferate. Government may legally affirm that single-parent families are "just as valid" as two-parent families, but it cannot declare that there will be no negative fallout from the choice to end a marriage or that fatherlessness will not leave its impact on the lives of the offspring.[34]

When these undesirable consequences do occur, rather than acknowledge

---

[31]For a recent defense of what I am calling fifth-stage liberalism within the domestic setting, see Michael Ignatieff, *The Rights Revolution* (Toronto: House of Anansi, 2000), especially chap. 4, "Rights, Intimacy, and Family Life," pp. 85-112. Here the author vindicates—though not unreservedly—the contemporary emphasis on personal authenticity, with its implied far-reaching extension of the right to choose, even in the most intimate of settings. What is missing from Ignatieff's account is a recognition that certain social formations exist not merely because autonomous individuals have called them into being but because they answer to a more fundamental, transhistorical order of some sort. Thus the choices we make as human beings are always constrained by the intrinsic limitations of a world not of our own making and, accordingly, have potentially deleterious ramifications for ourselves, those around us and the larger society when these constraints are not recognized.

[32]See, e.g., Barbara Dafoe Whitehead, *The Divorce Culture: Rethinking Our Commitments to Marriage and Family* (New York: Vintage, 1998).

[33]For a study of such effects on children, see Judith Wallerstein, Julia Lewis and Sandra Blakeslee, *The Unexpected Legacy of Divorce* (New York: Hyperion, 2000), and their earlier *Second Chances: Men, Women, and Children a Decade After Divorce* (New York: Ticknor & Fields, 1989).

[34]See David Popenoe, *Life Without Father: Compelling New Evidence That Fatherhood and Marriage Are Indispensable for the Good of Children and Society* (Cambridge, Mass.: Harvard University Press, 1999), and David Blankenhorn, *Fatherless America: Confronting Our Most Urgent Social Problem* (New York: Basic-Books, 1995).

that the quest to validate all lifestyle choices equally is a utopian one doomed to failure, fifth-stage liberals increasingly call on government to ameliorate, if not altogether eliminate, such consequences so they can continue to engage in this fruitless quest. This inevitably leads to an expansion in the scope of government that is difficult to contain within any boundaries whatever. As George F. Will observes, "The fundamental goal of modern liberalism has been equality, and it has given us government that believes in the moral equality of appetites. The result is a government that is big but not strong; fat but flabby; capable of giving but not leading."[35] This is the liberalism so often castigated by self-styled conservatives in the United States and Canada. Rather than calling on citizens to live up to their commitments and to fulfill their responsibilities throughout the range of communal contexts, this final stage of liberalism demands that government effectively subsidize irresponsible behavior for fear that doing otherwise risks making government into a potentially oppressive legislator of the good life.

Of course, not all professed liberals are willing to follow liberalism into its fifth stage, and many are not even inclined to move beyond its second. Indeed the harshest critics of fifth-stage liberalism come out of the twentieth-century classical liberal revival, often clothed in conservative garb. However, the classical liberal response to the bloated state, namely, the reaffirmation of the night watchman state, is fundamentally inadequate because it seeks merely to reverse a lengthy—and possibly inevitable, given liberalism's presuppositions—historical process rather than to question in the first place liberalism's reduction of the state to a mere voluntary organization charged only with fulfilling the shifting terms of a social contract.[36]

It is painfully evident, then, that liberalism as a *political* theory fails precisely on its view of the state as a distinct institution with its own appointed task in

---

[35] George F. Will, *Statecraft as Soulcraft: What Government Does* (New York: Touchstone/Simon & Schuster, 1984), pp. 158-59.

[36] A number of observers, even those firmly rooted in the Christian tradition, fail to note or at least downplay the continuities among the various strains of liberalism. See, e.g., Robert P. George, *The Clash of Orthodoxies: Law, Religion, and Morality in Crisis* (Wilmington, Del.: ISI Books, 2001), and particularly the essay contained therein, "Religious Values and Politics." Here the author distinguishes among three varieties of liberalism, "old fashioned liberalism," "Rooseveltian liberalism" and "personal liberationism," roughly corresponding to my second, fourth and fifth stages, yet he argues that "there is no necessary connection between these strands of liberalism" (p. 252), a position he ascribes to Pope John Paul II (p. 239). Thus George can express greater sympathy for old fashioned liberalism than for the other two strains and goes so far as to assert that, at least on certain issues, "to be a good Catholic one must be a kind of old-fashioned liberal" (p. 236). However, the continuity is precisely to be found in a shared voluntaristic notion of community, including the state, as I argue here.

God's world. If the state is merely a product of contract, then the contracting individuals are fully within their rights to alter the state's task as they see fit. There is a seemingly vast distance between the classical liberal night watchman state and the late liberal bureaucratic state undertaking to subsidize freedom of choice. Yet what they have in common is that both are reducible to the aggregative wills of their constituent members. To the extent that this is so, liberals are unable to recognize the state to be essentially different from the church, the school, the business enterprise, the labor union or the amateur baseball team. In this vision government exists not so much to adjudicate properly the multiple diverse interests in society, as to fulfill the aspirations of individuals, whatever form these may take at a given historical moment.

The Spiritually Vacant State: The Privatization of Ultimate Belief

The spiritually vacant state undoubtedly achieves its highest level of abstraction in John Rawls, whose "justice as fairness" can be seen as a way of securing general agreement on the principles of justice amid a plurality of ends chosen by individuals. To insure that these principles are chosen in an unbiased way, Rawls places this collective act of choosing in an artificial context called the "original position of equality," which corresponds to the early liberals' "state of nature." In this original position all participants are hidden behind a "veil of ignorance" which prevents not only others, but even themselves, from knowing anything about themselves, other than that they are rational and self-interested. Participants do not, therefore, know whether they themselves are male or female, rich or poor, white or black, Christian or Muslim, tall or short; indeed they have no knowledge of any of the ordinary characteristics that go into making them the unique human persons they are. Rawls is confident that if people could imagine themselves in this original position they would all uniformly choose certain principles of justice that would provide for a maximum amount of freedom while insuring that no one person could fall through the cracks and thereby lose the benefits that are attached to membership in society.[37]

Rawls's undertaking is based on the questionable supposition that it is possible to detach human persons from their subjective worldviews and that their reasoning abilities are capable of being exercised in a religiously neutral

---

[37] See once again Rawls's *Theory of Justice* and his more recent *Political Liberalism*, in which, responding to critics of his original formulation, Rawls attempts to detach his principles of justice from a Kantian metaphysic. For a critique of the latter, see Edward A. Goerner, "Rawls' Apolitical Political Turn," *Review of Politics* 55 (fall 1993): 713-18.

manner.[38] It assumes, further, the possibility of constructing a political order which is purely formal and is unaffected by the diverse and conflicting substantive commitments of its members. For the liberal there is to be no "Christian" state, no Islamic republic, not even an atheistic regime. Ultimate issues pertaining to the good and to God fall outside the legitimate sphere of the state, which must instead leave such issues to the individual.[39]

But an appeal to justice as fairness is not enough. As Alasdair MacIntyre has pointed out, there are rival conceptions of justice dependent on specific traditions of reasoning conditioned by divergent conceptions of the good.[40] If so, then even a liberal conception of justice is based on a notion of the good— something that the liberal is compelled by her own convictions to deny. In other words, the liberal belief in the priority of right is rooted in an underlying assumption that advancing such a priority is for the *good* of society.

Of course, this central difficulty within liberalism can be expressed in other than Aristotelian, teleological language. Liberalism makes a pretense of benign neutrality within the political realm toward such ultimate convictions commonly labeled religious.[41] Because traditional religions are deemed inherently divisive of the body politic, liberals would prefer—no, demand—that they be limited to the realm of private conviction. In contrast to the theocratic pretensions of earlier monarchies,

---

[38]In his *Political Liberalism*, however, Rawls is more congenial to the possibility of appealing to "comprehensive doctrines," i.e., religious principles, to support the conclusions of public reason when historical conditions warrant it, as in the antebellum abolitionist movement and the civil rights movement of Dr. Martin Luther King Jr. (pp. 247-54). Yet in these cases public reason must be accorded the clear priority, and traditionally religious people are in effect banned from introducing their doctrines a priori, especially if they conflict with public reason. They may bring them in only in the event of a general crisis in understanding public reason and its political implications. However, as Peter Berkowitz points out, Rawls's apparently freestanding liberalism is itself rooted in an act of *faith*. See Berkowitz, "John Rawls and the Liberal Faith," *Wilson Quarterly*, spring 2002, accessed July 25, 2002 <http://wwics.si.edu/outreach/wq/wqselect/rawls.htm>.

[39]Something of this approach can already be seen in Hobbes, who undertook to reinterpret Christianity in a liberal direction to domesticate it and make it more compatible not only with uncontested political sovereignty but with his individualism. See, e.g., the argument in John Seaman, "Hobbes and the Liberalization of Christianity," *Canadian Journal of Political Science* 32 (June 1999): 227-46.

[40]See once more MacIntyre, *Whose Justice? Which Rationality?* esp. pp. 1-11.

[41]For a trenchant exploration of liberalism's privatizing approach to religion, see Jean Bethke Elshtain, "The Bright Line: Liberalism and Religion," in *The Betrayal of Liberalism: How the Disciples of Freedom and Equality Helped Foster the Illiberal Politics of Coercion and Control*, ed. Hilton Kramer and Roger Kimball (Chicago: Ivan R. Dee, 1999), pp. 139-55. Although the title of the book expresses the editors' thesis that the distortions of late liberalism represent a betrayal of its original impulses, Elshtain herself questions this interpretation at the outset of her essay. The discussion in this chapter should make it clear that, although the early liberals would probably not have liked what liberalism has become in recent decades, the latter's distortions were already implicit in the logic of liberalism per se. See the last section of this chapter.

the liberal polity no longer attempts to prescribe an official creed for its citizens. Yet as a price for granting religious freedom, the followers of traditional religions must limit their beliefs to the realms of family, home and church, and must concomitantly keep them out of the public square. Undergirding this approach lies the assumption that traditional religious beliefs are fundamentally subjective and irrational, and thus not subject to thoughtful public discourse. In large measure this explains recent Supreme Court decisions in the United States intended to shore up Jefferson's oft-cited "wall of separation" between church and state. In the midst of a pluralistic society, it is argued, the state is obligated to exclude from the public square all beliefs that might have the effect of tearing apart the body politic.

At the same time, something must hold the political community together. In early modern and premodern times this something was religion. The axiom governing the relationship between religion and politics prior to the seventeenth century was *Cuius regio eius religio* (whose territory, his religion): the prince determined the religion of his realm, and his subjects must conform, risk being branded disloyal or leave. In this context the advent of liberalism undoubtedly seemed a liberating force because it offered a way of maintaining unity amidst diversity. Liberalism cemented the unity of the state by appealing to common principles of reason to which all human beings could theoretically adhere. Following Locke, Jefferson's Declaration of Independence speaks of the laws of nature and of nature's god as "self-evident," that is, available to all thinking human beings.

Yet the spiritually vacant state is, after all, nothing of the sort. As Richard John Neuhaus observes, the "naked public square" cannot remain naked for long: "When the value-bearing institutions of religion and culture are excluded, the value-laden concerns of human life flow back into the square under the banner of politics. It is much like trying to sweep a puddle of water on an uneven basement floor; the water immediately flows back into the space you had cleared."[42]

Neuhaus is surely right as far as he goes. But his argument must be taken a step further: the naked public square is not only quickly filled, but is itself an illusion. The spiritually vacant state is never such in reality. If liberalism is rooted in an idolatrous religion, as I am arguing here, then even when its followers presume to have banished the spirits from the public square, they have done no more than to infuse it with their own spirit. In other words, they have successfully privatized

---

[42]Richard John Neuhaus, *The Naked Public Square: Religion and Democracy in America* (Grand Rapids, Mich.: Eerdmans, 1984), p. 157.

all religions except their own, which they have in fact privileged above all others.

But perhaps through an ingenious sleight of hand, they have persuaded the followers of these other religions that liberalism is not rooted in any religion and, quite against the testimony of their own traditions, that the privatization of their ultimate beliefs is right and proper and in the public interest. When people finally see through the ruse and decide to accept no longer the terms of this Faustian bargain, liberalism's ascendancy is likely to end. Until then its assumptions appear incontestable and it continues to set the ground rules.

Sin and Salvation in Liberalism

If the various ideologies are based on a gnostic view of reality ascribing evil to something in God's creation, and if they further look to something else in that creation to effect salvation, to what extent is this true of liberalism? Does liberalism have salvific pretensions? To be sure, few flesh and blood liberals would make this sort of claim for their theory and its attendant policy programs. Most liberals would not recognize in liberalism a comprehensive worldview as such. Unlike, for example, Marxism, whose "worldviewish" character is more obvious, liberalism at its best does not claim an all-inclusive philosophy of history, nor does it necessarily attempt to analyze all human motivations in terms of a single animating factor. And if Marxism has a more overtly eschatological expectation, as we shall see in chapter six, liberalism's eschatology is more tacit and rarely articulated as such. The most thoughtful of liberals claim only that, say, their contractarian approach applies at least to the economic and political realms, while other principles are properly operative in other areas of life.

For example, Michael Novak supports a classical liberal approach to economics and society that he provocatively labels "democratic capitalism."[43] Championing the free market as the surest road to material prosperity, he nevertheless takes care to avoid subjecting the whole of life to market values, positing instead a society consisting of a triad of political, economic and moral/cultural systems. In the political system democratic institutions are paramount. In the economic system voluntary exchange within a market framework is the dominant element.

---

[43]But see Russell Kirk's response to Novak's use of this label: "Now in truth our society is not a 'capitalist system' at all, but a complex cultural and social arrangement that comprehends religion, morals, prescriptive political institutions, literary culture, a competitive economy, private property, and much more besides" (*The Politics of Prudence* [Bryn Mawr, Penn.: Intercollegiate Studies Institute, 1993], p. 184). This response comes from someone usually regarded as a "paleo-conservative" as opposed to Novak's "neo-conservatism."

By contrast, the moral/cultural system admits a variety of principles, depending on context. Healthy families, churches, professional associations and the like are keys to the success of democratic capitalism, though their undergirding principles may be quite distinct from that of voluntary exchange. Thus as a Roman Catholic Novak can defend his church's teaching authority, despite the fact that its hierarchical character and authoritative claims seem the very antithesis of liberal values.[44] In similar fashion Novak's associate Richard John Neuhaus argues that Pope John Paul II and the larger Catholic tradition are supportive of a liberalism rightly understood in this limited and apparently nonideological sense.[45]

What this indicates, however, is not that liberalism is anything less than an ideology rooted in a fundamentally secular worldview, but that not all professed liberals are willing to take its logic as far as it might otherwise lead them, particularly with respect to nonpolitical and noneconomic spheres of life. For this we can be grateful to God, since it testifies to his common grace. Nevertheless, as David L. Schindler correctly points out, liberalism is imbued with a spirit whose logic is antithetical to a public Christian witness and whose individualism is difficult to contain within normative limits.[46] Even Locke, though moderate in his adaptation of Hobbes' radical nominalism and legal positivism, implicitly extends the logic of the social contract from political association to marriage, which, far from being an intrinsically lifelong union, he deems dissoluble at the discretion of the partners once the offspring whom it serves are fully grown and on their own.[47] Whether this represents

---

[44]See Michael Novak, *The Spirit of Democratic Capitalism* (New York: Simon & Schuster, 1982). For trenchant critiques of Novak's argument, see Lesslie Newbigin, *Foolishness to the Greeks: The Gospel and Western Culture* (Grand Rapids, Mich.: Eerdmans, 1986), pp. 111-14; and David L. Schindler, *Heart of the World, Center of the Church* (Grand Rapids, Mich.: Eerdmans, 1996), esp. pp. 116-33.

[45]See, e.g., Richard John Neuhaus, "The Liberalism of John Paul II," *First Things* 73 (May 1997): 16-21; and once more the argument of George, *Clash of Orthodoxies.*

[46]Schindler, *Heart of the World,* esp. pp. 35-37.

[47]Locke *Of Civil Government* 2.7.77-81. For an analysis of the liberal approach to marriage, see Christopher Wolfe, "The Marriage of Your Choice," *First Things* 50 (February 1995): 37-41. Wolfe argues that the professed liberal commitment to freedom of choice and its pretense of neutrality in the public realm are contradicted by its unwillingness to permit prospective spouses to enter legally indissoluble marriages. On the other hand, in 1997 the state of Louisiana legally permitted couples the option of "covenant marriage," i.e., a marriage that is more difficult to end than that subject to a no-fault divorce. Arizona and Arkansas have subsequently adopted similar laws. For a journalistic account of the impact of the covenant marriage law in Louisiana, see Siobhan Roberts, "'God Hates Divorce': Covenant Marriage Allows Couples to Safeguard Their Commitment," *National Post* (Toronto), December 30, 2000, B1-2. For a more scholarly assessment, see Joel A. Nichols, "Louisiana's Covenant Marriage Law: A First Step Toward a More Robust Pluralism in Marriage and Divorce Law?" *Emory Law Journal* 47 (summer 1998), <www.law.emory.edu/ELJ/volumes/sum98/nichols.html>. Nichols would expand the range of choice beyond individuals to include the diverse faith communities themselves.

an extension of voluntaristic individualism from the political realm into marriage or from the market into marriage is perhaps a matter of interpretation.
I would be prepared to argue that *political* liberalism in fact already stretches
the logic of the economic marketplace, where exchange relationships are
quite properly transitory and noncommunal, into the political realm, where
the substance of both authority and community is eviscerated by being reduced to a similar exchange relationship. Thus for all their care to uphold and
to circumscribe the free market, which in itself is right and fitting, it is precisely the *liberalism* of Novak and Neuhaus that has difficulty understanding
why political community must be based on something other than the voluntarism of social contract theory.[48]

Thus, even if liberalism at its best is not as overtly totalitarian as, say, Marxism-
Leninism or national socialism, and even if most of its adherents would be
modest in their claims in its favor, there is within it, nevertheless, a tendency
to extend the voluntary principle too far—to assume that community and the
obligations it inevitably imposes on individuals can be reduced to the consent
of the component members, as we have repeatedly noted above. In other
words, in typical gnostic fashion evil is located in heteronomous authority,
namely, in authority originating outside one's own will, and thus in any collectivity whose claims are independent of the wills of its members. That human beings are created for life in community is a truth liberalism has difficulty
comprehending. Similarly, liberals find it difficult to admit that people may
be under legitimate obligations and other constraints irreducible to their voluntary agreement.

Again, although few liberals would assert, at least overtly, that they follow a soteriology of freedom, they work with an implicit assumption that we are progres-
sively saved insofar as the claims of community and external authority are
diminished and the authority (read: liberty) of one's own will is maximized. This
soteriological approach probably reaches its apogee in the near cultic libertarian-

---

[48]See, e.g., the controversial "Symposium: The End of Democracy? The Judicial Usurpation of Politics,"
First Things 67 (November 1996): 18-42, whose introductory essay manifests an obvious debt to
Locke's contractarian political theory. It is reasonable to assume that both Neuhaus and Novak played
a large role in drafting this essay. Similarly, Charles Colson and Nancy Pearcey, in *How Now Shall We
Live?* (Wheaton, Ill.: Tyndale House, 1999), revealingly argue "that government is not simply a social
contract between the people and those who govern, but a social contract made under the authority of
a higher law" (p. 400). What is interesting in this statement is not the authors' proper emphasis on law,
but their retention of contractarian language, even in their otherwise commendable attempt to understand government from a biblically Christian standpoint.

ism of an Ayn Rand[49] or a Murray N. Rothbard[50] or a Hayek. For all three the progress of civilization depends unambiguously on government exercising as little coercive power as possible and on individuals being permitted to pursue their self-interest to the greatest feasible extent. Here is where liberalism begins to take on eschatological dimensions approaching those of Marxist socialism. Here too is where liberalism, rather than simply working out of a larger secular worldview, appears itself to *become* a religiously based worldview whose practical implications daily play themselves out in a society where traditions are reflexively and uncritically despised as oppressive, marital obligations are deemed to inhibit free sexual expression, and "rights talk"[51] substitutes for genuine political deliberation.

Thus liberalism, for all the good it has accomplished in encouraging the protection of genuine human rights, fails on two counts. First and foremost, it offers a false salvation rooted in a fundamentally religious assertion of human autonomy against external authority. As Schindler correctly observes concerning the liberal quest to expand this autonomy to increasing numbers of people, a "freedom whose nature is wrongly understood does not become good simply because it is widely distributed rather than restricted to a few."[52] This observation cuts to the heart not only of liberalism, but of several ideologies working to achieve what their followers would see as emancipation or liberation from various forms of outside "domination," as we shall see further below. Second, and most significant for our purposes, liberalism is unable to distinguish adequately the state as an authoritative community irreducible to the voluntary consent of its constituent individuals. This suggests that we must look elsewhere if we are to articulate a genuinely political theory rooted in a nonidolatrous worldview.

---

[49] Ayn Rand (1905-1982) is best known for her philosophy known as objectivism, which brings together egoism, libertarianism and atheism. This philosophy is exemplified in her novels *We the Living* (1936; reprint, New York: Random House, 1959), *Anthem* (1938; reprint, New York: New American Library, 1946,), *The Fountainhead* (New York: New American Library, 1943), and *Atlas Shrugged* (New York: Random House, 1957). She later authored nonfiction works including *The Virtue of Selfishness: A Concept of New Egoism* (New York: New American Library, 1964) and *Introduction to Objectivist Epistemology* (New York: Objectivist, 1967).

[50] Murray N. Rothbard (1926-1995) was a prolific author whose writings include *Man, Economy, and the State: A Treatise on Economic Principles* (1962; reprint, Los Angeles: Nash, 1970); *For a New Liberty* (New York: Macmillan, 1973); and *The Ethics of Liberty* (Atlantic Highlands, N.J.: Humanities, 1982). He argues for as little government intervention as possible in economic activity, including a return to the gold standard and the abolition of central banks.

[51] See Mary Ann Glendon, *Rights Talk: The Impoverishment of Political Discourse* (New York: Free Press, 1991).

[52] Schindler, *Heart of the World*, p. 119.

3

CONSERVATISM

History as Source of Norms

In the previous chapter we saw that in popular political discourse, conservatism and liberalism are often seen as polar opposites. I would like to suggest here that this is not an accurate assessment. In the first place, it is not apparent that liberalism *has* a clear opposite. If it is synonymous with individualism, then it is possible that its antithesis would be some form of collectivism. But since collectivism takes socialist, nationalist, democratic and fascist forms, to speak of a single ideology contrary to liberalism is almost certainly incorrect. In the second place, and perhaps more significantly, conservatism is itself not a single unified ideology capable of being evaluated as an identifiable doctrinal position. Some, such as the late Russell Kirk (1918-1994), have gone so far as to argue that conservatism is not an ideology at all, partly because it lacks this common creedal formulation and partly because he identifies conservatism with a nondogmatic "politics of prudence" that eschews ideological visions.[1] Recognizing to some extent the persuasiveness of this argument, I am inclined to admit that conservatism is at least a

---

[1] See Russell Kirk, *The Politics of Prudence* (Bryn Mawr, Penn.: Intercollegiate Studies Institute, 1993), esp. pp. 1-14, and *The Conservative Mind: From Burke to Eliot*, 7th rev. ed. (Chicago: Regnery, 1986), p. iii. See also the arguments of Edward E. Ericson in "Conservatism at Its Highest," and of Gerhart Niemeyer in "Russell Kirk and Ideology," *Intercollegiate Review: A Journal of Scholarship and Opinion* 30, no. 1 (1994): 31-34, 35-38, a special issue devoted to the life and thought of the late Russell Kirk.

different sort of ideology than the others we are exploring here. While liberalism makes a god out of the individual, and while socialism (especially in its Marxist form) deifies the economic class, conservatism seems to be a tendency found in the several ideologies themselves. After all, a classical liberal who wishes to recover the Lockean and Smithian roots of his ideology might well be labeled a "conservative liberal." Similarly, a socialist who opposes his community's move toward a market-based economy can justifiably be called a "conservative socialist." Perhaps conservatism, then, is not an ideology in its own right, but is instead a tendency that feeds off of other ideologies. Nevertheless, as we shall see, conservatism does indeed bear many of the hallmarks of an ideology.

To conserve something means to keep it, to maintain it, in the face of forces that might tend to eliminate it over time. A conservative has a heightened sense that with change of any sort comes inevitable loss—often the loss of something good which cannot be replaced. In a Hollywood film some years ago, a teenage boy travels thirty years into the past and is greeted by, among other things, a peculiar spectacle: a car pulls into a "service station" (not just a "gas station") and is immediately looked after by several uniformed attendants who not only fill the tank, but check the oil and tires and wash the windshields.[2] This scene is obviously intended to invoke a sense of amusement and nostalgia in an audience accustomed to self-serve gas bars where the driver pumps her own gas, pays for it and then leaves. The viewers laugh, but they do so with some regret at the passing of a vanished world where ordinary customers were treated with a bit more attention and courtesy than they are today. Such regret is the foundation of the conservative mentality.

But perhaps conservatives regret nothing more than the loss of their own power and privilege. If there are conservative capitalists and conservative socialists, perhaps these are simply people who lament the erosion of a political or economic system from which they have long benefited. If a William E. Simon or a Milton Friedman defends a laissez-faire economic arrangement, then perhaps it is because this is the system that enables them to live comfortably and enjoy a privileged position in their own society, and indeed in the world as a whole.[3] If a Yegor Ligachev defends traditional Marxism-Leninism in Gor-

---

[2]Robert Zemeckis and Bob Gale, *Back to the Future*, dir. Robert Zemeckis (Universal City, Calif.: Universal Pictures, 1985).

[3]See William E. Simon, *A Time for Truth* (New York: McGraw-Hill, 1978); and Milton Friedman, *Capitalism and Freedom* (Chicago: University of Chicago Press, 1962); and *Why Government Is the Problem* (Stanford, Calif.: Hoover Institution Press, 1993).

bachev's declining Soviet Union, then it is because he is part of the privileged class, the *nomenklatura,* which is the backbone of the communist system.

Recall that, according to Marx and Mannheim, all ideologies are conservative and aim at maintaining existing power relations. Following this interpretation, many observers apply a certain "hermeneutic of suspicion" to all professed conservatives, looking behind their carefully articulated arguments and reasons to seek an underlying real life situation which may influence—or even determine—the way they think and express their views. Defenders of the so-called traditional family (by which is usually meant the twentieth-century nuclear family) are thus in the grip of patriarchal thinking which is enforced by the larger male-dominated society. Similarly, apologists for the Western canon of classic texts, such as Mortimer Adler or Allan Bloom, are influenced to think as they do out of their own position as "European" white males, the very group which has used its power to create and "canonize" these texts.[4]

Although there may be some validity to employing this hermeneutic of suspicion, it often flows out of a worldview that robs truth of any intrinsic meaning and sees it as reducible to mere will backed by superior power. As such, its use is frequently a way to avoid having to deal with arguments that may themselves have some legitimacy. But for every Archie Bunker, the bigoted television character of the 1970s, there is a George Grant who eloquently defends the unique traditions of virtue he believes once characterized his country's political culture.[5] For every Joseph McCarthy, the late U.S. senator who recklessly exploited the popular fear of communism, there is an Aleksandr Solzhenitsyn, the famed dissident Russian novelist who suffered personally through the oppressions of communism and has good, solid reasons to oppose it.[6] In short, we need to take seriously what conservatives have to say and to refrain from dismissing

---

[4]Mortimer Adler (1902-2001) was associate editor of the multivolume series *Great Books of the Western World* (Chicago: Encyclopaedia Britannica, 1952). Allan Bloom (1930-1992) was best known for his translation and interpretive essay of *The Republic of Plato* (New York: Basic Books, 1968) and for his best-selling *The Closing of the American Mind* (New York: Simon & Schuster, 1987). Bloom was a disciple of Leo Strauss, whose own academic career at the University of Chicago was devoted to understanding and disseminating knowledge of the classics of political philosophy. See Leo Strauss and Joseph Cropsey, eds., *History of Political Philosophy*, 3rd ed. (Chicago: University of Chicago Press, 1987), for an anthology of essays on individual political philosophers written by students of Strauss.

[5]See George Grant, *Lament for a Nation* (Toronto: Anansi, 1965); *Technology and Empire: Perspectives on North America* (Toronto: Anansi, 1969); *English-Speaking Justice* (Sackville, New Brunswick: Mount Allison University Press, 1974); and *Technology and Justice* (Toronto: Anansi, 1986).

[6]See, for example, Aleksandr Solzhenitsyn, *Warning to the West* (New York: Farrar, Straus & Giroux, 1976); *A World Split Apart* (New York: Harper & Row, 1978); and *The Mortal Danger: How Misconceptions About Russia Imperil America* (New York: Harper & Row, 1980).

them too glibly as simple apologists for their own positions of power. Like the other ideologies covered in this study, conservatism constitutes a significant intellectual trend in its own right, worthy of thoughtful consideration.

What makes conservatism more difficult to analyze than other ideologies is the fact that its contents vary from time to time and from place to place, often dramatically. If we were to ask a typical American what it means to be a conservative, he would likely answer in the following manner: A conservative respects the United States Constitution and the system of government it brought into being in 1787. He admires the carefully crafted balance of powers it prescribes among the executive, legislative and judicial branches, as well as among the federal, state and municipal levels of government. The conservative, moreover, is likely to support the Republican Party and almost certainly favors a noninterventionist state leaving the forces of the marketplace to operate to the widest extent possible. The conservative cherishes individual freedom and is vigilant in opposing any efforts at infringing on that freedom. It is probable that he voted for Ronald Reagan, George Bush, Bob Dole and George W. Bush in their respective presidential campaigns.

But this is too facile a definition of conservatism. It ignores the fact that much of the American political tradition itself was spawned in revolution and the deliberate repudiation of tradition. This is perhaps not a particularly trenchant observation, since by its very nature conservatism must seek to maintain something that was originally the product of innovation. Conservatives must face up to this tension within their own stance. But, perhaps more seriously, this definition of conservatism cannot cover everyone on earth claiming to follow this ideology. In an Islamic political culture, such as that of Saudi Arabia or Iran, a conservative would scarcely be enthusiastic about individual freedom, especially if it permitted a Salman Rushdie to publish *The Satanic Verses* or a Taslima Nasrin to advocate a wholesale revision of the Islamic religious codes. A conservative living in a traditional monarchy would hardly advocate an American style system of checks and balances that might diminish the prerogatives of the monarch. In short, if someone claims to be a conservative, the first order of business is to ask her exactly what it is she wishes to conserve. Depending on where and when she lives, we will naturally receive quite different responses.

Babies and Bathwater: The Conservative Creed

In what sense, then, can conservatism be considered an ideology if those bearing the label cannot bring themselves to agree on the specifics of a conservative

creed? If a twentieth-century American conservative believes in small government and the free market, while a nineteenth-century Russian conservative believes in the authority of the tsar and the Russian Orthodox Church, then
perhaps we must recognize that conservatism is an entirely historicist phenomenon and thus unable to offer anything in the way of a coherent worldview,
much less a concrete program for political action. This conclusion is not far
from the truth, but once again it is a bit too facile. For conservatives are not
ultimately united by their views on the role of government, the nature of community or the status of the individual. They certainly have opinions on all these
matters, but this is not what makes them conservative. What makes them conservative is their common attitudes toward tradition and change in the context
of the developing human community.[7]

More basically, conservatives have a heightened awareness of the fragility of
human undertakings and the tendency of human beings to fall into evil and
chaotic ways. Christians have labeled this tendency "original sin." Conservatives part ways with utopians of all stripes and are frequently at one with political realists in understanding that people tend to grasp as much power as they
can, often at the expense of others. People are filled with pride and other destructive passions, and the political order that pretends otherwise or tries to
make them something they are not risks overturning the entire edifice of civilization and plunging mankind into something approaching anarchy. It is for
this reason, in the face of these chaotic forces, that conservatives value every
small achievement on behalf of the community. But it is precisely the *achievements* they value, and not the abstract proposals for reform or revolution that
promise much but deliver little. Hence Edmund Burke's (1729-1797) preference for the rights of the English, with their time-tested guarantees, to the abstract notions of the rights of man, as preached by the French revolutionaries.
Better an imperfect law offering some genuine protections than a law perfect
on paper but without effect in the real world.

This sense of the frailty of the ongoing human endeavor has given conservatives a certain skepticism toward change, especially radical change. Granted,
society is not perfect. Nevertheless, if a certain social practice or custom is
working adequately, then the conservative assumes that the burden of proof lies
with those wishing to change it. To argue that society's imperfections necessi-

---

[7]For a good account of the conservative tendency, see Michael Oakeshott, "On Being Conservative," in
Rationalism in Politics and Other Essays (London: Methuen, 1962), pp. 168-96. See also Kirk, *Politics of
Prudence*, pp. 15-29.

tate a deliberate attempt at improvement is not sufficient for the conservative. Would-be reformers must demonstrate that their efforts will effect so significant an advancement that it will compensate for the inevitable negative side effects that are sure to accompany them. The abolition in 1917 of the monarchy in Russia, with all of its undoubted abuses and injustices, led to the outright horrors of totalitarianism and genocide. The well-intended attempt to move Russia forward ended up causing it to take a giant leap backward, plunging it into seven decades of darkness. But even U.S. President Lyndon Johnson's war on poverty, despite the best of intentions, seems to have made hardly a dent in the problem and instead created a class of perpetual dependents and successive years of public deficits, which arguably threatened the entire country with poverty.

If reforms are to be attempted, then they must be small in scale, incremental in pace and firmly grounded in past experience. The conservative prefers to see people attempt to alleviate poverty in their own neighborhoods than to try to eliminate it throughout the entire nation. Because of its local nature, the former is a much more realistic and manageable effort than the latter and is thus more likely to meet with success. Establishing a soup kitchen servicing five hundred to a thousand people is an enterprise with practicable goals, the attainment of which participants are likely to see with their own eyes over a definable period of time. By contrast, creating by legislative fiat a massive antipoverty program, from which countless millions may possibly benefit, is to undertake a reckless venture whose aims are so broad and indefinite as to entail a high risk of failure.

Of course, even small reforms carry the risk of failure. But if they stay small, the consequences of such a failure remain limited and the loss is contained. One of the reasons why conservatives tend to favor considerable local or regional autonomy in the face of large, centralized national governments is that the former provide an appropriate setting for experimenting with untried proposals. In 1944 the social democratic Cooperative Commonwealth Federation was elected to form the government in the Canadian province of Saskatchewan. Led by Premier Tommy Douglas, the CCF government decided to institute universal public health insurance in that province. If the program had failed, only a few thousand people would have had to bear its effects. But because it was successful, it provided a model to be adopted by the other provinces as well. Putting aside the larger issue of the advisability of public health insurance, this, according to the conservative, is the proper way of instituting reform: start locally and work outward from there.

In Ivan Turgenev's celebrated novel *Fathers and Sons*, the nihilist Bazarov, a literary prototype of the nineteenth-century Russian revolutionary, clashes with his friend Arkady's father and uncle, conservative aristocrats of the old school. In a memorable exchange between the antagonists, Arkady's skeptical father challenges the young Bazarov to consider the need for rebuilding society following his generation's revolutionary efforts. Bazarov declines, responding that this is not his generation's business. "The ground wants clearing first," he says provocatively.[8] Bazarov's assumption, of course, is that society's institutions and mores are so corrupt that there is nothing worth saving. Thus we do humanity a favor by destroying them and creating the space upon which future generations can build new institutions along more rational and humane lines. Needless to say, the conservative will have none of this sort of reasoning, which is at once too pessimistic about the present state of affairs and too optimistic about man's ability to mold an ideal social order. By contrast, conservatism teaches that no existing social, political or economic arrangement is ever completely without redeeming features. Those who would summarily dispense with it risk "throwing out the baby with the bathwater," as that hoary and overused cliché so inelegantly puts it.

But if the status quo is never completely beyond redemption, neither do rational plans for the remaking of society unquestionably represent an improvement for humanity. Conservatives have an instinctive distrust of grandiose, abstract schemes for the betterment of society. In contrast to change-oriented ideologies such as liberalism and socialism, conservatism recognizes the limitations of human reason and eschews those proposals that would, say, reorder marriage and the family in accordance with contemporary egalitarian sensibilities, or subject the state to the arid contractarianism of a Kant or Rawls. For this reason conservatives place a high value on something for which they are probably best known: tradition. Tradition is whatever we have inherited from the past, from our forebears. It is something that has proven itself against the test of passing time to be useful to society. Traditions are often incapable of being explained rationally, but they have nevertheless been vindicated in the arena of human experience. In the estimation of conservatives, tradition represents the accumulated experience and wisdom of previous generations. As such, we do well to work *with* tradition rather than *against* it.

---

[8]Ivan S. Turgenev, *Fathers and Sons*, trans. Constance Garnett (New York: Random House Modern Library, n.d.), p. 56.

The Grass Is Greener on Our Side

Given the conservative orientation toward tradition, one is naturally justified in asking which traditions adherents wish to conserve. The answer is likely to be "our *own* traditions." Conservatives are generally thought to be localists rather than globalists, patriotic rather than cosmopolitan, family- and village-oriented rather than state-oriented. Again, this is not necessarily true of all conservatives, some of whom might well be classified as nationalists or political centralists.[9] Yet the preference for tradition over innovation certainly predisposes the conserva-tive to favor the concrete and particular over the more abstract. The local neigh-borhood is something immediately tangible and accessible to the individual. The nation-state is not and it takes something of a leap of imagination to iden-tify personally with such a huge and far-flung community. The conservative is likely to sympathize with General Robert E. Lee's dilemma in the opening days of the American Civil War. Offered commissions by both the Union and the seceding Confederate armies, Lee finally chose to go with his native Virginia and hence with the Confederacy, painful though he found this decision. To Lee and many of his fellow Virginians, loyalty to a continental nation-state was too abstract to be genuine patriotism.

In this respect, conservatism is likely to be opposed not only to liberal and socialist ideologies, but also to any movement with cosmopolitan roots and im-plications, including continental or global federalisms. It will likely be nation-alist to the extent that the nation is a limited community embracing a limited number of citizens. But it may also reject nationalism insofar as the latter im-plies the dissolution of local allegiances and the imposition of broader, less proximate loyalties. Lasch suggests "that the capacity for loyalty is stretched too thin when it tries to attach itself to the hypothetical solidarity of the whole hu-man race. It needs to attach itself to specific people and places, not to an abstract ideal of universal human rights. We love particular men and women, not hu-manity in general."[10]

In similar fashion, Aristotle suggests that the civic friendship needed to bind the city together cannot be expanded too far; otherwise it becomes watered down and meaningless. It is, after all, "impossible to be a great friend to many

---

[9] One thinks, for example, of the first Canadian prime minister, Sir John A. Macdonald, who prior to 1867 preferred to see a British-style legislative union in British North America rather than an Ameri-can-style federation. See Janet Ajzenstat et al., eds., *Canada's Founding Debates* (Toronto: Stoddart, 1999), pp. 279-84.

[10] Christopher Lasch, *The True and Only Heaven: Progress and Its Critics* (New York: Norton, 1991), p. 36.

people."[11] If civic friendship is to play its crucial role in maintaining a genuine community where citizens feel they have a stake in the welfare of their fellow citizens, it must find its natural setting in the small polis where citizens meet face-to-face and have sufficient opportunities to know and to develop mutual feelings of attachment. Such opportunities are not available in the large state or empire.

On the other hand, conservatives may become de facto nationalists if the existence of a particular nation is wedded to local traditions threatened by more encompassing political entities. Such is the conservatism of Canadian philosopher George Grant, whose *Lament for a Nation* sparked a revival of a kind of "neo-toryism" among that country's intellectuals.[12] Alarmed by the perceived rise of a U.S.-dominated continental empire in North America, Grant defended a Canadian conservatism founded both on British Anglican traditions of virtue and on the traditional French Catholic culture in Quebec. Reflecting Jacques Ellul's influence, Grant argued that technological civilization is inescapably tied to liberalism and that together they pose a threat to any notion of limits in human life. Technology and freedom are constantly stretching the boundaries and cannot take seriously a political philosophy centered on virtue or an eternal order prescribing human actions.[13] Because of the leveling tendencies of technology, liberalism leads inexorably toward what the neo-Hegelian philosopher Alexandre Kojève has labeled the "universal and homogeneous state."[14] Here in North America this means that Canada, which was built on traditions of localism, virtue and loyalty to European civilization, is being drawn continually into the orbit of the United States, a country built on continentalism, individual liberty and the deliberate repudiation of tradition.

The tory conservatism of Grant stands in marked contrast to what usually goes by the conservative label in the United States. The more astute observers have long noted the tensions between so-called traditional conservatism and libertarianism, two tendencies that coexist within the American conservative movement. Pro-family and pro-life people would find themselves in the former category, while monetarists and free-marketeers would fall into the latter. Dur-

---

[11] Aristotle *Nicomachean Ethics* 9, 10; in *The Basic Works of Aristotle*, ed. Richard McKeon, trans. W. D. Ross (New York: Random House, 1941), p. 1091.
[12] See, for example, Larry Schmidt, *George Grant in Process: Essays and Conversations* (Toronto: Anansi, 1978); Yusuf K. Umar, ed., *George Grant & the Future of Canada* (Calgary: University of Calgary Press, 1992); and William Christian, *George Grant: A Biography* (Toronto: University of Toronto Press, 1993).
[13] Grant, *Lament for a Nation*, pp. 72-73.
[14] Ibid., pp. 53-54.

ing much of the post-World War II era, these tensions were largely submerged, and self-styled conservatives often behaved as if these two agendas were not only compatible but logically related.[15] But according to Grant, the libertarian agenda would come to dominate the visions of American conservatives, who are really "old-fashioned liberals." "Their concentration on freedom from governmental interference has more to do with nineteenth-century liberalism than with traditional conservatism, which asserts the right of the community to restrain freedom in the name of the common good."[16]

The election of 1980, which brought Ronald Reagan to the presidency and six years of Republican control to the Senate, was often called a conservative revolution. Many American Christians saw the Reagan administration as an ally in their cause. But Lasch disputes this assessment in a passage worth quoting in full:

> The "traditional values" celebrated by Reagan—boosterism, rugged individualism, a willingness to resort to force (against weaker opponents) on the slightest provocation—had very little to do with tradition. They summed up the code of the cowboy, the man in flight from his ancestors, from his immediate family, and from everything that tied him down and limited his freedom of movement. Reagan played on the desire for order, continuity, responsibility, and discipline, but his program contained nothing that would satisfy that desire. On the contrary, his program aimed to promote economic growth and unregulated business enterprise, the very forces that have undermined tradition. A movement calling itself conservative might have been expected to associate itself with the demand for limits not only on economic growth but on the conquest of space, the technological conquest of the environment, and the ungodly ambition to acquire godlike powers over nature. Reaganites, however, condemned the demand for limits as another counsel of doom.[17]

Historian Eugene D. Genovese similarly argues that Reagan was

> a rightwing liberal, indeed a progressive. His optimistic view of human

---

[15]A good example of contemporary conservatives unable to distinguish these two agendas is the Liberty University publication *Christian Perspectives: A Journal of Free Enterprise*. A typical issue contained articles indiscriminately reflecting both tendencies. See William J. Bennett, "Revolt Against God: America's Spiritual Despair," and Malcolm S. Forbes Jr., "Three Cheers for Capitalism," *Christian Perspectives* 6, no. 2 (1994): 1, 12-19. For an astute analysis of the division within the larger conservative movement see Robert Nisbet, "Conservatives and Libertarians: Uneasy Cousins," *Modern Age* 24 (winter 1980): pp. 2-8.

[16]Grant, *Lament for a Nation*, p. 64.

[17]Lasch, *True and Only Heaven*, pp. 38-39.

nature should warm the heart of liberal theologians; his celebration of limitless material progress reaches poetic heights; and his devotion to the free market and to finance capitalism could hardly be stronger.[18]

Lasch and Genovese are surely correct in their assessments, yet, as Louis Hartz has pointed out, it is difficult for a country which has never known feudalism, aristocracy or monarchy to embrace a preliberal conservatism.[19] Hence in the United States, conservatism can only strive to conserve an earlier form of liberalism, even if flesh and blood conservatives do indeed manage to defend existing institutions with nonliberal origins, for example, marriage and family.

This explains in large measure why at the polls repeated conservative attempts to win the day over the interminable liberal foe have inevitably met with frustration and with less than ringing success over the long term. At the end of the 1990s conservative fundraiser Paul M. Weyrich announced that the battle had been lost in the United States and that professed conservatives had little choice but to withdraw into their own parallel institutions—and so soon after the apparent victories of 1980 and 1994.[20] However, if American conservatism is already rooted in liberal principles, then conservatism is hardly the alternative its partisans think it is. It is, rather, an attempt to reverse what they see as the deleterious effects of liberal policies but without abandoning liberal first principles. That Grant's toryism would take issue with this American "upstart" and appeal instead to an older preliberal tradition only illustrates the lack of enduring principial content in conservatism as such. Because of this, any supposed victories scored by conservatism are likely to be temporary and without a sufficiently firm foundation. After all, an appeal to tradition per se tends to ignore what might be called the *temporal multiplicity of traditions*, a phenomenon that we shall now briefly explore.

Which Traditions and When?

Many people enjoy visiting the Parthenon in Athens or the Coliseum in Rome because they are part of our Western cultural heritage. They are the shared legacy of our civilization, and viewing them gives us access in some sense to our own

---

[18]Eugene D. Genovese, *The Southern Tradition: The Achievement and Limitations of an American Conservatism* (Cambridge, Mass.: Harvard University Press, 1994), pp. 82-83.

[19]Louis Hartz, *The Liberal Tradition in America: An Interpretation of American Political Thought Since the Revolution* (New York: Harcourt Brace Jovanovich, 1955), esp. pp. 145-77.

[20]"A Moral Minority? An Open Letter to Conservatives from Paul Weyrich," Free Congress Foundation, February 16, 1999 <www.freecongress.org/fcf/specials/weyrichopenltr.htm>.

past. We thereby come to know that our ancestors worshiped in pagan temples like the one we are viewing, or were entertained by the spectacles staged in arenas similar to the one before us. Many of us go to museums for similar reasons. There we may perhaps view the remains of Celtic settlements in Spain, medieval European chain mail, or Dionysian religious artifacts. But in connecting with our own past, we become aware that it has long since vanished and that what we are seeing is rather like the bones of an ancient mastodon extinct for millennia. Recognizing that these "ruins," as they are fittingly called, are subject to corrosion and decay, officials of the Greek government are frantically racing to save the buildings on the Acropolis and elsewhere from the ravages of urban pollution. In short, they are trying to halt the further ruination of their ruins.

On the other hand, if we go to the Greek countryside and step inside a village church, with its Byzantine domes and its inner walls covered with painted icons of Jesus Christ, the Mother of God and the saints, we are once more aware that we are in the presence of something very ancient. The building itself may not be more than a few decades old, but as we stand through the Divine Liturgy of St. John Chrysostom and observe the faithful singing the Creed and crossing themselves at appropriate moments in the service, we are immediately conscious of something much older than the participants themselves. Yet from the fervent prayers and acts of piety of those present, it should be evident that we are hardly seeing a fossil or relic of something long dead. We are, rather, experiencing something very much alive in the hearts of the people, which not only ties them to earlier generations, but manifests the latter's presence with them in a particularly vivid manner.

According to Jaroslav Pelikan, "tradition is the living faith of the dead" while "traditionalism is the dead faith of the living."[21] A vital tradition cannot simply be a keepsake or memento handed down from previous generations, but must continue to play an important role in the lives of those following it. Tradition*alism*, however, is simply rote, uncritical adherence to ideas and practices that have long ceased to have any meaning for the practitioners. For possibly two or three decades prior to the collapse of communism in the former Soviet bloc, the tenets of Marxism-Leninism had decayed to such an extent that they were merely an empty shell. The citizens continued to mouth the expected shibboleths, but they had long since stopped believing in their truth. Communism had, in short, degenerated into mere traditionalism, which could not ultimately

---

[21]Jaroslav Pelikan, *The Vindication of Tradition* (New Haven, Conn.: Yale University Press, 1984), p. 65.

withstand the impact of other spiritual forces, such as liberalism, nationalism, radical Islamism and Christianity.

But here we are confronted with a dilemma. What about traditions that have been largely lost and ought perhaps to be recovered? In the sixteenth century the Reformers sought to do precisely that in the face of an institutional church that they deemed to have abandoned in large measure the Christian gospel. Over against a number of existing traditions—such as the claims of the papacy, the sale of indulgences, infrequent participation in the Eucharist and popular ignorance of Scripture—Martin Luther, Thomas Cranmer, John Calvin and others sought to reach behind the traditions of their day to recover a much earlier tradition found in the written Scriptures and, to a lesser extent, in the church fathers. Both the reformers and their opponents in the official church thus could make a plausible claim to be conserving tradition. The Reformation sought to restore biblical religion and conserve what perhaps already existed in certain segments of the church. The Counter Reformation sought to conserve the role of the institutional church in setting the parameters of the faith and in guarding the larger Christian tradition. Each party saw the other as unduly innovating and in some sense altering or departing from the tradition handed down from the fathers.

Thus we are faced with what we might call the temporal multiplicity of traditions—the fact that over time even a specific local or religious tradition develops and mutates to such an extent that in its later form it may look quite different from its earlier manifestation. This phenomenon has had an impact in the political realm as well. Political conservatives in North America often forget that traditions exist in temporal layers and that the defense of one need not imply the defense of another, much less all. Many Renaissance and Enlightenment political theorists did not see themselves as introducing an entirely new and unprecedented political program into their respective settings. They certainly saw themselves breaking with the remnants of European feudalism and Christendom, but in so doing they believed they were simply recovering the classical republicanism of ancient Greece and Rome. Early liberals or protoliberals, such as Machiavelli and Montesquieu, devote much of their writings to political practice in the ancient world, from which they intend to draw lessons for contemporary statesmanship. Thus even these liberals, who in one sense saw themselves in the vanguard of change—sometimes even revolutionary change—also claimed to be recovering a forgotten tradition for the benefit of their societies. Thus they might fittingly be labeled conservative.

Even the reaction against the Enlightenment, which was the genesis of the modern conservative movement as we know it, took different directions depending on where it came into being. In the Anglo-Saxon world Edmund Burke founded a conservatism that owed much to the Whig settlement of 1688 in England and emphasized the maintenance of historical continuity. He had no desire to turn the clock back to an earlier, supposedly better era. Nor did he wish to halt the historical process. He simply sought to emphasize the need to proceed with caution and to respect existing conventions and mores. In contrast to liberal contractarianism, Burke argued that the state is "a partnership not only between those who are living, but between those who are living, those who are dead, and those who are to be born."[22] The French revolutionaries had broken this partnership in favor of the narrower conception of contract championed by liberalism.

The English constitution seemed to provide an ideal context for the Burkean approach. Although there have been times when the former's evolution was interrupted, most notably by the Commonwealth between 1649 and 1660 and by the Glorious Revolution of 1688, the regnant mythology surrounding England's constitution is one of unbroken continuity. Nearly a century after Burke, Walter Bagehot published his classic *The English Constitution* (1867), in which he argued that through the peaceful development of British political institutions, "A Republic has insinuated itself beneath the folds of a Monarchy."[23] Or, as Samuel E. Finer more recently put it, "The British constitution is a democratic one, but poured into a medieval mold."[24] In other words, Britain has adapted to the modern world without explicitly repudiating the old ways of doing things. At present the United Kingdom is one of a very few countries with an unwritten constitution, consisting very largely of conventions which, though highly persuasive and thus in some sense binding on political actors, are not enforceable in the strict legal sense.

On the European continent, by contrast, where continuity with the past had been disrupted by the Revolution, it was more difficult to be conservative in the Burkean sense. Many of these continental conservatives admired Burke as well as the English constitution that he defended. Joseph de Maistre (1753-

---

[22]Edmund Burke, *Reflections on the Revolution in France* (1790), in *The Harvard Classics*, ed. Charles W. Eliot (New York: P. F. Collier & Son, 1937), p. 232.

[23]Walter Bagehot, *The English Constitution* (Ithaca, N.Y.: Cornell University Press, 1963), p. 94.

[24]Samuel E. Finer, "Politics of Great Britain," in *Modern Political Systems: Europe*, ed. Roy Macridis, 6th ed. (Englewood Cliffs, N.J.: Prentice-Hall, 1987), p. 21.

1821), for example, wrote that the unique genius of the English constitution is that it moves while standing still. A constitution is a "divine work" whose strength is increased insofar as it remains unwritten. A genuine constitution is not a written document at all, but the sum total of customs and mores binding together the people of a nation. It is that "admirable, unique, and infallible public spirit which transcends all praise."[25] To try to codify such a spirit—or what we might today call a *political culture*—is to risk weakening or even destroying it.

Other continental conservatives, such as the Vicomte de Bonald (1754-1840) and Juan Donoso Cortès (1809-1853), approached the political realm in a similar fashion.[26] But they also understood that institutions that work well in one setting cannot simply be transplanted into another. Unable to accept the revolutionary status quo of fin-de-siècle Europe either, they could only call for restoring in some fashion the several *anciens régimes* systematically uprooted during the 1790s. This orientation to a more remote, vanished past prompts many contemporary observers to label these continental conservatives "reactionary." Far from looking backward to the civic republicanism of the ancients, these conservative restorationists sought to recover the vanished royal constitutions of medieval Europe. The common assumption of most restorationists was that society is hierarchically arranged with church and state, and king, nobles and commons having their divinely assigned places within the total structure. The departure from these constitutions, whether by gradual reform or by revolutionary activity, was nothing less than disobedience to the will of God as manifested through the historical process.

The danger of this kind of conservatism, of course, is that it easily becomes romantic—romantic in the sense that it reconstructs an ideal past that never really existed in the sense imagined. It partakes of a kind of reverse utopianism, positing a primeval golden age, the movement away from which is nothing less than a fall from divine grace. In 1815, after a generation of instability, a deliberate attempt was made to restore the old Europe. Reactionary conservatism became the regnant ideology of the day, but the Congress of Vienna created a Europe that, despite the attempt to the contrary, in large measure failed to reproduce pre-revolutionary realities. By romanticizing relations among king, nobles and commons, restorationists apparently forgot that these classes had often been in

---

[25]Joseph de Maistre, *On God and Society: Essay on the Generative Principle of Political Constitutions and Other Human Institutions* (South Bend, Ind.: Gateway, 1959), 5:11.
[26]For excerpts from their writings, see Béla Menczer, ed., *Catholic Political Thought, 1789-1848* (Notre Dame, Ind.: University of Notre Dame Press, 1962).

conflict with each other. Church and state, too, had hardly been allies throughout the "Christian" middle ages, but had each frequently sought to establish its supremacy over the other. Moreover, even the revolution of 1789 had not itself put an end to the medieval constitution in France, with its balance of competing estates. Nearly two centuries of Bourbon absolutism had already effectively done this. After all, when the États-Généraux (Estates-General) were convened that year, they had not met since 1614. The place of the clergy, nobles and commons in the French constitution had long been supplanted by the pretensions of the king. So much for a prerevolutionary "golden age."

Conservatives, therefore, do not agree which traditions they wish to maintain and often seem to ignore the fact of their temporal multiplicity. This demonstrates a central difficulty with the conservative creed. Any tradition or collection of traditions is inevitably a "mixed bag" from virtually any standpoint. The wisdom of past generations is intermingled with a large measure of folly. The Burkean conservative, that is, the one emphasizing continuity and maintenance of the status quo, typically underestimates the extent to which current usage and recent precedent embody the destructive and harmful. By contrast, the restorationist conservative understands that the *status quo* is not everything it should be, but in desiring to turn the clock back, overestimates the wisdom of earlier bygone traditions.

What conservatism as a whole seems unable to do is to formulate a generally accepted, *transhistorical* criterion by which to distinguish what in a tradition is worth saving and what ought to be discarded. To be sure, many conservatives profess to believe in the existence of what Kirk calls "an enduring moral order" in which "human nature is a constant, and moral truths are permanent,"[27] and by which our multiplicity of traditions might be judged. In this respect such conservatives are closer to a Christian understanding of the world than to an ideological belief in the unlimited malleability of the world to suit our own human ends. Yet even on this issue conservatives err: first, by failing sufficiently to distinguish the traditions, institutions and mores of their own society from the transcendent order they claim to uphold; and second, by underestimating the dynamic character of that order. Change and development are not defects; they are an integral part of creation as God has structured it. Conservatives have difficulty recognizing that structure and change, far from being opposed, in fact presuppose each other.

---

[27]Kirk, *Politics of Prudence*, p. 17.

Here is where we perhaps see how conservatism, like liberalism, partakes of the gnostic heresy which we have argued characterizes the several ideologies. Conservatism's gnostic character may not be immediately obvious, and many professed conservatives, following Voegelin, explicitly repudiate this gnosticism. Indeed a great part of conservatism's persuasiveness lies in its critique of those transformative ideologies that would redesign the world in their own images and ignore what might be called the natural constraints built into it. Conservatives are far more likely than, say, liberals or socialists, to call on policymakers and would-be reformers to subject their proposals to what is nowadays known as a "reality check," that is, to test their ideas against the real world. They would be the first to criticize social engineers who would, for example, move from a well-intended rejection of racism to a policy of forced busing of school children, irrespective of parents' wishes to the contrary, or would destroy longstanding local communities in the interest of "urban renewal." To the extent that conservatives are more aware of both the finitude and the fallibility of human efforts at social improvement, they have correctly seen through the gnostic pretensions of those elites claiming greater enlightenment than those they seek to govern.[28]

On the other hand, there is a distinct preference on the part of many, though by no means all, conservatives for a static, organic conception of society that confuses legitimate *differentiation*, that is, the tendency for different societal functions to disperse themselves among a variety of communal settings, with an antinormative fragmentation harmful to social order. In other words, many conservatives look back nostalgically to the days when society was ostensibly characterized by a pristine communal wholeness, and a person's loyalties were fewer, more narrowly focused and less complex. Children were educated in the household rather than in the school. Businesses were operated by families and handed down from one generation to the next. The institutional church ran everything from orphanages and universities to labor unions and hospitals. The nation as a whole was conceived as a great family, with relations between monarch and subjects mirroring on a much larger scale the relations between parents and children. Individuals knew their place in the social hierarchy and were less likely to assert themselves and their own interests therein. Aside from the fact that this apparently pristine "golden age" was undoubtedly less rosy than believed in retrospect, as we noted above, there is nothing to be deplored in this

---

[28]See, e.g., the argument of Thomas Sowell, *The Vision of the Anointed* (New York: BasicBooks, 1996).

entirely normal process of the differentiation of society. In fact, efforts to over-turn or reverse this process have troubling totalitarian implications. We shall re-turn to the concept of differentiation in chapters seven and eight.

Even those conservatives less fearful of differentiation nevertheless often har-bor an unreasoned distrust of reform in general. As Maistre puts it, "The word *reform*, by itself and prior to any scrutiny, will always be suspect to wisdom."[29] Current or past social norms are deemed almost wholly good, because they are rooted in the wisdom of the past, while efforts at deliberate change, as opposed to the more evolutionary change thought to operate independently of individ-ual wills, are deemed at least suspect because they depart from this apparent wis-dom. Of course the world is not static, as the more thoughtful conservatives already understand. More to the point, God's creation is not static but contains great potential for development and improvement, though certainly within sta-ble limits and always subject to norms that he himself has given. Yet the conser-vative is not wrong to counsel caution in assessing *actual* proposals for reform.

Nor does the conservative erroneously value tradition, without which we could not live. Even those who claim to repudiate tradition in general inescap-ably presuppose countless traditions that make up the fabric of their lives, both as individuals and as members of communities. We may rightly question certain *specific* traditions, for example, racial segregation or the exclusion of women from certain professions, but we can no more live without traditions in general than we could now live without clothing, tableware and bed linens, universi-ties, orchestras and legislatures, that is, the very things that are products of long centuries of cultural formation and are the fiber of a civilized existence. More-over, as Pelikan rightly observes, critics of a specific tradition deemed defective mount their critique, not so much in the name of an abstract Platonic ideal hovering above our traditions, but measured against a principle to some extent already embedded in and communicated by a larger tradition or set of tradi-tions.[30] After all, Dr. Martin Luther King Jr. fought segregation on substantive constitutional grounds, and Amnesty International tirelessly defends a concep-tion of human rights mediated by a Western tradition rooted in Christian and stoic antecedents. Similarly, Christians working to end slavery in the nineteenth century did so based on principles of justice taught by the biblical tradition.

Nevertheless, we obviously cannot defer to any and all traditions as though

---

[29]Maistre *Constitutions* 40.55-56.
[30]Pelikan, *Vindication of Tradition*, pp. 43-61.

they *entirely* embody God's norms for life. Even if we do critique one tradition based on another, we are still in need of some overarching criterion to determine how and why we should do so. In particular, if we are to understand the nature of politics in a discerningly Christian way, we shall have to look beyond our traditions, which precisely because they are human not only are fallible but also inevitably speak in several, often conflicting voices. This suggests already that we need to look elsewhere if we are to locate a normative vision for politics in God's world.

Conservatism and Christianity

Given our observation above about the variability of conservatism's contents, it should be evident that there is no necessary connection between this ideology and any particular religion. Nevertheless, because traditional religions are part of the heritage of particular civilizations, conservatives are often appreciative of the role they have played. In the Western world most professed conservatives are Christians in some sense and, more recently, they are wont to speak of the "Judeo-Christian" tradition as the basis of their society and culture. There are two principal reasons why conservatives would likely profess Christianity. The first and most obvious is that they genuinely believe its teachings are true. They believe that God has revealed himself uniquely in Jesus Christ and in the pages of Scripture, and they seek to follow his precepts as revealed therein. The second reason for professing Christianity is that it is part of the Western cultural heritage. For those conservatives who are Christians for this reason, the issue of the truth of the faith is secondary to the social utility of its ethical teachings. Like all traditions, Christianity has proven itself useful to the maintenance of social stability and for this reason the good conservative adheres to it. But for such conservatives Christianity is clearly one among several traditions that have come together to form Western culture, including the Roman legal and Greek philosophical traditions, and within this grand synthesis all are equally normative.[31]

The affinity between Western conservatism and Christianity seems to be mutual. Many Christians openly label themselves conservatives for what may appear initially to be solid reasons. Christianity itself is a religion based on the handing down, reception and maintenance of what many call the Great Tradition, either

---

[31]A small university in the American Midwest exhibits this synthesis in its claim to be "a trustee of modern man's intellectual and spiritual inheritance from the Judeo-Christian faith and Greco-Roman culture, a heritage finding its clearest expression in the American experiment of self-government under law" <www.hillsdale.edu/dept/english/hc%20missionstmt.html>.

in the form of a written Holy Scripture or in the larger sense of the unwritten tradition of the church, as taught by Eastern Orthodoxy and Roman Catholicism. For Christians this tradition represents not merely the wisdom of past generations but the very Word of God as revealed to the prophets and apostles. Although there is a persistent form of liberal Christianity that seeks to bring its tenets into line with contemporary ways of thought and behavior, the mainstream of Christianity has in some fashion attempted to maintain its tradition in the face of contemporary social and intellectual trends, while at the same time trying to address these trends in a meaningful and relevant way from within that tradition.

But of course historic Christianity, whether Protestant, Catholic or Orthodox, understands that the scope of this tradition is strictly delimited and cannot possibly include everything in the larger culture that has been handed down by previous generations. The Great Tradition includes at least: Scripture, doctrines such as the Trinity, the incarnation and the resurrection of Christ, the Apostles' and Nicene Creeds, and perhaps even the historic liturgies of the church, the writings of the fathers and so forth.[32] It does not include belief in democracy or monarchy as *the* biblical form of government or in capitalism or socialism as *the* biblical economic system. Yet on some level most Christians correctly understand that biblical Christianity does address the whole of life, including politics and economics. Moreover, due to the historic role played by Christianity in the ongoing development of our culture, it is reasonable to assume that such political and economic systems would already bear the stamp of Christianity's influence. It is not surprising therefore, that many ordinary Christians seek above all to conserve the traditions of their culture in the name of the Christian tradition that has helped to shape them. At its worst, this Christian conservatism can degenerate into an unthinking "God and country" form of nationalism that

---

[32]There is, of course, a difference between Roman Catholic and Eastern Orthodox conceptions of canonical authority, on the one hand, and Reformation conceptions, on the other. The former see the Great Tradition as more encompassing than do the latter, who adhere to the principle of *sola scriptura,* that is, "Scripture alone." For example, in principle Protestants do not regard their confessional documents and liturgies as canonical, although in practice they accord them a certain secondary canonicity under the primary authority of biblical revelation. Moreover, the doctrine of the Trinity is regarded by conservative Protestants as an undoubted tenet of the faith, although in its mature form it was formulated only in the postbiblical era. For a Protestant account of the evolving historic relationship between Scripture and tradition, see Stanley J. Grenz and John R. Franke, "Theological Heritage as Hermeneutical Trajectory: Toward a Nonfoundationalist Understanding of the Role of Tradition in Theology," in *Ancient & Postmodern Christianity: Paleo-Orthodoxy in the 21st Century: Essays in Honor of Thomas C. Oden,* ed. Kenneth Tanner and Christopher A. Hall (Downers Grove, Ill.: InterVarsity Press, 2002), pp. 215-39. For a Roman Catholic perspective, see Rino Fisichella, "*Dei Verbum Audiens et Proclamans*: On Scripture and Tradition as Source of the Word of God," *Communio* 28 (spring 2001): 85-98.

is unable to distinguish the Great Tradition from traditions. At its best, it correctly discerns which of our traditions agree with *the* Tradition, and attempts to keep them and build upon them.

This building upon tradition further suggests that, for the spiritually discerning Christian, conserving and progressing cannot properly be conceived as dialectical polarities. We observed that liberalism and conservatism are popularly held to be opposites, but I hinted that this is not accurate. Liberalism is a particular ideology holding to the sovereignty of the individual, while conservatism has to do with one's attitudes toward tradition and change. These two agendas are not mutually incompatible and are not even logically related to each other. It is, after all, quite possible to be an ontological individualist and yet be skeptical toward political and social reform. As Grant correctly recognizes, the true opposite of conservatism is not liberalism but progressivism. While conservatism wishes to keep and maintain something existing from the past, progressivism is oriented toward change, and above all desires to move forward. In Mannheim's terms, conservatism is an ideology, while progressivism—in whatever form it might take—is a utopia.

But even progressives are conservative in some sense, and this should indicate that conserving and progressing are not as irreconcilable as they might initially seem. In any civilization the elements of continuity tying the generations together are far greater than the discontinuities separating them. The vast majority of progressives are unwilling to go as far as Bazarov and destroy completely all existing human customs and institutions in the interest of building new and ostensibly better ones. Most presuppose the huge store of human achievements and cultural developments preceding them. Those wishing to reform health care could hardly wish to repeal such undoubted accomplishments as the discovery of penicillin or of the polio vaccine. Nor, more basically, are they likely to desire abolishing the division of labor whereby some are specially trained in the art of medicine and most are not. In other words, most reformers properly recognize that the huge store of civilization is worth keeping and building upon. Future progress could not occur without the foundation laid by past progress.

Where conservatives differ from progressives is in their understanding of the fragility of this vast cultural enterprise. There are no guarantees that the latter will continue as before into the future, and the possibility of reverses in progress are very real. This is the source of that caution so frequently associated with conservatism. Yet the very possibility of conserving a particular human achievement requires that someone have brought it into being in the first place. Someone took the risk and made the grand effort to do something unprecedented. American schoolchildren are taught to revere the likes of Samuel Morse, Thomas Edison and Alexander Graham Bell—each of whom is assigned the distinguished title "inventor." Inventors create new technologies that fundamentally change the way people live their lives, enabling them to produce more than they could before or to communicate and travel across vast distances. Except perhaps for those with Luddite tendencies, the vast majority of conservatives wish to maintain these technical accomplishments.

Many conservatives dislike "pop" or "rock" music and prefer, say, the baroque pieces of Bach or Telemann. Yet the early baroque composers were themselves "inventors" of sorts, creating such innovative musical techniques as counterpoint. The very label "baroque" was used in a derogatory fashion by conservatives of that day to describe what they felt was ugly music. Similarly, Thomas Aquinas's incorporation of pagan Aristotle into his own Christian philosophy was controversial in his day and antagonized the thirteenth-century equivalent of conservatives. Yet today conservative Roman Catholic philosophers, who ironically dislike liberation theology's use of Marx, prefer to stay with Thomas's scholastic philosophy, which they now view as tried and true and worthy of their loyalty. In short, for the discerning Christian, progressing and conserving properly belong together. One cannot exist without the other.

H. Evan Runner correctly points out that in the cultural mandate (Gen 1:28), which defines our earthly task, "there is both a conserving and a dynamic or progressive element." "Adam was commanded to keep the garden and to dress it. Conservation and progress are not alternative choices of a disjunction (which together exhaust the possibilities and are mutually exclusive); they are, in fact, complementary aspects of the integral human Task."[33]

To absolutize one or the other of these elements is to fall into a kind of idolatry, which, as we have been arguing, is at the root of all ideologies. Discerning Christians understand that God's good creation contains possibilities for further development, as noted previously, and this alone should be enough to keep them from embracing an unadulterated conservatism. More important, however, than concern over the pace of change should be the question of the basic *direction* of such change. On this issue Christians have resources which simple-

---

[33]H. Evan Runner, *Scriptural Religion and Political Task* (Toronto: Wedge, 1974), p. 86. See chapter seven for a somewhat fuller treatment of the cultural mandate.

minded conservatives and progressives do not. We shall examine these in more detail in chapters seven through nine.

Conservatism and the State

What is the conservative view of the state? Given our discussion thus far, it should be obvious that there is no single theory of the political community that can claim the conservative label. Most conservatives would argue, in any case, that political questions are not the most important ones to be addressed. Solzhenitsyn has written more than one tract addressing the political situation in his native Russia. Yet in all these he repeatedly affirms the primacy of the spiritual over the political, or that "the structure of the state is secondary to the spirit of human relations."[34] None of the current reform efforts in Russia will be an adequate substitute for a needed revival of the people's spiritual energies. To a large extent the believing Christian would have to agree with the thoughtful conservative on this point. Nevertheless, if politics is a part of life in God's world and if it has an important role to play in ordering the lives of its people toward justice, then political theory cannot be so easily dismissed as something dealing with the merely superficial. In fact, failure to reflect on the nature of government and the state could ultimately lead to the very things so many conservatives warn against, such as the leviathan state and ill-considered, possibly disastrous, reform efforts. Thus most conservatives have indeed undertaken to include something of their approach to politics in their creed.

According to Anthony Quinton, there are three principles of conservatism: a traditionalism that respects established customs and institutions, an organicism that views society as a natural growth rather than a mechanical invention, and a skepticism toward abstract theoretical speculations.[35] Above all, the conservative admits that human beings and their society are incapable of achieving perfection—especially intellectual perfection. As for government, the conservative believes in strong government, but not an "absolutely comprehensive" government. In contrast to various forms of idealism, conservatives do not identify the state with society, nor do they attempt to absorb society into the state.[36] This

---

[34]Alexander Solzhenitsyn, *Rebuilding Russia: Reflections and Tentative Proposals* (New York: Farrar, Straus & Giroux, 1991), p. 49. See also his *Letter to the Soviet Leaders* (New York: Harper & Row, 1974), representing an earlier version of his ideas. For a recent secondary treatment of Solzhenitsyn's political ideas, see Daniel J. Mahoney, *Aleksandr Solzhenitsyn: The Ascent from Ideology* (Lanham, Md.: Rowman & Littlefield, 2001).

[35]Anthony Quinton, *The Politics of Imperfection: The Religious and Secular Traditions of Conservative Thought in England from Hooker to Oakeshott* (London: Faber & Faber, 1978), pp. 16-17.

[36]Ibid., pp. 20-21.

might suggest at least a tacit recognition of the distinctness of the state.

Russell Kirk argues in favor of ten canons of conservative thought. The conservative believes, above all, in (1) an enduring moral order; (2) custom, convention and continuity; (3) the principle of prescription, that is, respect for those things established by long usage; (4) the principle of prudence, that is, thoughtful choices exercised with a view to long-term consequences; (5) the principle of proliferating variety and complexity over uniformity; (6) a recognition of human imperfectibility; (7) the connection between private property and liberty; (8) voluntary community as opposed to involuntary collectivism; (9) the need for restraints on power and the passions; and (10) the need to reconcile permanence and change in society.[37] What should be noted about these features is that, in and of themselves, they do not add up to a comprehensive political theory capable of understanding the nature of the state as a differentiated institution. To be sure, the fifth feature seems to contain the seeds of that phenomenon known as *civil society,* to which we shall return in chapters five and eight. This implies that there are a multiplicity of communal structures that *are not the state* and fall outside of its structural boundaries. The ninth element could be said to reinforce this limited character of the state, although the institution as such is not mentioned. But the eighth element fails to acknowledge that, although many communities are properly voluntary in nature, some, including those most foundational for human society, cannot be reduced to the wills of their members. This quite evidently includes the state, within which inhabitants are born to the rights and responsibilities of citizenship. On this point Kirk's conservatism is obviously in debt to classical liberalism, which once again illustrates the lack of sufficient substantive content in the conservative vision.

Clinton Rossiter observes that the conservative formulates his ideas in contrast to his opponents: "For example, in discussing the nature of government, he likes to point out to radicals that it is natural rather than artificial, to individualists that it is good rather than evil, and to collectivists that it is limited rather than unlimited in potentialities and scope."[38] Rossiter perhaps comes close to a differentiated view of government insofar as he believes it has the following, limited responsibilities: to defend "the community against external assault"; to serve as a symbol of national unity; to establish and administer "an equitable system of justice, which alone makes it possible for men to live and do business with one

---

[37] Kirk, *Politics of Prudence*, pp. 17–25.
[38] Clinton Rossiter, *Conservatism in America* (Cambridge, Mass.: Harvard University Press, 1982), p. 31.

another"; to protect people against violence, with the use of force if necessary; to protect people's rights, including that to property; to adjudicate "conflicts among groups and [regulate] their activities, thus acting as the major equilibrating force in the balance of social forces"; to promote public and private morality, including the encouragement of organized religion and education; to assist people in their pursuit of happiness by removing obstacles to this; and, finally, to perform a humanitarian function in "cases of clear necessity."[39]

Yet many of these tasks of government stand in some tension with each other and are not clearly related to a comprehensive sense of how one might establish the necessary priorities among them. The conservative, in Rossiter's view, is able to hold onto all of these features, refusing to take a doctrinaire stand in favor of any one over all the others. "In general, he tries to strike a workable compromise between the needs of community and the rights of the individual, both of which he champions eloquently whenever they are ignored or despised."[40] The guiding principle is thus a pragmatic one, addressing itself to the solution of particular problems in accordance with preexisting traditions at the very most. But given that these traditions vary from time to time and from place to place, simply tallying up several plausible tasks of government will hardly make for a satisfactory political theory.

As a possible Christian political theory, then, conservatism ultimately fails on two counts. First, there is nothing intrinsically Christian about it. Conservatives in some places and times may call themselves Christians, but it is hardly required by their conservatism as such. Second, it offers nothing in the way of a coherent view of the state as a specialized, differentiated community within human society. A simple deferral to tradition gives us no substantive guidelines as to what politics is all about or where it properly finds its place within God's creation. Conservatives surely do an invaluable service by counseling a certain degree of caution to those whose zeal for reform might inadvertently lead to the overturning of the ship of state. A polity lacking such persons is likely to get itself into considerable dangers. But conservatism by its very nature is unable to offer anything in the way of a positive direction for such a polity. All it can do is to apply the brakes occasionally in a vehicle that may well be on the way to the abyss. If, finally, conservatism cannot of itself provide a positive direction for state action, then it seems we must look elsewhere.

---

[39]Ibid., p. 34.
[40]Ibid., p. 35.

4

NATIONALISM

The Nation Deified

Perhaps the chief deficiency of liberalism is its inability to account fully for community as a distinct ontological category. Because liberalism sees the individual as the primary datum of human experience, it must see community as ultimately reducible to the individuals of which it is composed. Thus liberal ideology is synonymous with individualism. Conservatism, on the other hand, generally values community as a source of social stability and as the repository of the traditions and mores undergirding society. Yet if a conservative wishes to protect a political order with liberal underpinnings, then it is very likely that she too will view community in a similarly reductionist fashion. It is hoped that the discussion of liberalism in chapter two has pointed to the fundamental inadequacy of individualism. It is further hoped that this discussion will underscore the necessity of a theory that makes room for community as something possessing a status in its own right.

Nationalism is the first of the ideologies treated to take community seriously. To this extent it can be said to have a certain theoretical edge over liberalism and conservatism alike.[1] Nationalism recognizes that people seek their identities

---

[1]There is certainly a communitarian form of conservatism; in fact it may well be the dominant form in the Western world as a whole. Yet see once again the comments of Grant, Genovese and Lasch in chapter three concerning the predominant conservative liberalism in the United States particularly. This

in communities, which make claims on their loyalties and demand varying degrees of personal sacrifice for their collective well-being. Although these communities offer much to their members, including a sense of purpose and camaraderie as well as more tangible economic benefits, they do not exist principally to satisfy the needs and wants of the members as individuals. Rather they are held to fulfill a broader, and possibly higher, function transcending their members' individual interests.

But a community must be delineated in such a way that we know who its members are and what its unique character is. In chapters eight and nine I shall define the state in terms of two elements intrinsic to its structure, namely, power and justice. The state, I shall argue, can be distinguished from other communities, such as church institution, family and business enterprise, by a proper understanding of the relationship between these two elements. Furthermore, the state is limited in its membership and in its competence. Only a limited number of people are members, or *citizens*, of this political community. And the state has a limited task mandated by its specific character as an institution of power and justice. It is not totalitarian; it cannot do everything. The state must respect both its own boundaries and the boundaries of other, nonstate communities, and it must also respect the legitimate sphere of individual freedom.

But what of that community known as *nation*? How shall we define this? I would suggest that formulating an incontestable definition of nation is not as readily done as for state. Certainly a nation binds people together in an enduring community of some sort, but what is the basis of this community? An answer to this question is not so easily forthcoming, and we are likely to be impressed by the sheer diversity of definitions for *nation*.

Americans probably have less difficulty than others with the term. The "American nation" encompasses all those who are citizens of the United States, whatever their ancestry, ethnic origins or religion. Yet for Americans *nationality* is more than common citizenship in the body politic. It means adherence to certain ideals, such as liberty, democracy and equality, which have come to be seen as the defining values of the nation. Furthermore, to be an American means to put one's faith in a particular ideology embodied in the Declaration of Independence and the Constitution. This ideology is the liberalism of John Locke, as articulated by Thomas Jefferson and James Madison, and as modified

---

brand of conservatism may well value community, but it still sees it as fundamentally voluntary and rooted in the contracting wills of participating individuals.

and adapted by Andrew Jackson, Woodrow Wilson and Franklin Roosevelt. Although a professed monarchist or socialist might formally be a citizen of the United States, there is widespread doubt that someone holding such "un-American" opinions can really be part of the nation.

By contrast, Canadian definitions of nation are much more ambiguous. Is Canada a nation? Most English-speaking Canadians will say yes to this. After all, Canadians live under a common flag and a common federal political order. Canadians carry the same passport and enjoy equal rights of citizenship. But French-speaking Canadians insist that Canada is two nations. After all, two different languages are spoken. And although all Canadians sing the same national anthem, they do so in separate French and English versions. The national broadcasting service is divided into the Canadian Broadcasting Corporation (CBC) and la Société Radio Canada (SRC). As early as 1839 Lord Durham wrote that he found in Canada "two nations warring in the bosom of a single state."[2] All of this suggests that some definitions of nation may not be dependent on a common political framework as the defining feature.

Indeed attempts to locate defining objective criteria for nation have not been famously successful. Among the suggested possibilities are shared language, ethnicity, religion, culture, customs, ancestry, race, homeland, history and constitutional order. Usually one or more of these factors are held to be foundational for the existence of a nation. Yet the attempt to apply these criteria to real nations usually indicates their inadequacy. Each of these criteria admits of exceptions that make it difficult to pin down a universally valid meaning of nation. For example, the defining feature of the Afrikaner nation in South Africa is usually held to be the Afrikaans language. But many South African "Coloureds," that is, those of mixed racial origins, also speak Afrikaans but have never been fully accepted by white Afrikaners because of their skin color.

This suggests a possible racial criterion for delimiting a nation. Prior to the Second World War, it was common in the English-speaking world to speak of a German race or a Greek race, as if these were biologically fixed subgroups of humanity. Yet French people in Normandy have Nordic facial features and light skin, while French people in Marseilles have darker coloring and Mediterranean features. Serbs, Croats and Bosnian Muslims speak a common Serbo-Croatian language, yet their separate group identities are anchored in religion.

---

[2]Gerald M. Craig, ed., *Lord Durham's Report* (Toronto: McClelland & Stewart, 1963), p. 23.

The Swiss may plausibly be considered a nation,[3] yet they are religiously and linguistically divided. Even a common homeland may not suffice to define a nation, because some self-conscious nations are scattered across a wide territory, interspersed with other nations. Diaspora Jews are an example of this. And to this day the Federal Republic of Germany recognizes claims to citizenship of people of German ancestry from Eastern Europe and Russia.

Discussions about the concept of nation often begin with Ernest Renan's 1882 essay, "Qu'est-ce qu'une nation (What Is a Nation)?" Against the prevailing currents of his day, he denies proposed bases for a nation in common race, language or religion. He even doubts that shared material interests or geography are sufficient to produce a common national identity. For Renan a nation is "a living soul, a spiritual principle" binding people together through common consent to be together and on the basis of shared historical memories. A nation exists by a "daily plebiscite," a perpetual will on the part of its members to remain a nation. Once this will ceases to exert itself, the nation is likely to come to an end, for nations are not eternal. In short, for Renan nationhood is something intangible and perhaps even a bit mysterious. How else can we account for the fact that Finnish- and Swedish-speaking Finns are a nation while Spanish-speaking Latin Americans are not? History is the decisive factor. Or, more to the point, consciousness of having experienced the same efforts, sacrifices and achievements is what binds a people together in a nation.[4]

Many observers have noted that *nation* is a phenomenon peculiar to the modern age, despite a persistent popular tendency to view it as something almost natural or innate to the human species.[5] Benedict Anderson argues that nations in the modern sense are "imagined communities" whose genesis and subsequent existence were made possible by "print capitalism," that is, by the rise of new technologies enabling the spread of standardized vernacular languages over a wide geographical area. The primary communities with which people most easily identify are families and villages because they are intimate enough to command their immediate loyalties. By contrast, the nation is

---

[3] I am told by a native of Switzerland, however, that the Swiss never speak of their federal government in Berne as a "national" government. Furthermore, the expression *la patrie* is applied by most Swiss to their individual cantons and not so much to Switzerland as a whole.

[4] Ernest Renan, "What Is a Nation?" reprinted in Mark O. Dickerson, Thomas Flanagan, Neil Nevitte, *Introductory Readings in Government and Politics*, 3rd ed. (Scarborough, Ontario: Nelson Canada, 1991), pp. 32-42.

[5] See, e.g., Hans Kohn, *The Idea of Nationalism* (New York: Collier, 1967), pp. 8, 13.

"imagined" insofar as its members "will never know most of their fellow members, meet them, or even hear of them, yet in the minds of each lives the image of their communion."[6] Nations, in short, are deliberate social constructions enabling members to imagine a common identity with those far removed from their own circle of family, friends and acquaintances.

Furthermore, in the modern era, nation has come to be connected with the state, or political community, which binds large numbers of people together under a single constitutional and legal framework. Eric Hobsbawm points out that the Spanish *Nación*, the French *Nation* and the German *Volk* once applied principally to a smaller grouping of people inhabiting a locally defined *patria*. It was not until well into the nineteenth century that nation and *patria* came to be defined politically. Now it is considered axiomatic that nationhood entails sovereign statehood, and the language of nation has now become inescapably political.[7] Herman Dooyeweerd argues that "every national community has the potency to become a real State."[8] Charles Taylor believes there to be a certain logic in the progression from nationhood to statehood as a working out of the democratic belief in self-government.[9] In the aftermath of the First World War this would come to be articulated in the principle of national self-determination, a right enshrined in the United Nations' International Covenant on Economic, Social and Cultural Rights.

On the other hand, José Ortega y Gasset argues that the relationship between state and nation moves in precisely the opposite direction. The common identity of the nation is a product of the consolidating efforts of the state over many centuries. "The state has always been a grand impresario and dedicated matchmaker."[10] An existing state has rarely "coincided with a prior identity of 'blood' or language." Rather, it is the state that has created the territorial national community within which people are persuaded to develop national loyalties and a common sense of identity. Against Renan, who sees nationhood as rooted in shared history,

---

[6]Benedict Anderson, *Imagined Communities: Reflections on the Origin and Spread of Nationalism* (London: Verso, 1983), p. 15.

[7]Eric Hobsbawm, *Nations and Nationalism Since 1780: Programme, Myth, Reality* (Cambridge: Cambridge University Press, 1990), pp. 14-20.

[8]Herman Dooyeweerd, *A New Critique of Theoretical Thought* (Philadelphia, Penn.: Presbyterian & Reformed, 1953-1958), 3:470.

[9]Charles Taylor, "Why Do Nations Have to Become States?" in *Reconciling the Solitudes: Essays on Canadian Federalism and Nationalism,* ed. Guy Laforest (Montreal: McGill-Queen's University Press, 1993), pp. 40-58.

[10]José Ortega y Gasset, *The Revolt of the Masses* (Notre Dame, Ind.: University of Notre Dame Press, 1985), p. 152.

Ortega contends that a nation is a deliberate projection into a shared future.[11]

Once again, however, as Bernard Crick points out, "no single objective criterion of the national unit has ever been found."[12] Even a combination of several factors has not proved adequate in all cases to delineate the boundaries of a nation. It is difficult to avoid the conclusion that a nation simply encompasses all those who feel themselves to be members. That said, however, membership in a nation is not simply left up to individual decision, but rests on the willingness of other members to accept an individual as such, usually on the basis of some sort of tangible, objective connectedness. Whatever criteria Lithuanians use to define themselves as a nation, I cannot plausibly claim membership, nor am I likely to be accepted as a fellow Lithuanian, because neither I nor my ancestors have had any prior attachment to the Lithuanian land, people or language. In short, nations exclude, both formally and informally, those whom they deem to be outside their boundaries. In this respect, a nation is essentially no different from any other community.

On the other hand, not all people bearing a tangible connectedness to each other, to their land or even to common political institutions necessarily think of themselves as a nation. Pennsylvanians are not a nation and do not see themselves as such. As Crick paraphrases Renan, a "nationality is formed by the decision to form a nation."[13] Right-wing Israelis have often averred that the cause of the Palestine Liberation Organization is illegitimate because Palestinians are not a nation but are simply part of a larger Arab nation stretching across the Middle East and North Africa. These Israelis have mistakenly assumed that there are obvious, universally accepted criteria for nationality which Palestinians fail to satisfy. But the fact that enough Palestinians believe themselves to constitute a nation would seem to be sufficient to accord them national status. Conversely, some have argued that modern European Jews are in some measure descended from the Turkic Khazars, who converted to Judaism in the middle ages.[14] If so, then this could place in doubt the Zionist claim to Palestine in the twentieth century. Yet both of these arguments miss the point. Quoting Crick again, "nothing can argue people who feel themselves to be a nation out of the belief that they are a nation."[15]

---

[11]Ibid., pp. 157-64.

[12]Bernard Crick, *In Defence of Politics* (Harmondsworth, U.K.: Penguin, 1993), p. 75.

[13]Ibid., p. 77.

[14]See, e.g., Arthur Koestler, *The Thirteenth Tribe: The Khazar Empire and Its Heritage* (New York: Random House, 1976); and Kevin Alan Brook, *The Jews of Khazaria* (Northvale, N.J.: Jason Aronson, 1999).

[15]Crick, *In Defence of Politics,* p. 74.

In short, nations seem to constitute themselves as such. This does not mean that objective characteristics play no role. They do indeed play an important role, although one cannot reduce a particular nation to any one or more of these. Nor does it mean that other nations play no role in the process. In fact, a nation is frequently formed in the crucible of oppression by a foreign power. Had it not been for the British mandate in Palestine and subsequent Jewish immigration, it is unlikely that the Arab residents of the territory would ever have developed a cohesive national identity. Dutch nationality developed during the eighty years war against Spain. American nationality was created by perceived British oppression, and Canadian nationality emerged out of a fear of American belligerence. Once a nation has come into being as a self-conscious community, it joins the world of political actors and becomes a force to be reckoned with, for good or for ill.

The difficulty of anchoring nation in objective factors already gives us an insight into the ideology of nationalism and its attendant dilemmas. Rather than coming up with an ironclad definition of nation, capable of withstanding the onslaughts of all other possible definitions, we shall perhaps have to content ourselves with a certain degree of ambiguity, understanding that no one definition is likely to account for all claimed manifestations of the phenomenon. I personally believe, along with Taylor, Ortega and others, that a nation is usually connected in some fashion with the concrete institution of the state, though not every self-conscious nation need—or even can—find expression in a state under its exclusive control. Nevertheless, the aspiration to self-government seems implicit in the idea of nationhood, however difficult this may be to accommodate in every case.

A Creed for a Century

Although it is a commonplace belief that the twentieth century belonged to democracy and socialism, historian John Lukacs believes it was most characterized by the conflict of nations and nationalisms.[16] Certainly the likes of Vladimir Lenin put an indelible stamp on the history of our era by ushering in a political and economic system that would dominate a large portion of the earth's surface for between forty and seventy years. Yet it was Woodrow Wilson's doctrine of national self-determination that ended up having the more enduring impact.

---

[16]John Lukacs, *The End of the Twentieth Century and the End of the Modern Age* (New York: Ticknor & Fields, 1993), esp. pp. 1-9.

Communism is a spent force, no longer capable of rallying large numbers of people to its cause. Nationalism, on the other hand, has continued to exercise its sway, first in the breakup of the European multinational empires after 1918, later in the anticolonial struggles after 1945, and finally in the fragmentation of modern culturally plural states and federations after 1989.

But nationalism is no easier a concept to grasp than nation itself. In fact, nationalism is less identifiable an ideology than, say, liberalism. While the latter is a coherent set of doctrines with a long and honored intellectual history, nationalism is a phenomenon differing from one time and place to the next. Nationalisms are utterly different from each other because the focus of each is utterly different.[17] Serbian nationalism is totally other than Croatian nationalism. Liberalism and socialism are, at least in theory, internationalist and cosmopolitan ideologies, commanding the allegiance of people around the world. Nationalism is not, with its focus on the peculiar traditions of a particular community of people, and to the extent that this is true it bears some similarity to conservatism.

Yet nationalism is not necessarily a conservative ideology, despite some shared characteristics with—and indeed even roots in—the historicism of Burke and Maistre. Throughout the two centuries of its existence, nationalism has been a revolutionary force, overthrowing ruling dynasties, unifying previously fragmented peoples, dismembering old empires, creating new ones, and killing off ailing ideologies. Although many nationalistic regimes have been autocratic, there is an intimate connection between nationalism and the characteristic democratic doctrine of popular sovereignty, the latter of which tends to erode conservative regimes constructed on a different principle. Furthermore, Hans Kohn argues that throughout its history, nationalism has often been a progressive force drawing disparate peoples together into broader and more encompassing loyalties. And although he believes the time has come to reorganize our liberties on a supranational basis, he nevertheless believes that in its time nationalism played a positive role in overcoming parochial loyalties narrower than the nation-state.[18]

According to Kohn, nationalism is a "state of mind" recognizing in the nation-state "the ideal form of political organization" and in nationality "the source of all creative cultural energy and of economic well-being."[19] For the na-

---

[17]William Pfaff makes this point in *The Wrath of Nations: Civilization and the Furies of Nationalism* (New York: Simon & Schuster/Touchstone, 1993), pp. 14–15.

[18]Kohn, *Idea of Nationalism*, pp. 22–23.

[19]Ibid., p. 16.

tionalist, the nation must claim the ultimate allegiance of its members, who are dependent on it for their welfare and even to some extent, their very existence. Charles A. Kupchan concurs that nationalism "elevates the nation-state to a place of primacy—one that transcends class, kinship, or regional affiliations in commanding popular loyalty."[20] One might also add religion to the list of loyalties that the nation strives to transcend. In fact, Kohn recognizes that nationalism imbues loyalty to the state with a certain religious fervor.[21]

Carlton Hayes carries this observation further and treats nationalism as itself a religion.[22] He notes striking similarities to traditional religions such as Christianity and Buddhism. Nationalism has engendered a cult of the nation, complete with its own liturgical ceremonies, Te Deums, sacraments, icons and feast days. Like Yahweh, the God of Israel, the nation is a jealous god whose worshipers are likely to be intolerant of all dissenters, including the adherents of rival religions. Nationalism is a bloody religion whose victims dwarf in number all the casualties of the late medieval crusades. As a religion, nationalism "represents a reaction against historic Christianity, against the universal mission of Christ; it re-enshrines the earlier tribal mission of a chosen people."[23] While Christianity aspires to draw people together on the basis of charity and humility, nationalism drives them apart on the basis of pride and tribal selfishness.

Obviously Hayes' analysis of nationalism comports well with our own thesis that ideologies are fundamentally idolatrous religions. Yet it is not simply the associated cultic practices that give nationalism its religious character, though they certainly make it more visible. Even if it were to lack such trappings as national anthems, holidays, parades, oaths of loyalty and the like, nationalism would still be religious insofar as it sees nation as a transcendent reality infusing ultimate meaning into the rest of life. A god need not demand that we literally bow the knee and sing its praises to claim divine status. It is sufficient that it demand unconditional loyalty overriding all other loyalties.

From what, then, does the god of nation claim to save us? If, once again, nationalism is an ideology, and if ideologies are guilty of the gnostic heresy, then it must find something structural within the world to be a source of evil and it

---

[20]Charles A. Kupchan, "Introduction: Nationalism Resurgent," in *Nationalism and Nationalities in the New Europe,* ed. Charles A. Kupchan (Ithaca, N.Y.: Cornell University Press, 1995), p. 2.

[21]Kohn, *Idea of Nationalism,* p. 4.

[22]Carlton Hayes, *Essays on Nationalism* (New York: Macmillan, 1926), pp. 93-125; and *Nationalism: A Religion* (New York: Macmillan, 1960), pp. 151-82.

[23]Hayes, *Essays on Nationalism,* p. 124.

must claim the power to save us from it. Most of the ideologies in this study view any heteronomous authority—that is, any authority outside of the sovereign will—as bad. Thus far we have seen this particularly with respect to liberalism. Nationalism is no different in this regard, except insofar as it expands the seat of the autonomous will to encompass the entire national community. Just as liberalism attempts to free the individual as much as possible from other wills impinging on her sovereignty, so also does nationalism undertake to emancipate the nation from the rule of others outside of its self-defined boundaries. Either implicitly or explicitly, nationalists identify ultimate evil with being ruled by someone unlike oneself, whether this unlikeness be racial, cultural, linguistic or religious. Thus Greek Cypriots objected to being ruled indefinitely by British high commissioners and governors from 1878 to 1960. Similarly Turkish Cypriots feared being ruled by ethnic Greeks in a Cyprus controlled by Athens. Ethnic Serbs in the Krajina took exception to being ruled by Croats in an independent Croatia between 1991 and 1995. Afrikaners feared being ruled by a black majority in South Africa after 1994, while nonwhites disliked being governed by a white minority before that year. Moreover, many contemporary feminists display a similar dislike for what they call patriarchy, that is, a society disproportionately ruled by men.

To some extent such fears are understandable. It is perhaps axiomatic that *like best represents like*—that our interests are best protected by leaders sharing significant personal qualities with us. In Anglo-Saxon democracies the operative assumption is that representation is primarily territorial: our legislators must either be from the district they claim to represent or have some tangible connection with it. If they do not, then they might not see themselves having any stake in the community for whose interests they ostensibly speak, which would tend to undermine their representative function, both in the legislature itself and in the eyes of constituents. Furthermore, most people deem it desirable that parliaments and cabinets in some measure be a microcosm of the body politic, that is, that they should include men and women, linguistic minorities, adherents of different religions, racial minorities and the like. If a parliament is occupied by a large number of lawyers or other professionals, people will tend to deprecate the body as insufficiently representative, however well intended the parliamentarians themselves may be and however many votes they may have received in the last election. More recently we have come to recognize that an excessively male-dominated legislature is less likely to consider the unique concerns of women in the making of public policy. There is, in short, a measure of legitimacy in the call for national and other forms of group liberation.

However, the desire never to have to answer to those unlike oneself is neither practicable nor theoretically defensible. In the first place, it is altogether impossible that we should be governed solely by ourselves or by those like us. The very nature of leadership demands that governors should at least be better educated than the governed, as Plato already understood more than two millennia ago. Even the most convinced nationalist does not demand that leaders be limited to the same educational qualifications as the general population. But even beyond what may seem obvious, we inevitably have to accept political authorities who may have French as their mother tongue while ours is English, who may be women while we are men, who may come from Iowa while we are from New York, or who may be urban while we are rural. There is in itself no injustice in the fact that Basques are ruled by Spaniards, Christians by Muslims, women by men, and Manitobans by Quebeckers. Such conditions are unavoidable in a normal political community, with its inevitable diversity of interests and uneven distribution of talents.

In the second place, it is simply untrue that only Francophones are capable of looking out for Francophones. During the negotiations leading up to Canada's failed Charlottetown Accord in 1992, there were calls for provincial Senate delegations to be legally divided in half between men and women.[24] If, it was reasoned, half the population is female, then we ought to mandate the same proportion for representatives to the upper chamber of Parliament. This would certainly accord with a microcosmic conception of representation. However it does not so easily accord with other, equally legitimate conceptions. In particular, it unduly limits the freedom of choice deemed essential to safeguarding the representative character of democratic polities. In the real world voters regularly cast ballots for candidates who may not share their gender, ethnicity, religion and so forth. In Canada during the 1990s Prime Minister Jean Chrétien was much more popular among Anglophones than among Francophones, a fact that nationalists and partisans of what might be called identity politics would

---

[24]The Charlottetown Accord represented the second attempt by the Conservative government of Brian Mulroney to secure Quebec's approval of Canada's Constitution Acts, which had been "patriated," or "brought home" from Great Britain a decade earlier. At that time Prime Minister Pierre Trudeau had obtained the approval of nine of the ten provincial governments, with the notable exception of his home province of Quebec. Neither of Mulroney's efforts met with success. For a good textbook account of "The Modern Era of Megaconstitutional Politics" in Canada, see Keith Archer, Roger Gibbins, Rainer Knopff and Leslie A. Pal, *Parameters of Power: Canada's Political Institutions*, 2nd ed. (Toronto: ITP Nelson, 1999), pp. 71-132.

find difficult to explain. If it is desirable that a legislature resemble in some measure the society it claims to represent, it is nevertheless true that real, flesh and blood persons are capable of protecting the interests of others unlike themselves. Our common humanity, augmented by our created capacity for sympathy with others, makes it possible for dissimilar persons to treat each other justly.

Moreover, nationalists at their most ideological tend to assume unduly that national liberation will bring about an end state free from the perceived evils of foreign rule. Unfortunately there is no guarantee that local elites in an independent national polity will be any more just or less despotic than the recently repudiated foreign rulers. In this respect the nationalist enterprise seems effectively to "emancipate" people by granting them the singular privilege of being oppressed in their own language by leaders sharing their ethnicity or race. It is not difficult to find examples of this unhappy phenomenon in the newly "liberated" postwar states of Asia and Africa, where domestic rulers have sometimes proved to be far more venal and vicious than former colonial administrators. There can be little doubt that the average Ugandan was better off under British rule than under Idi Amin's tyranny in the 1970s, yet nationalism is unable to account for this apparently anomalous situation. Furthermore, as Philip Mansel argues in his fascinating account of Constantinople during the Ottoman era, diverse ethnic and religious communities were often more tolerated under dynastic regimes, such as the Ottomans or Hapsburgs, than under the successor nationalist governments that sought to impose an artificial uniformity within equally artificial borders.[25] While none of this should be construed as an argument for continued European imperial or hereditary monarchical governance, it is the better part of wisdom to avoid attaching redemptive, eschatological expectations to otherwise legitimate aspirations for national independence and self-government.

Civic and Ethnic Nationalisms: State Versus Tribe

Even the casual observer of such phenomena will note that not all nationalisms are of the same kind. For example, what George Grant labels "Canadian nationalism" has little in common with the Serbian nationalism of former Yugoslav president Slobodan Miloševic. In South Africa the multiracial nationalism of the African National Congress is sharply opposed to the exclusivist black na-

---

[25]Philip Mansel, *Constantinople: City of the World's Desire, 1453-1924* (New York: St. Martin's, 1995), especially pp. 415-32.

tionalism of the Pan African Congress. The French nationalism of the late
Charles de Gaulle and his successors is a quite different phenomenon from the
Kurdish nationalism of the Middle East. What distinguishes these varieties from
each other? Principally, it is their respective definitions of nation and its relation
to the state. Michael Ignatieff and William Pfaff, for example, work with a twofold distinction between civic and ethnic nationalisms.[26]

Civic or *political nationalism* has as its specific focus of allegiance the state, or
the political community, of which all citizens are members. The world's first national revolutions were animated by this civic variety of nationalism. The
American Revolution (or, more modestly, the American War of Independence)
aimed to establish thirteen new bodies politic separate from the British Crown.
Eventually a single federal political system was set up in 1787, and nationalism
finally triumphed over the vestiges of state sovereignty in 1865 or possibly as
late as 1917.[27] Gradually, over the course of successive decades, American nationality attained a larger than life, mythical stature in the hearts of its citizens.
Its symbols, such as the Constitution and the "stars and stripes," acquired a sac-
rosanct and inviolable status. The American nation, whose "manifest destiny" it
was thought to be to occupy the whole of North America, assumed an imperial
role in Central America, the Caribbean and the Pacific. And of course after the
Second World War it took on the mantle of international superpower.

For all the abuses that this form of civic nationalism generated, and despite
the occasional expression of "nativist" (white, Anglo-Saxon, Protestant) sentiments, American nationalism had the virtue of being inclusive of a variety of
ethnic, religious and racial groups. Citizenship was recognized and granted on
the basis of professed loyalty to the country and its constitution, not of membership in a particular ethnic community. Emma Lazarus's famous poem "The
New Colossus" on the base of the Statue of Liberty is testimony to a nationalism that in principle encompassed would-be Americans from all corners of the
globe, bound together by the common desire for freedom in a new land.[28] Of

---

[26]See Michael Ignatieff, *Blood and Belonging: Journeys into the New Nationalism* (Toronto:Viking/Penguin,
1993), pp. 3-6, and Pfaff, *Wrath of Nations*, pp. 1-40.

[27]Jean Bethke Elshtain argues that the triumph of nationalism over particularism in the United States did
not occur until the era of the First World War, when President Woodrow Wilson invoked it to secure
public support for the war effort. See Elshtain, *Women and War* (Chicago: University of Chicago Press,
1987, 1995), pp. 113-20.

[28]The poem ascribes the following to the lady Liberty portrayed in the statue: "Give me your tired, your
poor, / Your huddled masses yearning to breathe free, / The wretched refuse of your teeming shore. /
Send these, the homeless, tempest-tost to me, / I lift my lamp beside the golden door!"

course, the reality for such groups as African- and aboriginal Americans was quite different, but its principles were eventually extended to include them as well. This is civic nationalism at its best.

The French launched the world's second nationalist revolution in 1789. Although France itself was founded on the dynastic principle inherited from the late Middle Ages, in its revolutionary manifestation it claimed to be a national community binding its citizens together into a single sovereign people with a unified will. Accordingly, after Louis XVI had convoked the Estates General in July of that year, the Third Estate abolished the first two estates and declared itself the National Assembly, claiming to represent and articulate the will of the nation. This notion of a unitary national community was an innovation that even the Americans had not attempted. Henceforth France was to be knit together by common allegiance, not to the king, who would shortly pass from the scene, but to a legal and philosophical abstraction that had yet to assume reality. Subsequent generations of French people sought to realize a French nation by mobilizing the citizens to participate in republican institutions, by standardizing and centralizing education, by disseminating knowledge of the French language, and by inculcating a belief in the principles of the Declaration of the Rights of Man and of the Citizen of 1789. Of course, these subsequent generations were sporadically dominated by restored monarchies and empires, illustrating the extent to which the French nation was still divided over a pivotal event in its own history and, therefore, far from conforming to the unitary national ideal.

The French Revolution and the subsequent Napoleonic conquests in Europe set off a wave of nationalism whose effects are still being felt on that continent nearly two centuries later. Both American and French citizens inherited state apparatuses from predecessor regimes. For them nationalism was simply a matter of redirecting the loyalties of the people from a dynastic ruler to a domestic body politic of which they were seen to be active members. Thus partisans sought to cement the unity of their respective countries by means of a new civic nationalism, that is, by means of an ideology whose ultimate focus is on the concrete institutions of an existing political community.

But in the years after 1815 nationalism spread to a part of Europe lacking, not only nation-states, but even the potential for nation-states. This "belt of mixed populations" extended from the Elbe to the Volga and beyond, and was governed by several dynastic empires, the boundaries among which were constantly shifting according to the respective strengths and weaknesses of their rulers. By the early nineteenth century the Ottoman Empire was in decline and its diminishing Balkan territory was coveted by Austria and Russia in particular, while the Western powers also claimed an interest. Yet a distinctive kind of nationalism began to assert the right of local populations to rule themselves insofar as they comprised distinct, self-conscious nations. Without specific territories or political institutions, these nations came to be defined ethnically, by a collection of qualities and attributes said to inhere in the people themselves. This contributed to the rise of *ethnic nationalism*, or what Hannah Arendt has aptly labeled "tribal nationalism."[29]

According to Arendt, the nation-state, though by no means the ideal form of political organization, nevertheless placed a certain limit on the potential expansiveness of nationalism. However, once divorced from stable political institutions, nationalism became tribal and began to focus on common cultural characteristics binding a people together in a higher spiritual unity. When German Romanticism was added to the mix, the conception grew of a rootless nation, animated by a distinctive spirit manifested in common language or even ancestry. The focus of loyalty here shifted from the fatherland to the *ethnos* or *Volk* itself, whose presence in the world transcended normal state boundaries and was thus subversive of existing states and empires. Tribal nationalism would eventually lead to various forms of imperialism such as pan-Germanism and pan-Slavism.[30] But it also led to a general desire to break up such empires as those of Austria and Turkey and to replace them with would-be nation-states on the west European model.

Modern Greek nationalism provides an excellent paradigm for ethnic or tribal nationalism. In the waning days of the Ottoman Empire, at the beginning of the nineteenth century, the Christian subjects of the Sultan began to become restive under the rule of their Muslim Turkish overlords. Many of these Christians began to describe themselves as Hellenes, or Greeks, and agitated to overturn Ottoman rule. Open rebellion broke out in 1821 and with the help of Britain, France and Russia, an independent Greek kingdom was established at the foot of the Balkan peninsula in 1830. Greek nationalists had scored an undoubted success, but a small independent state was not what they had originally sought. Influenced by the nationalistic *Meghali Idhea* ("Great Idea"), partisans had sought at most to reestablish the ancient Byzantine Empire and at least to

---

[29]Hannah Arendt, *The Origins of Totalitarianism* (New York: Harcourt Brace Jovanovich, 1973), pp. 227-43.

[30]Ibid.

recover for the Greek nation the historic lands deemed once to have belonged to it. The new Greek kingdom—which was considerably smaller than present-day Greece—was hampered from the outset by the fact that the majority of ethnic Greeks lived outside its boundaries. Thus the government in Athens embarked on an irredentist policy of "restoring" as much as possible of the territory of the Balkans, Asia Minor and the islands to its own jurisdiction. The monarch styled himself not King of Greece, but King of the *Greeks*, a deliberate choice of words indicating a claim to rule over all members of the Greek *ethnos*, wherever they might live.[31]

This *Meghali Idhea,* as well as the irredentist policies flowing from it, eventually led to a series of human tragedies, including the massacre and expulsion of Anatolian Greeks in 1922, the ensuing compulsory exchanges of populations mandated by the Treaty of Lausanne and the forced partition of Cyprus in 1974. Ethnically conceived nations evidently find it difficult to live with fixed territorial boundaries and a culturally plural citizenry. Whereas the civic variety of nationalism begins with a given land possessing known borders and goes on to assume that all those born or domiciled within are real or potential citizens, ethnic nationalism begins with a homogeneous group of people scattered in different places and tries to find for them a homeland with expandable boundaries. It is not surprising then that ethnic nationalism has often contributed to the proliferation of conflict, including two world wars, three Balkan wars and four Middle Eastern wars.

But even the civic variety of nationalism can be as expansive as ethnic nationalism, though for different reasons. While the latter is tempted to engage in reckless irredentist ventures or to seek lebensraum from the territory of neighboring states, the former is more likely to try to extend the "benefits" of its own political system or civilization to other "less advantaged" peoples in far-flung corners of the globe. British and American imperialists viewed their own constitutions as embodying eternally valid principles of which others were thought to stand in need. Hence the British dominions of Canada, Australia and New Zealand were granted parliamentary-cabinet systems on the Westminster model, despite the fact that local conditions might have called for something better suited to the diverse cultural geographies of these newly emerging na-

---

[31]See Hugh Seton-Watson's discussion of Greek nationalism in *Nations and States: An Enquiry into the Origins of Nations and the Politics of Nationalism* (London: Methuen, 1977), pp. 110-17. See also Richard Clogg, *A Concise History of Greece* (Cambridge: Cambridge University Press, 1992), esp. pp. 47-99, for an account of the impact of the *Meghali Idhea* on the building of the Greek kingdom.

tions. Believing as well in their own civilization's obvious superiority, many loyal Britons saw it as their nation's mission to bring as much of the world as possible not only under the benevolent rule of their own Parliament but also under the influence of English manners and mores.

In similar fashion, Americans, after severing their ties with the Crown, quickly moved to conquer much of their continent and to extend their sphere of influence over the entire western hemisphere. Though overt imperialism fell out of favor after the beginning of the twentieth century, the United States nevertheless saw itself possessing a mission to export its own representative institutions, and eventually even its popular culture, to the rest of the world. Whether in the guise of making the world safe for democracy, containing communism, establishing a new world order or combating terrorism, such expansionist sentiments eventually led that country into policies that stretched its resources too thinly and bitterly divided its own electorate. In Vietnam, most notably, the United States effectively assumed the imperial mantle abandoned by France in 1954 and over the course of the next two decades ran up against the limits of its own political prudence. Nationalism, in short, is potentially expansionist, whether in its civic or in its ethnic form.

The Nationalist View of the State

Although the distinction between civic and ethnic varieties of nationalism is an important one, not every nationalistic movement can be neatly placed in one or the other category. Moreover, some observers, such as Bernard Yack, Kai Nielsen and Will Kymlicka, dispute the distinction altogether on the grounds that even so-called civic nations possess a culture of some sort involving the handing down of inherited political traditions.[32] To be sure, virtually every nationalism has an overriding political goal of some sort, so even the ethnic nationalist movement aspires to control state institutions of some sort. Nevertheless this political goal is likely to differ from one movement to the next. Some aim

---

[32]See, e.g., Bernard Yack, "The Myth of the Civic Nation," Kai Nielsen, "Cultural Nationalism: Neither Ethnic nor Civic," and Will Kymlicka, "Misunderstanding Nationalism," in *Theorizing Nationalism,* ed. Ronald Beiner (New York: SUNY Press, 1999), pp. 103-40. I would agree with these writers that a so-called civic nation is not necessarily democratic or characterized by the rule of law, yet this fact in itself does not invalidate the distinction between civic and ethnic nations, if one understands that the inherited culture of a so-called civic nation revolves around loyalty to concrete *political* institutions rather than to primarily nonpolitical attributes such as language, race or religion. Like ethnic nationalism, then, civic nationalism does indeed bequeath a common cultural heritage, if one understands that this is precisely a *political* culture.

to maintain and strengthen the unity of an already existing nation-state such as
the United States or Canada. Some aim to secure the independence of a subordinate overseas territory from a controlling metropolitan power. The anticolonial movements of the 1950s and 1960s are examples of this. Others aim to break
up an existing multiethnic state into smaller, ethnically homogeneous states. The
movements for Croatian and Slovenian independence in 1991 fall into this category. Yet others desire to unify a politically fragmented ethnic group under a
single government, such as Italy and Germany in the nineteenth century.

Nevertheless, each of these nationalisms shares a single view of the state. I
shall argue that a normative Christian political theory sees the state as an institution built on the exercise of power and guided by the principle of justice. We
shall examine the normative content of justice in chapter nine, but at this point
it is sufficient to note that it calls for the legal protection of all individuals and
communities domiciled within the state's borders. By contrast, nationalism sees
the state as the instrument of the nation's aspirations and the expression of its
will. Civic nationalism identifies nation and state and attempts to use the state
to solidify national unity through the use of communications media and
through its educational monopoly. In other words, the state precedes and creates the nation. In most Western democracies civic nationalism takes a fairly
mild form and is subject to constitutional constraints, to the influence of other,
competing ideologies, such as liberalism, and, of course, to the limits built into
creation. But civic nationalism can take a more destructive, totalitarian form, as
in Benito Mussolini's Italian fascism. In fascism, loyalty to the state becomes the
highest loyalty a person can have, and this idolatrous allegiance becomes the defining characteristic of the national community. To dissent from this religious
devotion is to place oneself outside the nation.

Ethnic nationalism, too, views the state as the vehicle for realizing the ambitions of the nation. In this case, however, nation precedes state and is identified primarily with a particular group of people—often, though not necessarily,
defined linguistically—who desire some form of political organization to satisfy
their need for security or even their desire for power over neighboring nations.

The changing self-definition of the French fact in Canada provides a good
case study for understanding the development of ethnic nationalisms. Prior to
the *Révolution tranquille* (Quiet Revolution) of the 1960s in Quebec, the aspirations of French Canadians were articulated in the form of a French Canadian
nationalism rooted in the traditions of a largely agrarian and Roman Catholic
population with strong ties to the land and a high birthrate. French Canadian

nationalists had an abiding affection for the province of Quebec, the only province in which they constituted a majority, but they also shared close fraternal feelings with their ethnic compatriots in New Brunswick, northern Ontario and Manitoba. The primary bases of French Canadian identity at this time were common loyalty to the Roman Catholic Church and a shared French mother tongue.

After the Second World War this began to change in favor of a more statist form of nationalism that attempted to fuse the civic and ethnic forms. During the 1960s both church attendance and birthrate plummeted, and loyalty to the Catholic Church began to wane. Having become increasingly urbanized and secularized, Québecois could fall back on the French language as the sole remaining ground of their distinct identity. It is not surprising, then, that the separatist Parti québécois, upon coming to power in 1976, moved to enact laws protecting the status of the French language and prohibiting the use of other languages on public signs. After the *Révolution tranquille*, French Canadian nationalism became Quebec nationalism. Still centered on a particular ethnic identity, Quebec nationalism nevertheless sought to shift the focus from the protection of a French Canadian "tribe" to the advancement and realization of a sovereign French-speaking nation-state in Quebec. French Canadians outside that province were now seen to be in exile and were told to "come home" if they wished to live their lives in their mother tongue.

The danger of the ethnic variety of nationalism lies, of course, in the pursuit of a double standard of justice. When ethnic nationalists come to power in a given state, they privilege the members of the titular ethnic group over those of other ethnic groups. Only ethnic Romanians can be considered "true" members of the Romanian nation, while the ethnic Hungarians and Germans of Transylvania come to be seen as at least resident foreigners and at most possible enemies of the nation. The desire for ethnic homogeneity has led to "ethnic cleansing" during the 1990s in the Balkans. Carried to its logical extreme, it led to the horrors of German national socialism, or Nazism, in the 1930s and 1940s. In one respect Hitler was not a good nationalist because he allowed his own grandiose ambitions to ruin the German nation. But in another respect, he simply took the logic of ethnic nationalism and carried it in an overtly racist and imperialist direction.

While every ideology has insights into human life as it relates to politics, each is nevertheless in error on some fundamental point. As indicated above, nationalism is right to alert us to the reality of community as something irreducible to the aggregate wills of freely contracting individuals. Nationalism also correctly understands, in contrast to liberalism, that a significant part of the state's task is to protect and advance the rights of community. Where nationalism fails, however, is in its inability to make room for a variety of communities with different structures and with overlapping claims on the person's loyalties. Assuming it is possible to determine the structure of the national community, there is still no justification in vesting that community with ontological ultimacy or in seeing it as the fount of people's overall sense of meaning and identity. In short, nationalism, in properly avoiding the perils of individualism, falls prey to the blandishments of collectivism.

Patriotic Loyalty: A Modest Devotion

Is there a legitimate place, however, for some form of loyalty to nation in a modest and nonidolatrous sense? There is indeed, whichever definition of nation we find ourselves working with.

Ethnic loyalty can degenerate into overt racism, as we have seen. Yet it is surely proper to encourage an interest and love for the cultural traditions of one's own *ethnic community*. One thinks, for example, of professor and physician Elias Lönnrot (1802-1884), traveling his own Finnish countryside collecting the pre-Christian epic folk poetry that had circulated for centuries and compiling them into the *Kalevala*, the Finnish national saga.[33] In the musical realm, Béla Bartók and Zoltan Kodaly made a similar journey through pre-Trianon Hungary, collecting the folk melodies of the ethnically diverse inhabitants and committing them to paper for posterity. Other composers, such as Mikhail Glinka, Bedřich Smetana, Maurice Ravel and Ralph Vaughan Williams, drew on their own or related ethnic heritages for their compositions, thereby enriching the larger Western musical tradition. We should surely be poorer without "Kamarinskaya," "Die Moldau," "Rhapsodie Espagnole" and the "English Folk Song Suite."

Nevertheless, the mere recovery of vanishing folk traditions, whether in literature, music or even the visual arts, need not logically entail a separate political community for each folk culture. Theoretically, a Smetana or an Antonín Dvořák could have celebrated the glories of their own Czech musical heritage

---

[33]With its distinctive trochaic tetrameter, famously imitated in Henry Wadsworth Longfellow's *Song of Hiawatha*, the *Kalevala* is difficult to render adequately in English translation. However, for one effort that preserves the metrical flavor of the original, see *Kalevala: The Land of Heroes*, trans. W. F. Kirby (London: Athlone, 1985).

while remaining loyal subjects of the Austro-Hungarian Empire. Yet, as we all know, Czechs would eventually come to create their own nation-state, in conjunction with Slovaks, out of the remains of Austria-Hungary.[34] A celebration of an ethnically defined nation seems historically to lead to the demand for national sovereignty within a sometimes ill-defined homeland. This is undoubtedly due to an understandable desire of the members of that group to protect their culture through political means. Although the quest for national sovereignty often has tremendous negative consequences for the continued peace of an ethnic community and its neighbors, the sense of solidarity based on shared traditions is, in itself, right and proper. This is perhaps the grain of truth to be found even in ethnic nationalism.

What then shall we do with the ethnic community, which is clearly a significant factor in human life and must be accounted for in some fashion? Here we must exercise some caution, because nationalists are often tempted to conceive the ethnic nation in totalitarian terms. German national socialism is certainly the most extreme example of this. In my view, the ethnically based nation ought to be described as an *aggregating* or *nontotalizing community* that may or may not coincide with the political nation. Unlike other forms of community, such as state and family, which have a certain degree of internal solidarity and are capable of being active responsible agents, the ethnic nation is simply a nonpurposive network of interrelated individuals, institutions and associations bound together by a common culture, however this be defined. It has no internal authority structure and is consequently incapable of acting as a unified body. Because it is a mere network of interrelations, it cannot supplant or envelop in totalitarian fashion other, more tangible communities, such as school, labor union, business enterprise and even state, yet all of these participate in some fashion in its cultural distinctives.

As for the politically defined *nation*, this is more immediately tied to concrete political institutions set over a well-defined territory. Nation in this sense can be seen as embodying what Dooyeweerd labels the ethical aspect of political community.[35] In other words, we are here referring to that community of citizens created by political power but deepened in the development of a shared commitment to,

---

[34]In 1993 the continuing outworking of the ethnic principle as a basis for state sovereignty led to the further breakup of Czechoslovakia into separate Czech and Slovak republics. The latter, however, is still not ethnically homogeneous, as some 10 percent of its population is made up of ethnic Hungarians.

[35]Concerning Dooyeweerd's theory of aspects or modes, see chapter eight.

and love of, that community. The name we often give to this love is *patriotism* or *patriotic loyalty.*[36] Such loyalty is not an idolatrous worship of nation; rather, it is a limited affection for a community of fellow citizens bound together for purposes of government and based in a defined territory.[37] A nation cannot be unified on the basis of mere mutual satisfaction of utilitarian needs. It must rather be bound together by an active dedication to the maintenance of the body politic. To call this dedication *love* is quite proper if we understand that this particular manifestation of love is distinct from that between close friends, husband and wife, or parents and children. Patriotic loyalty is thus inextricably tied to the shared commitment to do justice within the context of political community.

This is where Renan's "daily plebiscite" enters the picture. The mere organization of coercive sword power is not sufficient to maintain political community. Nor is the mechanical operation of a constitutional structure enough to command popular compliance in the absence of a corresponding sense of community among the governed. When states break up, it is often because the people of the successor states did not believe they were receiving justice under the old system. But such fragmentation is as frequently due to a lack of fellow feeling among the citizens of the larger state. Although Canada is by any criterion a successful and prosperous country, many Québecois would like to claim independence simply because, for them, Canada is an abstraction unable to command their loyalty. Even many of those favoring Canadian unity in that province see themselves as Québecois first and Canadians second. In the absence of an active commitment to maintain the body politic, the sense of nationhood will be slow to develop or may even cease to exist. For this reason patriotism is a necessary concomitant to the state's central task of doing justice. Nationalism, on the other hand, is a perversion of a legitimate human affection and ultimately runs contrary to justice.

---

[36]Here again we are confronted with the problem of labeling and definitions, since conventional wisdom tells us that ideologies are "-isms." One might argue the preferability of the expression *patriotic loyalty* for the legitimate, nonidolatrous love of country, since it is free from this otherwise tainted suffix. However, since it is unlikely the word *patriotism* will be abandoned any time soon, I shall assume the two terms are synonymous.

[37]In theory patriotism could perhaps also be applied to the ethnic nation, though in practice this appears to be a rare usage. Rather more frequently patriotism is directed at the territory itself—at the land in which a people lives. The unofficial American anthem "America the Beautiful" is a good example of this territorial or geographic patriotism, as is Smetana's *Má Vlast*, his cycle of symphonic tone poems celebrating, among other things, "Bohemia's Woods and Fields" and the winding river "Vltava." Moreover, there is something to be said for defining this territorial patriotism in a purely local sense, i.e., as an attachment to the immediate land of one's birth and upbringing as opposed to the larger territory of the political community. Yet in both these wider and narrower senses, patriotism's beloved "land" is created by a human community and its history.

Christians and Nationalism

Once again we note that even Christians have a tendency to fall prey to the appeal of ideologies, despite their commitment in principle to the exclusive claims of the gospel. It is not surprising, therefore, that many believers have willingly embraced nationalism. Moreover, some have so closely tied their faith to nationalism that the two have become almost indistinguishable in their minds. There is some irony in the fact that many Christians, who are otherwise able to see through the pretensions of liberalism and socialism, are nevertheless among the first to jump on the "God and country" bandwagon. This is particularly true in countries that have enjoyed some degree of formative influence from the Christian faith. To a large extent this "Christian nationalism" has roots in the Constantinian conversion of the pagan Roman Empire to Christianity. It further claims roots in the Old Testament covenant between God and his chosen people Israel. Christian nationalists usually claim that their own nation—whether defined politically, as in the United States, or ethnically, as in the Afrikaners of South Africa—is specially called by God to fulfill some larger divine purpose in the world.

Protestants seem to be more susceptible than Catholics to the temptations of Christian nationalism, possibly because the supranational character of the Roman Church constitutes a certain antidote to the particularisms of nationalism. During the 1960 election campaign in the United States, many Protestants objected to a Roman Catholic president out of fear that the Pope might come to dictate national policy and thereby violate the sovereignty of the nation. Protestant Ulstermen have for generations sought to maintain their country's union with the United Kingdom, fearing the consequences of being abandoned to Ireland's Catholic majority. Yet in southern Ireland, Poland and Ukraine, Catholicism has played a nationalistic role in sustaining its followers in the long struggle against British and Soviet imperialisms.

However, more than either Catholics or Protestants, Eastern Orthodox Christians have been particularly prone to identify their faith with various East European ethnic nationalisms. This can be seen already in the names of their churches: *Greek* Orthodox, *Russian* Orthodox, *Serbian* Orthodox, and so on. Although an Orthodox local Council of 1872 condemned as heresy "phyletism," or the establishment of local churches on an ethnic basis, Orthodoxy has nevertheless been divided precisely along territorial national lines in the old world and overlapping ethnic lines in the new. At least part of the reason for this state of affairs lies in a perversion of the traditional ecclesiastical polity, in which autocephalous regional churches, headed by a local bishop or patriarch, have become independent national churches, closely tied to the political fortunes of the nation and its rulers.[38]

However, apart from the influence of church polity, Eastern Orthodoxy is also the direct heir of the Constantinian settlement between church and empire, in which not only was Rome Christianized but Christianity Romanized. The traditional Orthodox conception of church-state relations is based on the ideal of a *symphonia*, or harmony, between the two institutions. What this has often meant in practice is that the church has lost its prophetic edge and has become handmaiden to the state and its imperatives. Former Soviet dissident Yevgeny Barabanov has affirmed that the subjection of church to state is a long-standing tradition in his own Christian East. "Surely we shall be obliged," he writes, "to acknowledge that in Byzantium and Russia ideas about the Kingdom of God and the kingdom of Caesar too often merged and became interchangeable."[39] It is not surprising, then, that Orthodox Christians, and even their church hierarchs, would come to tie the fortunes of the kingdom of God to those of their respective nations.[40]

American conservative Protestants have often been vulnerable to a different sort of nationalism with more evident Old Testament associations. Applying references to biblical Israel to the contemporary American polity, such Christians believe that the latter is heir to the promises made by God to the former. According to the biblical author of the Chronicles, God promises that "if my people who are called by my name humble themselves, and pray and seek my face, and turn from their wicked ways, then I will hear from heaven, and will forgive their sin and heal their land" (2 Chron 7:14). Because this promise, issued on the occasion of the dedication of Solomon's temple, was made by God to his people of the old covenant, it would be logical to assume that, after the appearance of Christ, the promise now applies to his people of the new covenant, namely, the church or the *corpus Christi*. After all, Peter writes, "you are a chosen race, a royal priesthood, a holy nation, God's own people" (1 Pet 2:9).

Yet the tendency of many conservative Protestants, who are otherwise fairly

---

[38]See the chapter "Ecclesiastical Regionalism: Structures of Communion or Cover for Separatism?" in John Meyendorff's *The Byzantine Legacy in the Orthodox Church* (Crestwood, N.Y.: St. Vladimir's Seminary Press, 1982), pp. 217-33.

[39]Yevgeny Barabanov, "The Schism Between the Church and the World," in Aleksandr Solzhenitsyn et al., *From Under the Rubble* (Boston: Little, Brown, 1974), pp. 172-93.

[40]For an analysis of the distinctive Orthodox approach to politics, see my own "Imaging God and His Kingdom: Eastern Orthodoxy's Iconic Political Ethic," *Review of Politics* 55 (spring 1993): 267-89.

literal in their interpretation of Scripture, is to see their own American nation as the potential beneficiary of this promise. To be sure, they have not invented this notion of America as a chosen nation, which finds its origins in the early years of English settlement in North America. John Winthrop, the first governor of the Massachusetts Bay Colony, affirmed the aspirations of his fellow Puritans to establish "a Citty [sic] upon a hill," which would be a shining example of a godly commonwealth to the rest of the nations.[41] In the nineteenth century, evangelical Protestants, who constituted a majority of Americans at that time, believed that the American experiment in measured liberty and self-government was intended by God to usher in his millennial kingdom and thus be a blessing to the rest of the world. During the Spanish-American War, President William McKinley claimed to have concluded, after several nights of anguished prayer to God, that the United States had a divine calling to annex the Philippines for the purpose of uplifting, civilizing and Christianizing its population.[42]

More recently, such groups as the Moral Majority and the Christian Coalition have appealed to nationalistic sentiments on the part of American fundamentalists and evangelicals.[43] America, it is said, is a "nation under God," charged by him with the awful responsibility of protecting freedom around the world. During the Cold War, this responsibility meant pursuing a policy of containment of godless communism. Now, after communism's collapse, American nationalists have had to find a new purpose to animate their country's overseas efforts, and this new purpose may have been provided in the ongoing fight against terrorism. In the meantime, there is plenty on the domestic front to keep them occupied. Many conservative Protestants have a sense of having lost a country that once belonged to their evangelical forebears. After the First World War and the tremendous cultural shifts of the 1920s, including the notorious Scopes trial in Dayton, Tennessee, fundamentalists withdrew into their own subculture with its network of independent church congregations and educational institutions. A generation later, after the Second World War, they emerged from their self-imposed isolation and sought to win back what they had lost, namely, the American nation.

Concern for one's political community is, of course, right and proper, and

---

[41] A. J. Beitzinger, *A History of American Political Thought* (New York: Harper & Row, 1972), p. 31.
[42] G. J. A. O'Toole, *The Spanish War: An American Epic, 1898* (New York: W. W. Norton, 1984), p. 386.
[43] The term *fundamentalist* is generally used by the North American media in a disparaging sense and is as often applied to radical Islamists as to Christians. I myself use the term here to apply only to those conservative Protestants calling themselves such. No negative meaning is implied by my use.

Christians can hardly be faulted for wishing to correct their nation's deficiencies. At the same time, this variety of Christian nationalism errs on at least four counts. First, it unduly applies biblical promises intended for the body of Christ as a whole to one of many particular geographic concentrations of people bound together under a common political framework. Once again this requires a somewhat dubious biblical hermeneutic.

Second, it tends to identify God's norms for political and cultural life with a particular, imperfect manifestation of those norms at a specific period of a nation's history. Thus, for example, pro-family political activists tend to identify God's norms for healthy family life with the nineteenth-century agrarian family or the mid-twentieth-century suburban nuclear family. Similarly, a godly commonwealth is believed by American Christian nationalists to consist of a constitutional order limiting political power through a system of checks and balances, rather than one based on, in Walter Bagehot's words, a "fusion of powers" in the hands of a cabinet responsible to a parliament. Thus Christian nationalists, like their conservative counterparts, tend to judge their nation's present actions, not by transcendent norms given by God for its life, but by precedents in their nation's history deemed to have embodied these norms.

Third, Christian nationalists too easily pay to their nation a homage due only to God. They make too much of their country's symbols, institutions, laws and mores. They see its history as somehow revelatory of God's ways and are largely blind to the outworkings of sin in that same history. When they do detect national sin, they tend to attribute it not to something defective in the nation's ideological underpinnings, but to its departure from a once solid biblical foundation during an imagined pre-Fall golden age. If the nation's beginnings are not as thoroughly Christian as they would like to believe, they will seize whatever evidence is available in this direction and construct a usable past serviceable to a more Christian future.[44]

Fourth, and finally, those Christians most readily employing the language of nationhood often find it difficult to conceive the nation in limited terms. Frequently, Christian nationalists see the nation as an undifferentiated community

---

[44]See, for example, John Eidsmoe, *Christianity and the Constitution: The Faith of Our Founding Fathers* (Grand Rapids, Mich.: Baker, 1987), pp. 39-49, in which he attempts to refute claims that the American founders were mostly deists by listing the formal church affiliations of the delegates to the Constitutional Convention. But see Michael P. Zuckert, *The Natural Rights Republic: Studies in the Foundation of the American Political Tradition* (Notre Dame, Ind.: University of Notre Dame Press, 1997), in which the author persuasively argues that, far from being a conservative Whig or Puritan enterprise, the American revolution had at its very center a Lockean concern for individual rights.

with few if any constraints on its claims to allegiance.[45] Once again this points to the recognition of a modest place for the nation, however it be defined, and away from the totalitarian pretensions of nationalism. Whether the nation is already linked to the body politic or to an ethnically defined people seeking political recognition, it must remain within the normative limits God has placed on everything in his creation.

---

[45]See, for example, James W. Skillen's analysis of "pro-American conservatives" in *The Scattered Voice: Christians at Odds in the Public Square* (Grand Rapids, Mich.: Zondervan, 1990), pp. 33-53. Cf. Skillen, *Recharging the American Experiment: Principled Pluralism for Genuine Civic Community* (Grand Rapids, Mich.: Baker, 1994), esp. pp. 26-30, 66-68.

5

DEMOCRACY

Vox Populi Vox Dei

The reader might initially be surprised to see democracy listed among the ideologies treated in this book. Is democracy actually an ideology? Does it really satisfy the criteria set forth in chapter one? More to the point, does it possess the character of an idolatrous religion, as I have argued with respect to liberalism, conservatism and nationalism? At first glance, one is tempted to say no. After all, democracy seems to be merely a form of government. It is simply a label used to describe a political system in which citizens are given the right to vote, to stand for public office and to discuss openly the issues of the day. Yet I shall argue in this chapter that, although democracy is indeed a form of government—and almost certainly the best currently available in our complex, differentiated society—it can take on ideological dimensions insofar as it embodies a belief in the near infallibility of the vox populi—the voice of the people. Where it is claimed that a policy is right simply because the majority is favorable, democracy has become a genuine ideology, subject to all the distortions, as well as the insights, characteristic of this phenomenon.

Structure and Creed

Democracy is conventionally defined as the "rule of the people," though beyond that it is infused with a variety of meanings with both positive and negative connotations. For the ancient Greeks, democracy was one of six basic forms of government, distinguished according to who rules and in whose interest. *Monarchy* means the rule of one in the general interest. *Tyranny* is the perversion of monarchy and signifies the rule of one in his own interest. *Aristocracy* literally means the rule of the best or most virtuous, but more basically it denotes the rule of the few in the community's interest. Its distorted form is called *oligarchy*, which designates the rule of the few in their own interest. The Greeks doubted that the rule of the many could ever be a good thing, although the term *politeia* was applied to this when it was regulated by well-framed laws. But *democracy* itself was seen as a nearly unadulterated evil and tantamount to mob rule, or the misrule of the untutored masses, which would, it was assumed, use the instruments of political power to benefit themselves at the expense of the minority.

Far better to the ancients was a constitution that combined the best features of the three legitimate forms of government. Rather than an unadulterated monarchy, aristocracy or democracy, most of the classic political theorists, ranging from Polybius to Montesquieu, believed that the best constitution was a mixed one in which rule of the one, the few and the many was embodied in carefully balanced institutions. It was not until the twentieth century that democracy acquired a wholly positive connotation in general parlance. By 1917 U.S. President Woodrow Wilson was telling his country's citizens that they were fighting in the First World War to "make the world safe for democracy," something which would have sounded strange to European ears in particular only a short time earlier. By the end of the century, democracy appeared to be the "only game in town," having supplanted—at least as an ideal, if not always in reality—the communist systems which were everywhere in retreat.

Although there are numerous theories of democracy, ranging from elitism to various forms of pluralism,[1] the principal distinction I shall make here is between *democracy as structure* and *democracy as creed*. As structure, democracy consists of a number of institutional arrangements incorporating the participation of citizens on a regular basis. Each of these arrangements may embody quite different relationships between the executive and legislative branches or among central, regional and local governments. They may embody strong or weak or even divided executives. They may have unicameral or bicameral legislative assemblies. Yet for all their differences—many of them substantial—they share in

---

[1] A good survey of such theories is found in Barbara Goodwin, *Using Political Ideas*, 3rd ed. (Chichester, U.K.: John Wiley & Sons, 1992), pp. 219-53. For a fuller treatment see Frank Cunningham, *Theories of Democracy: A Critical Introduction* (London: Routledge, 2002).

common the fact that all make provision for the citizenry to choose the office-holders in at least the most crucial of these institutions. Some polities even go beyond the periodic election of representatives and permit citizens to vote directly on specific proposals in a referendum or plebiscite.

Western-style democracies can be observed to have the following shared characteristics. First, there is a universal franchise. All citizens over a designated age of majority possess the right to vote irrespective of class, race, ethnic origin, sex and religion. Second, the franchise is possessed by all equally. In the modern democracy there are no weighted votes according to property ownership, class, education or profession. Each citizen has one vote and one vote alone. Third, decisions are made according to the principle of majority rule. If everyone has an equal vote, then it follows that numerical weight must carry the day, and not, once again, property ownership, social status, education or professional competence. Fourth, with the right to vote usually comes the right to stand for public office, which implies competitive elections. Where electoral outcomes are predetermined, democracy cannot be said to exist in any meaningful sense. Fifth, there is a considerable amount of freedom of speech and of the press to enable the populace to vote and otherwise participate intelligently. Sixth, most democratic political systems provide for citizens' liberties and the protection of minority rights, which are often embodied in a bill or charter of rights. Seventh, and perhaps most basic of all, Western democracies are almost always subject to the general principles of the rule of law as embodied, at least in part, in either a written or unwritten constitution. There is, of course, nothing intrinsically democratic about the rule of law, an ancient principle with Mesopotamian, Hebrew, Greek and Roman roots. However, it certainly must be admitted that without this predemocratic and perhaps even nondemocratic principle, democracy would quickly degenerate into a tyranny of the majority, which we shall explore further below.

In the sense just outlined, democracy can be said to represent a genuine advance in the unfolding historical process. Because the state or body politic is not, normatively speaking, the private patrimony of a feudal ruler, but the community of citizens and their government called by God to do public justice, it seems particularly appropriate that those citizens should exercise some responsibility within and over that community. Furthermore, because of the temptation for political leaders to abuse their authority and to act in ways contrary to the public interest, it makes sense to place checks on those leaders by requiring them to submit to the periodic verdict of the voters. As Reinhold

Niebuhr famously puts it, "Man's capacity for justice makes democracy possible; but man's inclination to injustice makes democracy necessary."[2] Because "irresponsible and uncontrolled power is the greatest source of injustice,"[3] democratic checks are needed to increase the likelihood of justice being done. C. S. Lewis similarly confesses, "I am a democrat because I believe in the Fall of Man." In contrast to those anchoring their support of democracy in an excessively rosy view of human nature, Lewis avers that human beings are "so fallen that no man can be trusted with unchecked power over his fellows."[4]

Among those defending democracy as structure on a similar modest basis are Walter Lippmann, Yves R. Simon, Hannah Arendt and more recently Christopher Lasch and Jean Bethke Elshtain. Both Lippmann and Simon seek to find a metaphysical foundation for democracy free from the absolutist implications of the Jacobin ideology of the French Revolution. Lippmann appeals to "traditions of civility" as a basic precondition for democracy's survival and ultimate prosperity.[5] Simon seeks to anchor modern democratic polities in an Aristotelian/Thomistic account of natural law and in that human reason to which it is accessible.[6] Hannah Arendt perhaps has more affinities with those direct democratic traditions engendered by Rousseau and the French Revolution, but she too repudiates popular sovereignty and favors the citizens' rights to speak and act as unique individuals within the public realm, free from the nonpolitical constraints of economic necessity on the one hand, or of abstract essentialist philosophies on the other.[7]

Lasch defines democracy as "a legal system that makes it possible for people to live with their differences."[8] It "is not an end in itself," but must be evaluated by its capacity to encourage excellence in its citizens. Elshtain agrees with Lasch that democracy properly shuns utopian thinking and the absolutist claims of abstract compassion, and fosters instead concrete compromises that avoid making

---

[2] Reinhold Niebuhr, *The Children of Light and the Children of Darkness* (1944; reprint, New York: Charles Scribner's Sons, 1960), p. xiii.

[3] Ibid., p. xiv.

[4] C. S. Lewis, "Equality," in *Present Concerns,* ed. Walter Hooper (New York: Harcourt Brace Jovanovich, 1986), p. 17.

[5] Walter Lippmann, *The Public Philosophy* (New York: Little, Brown, 1955), esp. pp. 79-81, 123-38. The expression "traditions of civility" is taken from Coventry Patmore by way of Sir Earnest Barker.

[6] Yves R. Simon, *Philosophy of Democratic Government* (Chicago: University of Chicago Press, 1951).

[7] See Hannah Arendt, *The Human Condition* (Chicago: University of Chicago Press, 1958), esp. pp. 175-247, and *On Revolution* (New York: Viking, 1962), esp. pp. 53-110, 153-64.

[8] Christopher Lasch, *The Revolt of the Elites and the Betrayal of Democracy* (New York: W. W. Norton, 1995), p. 85.

citizens into winners and losers in a needlessly adversarial zero-sum game. Democracy, argues Elshtain, is "an institutional, cultural, habitual way of acknowledging the pervasiveness of conflict and the fact that our loyalties are not one, our wills are not single, our opinions are not uniform, our ideals are not cut from the same cloth."[9] Democracy, in short, calls for the harmonization of legitimate human diversity.

Remarkably, Elshtain's compelling account of democracy bears striking similarities to Bernard Crick's definition of politics, which also entails the peaceful conciliation of potential conflict among diverse interests.[10] But Crick understands that democracy itself can take on an ideological form that threatens this ongoing conciliatory process. Here is where we begin to catch the first glimpse of democracy as creed, as a belief system rooted in a faith commitment of the believer. According to Crick, democracy threatens politics itself, understood as the ongoing conciliation of diverse interests. If by democracy we mean popular sovereignty in the monolithic sense, then it threatens "the essential perception that all known advanced societies are inherently pluralistic and diverse, which is the seed and root of politics."[11] Democracy, in short, can endanger politics by attempting to impose a single majoritarian interest on a diverse and pluriform political community. It seems that democracy as creed—the belief in popular sovereignty—can come to infuse democracy as structure—the ordinary processes of contemporary participatory politics—and may even threaten the latter's continued ability to function over the long term.

We shall for the moment put aside democracy as structure and concentrate on democracy as creed, or democratic ideology, which is the primary focus of this chapter. Before proceeding, however, it is worth mentioning that the fact that structure and creed can be distinguished logically does not mean that structure operates independently of spiritual foundation. Had it not been for Locke, Rousseau, Kant and the French Revolution, it is probable that our democratic polities would look quite different from their present shapes. In this respect, we are justified in isolating a causal connection between democratic ideology and our current, less-than-ideal democratic political systems.

But once again, as we observed in chapter one, the ideologies are incapable of entirely distorting the real world, which remains the good creation of God, despite the undeniable presence of sin. Although an increasing belief in popular

---

[9]Jean Bethke Elshtain, *Democracy on Trial* (Toronto: Anansi, 1993), p. 114.

[10]Bernard Crick, *In Defence of Politics* (Harmondsworth, U.K.: Penguin, 1993), pp. 15-33.

[11]Ibid., p. 62.

sovereignty served to pave the way for the extension of the franchise in most Western countries, it has generally not succeeded in supplanting the counter-vailing principle of the rule of law, which long antedates democracy. Nor has it been able to replace altogether the Christian confession that democratic cit-izenship is a responsibility entrusted to us as servants of God and of humanity. God's grace continues to come to us, even in the midst of widespread belief in alternative gods. This means that democracy as structure falls under both judg-ment and redemption in Jesus Christ, even if democracy as creed is rooted, as we shall see, in an apostate spirit with which we must break at a basic religious level. We shall explore some of the relationships between democracy as struc-ture and democracy as creed in another section.

From Liberalism to Democracy

There is much overlap between the respective assumptions of liberalism and of democracy. In fact, some observers are inclined to group the two under the sin-gle rubric of "liberal democracy" and to conclude that the one inevitably im-plies the other.[12] There is much to be said for this approach. In chapter two we noted that one of the principal characteristics of liberalism is that it views the state, as well as a variety of other communities, as the product of contract among sovereign individuals. In early liberalism this did not yet imply democ-racy in the full sense, but it can hardly be denied that it served to lay the foun-dation for the expansion of participatory rights within the body politic.

The assumption underlying social contract theory, and thus both liberalism and democracy, is that my obligation to do something rests solely in my having assumed it voluntarily. It implies, in particular, that my obligation to obey the law originates in my having had a hand in making it, whether directly or indi-rectly. If I have not been consulted in some fashion then there is cause to doubt I am bound by it. Authority, in short, can claim no intrinsic right to command obedience unless those under it consent to it. Failing such consent, authority is deemed oppressive for that reason alone. The net effect of this is to invalidate the entire tradition of the rule of law prior to and apart from the institution of the universal franchise. The historic distinction between the rule of law and ar-bitrary rule is thus rendered meaningless.

---

[12]See again, for example, Mark O. Dickerson and Thomas Flanagan, *An Introduction to Government and Politics: A Conceptual Approach*, 6th ed. (Scarborough, Ontario: Nelson Thompson Learning, 2002), pp. 217-44; and Leon P. Baradat, *Political Ideologies: Their Origins and Impact*, 7th ed. (Englewood Cliffs, N.J.: Prentice-Hall, 2000), pp. 64-84.

Liberalism assumes, once more, that the enjoyment of perfect freedom untrammeled by any demands outside the will is in some sense the more "natural"
condition of man, even if it is not particularly advantageous to the development
of social cooperation. All social and political bonds are deemed artificial and
somewhat arbitrary. Hobbes, for example, is not usually considered to be either
a liberal or a democrat in the contemporary sense, yet he concurs that human
individuals prefer freedom to unfreedom. However, because freedom brings
people into conflict and leads inescapably to general warfare, and because people prefer even unfreedom to anything that would threaten their lives, they will
put up with absolute rule by an omnicompetent sovereign with the physical
power to keep them in line. Yet there is no real normative status attached to the
subjects' obligation to this sovereign, which comes to an end the moment it
loses the power to protect them.[13] For Hobbes, then, right is perfectly coexten-
sive with might.

For all his undoubted theoretical similarities to Hobbes, Locke is somewhat
closer to the modern democratic spirit. Locke agrees with his predecessor in
speaking of "that equal right that every man hath to his natural freedom, without being subjected to the will or authority of any other man."[14] In arguing that
"[t]he natural liberty of man is to be free from any superior power on earth,"[15]
Locke is demonstrating himself to be not only a liberal concerned to defend
human freedom, but potentially a democrat wishing to establish a form of authority rooted in consent and sufficient to prevent open conflict and thereby to
secure more surely the enjoyment of that freedom.

In contrast to Hobbes, Locke places his political theory in a normative
framework, arguing that human beings have certain rights—principally those
of life, liberty and property—which government is obligated to protect. In
other words, right cannot be reduced to might. Once the government no
longer defends these rights, the concomitant obligation of the people to the
government comes to an end and they are justified in reassuming their original
freedom or in establishing a new government that will safeguard their rights.
The implications of this part of Locke's thought for democracy seem obvious,
yet Locke himself was quite comfortable with a restricted franchise based on
the ownership of property. If the chief end of government is the defense of
property, then it is the propertied who are chiefly concerned to establish such

---

[13]Hobbes *Leviathan* 2.21.
[14]Locke *Of Civil Government, Second Treatise*, 6.54.
[15]Locke *Of Civil Government* 4.21.

government. Thus the equal right to freedom need not, and probably should not, entail an equal franchise. Yet it seems undeniable that Locke's emphasis on consent of the governed, picked up a century later by Thomas Jefferson in his Declaration of Independence, exerted a large influence on the eventual development of democratic polities in the Western world and elsewhere.

In similar fashion, Rousseau writes that "since no man has a natural authority over his fellow, and force creates no right, we must conclude that conventions form the basis of all legitimate authority among men."[16] Conventions are in turn rooted solely in the human will and therefore need answer to no higher standard, much less to one rooted in a creation order positing norms independent of that will. In other words, the existence and legitimacy of authority are entirely dependent on the agreement of those under it. Failing such consent, all that is left to establish authority is brute power, which does not provide an adequate basis.

In other words, freedom is the more pristine condition of humanity, though the very possibility of continued survival calls for cooperative ventures inevitably placing limits on this freedom. In Rousseau's famous expression, "Man is born free; and everywhere he is in chains." The only way to legitimate these "chains," or limits to freedom, is to ensure that the individual, as member of a sovereign people, retains the power to make the laws under which he must live. If the general will which creates the sovereign should pass out of existence, then the individual loses his freedom and is within his rights to try to liberate himself from these chains, which are no longer legitimate but are now oppressive.

It is at this point in the argument that we see the social contractarian position of liberalism undergo an almost imperceptible spiritual shift in the direction of democracy. Following Locke, most classical liberals were content to live with a restricted franchise based on property and other qualifications. However, their political theories laid the groundwork for an expansion of the franchise that would become the foundation for modern democracy.

Moreover, while early social contract theorists were ontological individualists with all this implies, later such theorists, including Rousseau and his Jacobin and Marxist heirs, moved in a decisively collectivist direction, viewing the sovereign people as a body transcending, and taking precedence over, the individuals making it up. In Locke's compact, human beings give up to the body politic only

---

[16]Rousseau, *On the Social Contract,* trans. G. D. H. Cole, in *Great Books of the Western World,* vol. 38, *Montesquieu, Rousseau,* ed. Robert Maynard Hutchins (Chicago: Encyclopaedia Britannica, 1952), p. 389.

those powers deemed appropriate to eliminate the inconveniences of the state of nature and to allow them to enjoy their property more securely. Accordingly government operates within strict limits bounded on all sides by the considerable freedom retained and jealously guarded by the contracting individual.

In Rousseau, by contrast, human beings give up their entire selves to the body politic and hold back nothing, not even the right to defend their own lives, which they do retain in both Locke and Hobbes. Because the collectivity known as the sovereign is so thoroughly identified with the interests of its members, it can have no interest contrary to theirs. Hence there is no need to limit the body politic or to place constraints around its ability to impinge upon its members' lives. In Rousseau's words, "the sovereign power need give no guarantee to its subjects, because it is impossible for the body to wish to hurt all its members," or even to harm any particular member.[17]

It was, of course, far from Rousseau's intention to establish a totalitarian government. In fact, the whole of his *Social Contract* revolves around efforts to prevent government from becoming oppressive and imposing its own corporate will upon the sovereign general will. Yet by failing to circumscribe the legislative power of the latter, he inevitably left the door open to the expansion of state power under the guise of pursuing the general will. It is often forgotten that there is a deep distrust of government in both Rousseau and Marx, at least insofar as it is said to embody the narrow interest of a ruling class. Yet because they are almost naively trusting of the people in the one case, and of the working class in the other, neither can see any need to limit their legislative power or the power of those claiming to speak in their behalf.

This is where liberalism and democracy begin to part ways. There is already something of a tension between liberalism and democracy—between an emphasis on the sovereignty of the individual and the sovereignty of the democratic people. Rousseau could not bring himself to understand this, but later theorists such as Alexis de Tocqueville and John Stuart Mill were more aware of this possibility, which caused them to be leery of democracy's initial appeal.

The Majoritarian and Totalitarian Temptations

Like the other ideologies on which I have focused, democracy too takes something out of God's created cosmos and ascribes to it an ontological ultimacy properly belonging to God alone. More to the point, this "something" is be-

---

[17]Rousseau *On the Social Contract* 1.7.

lieved to possess a sovereignty over all other existing and possible authorities. In *liberalism* God-given individuality—a created good—becomes individual*ism*, in which all social institutions are seen as derivative from and subject to the sovereign wills of the individuals. In *conservatism,* tradition, without which we could hardly live as social creatures embedded in particular cultures, comes to be seen as sovereign over the broad range of human activities, associations and communities. In *nationalism* a particular human community known as the *nation* is accorded divine status, and all other communities are seen as little more than parts of this larger whole. Families, schools, automobile clubs, labor unions, private businesses and consumers cooperatives are deemed ancillary to the national community and, accordingly, must serve its larger ends.

Democratic ideology bears some similarity to each of these three ideologies while it assumes distinctive characteristics of its own. In its mature form it is probably closest in spirit to nationalism. In the previous chapter we noted the difficulty of defining the object of nationalism's faith, namely, the nation, which is based on a shared sense of identity, possibly rooted in common characteristics (or at least perceived characteristics), and aiming at self-government in some fashion. Although nationalism is compatible with an autocratic form of government, it seems particularly suited to a system in which the members of the nation are granted a direct voice in choosing their leaders. Indeed, like nationalism, democratic ideology also claims to confess the sovereignty of the people, the latter of which may or may not coincide with the nation.

Furthermore, like nationalism, democratic ideology also eschews heteronomous authority, identifying salvation with liberation therefrom. However, evil is identified, not merely with being ruled by someone unlike oneself, but with being ruled by someone else, period. If nationalists are content with being ruled—or possibly misruled—by someone sharing their language, race or ethnicity, ideological democrats strive, as much as possible, to diminish the need to obey anyone at all without input into the authoritative command. Here the emphasis is less on shared characteristics between rulers and ruled than on a shared will. From this perspective, in order for democracy to be effective in preserving my autonomy, it must be demonstrated that those making the laws on my behalf—the same laws under which I must live—are in some sense following my will. In this fashion I will be constrained to obey only those laws to which I have assented voluntarily. Ideological democrats thus have a pronounced affinity for those direct democratic mechanisms, which we shall explore further below.

There is a further similarity between nationalism and ideological democracy. If nationalism contains the seeds of the more destructive ideologies of fascism and national socialism, or Nazism, democracy too is fully capable of becoming tyrannical and perhaps even totalitarian. At such a point structure and creed become difficult to disentangle, and popular sovereignty begins to endanger not only those rights of individuals championed by liberals, but also the integrity of the political system itself and of nonpolitical communities within its jurisdiction. It does so principally by positing the democratic community, or "the people," as an undifferentiated community that is difficult to contain within normative boundaries.

We see this most clearly in Rousseau, whose *volonté générale* (general will) is the fount of political legitimacy. Like Plato, Rousseau places a premium on the unity of the body politic, and he does so by maximizing the status of the latter and minimizing the place of particular communities and loyalties that might tend to detract from loyalty to the whole. Marx and Engels too can be considered democratic in the ideological sense. Both see the future socialist society being established by the superior force of numbers of the proletariat, who will use their power to dispossess the bourgeoisie of the means of production, to redistribute its fruits to the whole society and to abolish all class-based interests in favor of a single overriding popular interest.

Ironically, during the era of the Cold War, both Western democracies and communist countries were wont to appeal to "the people" as the highest authority for policies pursued by their respective governments. In 1892 and 1896 William Jennings Bryan stood for the American presidency as a candidate for the People's Party, better known as the Populists. Since then successive presidential and congressional candidates have gone to great lengths to demonstrate that they are in tune with the people and thus close to the spirit of the American democratic system. The implication, of course, is that their opponents are enslaved to "special interests" bent on derailing democracy as we know it and replacing it with some form of oligarchy. This form of ideological democracy is especially hospitable to the use of referenda and plebiscites to decide political issues. It would tend to be more hostile to federalism or any form of government that might in some fashion divide political authority.

There is, however, an obvious problem with such a notion as "the people" as fount of political authority: who precisely is this people? Is it the entire body of citizens? Is it the leading opinion-makers capable of molding the attitudes of these citizens? Is it the majority of the body politic? Or is it perhaps a mythical, shadowy entity that needs to be continually created and recreated by whoever wants to use it for his own purposes at any given time? When communism collapsed in Eastern Europe and the former Soviet Union, it became obvious to nearly all that "the people" had never really existed as an identifiable, responsible agent. Generations of appeals to the people simply masked (and not very convincingly, at that) the dictatorial and totalitarian rule of a single oligarchical party. In this respect, "the people" is as nebulous and insubstantial an entity as "society" or even "nation."

Other conceptions of democracy are more realistic in acknowledging the legitimate diversity of the body politic and the multiple interests contained therein. Federalisms such as those of Canada, the United States and Australia were set up precisely on the understanding that a pluralistic population cannot be represented adequately by a single government located in one central capital city. In a federal system, sovereignty is shared by two or more levels of government, none of which can legally abolish the others.[18] When, for example, Ottawa comes into conflict with the provincial government of Alberta, it is understood not that the democratic people are contending with oligarchy, but that legitimate local interests are at variance with legitimate national interests and stand in need of conciliation. Because both federal and provincial governments properly represent distinct interests, the conflict cannot be resolved by an appeal to the democratic people. If, to shift the example, Washington, D.C., possessed all political power in the United States, the various interests of people living in Illinois, Massachusetts and California would suffer. Justice, in short, would not be done.

Consociational democracy represents another approach recognizing the pluriformity of the body politic. According to consociational theorists, such as Arend Lijphart, Hans Daalder, Gerhart Lehmbruch and others, there is no such thing as "the public." There are, rather, different "publics" coexisting within the body politic, whose separate interests need to be taken into account in the policymaking process. Any number of mechanisms can be established to prevent

---

[18]Although both Canadian and American federalisms formally and constitutionally consist of only two levels, the autonomy of regional and municipal governments can be said to have a certain conventional status in what may be labeled the unwritten constitutions of the two countries. It may be the case, however, that the autonomy of municipal governments is more deeply rooted in American than in Canadian experience. For example, the Ontario government has at various times experimented with the establishment of regional government and with municipal consolidation. On the other hand, it would be all but politically impossible for the state of Illinois to abolish or consolidate the hundreds of cities and villages surrounding Chicago.

the majority's riding roughshod over the several minorities, including (in addition to federalism) bicameralism, concurrent and qualified majorities, proportional representation, multiple parties, coalition governments and grand coalition governments. These are especially important in contexts characterized by pronounced and enduring cleavages, such as those between Protestants and Catholics in Northern Ireland, English and French in Canada, and Greeks and Turks in Cyprus. However, even where social segmentation is not as obvious or potentially divisive, all bodies politic contain enough diversity to warrant measures other than the continual rule of the majority.[19]

Furthermore, if ideological democracy tends to favor majoritarian tyranny, it also carries a totalitarian potential. A number of observers have noted the dangers of a Rousseauan conception of society, in which isolated individuals confront a single, monolithic, sovereign state, whose power is unchecked by other authorities. Sovereignty itself is problematic for Arendt because it denies the human condition of plurality and pretends that only one person inhabits the world.[20] Jacques Maritain, too, prefers to ascribe sovereignty to God alone and not to a human institution such as the state or even to the people.[21] Richard John Neuhaus and Peter Berger have emphasized the importance of what they refer to as "mediating structures" to a healthy society.[22] These structures are the plethora of communities that can be said to exist "between" the state and the individual, mediating the authority of the former and maintaining the freedom of the latter. They include the likes of families, schools, private businesses, labor unions, housing cooperatives,

---

[19]The literature of consociationalism includes *inter alia* Arend Lijphart, *The Politics of Accommodation: Pluralism and Democracy in the Netherlands* (Berkeley: University of California Press, 1975); *Democracy in Plural Societies* (New Haven, Conn.: Yale University Press, 1977); Kenneth McRae, *Consociational Democracy: Political Accommodation in Segmented Societies* (Toronto: McClelland & Stewart, 1976); *Conflict and Compromise in Multilingual Societies: Switzerland* (Waterloo, Ontario: Wilfred Laurier University Press, 1983); *Conflict and Compromise in Multilingual Societies: Belgium* (Waterloo, Ontario: Wilfred Laurier University Press, 1986); and *Conflict and Compromise in Multilingual Societies: Finland* (Waterloo, Ontario: Wilfred Laurier University Press, 1997); Kurt Richard Luther and Kris Deschouwer, eds., *Party Elites in Divided Societies: Political Parties in Consociational Democracy* (London: Routledge, 1999); and Jeffrey L. Obler, Jürg Steiner and Guido Dierickx, *Decision-Making in Smaller Democracies: The Consociational "Burden"* (Beverly Hills, Calif.: Sage, 1977). Lijphart's name is probably most associated with consociationalism, although in recent years his work has broadened somewhat to cover a number of comparative institutions, particularly electoral and party systems.

[20]Arendt, *Human Condition*, p. 234.

[21]Jacques Maritain, *Man and the State* (Chicago: University of Chicago Press, 1951), pp. 28-53.

[22]Peter Berger and Richard John Neuhaus, *To Empower People: The Role of Mediating Structures in Public Policy* (Washington, D.C.: American Enterprise Institute, 1977). See also Michael Novak, ed., *Democracy and Mediating Structures: A Theological Inquiry* (Washington, D.C.: American Enterprise Institute for Public Policy Research, 1980), which contains several essays devoted to this concept.

gardening clubs and professional associations. Tocqueville refers to such phenomena as "civil associations," which are distinguished from political associations in having "no political object." But where government attempts to usurp these associations, it threatens the well-being of the people.[23]

Other observers, following Hegel (1770-1831), refer to the broad range of these phenomena as "civil society," which they invest with considerable significance in upholding human liberty. According to Elshtain, civil society is "defined against overweening state power, on the one hand, and debilitating individualism, on the other."[24] After the collapse of communism in Eastern Europe and the former Soviet Union, many observers, both within and without, have placed their hopes for the future of this huge region in a recovery of civil society, that is, in a rehabilitation of spontaneous communal initiatives springing from the energies of the citizens themselves and not imposed from above by the dead weight of a bureaucratic party apparatus. Those countries already possessing the traditions of a vibrant civil society, such as Poland, Hungary and the former Czechoslovakia, have been better able to move out from under the shadows of totalitarianism than have those countries lacking these traditions, such as Russia, where the totalitarian project had gone much further in stifling independent initiatives.[25]

It seems then that democratic checks on political power are insufficient to prevent a totalitarian expansion of that power, especially if there are no countervailing checks on democracy itself. As Tocqueville puts it, "There is no power on earth in itself so worthy of respect or vested with such a sacred right that I would wish to let it act without control and dominate without obstacles."[26] Simon argues that liberty is endangered where a democratic state is not also a political regime, that is, one "which gives the governed a legal power of resistance" to state authority.[27] Whether they are democratic or not, all polities must allow for external forces to check the state's expansive power. For Simon, the foremost of these are freedom of the church, freedom of the press and the

---

[23] Alexis de Tocqueville *Democracy in America* 2.5.

[24] Jean Bethke Elshtain, "'In Common Together': Christianity and Democracy in America," in *Christianity and Democracy in Global Context,* ed. John Witte Jr. (Boulder, Colo.: Westview, 1993), p. 68.

[25] But see Nicolai N. Petro, *The Rebirth of Russian Democracy: An Interpretation of Political Culture* (Cambridge, Mass.: Harvard University Press, 1995), in which the author argues for the existence of an alternative political culture in Russia placing constraints on traditional autocratic rule and carrying the seeds of what others call civil society.

[26] Tocqueville *Democracy in America* 2.7.

[27] Simon, *Philosophy of Democratic Government,* p. 74.

institutional freedoms of private schools, independent labor unions, autonomous cooperatives and private property.[28] Without these, even the democratic
system will tend to become nonpolitical or despotic. We shall return to the notion of mediating structures or civil society in chapter eight, when we discuss
the historic alternatives to the ideologies.

Democratization Without Limits

If democratic ideology is unable to posit normative limits to the power of the
democratic state, there is also a second way in which democracy can become
totalitarian: by attempting to extend the democratic principle throughout the
entire political system and even into the whole of life, including an array of
spheres where for various reasons it is simply not appropriate. Here democracy
becomes not simply a form of government, but a way of life with definite idolatrous religious roots.

Within the sphere of government itself, this implies that as many institutions
as possible should be governed on democratic principles. In the United States,
in particular, a longstanding commitment to democracy has implied that both
houses of Congress, the presidency and, to some extent, even the courts should
be subject to direct popular election, though this was clearly not the intention
of the country's eighteenth-century founders, who had been steeped in the tradition of the classical mixed constitution. At the beginning of the twentieth
century a series of progressive reforms attempted to solve the country's problems by increasing popular participation in the institutions responsible for dealing with them. Thus in 1913 the seventeenth amendment to the Constitution
made Congress' upper chamber, the Senate, subject to direct election, whereas
senators had previously been appointed by the state legislatures. Primary elections were instituted in a select number of states to give ordinary people a say
in the choice of their party's presidential candidate. Even local judges were often subject, if not necessarily to competitive election, at least to popular con-
firmation at the polls.[29]

---

[28]Ibid., pp. 137-38.
[29]Efforts in the United States to abolish the electoral college and to institute direct election of the president have not thus far met with success. However, by convention, and in many cases by state law, the
  members of the college nearly always vote en bloc as they are instructed by a plurality of voters in their
  respective states, thereby giving a presidential election most of the features of a direct popular election,
  without the time-consuming necessity of a second ballot in the absence of an absolute majority. Very
  occasionally, however, the popular and electoral votes come into conflict, as in the case most recently
  of the 2000 U.S. presidential election.

A notable exception to this gradual democratization of American government was the adoption of the merit principle in hiring the civil service after 1883. Remarkably, and somewhat ironically, in recent decades the powers of unelected administrators have increased at the same time that the two major political parties have expanded the number of primary elections in the selection of their presidential and other candidates for public office. Moreover, the past thirty years have seen an increase in what has come to be called judicial activism, whereby unelected Supreme Court justices have effectively made policy on such divisive political issues as abortion on demand and prayer in the public schools. Whatever one may think of these trends, they can be seen as a possibly inevitable concession to the need for aristocratic institutions to balance the democratic ones. The classical mixed constitution may in fact have survived to the present despite the popular myth that our Western polities are unadulterated democracies.

There is, of course, nothing intrinsically unseemly in this extension of popular participation into such institutions as the Senate and the presidency (though one might well question the wisdom of electing judges, because this might tend to compromise their vaunted impartiality). Where the danger lies is in the underlying assumption that democracy is a panacea—a cure for all the ills afflicting an institution or even an entire political system. Those following one-time presidential aspirant Alfred E. Smith's dictum that "all the ills of democracy can be cured by more democracy"[30] risk investing democracy with salvific pretensions and thereby expecting far too much from an otherwise beneficial institutional arrangement.

For example, efforts at party reform during the late 1960s and early 1970s aimed to remove the presidential nomination process from the hands of the politicians and turn it over to "the people." The unintended result was not the president's increasing awareness of his responsibility to the electorate, but a chief executive who is less able than his predecessors to govern because he enjoys little support in Congress or among local officials of his own party. In this particular case, efforts to augment democratic control within the respective parties may have inadvertently increased popular disaffection with both the president and Congress, who find themselves unable to cooperate in the policymaking process. Clearly, the American example illustrates that while democratic checks

---

[30]Alfred E. Smith, in a speech delivered in Albany, New York, June 27, 1933. Smith ran for the American presidency in 1928 as the Democratic candidate.

on power are positive and beneficial, they cannot be applied indiscriminately throughout a political system without incurring negative consequences.[31]

Moreover, the followers of democratic ideology have sought not simply to extend democracy throughout the broad range of governmental institutions, but also beyond the structural bounds of the body politic into nonstate communities. Hence it is taken as axiomatic that in a democratic society, not only ought the political system to be democratized, but also the economy. This is where we begin to see some of the connections between democracy and socialism, the latter of which claims simply to be extending the logic of democracy beyond the political community. Socialists have, however, been divided as to the implications of this democratization. Does it perhaps imply that all of the voting citizenry should have control over the means of production, in which case the policy of choice is likely to be nationalization, or at least heavy regulation, of industries? Or does it imply that only the workers employed by a particular company should exercise democratic control over that company? Both alternatives are plausibly democratic, but each presupposes a different conception of what is meant by "the people" and even a different conception of the proper role of the state.

Once again there is much to be said for giving workers a say in the operation of an economic enterprise, especially a large manufacturing concern, in which their contribution to the whole may tend to be overlooked by managers preoccupied with the need to make a profit and to ensure a satisfactory return to the owners of capital. But such a participatory role for workers must be defended on grounds other than those of a continual extension of democracy throughout society. They must be justified for reasons clearly related to the structure of the enterprise itself and not from the supposed sovereignty of an undifferentiated democratic people. Workers' participation is better defended on the grounds that they are an integral part of the work community and thus have a stake in its continuing welfare.

---

[31]For brief textbook accounts of efforts to reform the presidential nomination process particularly within the Democratic Party and the unintended results of these reforms, see Larry Berman and Bruce Allen Murphy, *Approaching Democracy*, 2nd ed. (Upper Saddle River, N.J.: Prentice-Hall, 1999), pp. 345-49; and Susan Welch, John Gruhl, Michael Steinman, John Comer and Susan M. Rigdon, *American Government*, 6th ed. (Belmont, Calif.: Wadsworth, 1998), pp. 186-95. For a more detailed account see Nelson W. Polsby, *Consequences of Party Reform* (New York: Oxford University Press, 1983). In 1984 the Democratic Party attempted to undo some of the negative effects of the reforms by appointing between 15 and 20 percent of convention delegates from the ranks of members of Congress and other party and public officials. This was intended to lessen slightly the influence of the primary-chosen delegates.

A similar assessment can be made of the educational institution, whether this be the primary or secondary school or the university. Efforts to democratize a school must be confronted with questions similar to those raised by democratization of the economy. Does democratization entail a role for teachers in electing administrators? Does it imply that students ought to have a voice in the hiring of teachers? Should students participate in shaping curriculum? Should parents have a vote on all these issues? Or does democratization mean, in Rousseauan style, that the democratic people, represented by their government, should control the schools? Certainly in the United States and other Western democracies, citizens have come to believe that the education of their youth properly lies within the jurisdiction of government. Hence local school districts provide for the election of school board members by the electorates within those districts. This all seems to accord with the best principles of democracy, but little thought has been given to the possibility that the educational task may not be intrinsically democratic and may not properly belong to government at all.[32]

Some efforts have also been made to democratize the institutional church. Particularly in the United States, where denominational pluriformity became the rule early and where an established church was prohibited by the federal Constitution in 1791, it is not accidental that, as democracy grew apace in the political realm, so also did those churches emphasizing voluntarism and individual conscience, which are closely related to the spiritual foundations of democracy. Baptists and Methodists were the immediate beneficiaries of the democratic sentiments of Americans, yet even the more hierarchically structured Episcopal Church modeled its two synodical chambers, the House of Bishops and the House of Clerical and Lay Deputies, after the bicameral U.S. Congress.[33] In this context, any church that was obviously undemocratic in its internal organization, for example, the Roman Catholic Church, was considered authoritarian, reactionary and thus generally suspect by the non-Catholic populace.

Yet even the most congregational of churches must admit that ultimate authority for faith and practice does not issue from the will of the parishioners (much less from the body politic), but from the Word of God as embodied in

---

[32]I will return to this issue in chapter nine.

[33]Mark A. Noll, *A History of Christianity in the United States and Canada* (Grand Rapids, Mich.: Eerdmans, 1992), pp. 148-51. See also Nathan O. Hatch, *The Democratization of American Christianity* (New Haven, Conn.: Yale University Press, 1989), for a more in-depth exploration of democracy's influence on the churches.

Scripture. Most churches have come to recognize a God-ordained teaching authority in a particular office, whether this be pastor, elder, bishop or pope. That such authority does not possess democratic legitimacy is often deemed scandalous to modern democrats, who would remake the churches in the image of the body politic. Once again, however, the democratic principle cannot be endlessly extended without undermining the integrity of the church as church.

Democratization is almost certainly least applicable to the nuclear family, composed as it generally is of two adults and one or more minor children. Because the family exists primarily for the training of children who are gradually increasing in maturity, the application of participatory mechanisms based on equality is not suitable to the institution and its central task. As Simon observes, parental authority within a family context is "substitutional" insofar as it substitutes for the as-yet-undeveloped maturity of the child under its care. Parental authority is pedagogical and "aims at its own disappearance," which will ensue once the child reaches the age of majority. Normatively, such authority seeks "the proper good of the governed."[34]

Given the nature of parental authority, two possibilities of abuse present themselves within the family context. First, parents may in fact seek their own good above that of their children and may even exploit the latter for their own purposes. Second, parents may attempt to continue to exercise their authority after the children have attained adulthood. In neither case will a democratization of the family offer a remedy. In the first case, giving the children an "equal vote" on a par with the parents represents an attempt not to correct an abuse of authority but to alter the nature of authority in such a way as to ignore the fact of juvenile immaturity. In the second case, once the children have attained maturity and are able to fend for themselves, the nature of the family itself has changed and authority is no longer exercised at all in its imperative form. Generally the children (or, perhaps more accurately, the adult offspring) are now out of the parental home and are embarking on the establishment of their own families and the rearing of a second generation of children.

Democracy as structure properly embodies citizens' participation in the most central institutions of government, including a legislative assembly and possibly a chief executive. However, democracy as creed, in accordance with its pivotal belief in popular sovereignty, attempts to extend the democratic principle throughout the whole of government and even into other nonstate institu-

---

[34]Simon, *Philosophy of Democratic Government*, pp. 7-9.

tions, such as business, school, institutional church and family. What is not understood here is that democracy, far from being a panacea for such ills as abuse of power, authoritarianism and corruption, becomes itself an oppressive intrusion of an undifferentiated social mass into communities normatively established on a variety of alternative principles. In this respect, democracy attempts to subject the whole of life to its chosen divinity, which is sufficient to place it into our larger category of ideology.

Creed and Structure Revisited:
Direct Versus Representative Democracy

Closely related to the distinction between democracy as creed and democracy as structure is that between direct democracy and representative democracy. Though the two distinctions are not precisely parallel, they do serve to indicate the extent to which a particular organizing principle of democracy as a form of government may be influenced, if not entirely determined, by an underlying belief in popular sovereignty. It demonstrates, once again, that structure and creed cannot be detached but must be seen as interdependent.

In a direct democracy, the citizens assemble together to vote directly on the issues of the day and can thereby be said to govern themselves. In a representative democracy, the citizens' participation consists largely of electing representatives who govern on their behalf. Because of the numerical and geographical constraints inherent in a direct democracy, living examples of this have historically been restricted to fairly small local communities, such as the ancient Athenian *polis*, the New England town meetings and several Swiss cantons. Large nation-states have been forced to abandon what many would consider the ideal of direct democracy, leaving legislative authority in the hands of an elite that is chosen (French: *élu*) by the voters in regular, periodic elections.

It is perhaps not coincidental that Rousseau, the seminal proponent of popular sovereignty, would find his ideal body politic in the small polislike community where the citizens could come together and give effect to their sovereignty in direct democratic fashion. Only in this way would the general will be able to carry the day over the corporate will of the government and the particular wills of individual citizens. Direct democracy in a local community potentially provides each citizen with a greater voice in public policymaking than is possible in a large state, where one's right to vote is exercised on a regular though infrequent basis and is drowned out by millions of other votes, each of which amounts to very little in itself. For Rousseau the very smallness of the body politic is key to each citizen maintaining a maximum amount of personal autonomy in the midst of social cooperation.

Rousseau's influence on contemporary democratic polities has not, of course, effected the breakup of existing nation-states into sovereign city-states. It has, however, moved some countries to adopt certain mechanisms of direct democracy, most notably the referendum, in which the citizens are given the opportunity to vote on issues placed immediately before them. France, Switzerland and member states of the United States are all polities that make regular use of referenda to decide important questions, often involving constitutional change.

Although literally assembling one hundred fifty million citizens to act as a Rousseauan sovereign is obviously impracticable, the recent information revolution, with its dramatic improvement in the means of communication, has made possible a kind of "virtual assembly" bringing people "together" on the basis of a shared connection to a nationwide electronic infrastructure. In the United States Ross Perot and others have proposed the establishment of an "electronic town hall," or what might be labeled "cyber-democracy," in which citizens, from the comfort of their own homes, would vote electronically on issues posed to them from their television sets or computer screens.[35] For the first time in human history, it is theoretically possible to poll large populations in fairly short order. Direct democracy seems finally to be within reach.

Yet there are two obvious difficulties with cyber-democracy that might cause us to doubt its supposed benefits. In the first place, merely allowing every individual citizen to cast a vote on a particular issue does not permit the sort of deliberation characteristic of a face-to-face assembly.[36] Cyber-democracy would atomize citizens, keeping them from interacting with each other and tying them instead to whoever was providing the information concerning the issue being decided. Far from being democratic, cyber-democracy could develop into a form of tyranny in which a central government claiming to follow the dictates of the people was in reality shaping popular opinion for its own purposes.

In the second place, and more importantly for our purposes, convening a continuously sitting electronic assembly of the whole citizenry would lead to a massive politicization of life in which both politics and other pursuits would inevitably suffer. We human beings are finite creatures. We cannot devote our-

---

[35]See, for example, Robert Wright, "Hyperdemocracy: Washington Isn't Dangerously Disconnected from the People; the Trouble May Be It's Too Plugged In," *Time*, January 23, 1995, pp. 15-21.

[36]See, e.g., the argument of Amy Gutmann and Dennis Thompson in *Democracy and Disagreement* (Cambridge, Mass.: Belknap, 1996).

selves to every possible endeavor. Life in community, particularly a large community, calls for a division of labor of some sort. Even if cyber-democracy is technically feasible, in the larger human sense it would not be possible to have a society in which, day after day, everyone sits in front of a screen and pushes buttons. Bread would not get baked. Houses would not be built. Cars would not be manufactured. Physicians would not get trained. Children would suffer from neglect. The whole array of human life in all its diversity and complexity would atrophy, leaving a stunted and (in several respects) impoverished society in its wake.

Yet even if it were possible for nearly all people to devote part of their energies to political life, they would never be able to develop the necessary expertise in it.[37] This is the moment of truth in Socrates' argument in Plato's *Republic*. It is also where Marx and Engels go wrong in their assumption that it is possible to dispense with a division of labor. The art of statesmanship requires a high level of proficiency that can be gained only by devoting the major part of one's life to it. Obviously only a few will be able to do this, while the vast majority will not. It seems then that we are stuck with a form of aristocracy in our political life, and perhaps this is how it should be if we expect people to fulfill their own diverse callings in accordance with their God-given gifts.

Thus cyber-democracy, and ultimately direct democracy in general, seems particularly conducive to the development of an ideological approach to politics and perhaps even to the whole of life. This is where representation enters the picture once again. Given the shortcomings of direct democracy, it would seem preferable to institute an arrangement whereby the advantages of aristocracy can be combined with those of democracy, along the lines of the classical mixed constitution. In other words, a better form of government would capitalize on the specialized skills of the few while ensuring that they remain accountable to the general public, but without implying that public accountability entails popular sovereignty in the ideological sense.

Representation: Followership or Leadership?

However, if the direct form is more conducive than the representative form to

---

[37]This is one of the central arguments Yves Simon makes in *A General Theory of Authority* (Notre Dame, Ind.: University of Notre Dame Press, 1962). Although the direct decision of the majority satisfies the criteria for authority's existence, the community is incomparably better off if authority is invested in particular persons with proven wisdom and leadership skills (p. 139). Here he labels authority's function as the "communication of excellence" (pp. 133-56).

the creedalization of democracy, the latter is nevertheless capable of being invested with ideological significance if representation comes to be infused with a faith in popular sovereignty. To elucidate this we must take note of two basic conceptions of representation and its role in relating the people to their government. The first of these is what may appropriately be called the *agent* or *delegate* theory, according to which a representative acts on instruction from her constituents. Assuming the people are sovereign, the representative must continually go back to them and attempt to learn their opinions on issues coming before the parliamentary body, ranging from taxation, expenditures and social services to foreign policy and perhaps even war and peace. Once she has learned these opinions, she is then obligated to reflect them in her voting, whatever her own convictions. In Rousseau's proposed republic, the government or the prince is precisely such an agent, hired by the sovereign—that is, the whole body of citizens—to act in its stead between public meetings. Following Paul-Louis Courier, Simon labels this notion of representation "the coach-driver theory."[38] Such a theory, he argues, "reduces the role of the government to that of a leader without authority." Government becomes a mere coach-driver, appearing to lead the passengers but in reality doing no more than to take them where they wish to go. Leadership thus becomes followership.

Simon argues that the coach-driver theory played a pivotal role in the French Revolution and in the development of Jacksonian democracy in the United States. More recently it has also played a role in the political process when practical politicians are confronted with difficult issues on which they prefer not to have to take a stand. When asked how they will vote on abortion or capital punishment, for example, some candidates for public office typically elude the question by promising to poll their constituents and vote accordingly. Thus they appear to be impeccably democratic and generally throw their interrogators off track, at least for a time.[39]

Yet the notion of the representative as agent or delegate is not the only one possible. A representative may see herself as a *trustee*, elected not so much to do the people's bidding as to act in their interest. This requires a certain amount of

---

[38]Simon, *Philosophy of Democratic Government*, pp. 146-54.

[39]I have seen this elusiveness occur at candidates' debates during the 1988 and 1993 Canadian federal election campaigns. Although Canadian Members of Parliament (MPs) are bound to vote with their parties in virtually all cases, on the more controversial and divisive issues free votes are generally permitted, which allow individual MPs to vote as they see fit without fear of party discipline. In the two candidates' debates in the Hamilton-Wentworth district I attended, candidates for the Progressive Conservative, Liberal and Reform Parties chose the approach described here.

knowledge and wisdom gained through education and experience, and it further demands that she exercise a large degree of independent judgment. The
trustee theory of representation is usually associated with Edmund Burke, discussed in chapter three. In addressing the electors of his Bristol constituency, he
articulated the meaning of the trusteeship he was seeking to retain from them
in classic words:

> His unbiased opinion, his mature judgment, his enlightened conscience,
> he ought not to sacrifice to you; to any man, or to any set of men living.
> These he does not derive from your pleasure. They are a trust from Prov-
> idence, for the abuse of which he is deeply answerable. Your representa-
> tive owes you, not his industry only, but his judgment; and he betrays
> instead of serving you, if he sacrifices it to your opinion.[40]

In Burke's conception the representative is more than a mere coach-driver.
She is a leader who has been entrusted with the authority to make public policy
in the general interest. Although her constituents may wish her to implement
a variety of programs that will be to their own private benefit, possibly even at
the expense of other citizens elsewhere, the representative understands that she
is charged with the responsibility of doing what is best for the entire political
community. This may necessitate her making decisions that are unpopular in
the short term on the understanding that her first duty is not to the voters' preferences but to the common welfare. Moreover, because they are not privy to
the same information to which she has access, and because her better judgment
tells her that following their express wishes may lead to the ruin of the state, she
may have no other alternative but to vote against these wishes.

In contrast to the coach-driver, the trustee is not likely to fall prey to an ideological faith in popular sovereignty. He properly recognizes that the general will
is not infallible and that the political art often requires making hard decisions that
may fly in the face of public opinion. Yet even the trustee cannot afford simply
to ignore public opinion; otherwise he is in danger of losing touch with those
he presumes to lead. A leader who gets too far in front of the people may look
behind only to see he has lost his followers. Here is where public opinion poll-
ing, which might otherwise seem to fit with a coach-driver theory of representation, continues to play a legitimate role, even for the trustee. The good leader

---

[40]Quoted in George Gallup and Saul Forbes Rae, *The Pulse of Democracy: The Public Opinion Poll and How
It Works* (New York: Simon & Schuster, 1940), p. 262.

is always concerned to know where the people are on a particular issue, not so he can slavishly follow their wishes, but so he can learn how far they are able and willing to follow his lead. He does not abdicate genuine leadership but exercises it with great care and sensitivity toward those he is leading. Proper leadership is thus an ongoing dialogue between leaders and led, with both parties taking seriously the respective callings and responsibilities of the other.

Of course, in a fallen world trusteeship is subject to abuse and can become high-handed and authoritarian,[41] as noted above. This is why regular elections are deemed necessary: they enable the people to maintain some form of check on their representatives, who might otherwise be tempted to ignore their opinions altogether. Thus even a trustee must eventually answer to the electorate, who has the power to withdraw this trusteeship if they dislike his performance in office. After Burke delivered his famous speech, his Bristol constituents nevertheless repudiated him at the polls, despite his eloquent pleas for their continued support. Yet this is not necessarily a vindication of the representative as coach-driver. If Burke had indeed sacrificed his judgment to his constituents' opinions, and if the policy thus pursued had not met with success, they might have defeated him anyway. As journalist Rick Groen perceptively points out, citizens of a democracy typically make "contradictory demands of their politicians and system of government . . . expecting politicians to be responsive to the wish of the people, but at the same time demanding strong leadership."[42] Such contradiction should be sufficient to establish that the people—understood as the aggregate of those making up the electorate—are far from infallible and that putting one's ultimate confidence in their sovereignty is a misplaced faith.

On the other hand, some political leaders have been able to govern as trustees while effectively maintaining the support of their constituents. U.S. Senator

---

[41] Although there is a tendency within the discipline of political science to apply the label "authoritarian" to virtually any autocratic form of government, I prefer to distinguish between the two. "Autocracy" I take simply and literally to mean the largely nonconsultative rule of one or more persons by themselves, while "authoritarianism" has connotations of an abuse of authority not necessarily entailed by the former. See, e.g., Richard De George's magisterial *The Nature and Limits of Authority* (Lawrence: University of Kansas Press, 1985), where he defines authoritarianism as "an abuse of the exercise of authority in which the bearer of authority uses his authority for his own good at the expense of the subject of authority" (p. 56). The distinction between autocracy and authoritarianism is thus roughly comparable to that made by the ancients between monarchy and tyranny or despotism, or perhaps even between aristocracy and oligarchy when applied to a small ruling group or junta. This said, it is probably nevertheless true that autocracy is more likely than constitutional democracy to degenerate into authoritarianism simply because of the absence of effective checks on the autocrat's authority.

[42] Rick Groen, *The Globe and Mail* (Toronto), December 8, 1990.

Mark Hatfield of Oregon enjoyed a long political career extending over nearly half a century, although many of the positions he took on specific issues were quite controversial, especially his early opposition to American involvement in Vietnam. Hatfield explicitly claimed to vote in accordance with his convictions whether or not his constituents always agreed.[43] Nevertheless, Oregon voters continually reelected him, twice as state governor and five times as senator, not because he followed their wishes, but because he acted on principle and in so doing earned their continued respect.[44] Refusing to bow the knee to the god of popular sovereignty is not necessarily a recipe for political failure. On the contrary, many citizens prefer to vote for someone willing to stand on principle.

Democracy and Justice: A Final Assessment

We return then to our original distinction between democracy as structure and democracy as creed. Granted we are at a stage in our Western historical development in which popular participation in government is an appropriate and positive thing. Granted, too, that giving citizens the opportunity to render effective judgment on the performance of a specific government constitutes a powerful check on its actions. Finally, it must be conceded that where authority and law do not enjoy popular consent a crucial element is missing from them, which may endanger their continued existence.

At the same time, it must be understood that it is not popular approval that creates law per se. Law, and indeed all authority—whether personal or institutional—is necessitated because of who we are as created, fallen and redeemed human beings. Christians have long understood that law and the authority behind it are needed to restrain the outworkings of our fallen nature. The apostles Peter and Paul emphasize this role of authority in observing that the civil magistrate is commissioned by God "to punish those who do wrong" (1 Pet 2:14) and "to execute his wrath on the wrongdoer" (Rom 13:4).

But Christians also recognize the need for law and authority due to our created finitude. Because our knowledge and capacities are limited, we cannot expect, even under the best of circumstances, to come to spontaneous agreement

---

[43]See the interview with Hatfield in *The Wittenburg Door*, October-November 1974, p. 8; and Lowell A. Hagan's interview with Hatfield in *Vanguard*, April 1976, pp. 18-20.

[44]Hatfield's writings include *Not Quite So Simple* (New York: Harper & Row, 1968), *Conflict and Conscience* (Waco, Tex.: Word, 1971); and *Between a Rock and a Hard Place* (Waco, Tex.: Word, 1976). See also the mid-career biography cowritten by Robert Eells and Bartell Nyberg, *Lonely Walk: The Life of Senator Mark Hatfield* (Chappaqua, N.Y.: Christian Herald Books, 1979).

on a communal course of action without the guidance of authoritative patterns known as rules or laws. A cooperative effort to construct bicycles, for example, would go seriously awry without some central coordination, even if all participants were perfect in virtue. The best of intentions, minus personal or impersonal guidance, would not prevent the building of parts that do not fit together or the proliferation of some parts over others. Law would thus be necessary, even in the hypothetical state of unfallen, sinless humanity, not to hold sin in check, but to compensate for the intrinsic limitations of human finitude that are unrelated to sin.

In other words, if laws are not precisely natural in the narrow physical or biological sense, they are nevertheless fully creational in that they are an integral part of our created social and communal nature. They cannot be reduced to the arbitrary dictates of a sovereign will. Laws are valid whether or not they have been formally approved by the people or their elected representatives; otherwise we cannot make sense of the ancient principle of the rule of law, as found in, say, Hammurabi's Code, the Mosaic Law or the Code of Solon, prior to the adoption of the universal franchise. Nevertheless, at our current stage in history it is appropriate to observe that the making of *just* laws is immeasurably enhanced by the participation and consent of those whose interests they are intended to protect.

Perhaps another way of stating it is that democracy is indeed but one possible form of government capable of doing justice. We are no longer accustomed to categorizing forms of government primarily according to the six ancient Greek models. We are now more likely to speak of federal systems, unitary systems, strong and weak presidential regimes, strong and weak parliamentary regimes, executive-dominated cabinet systems, military dictatorships and nonmilitary autocracies. Some of these forms of government are plausibly democratic insofar as they successfully embody popular representation to a greater or lesser extent. Others are not so democratic and may be led by a dominating individual or junta not directly accountable to the citizens. Yet even the latter are called by God to fulfill the normative task of government: to do justice to all persons and communities residing within the state's territorial jurisdiction. Only when a government takes on totalitarian dimensions, that is, when it claims to control the whole of life and pretends to possess a godlike sovereignty, can we conclude that it has forsaken its task of doing justice and has arrogated to itself a position to which it has no legitimate right. As we have noted above, this totalitarian potential is one to which even democratically elected governments are not immune.

Ultimately then we are justified in appreciating constitutional democracy and the opportunities it affords citizens to participate in the political process. The achievements of universal and equal suffrage, truly competitive elections, and the freedom to engage in public debate, are well worth celebrating. After all, as noted above, it gives effect to the notion of citizenship as membership in the body politic better than other, less democratic forms of government. Yet we must avoid the assumption that democracy is identical to just government. We should refrain from assuming that democracy represents the final stage of history and the culmination of the development of all political constitutions. Accordingly, we must escape the temptation to deify what is otherwise a good political system with its own undoubted virtues. Democracy may indeed be good, but it is not god.

6

SOCIALISM

———

Common Ownership as Salvific

There are few people in the world today without strong opinions one way or the other on socialism. In some quarters it has come to mean all that is right and good. It means cooperation rather than competition, altruism rather than egoism, generosity rather than greed. It means sharing the wealth, ending poverty and ensuring that the fruits of production are fairly distributed throughout the whole of society. More broadly it means that the needs of the community take precedence over the wants of the individual. It even means, in the words of Wilhelm Liebknecht, to "extend civilization to all humanity."[1] This is the vision of socialism that has held sway at various times in countries ranging from the Scandinavian social democracies to the Soviet- and Chinese-style communist countries.

For others, however, socialism has downright sinister connotations.[2] In many Western countries, to profess an allegiance to socialism is tantamount to claiming a penchant for strangling puppies or pulling the wings off flies. According to

---

[1]Eugene E. Brussell, ed., *Dictionary of Quotable Definitions* (Englewood Cliffs, N.J: Prentice-Hall, 1970), p. 536.

[2]Pun intended—the word *sinister* is the Latin word for "left." According to conventional categorizations, socialism is classified as a "leftist" ideology, meaning that it champions greater equality, particularly economic equality. See chapter one on the left-right spectrum.

Cecil Palmer, socialism is a system "workable only in heaven, where it isn't needed, and in hell, where they've got it."[3] Or as Elbert Hubbard puts it, it entails "participation in profits without responsibility as to deficits."[4] In the United States especially, socialism's greatest perceived vice is that it is foreign or un-American. For most Americans socialism means a stagnant economy with no incentives for ordinary people to work. It means bureaucratic interference in a wide variety of venues where it probably does not belong. It means confiscatory taxation that penalizes the industrious and rewards the idle. Worse, it could entail an arbitrary government with little respect for personal liberty. This is the specter raised in most Americans' minds when they hear the word *socialism*.

A World of Socialisms

Like the other ideologies we have explored, socialism allows a variety of possible meanings. Indeed Michael Harrington argues that although people generally speak of socialism as though it were a singular phenomenon, we ought to speak of socialism*s* in the plural.[5] At the outset of the present discussion, it is necessary to make several categorical distinctions that will aid us in understanding these socialisms. First and most basically, we need to distinguish between the empirical phenomenon of communal ownership of property and the ideology of socialism. The former is little more than a continuing part of reality whose legitimacy has been recognized by most people beginning at least with Aristotle. We shall explore this phenomenon further below. The latter, by contrast, is rooted in a secular faith that attempts to extend the principle of communal ownership, and the economic equality thought to follow from it, beyond its normative limits.

Second, we need to distinguish between socialism as a system external to the person and socialism as a state of mind in the person herself. Most socialists, whether theoretical socialists in the mode of Marx or the Fabians, or practical socialists like Robert Owen and Vladimir Lenin, have operated under the assumption not only that human beings are embedded in systems operating distinct from their own wills but that human virtues—particularly those relating to productive capacities—will flourish in a radically changed environment. Thus any attempt to change the world for the better must concentrate on changing this system in some fashion so as to release these suppressed virtues. For other socialists, such as the late Tanzanian president Julius Nyerere, social-

---

[3]Brussell, *Dictionary of Quotable Definitions,* p. 536.
[4]Elbert Hubbard, *Roycroft Dictionary and Book of Epigrams* (East Aurora, N.Y.: Roycrofters, 1923), p. 55.
[5]Michael Harrington, *Socialism: Past and Future* (New York: Mentor/Penguin, 1989), p. 31.

ism is not primarily a system but a state of mind predisposing the person in an altruistic direction. Indeed the socialist puts aside acquisitiveness and devotes herself to the care of the larger community. Nyerere's African socialism, or *Ujamaa*, is not a proposal for radical systemic change in his own country, but rather an expression of hope that already existing socialist attitudes, which he believes are indigenous to traditional African society, can be drawn upon and extended to cover the entire continent and beyond.[6]

For most socialists, however, the socialist system and the socialist attitude are inextricably bound up with each other. Not everyone shares Nyerere's confidence in the socialist orientation of ordinary citizens. Here we encounter one of the central paradoxes of most brands of socialism. On the one hand, socialism often seems based on the assumption that human beings are spontaneously virtuous when emancipated from vicious social, economic and political systems. This belief is especially pronounced in anarchism, where it implies the persistence of social order without external governance. Yet many socialisms are also based on the conviction that human persons are infinitely malleable, that is, capable of being fashioned in accordance with the imperatives of the new system. For socialists *out* of power, the paradox is not so pronounced because they are confident that an eventual alteration in the external environment will inevitably transform human nature, insofar as it can be said to exist. For socialists *in* power, the paradox threatens to become outright conflict as this new socialist person stubbornly refuses to make her appearance and they are forced to assume total control of the means of socialization to try to produce her. Successive generations of Soviet leaders tried unsuccessfully to create "the New Soviet Man" fully emancipated from residual bourgeois motivations. This grand effort finally collapsed in 1991 as history demonstrated that human nature is, if not fixed or static, at least more stable and complex than socialist planners were willing to admit.

Third, we need to distinguish between statist and nonstatist varieties of socialism. This introduces the distinction between socialism per se and anarchism. Many of the ideologies in this study believe, either implicitly or explicitly, that heteronomous authority is a necessary evil. Anarchism takes this antiauthority conviction even further by averring that this evil may not even be necessary. Liberalism and ideological democracy believe that individual autonomy is the

---

[6]Julius Nyerere, *Ujamaa—Essays on Socialism* (Oxford: Oxford University Press, 1968), pp. 1-12. On the other hand, Nyerere's *Ujamaa* certainly had practical implications for the people of Tanzania, as his policies, while producing one of the highest literacy rates in Africa, nevertheless led to the uprooting of stable communities and failed to stimulate economic growth.

"natural" state of man and that only voluntary consent can legitimize any authority. Anarchism concurs that voluntary consent legitimizes authority, but only nonhierarchical authority that is noncoercive. Such anarchists as Mikhail Bakunin envision the advent of a society characterized not by "fixed, constant, and universal authority" but by "a continual exchange of mutual, temporary, and, above all, voluntary authority and subordination."[7] Although there is a pronounced antistatist element in other types of socialism, most notably the Marxian variety, most socialists have not been willing to go as far as anarchists in disavowing political authority. In fact, as we shall note, there is a tendency for a socialism antistatist in theory to become heavily statist in practice.

Fourth, socialisms can be distinguished by their varying strategies for implementing their programs. At one end lies the British Fabian Society, founded in 1883 by George Bernard Shaw, Sidney and Beatrice Webb, and H. G. Wells, whose approach was so gradual that the group threatened to remain little more than a talking shop. The Fabians seemed to vindicate Hubbard's wry comment that a socialist is someone who "considers a thing done when he has suggested it."[8] At the other end lie the communist parties following the doctrines of Marxism-Leninism and preaching revolutionary change on behalf of the oppressed proletariat. The assumption of Marxist-Leninists, including their Stalinist, Maoist and Titoist successors, is that the advent of socialism is an all-or-nothing, irreversible event impelled by the imperatives of history. Residual bourgeois tendencies present in the ostensibly postcapitalist society require a strong state apparatus to keep history moving forward and to prevent a return to the earlier historical stage. In between the extremes of the Fabian Society and revolutionary socialism lie most of the world's democratic socialist or social democratic parties, which are content to pursue specific ameliorative policies within the context of normal parliamentary politics. Like Bernard Crick, who claims the socialist label for himself, they eschew an antipolitical socialism that would impose a uniform vision on a diverse body politic.

Fifth and finally, socialisms can be grouped into utopian and scientific varieties. Utopian socialists attempt to reorganize small communities and generally refrain from establishing political parties and programs to implement their ideas on a wider scale. Their visions are often based on an overtly religious worldview rooted in one of the traditional faiths, such as Christianity. Even those utopian

---

[7]Michael Bakunin, *God and the State* (New York: Dover, 1970), p. 33.
[8]Hubbard, *Roycroft Dictionary and Book of Epigrams*, p. 54.

socialists who explicitly reject Christianity frequently work out of strong ethical commitments flowing from a devout belief in the goodness and brotherhood of humanity.

Scientific socialism is associated with the theories of Karl Marx, although the term itself is more closely associated with his colleague Friedrich Engels.[9] Marx and Engels made no secret of their contempt for utopian socialism, which they believed to be based on a sentimentality fundamentally out of touch with the realities of productive processes and class struggle. Marx and Engels believed that their own philosophy of history had a scientific basis insofar as it was rooted in an empirical observation of actual historical developments and made predictions for the future based on these past patterns. Thus neither Marx nor Engels believed it was incumbent upon them to forecast the precise contours of the future classless society, a task they were largely content to leave up to the working class. They understood their own task as demonstrating scientifically that such a society would indeed come about through the operation of historical forces of an economic character.

Yet there is a certain disingenuous quality to Marx's and Engels's repudiation of utopianism and their claim to scientific status for their own theories. After all, as we have been arguing from the outset of this study, all human knowledge is rooted in an underlying religious worldview with its own gods and distinctive soteriology. Despite their professed view that capitalism is simply one more stage in the historical process, it is difficult to read Marx and Engels without concluding that their own theories are rooted in a commitment to the emancipation of the oppressed and that whatever facilitates or obstructs this emancipation is deemed good or evil respectively. As is well known, Marx and Engels professed atheism. Not all Marxists are necessarily atheists, as can be seen in the so-called liberation theologians, yet their tenets are rooted simultaneously in a philosophical materialism and a commitment to human autonomy that are themselves religious in character, not to mention in tension with each other. We shall return to the Marxian vision later.

A Transformative Vision

Possibly more than the other ideologies in this study, socialism claims to em-

---

[9]Paul Thomas, "Critical Reception: Marx Then and Now," in *The Cambridge Companion to Marx,* ed. Terrell Carver (Cambridge: Cambridge University Press, 1991), p. 25. See Friedrich Engels, "Socialism: Utopian and Scientific," in *Karl Marx and Frederick Engels: Selected Writings* (New York: International Publishers, 1968), pp. 379-434. Engels wrote this essay in 1880, three years before Marx's death.

body a radical social critique promising fundamental change, and thus salvation, to society as a whole. Socialism is not content to reform the political community by, for example, guaranteeing greater personal freedoms, securing national independence or expanding the franchise. At its most ambitious, socialism offers a comprehensive program of architectonic change extending well beyond the boundaries of the body politic. As a theoretical system, its lineage can be traced back to Thomas More's *Utopia* and, much earlier, to Plato's *Republic*, in which Socrates and his companions construct a city-in-speech characterized by a maximum amount of social solidarity and a minimum degree of privacy. Yet even this ancient intellectual exercise in social transformation did not touch the farmers and merchants but limited itself to the guardians of the city. Moreover, in writing the *Republic*, Plato never envisioned that his proposals were actually capable of implementation. Socialism in its various forms, however, is intended by its followers precisely to be put into effect, either in small alternative communities or in the larger society, and usually by political means.

Along with this transformative approach comes a root-and-branch repudiation of the existing social arrangement, which, like socialism itself, is usually conceived as an all-encompassing whole characterized by a single economic principle, often labeled capitalism. For some socialists, this repudiation demands nothing short of a revolution that goes beyond the mere overthrow of one set of political leaders by another. Revolution entails overturning the basic structures of society, possibly including such institutions as family, marriage and church, which are deemed to have been imprinted with a capitalist character. Because capitalism is deemed to have tainted the whole social order, the latter must be radically reordered to bring the former to an end. For some, capitalism is an evil to be expunged, because it embodies an intrinsically oppressive economic system. For others, including Marx and his heirs, capitalism represents a particular stage in the historical process—one that has brought undoubted progress to humanity in its day but which is now destined to be supplanted by a new classless society transcending the old antagonisms it has spawned. Still others, seemingly unaware of the logical tension between them, combine the two arguments: capitalism is both immoral and outmoded.[10]

As we have seen in previous chapters, socialism is not the only ideology to mount a critique of capitalism. Both conservatism and nationalism have anti-

---

[10]In fact, this very contradiction constitutes a subtext even in the Marxian corpus. Despite Marx's unwillingness to use such an unscientific word as *immoral*, it is not difficult to detect in his writings what most people would label a moral outrage at the injustices of early industrial capitalism.

capitalist components, but their critiques are based on capitalism's threatened dissolution of local and national traditions, including settled ways of life characterized by social stability. Conservatives are unlikely to see capitalism as an all-embracing totality, although they certainly recognize in it the excessive dominance of economic and commercial interests over other legitimate concerns.[11] For conservatives capitalism changes too much and weakens valuable traditions that ought to be maintained for the sake of a richer social life. For socialists, on the other hand, capitalism is too conservative of existing power arrangements and undergirds an inegalitarian society. Capitalism is not progressive enough and *impedes* the development of a rich social life. Continued progress therefore demands its replacement with a system ensuring greater economic equality.

With its heavy focus on economics, it might be doubted plausibly that socialism can be considered a *political* ideology at all and perhaps ought not to be treated in a book on the subject. After all, Marx and Engels viewed politics and the state as little more than ideological byproducts of the concrete productive processes in which human beings find themselves caught up. We shall examine Marx and Engels in more detail later. At this point suffice it to note that Marxian socialism is by no means the only ideology to view politics as derivative from something fundamentally nonpolitical or extrapolitical. Locke believed that political authority exists largely, if not wholly, to protect private property. Nationalists routinely subordinate the state's task of doing justice to all to their own agenda of advancing the cause of their national community. Conservatives often fail to think through the central task of the state, deferring instead to whichever political and other traditions they believe have proven their social utility. And ideological democrats view politics and the state as ancillary to the passions of popular majorities. If these other ideologies are appropriately treated here, so also is socialism. Moreover, given the fact that socialism is so often defined by its political agenda, whether this be the nationalization of industries, the progressive income tax or other courses of action, we are justified in treating it as a *political* ideology, even if its view of politics may prove to be deficient in some fashion.

Like the other ideologies we have dealt with in this study, socialism too is subject to more than one interpretation. At a basic level socialism can be defined by its attachment to economic equality, that is, by a desire to distribute

---

[11]On the other hand, so-called *neo*conservatives such as Michael Novak are wont to reclaim and endorse the term *capitalism*, ironically agreeing with Marx in seeing it as something characterizing the society as a whole. But see once again Russell Kirk's comments in *The Politics of Prudence* (Bryn Mawr, Penn.: Intercollegiate Studies Institute, 1993), p. 184.

the fruits of the earth more evenly throughout a given community. But beyond this basic predilection, as noted earlier, definitions differ, as do the strategies for achieving this sought-after equality. Moreover, some observers argue that we now live in a postsocialist age, principally because one of its chief manifestations in the twentieth century, namely Marxism-Leninism or communism, came to a rather dramatic, if largely peaceful, end beginning in 1989. In the prosperous Western democracies, the welfare state, which was a product of late liberal and democratic socialist efforts after the Second World War, has been scaled back by both neoliberal and social democratic governments for fiscal reasons. Yet the egalitarian impulse remains alive and has spread into other areas of life, even if the class basis of socialism is not as persuasive as it once was.

From Democracy to Socialism

In chapter five we traced the pedigree of democracy as creed, pointing out its roots in the liberalism of Hobbes and Locke and following it up to Rousseau, whose radical democratic twist on social contract theory led in a strikingly anti-liberal direction. Rousseau was by no means a socialist as that term has come to be understood over the past two centuries. Yet there are a number of elements in his thought that could be seen to support its eventual development. To begin with, Rousseau believed that human beings in the prepolitical state of nature are at once equal and unequal. To be sure, they are unequal in their respective physical strengths and capacities, but they are equal in their right to enjoy the fruits of the earth. The bulk of human inequalities that we observe today are due in large measure to the conventions of society, which are in turn based on private property. Civil society began when someone first enclosed a piece of ground and claimed it as his own and nobody bothered to stop him.[12] From this followed the eventual development of governments with their rules and laws, and the rivalries and conflicts attendant upon the division of the earth into discrete parcels controlled by the few. With increasing inequality came a proliferation of warfare.

Following Plato, Rousseau's political theory is haunted by the threat of private concerns overwhelming the public good. His solution to this dilemma is not to abolish societal conventions and revert back to the prepolitical state, which is neither feasible nor desirable at this stage, but to try to diminish all allegiances that might conflict with the ultimate loyalty of citizens to the sover-

---

[12]Rousseau *A Dissertation on the Origin and Foundation of the Inequality of Mankind* part 2.

eign. The principal means is by establishing a civil religion consisting of "social
sentiments without which a man cannot be a good citizen or a faithful subject."[13] This civil religion would be tolerant of all other religions except those
that prove their intolerance by distinguishing between saved and unsaved and
thereby introducing an intolerable division into the body politic. Needless to
say, Rousseau's "tolerant" civil religion must exclude virtually all traditional religions such as Christianity, Judaism and Islam.

On the issue of property, Rousseau does not oppose its private possession
and generally agrees with his liberal predecessors that its preservation is a chief
reason for establishing the civil commonwealth.[14] Yet extreme disparities in the
distribution of property are as divisive of political unity as is diversity of religions. As soon as the few become wealthy and the many poor, civic virtue is
likely to yield to corruption and the general will is certain to be extinguished.
Even the quest to accumulate wealth is a preoccupation that diverts one from
attention to the public business. Better a republic characterized by limited resources evenly distributed than by great wealth concentrated in too few hands.
This would exclude from the body politic the threats of envy and covetousness
and the conflicts they inevitably engender.

Furthermore, in the Rousseauan republic, if property is not precisely possessed in common, the citizens have nevertheless given themselves up entirely
to the body politic, and whatever rights they enjoy, including that to property,
are at the pleasure of the general will. As long as the general will remains truly
general, Rousseau is persuaded that it cannot harm its members. Nevertheless,
"the social compact gives the body politic absolute power over all its members,"
and it is up to the body politic to determine the extent to which a citizen's life
and goods are required by the needs of the larger community.[15] This is the
meaning of that sovereignty which Rousseau ascribes to the body politic. Even
if the state requires that a person die, then die he must, "because his life is no
longer a mere bounty of nature, but a gift made conditionally by the State."[16]

It is perhaps a small step from Rousseau's notion of the general will and its
sovereignty over its members to the socialist conception of common property

---

[13]Rousseau *On the Social Contract* 4.8.
[14]Rousseau *On Political Economy*, trans. G. D. H. Cole, in *Great Books of the Western World*, vol. 38, *Montesquieu, Rousseau*, ed. Robert Maynard Hutchins (Chicago: Encyclopaedia Britannica, 1952), pp. 381,
439.
[15]Rousseau *On the Social Contract* 2.4.
[16]Ibid., 2.5.

held in trust for its citizens by the state. If it is up to the state to determine autonomously what belongs to itself as guardian of the public interest, and if unequal property ownership comes to be deemed a threat to that interest, then
the state may take it upon itself, not simply to limit the right to property, which
is consistent with its normative task of doing public justice, but to abrogate it
altogether, which is not.

Eleven years after Rousseau's death, the French Revolution attempted to reorder the political system based on the radical democratic principle of popular
sovereignty. But for many French people the changes wrought by the Revolution were not thorough enough because the resultant institutions left people
unequal in their respective material stations. François-Noël Babeuf went further than Rousseau in arguing that private property is usurpation and that all
the ills of society flow from it. Or, as Pierre-Joseph Proudhon would later put
it, "Property is theft." Pierre Sylvain Maréchal's *Manifesto of Equals* predicts another revolution that will complete the work of the French Revolution by extending equality before the law into the lives and homes of the people. What
has thus far been merely abstract and remote will one day become concrete and
tangible. All of this depends on a recognition that land in particular is rightfully
nobody's property but is the common property of humanity as a whole.

But, of course, "humanity as a whole" no more exists as an identifiable and
responsible agent than does "the people." To argue that property belongs to so
indefinite and nebulous a collectivity inevitably entails that some particular institution exercise actual control on its behalf. For many, if not most, socialists
this institution is not necessarily the state or government. In fact, many socialists, particularly those of an anarchist bent, would prefer to dispense with the
state altogether. Even Marx and Engels envisioned the state at least losing its political character and at most withering away completely. Utopian socialists such
as Robert Owen and Charles Fourier did not advocate a state-sponsored socialism such as would later emerge in both the Soviet Union and the Western social
democracies. They saw their proposals being achieved through private efforts
on a small scale in such experimental communities as New Lenark, Scotland,
or New Harmony, Indiana, in the case of Owen, and in the hypothetical
phalanstère (phalanstery or phalanx) in the case of Fourier. Yet all but the most
anarchistic of socialists understood that their designs for the future depended on
more than simply the spontaneous cooperative efforts of the participants. Some
sort of elite within the whole must direct the community toward socialist ends.

Although Marx's cosmopolitanism would seem to point him in the direction of an abstract humanism, in fact he sees the salvation of humanity lying not in humanity as such, but in a particular segment of the species defined by its relationship to the means of production known as the proletariat. Marx is confident that through the development of capitalist production, the proletariat will one day constitute a majority of society. Through its superiority of numbers, the oppressed proletariat will eventually "win the battle of democracy"[17] by expropriating the oppressing bourgeoisie or capitalist class and redistributing its property to the community as a whole. The net result will be a classless society in which the ancient division between propertied and dispossessed will disappear. The proletariat is thus not only of salvific significance for the whole of humanity, but it is destined to *become* the whole of humanity in the new dispensation.

Nevertheless, even the proletariat is too abstract a collectivity to be a responsible agent. It is hardly surprising then that Lenin's adaptation of Marxism posits a vanguard of the proletariat in the form of an elite party acting on its behalf. In classic socialism proponents see the members of the community turning over the products of their labor to a central authority of some sort, which would in turn redistribute them on an equal basis back to the members. On a small scale this could conceivably work, and throughout history many communities, such as monasteries and Israeli kibbutzim, have operated on precisely this basis. But if one expands the communal-ownership principle to cover an entire community of citizens, then the question arises as to who would take responsibility for this redistribution. In virtually all cases it turns out to be the organs of government that must then undertake to plan the economy from the top down. Since most governments are unwilling to take on such a herculean task, a socialist or communist party must aspire to assume direct control over the government for this purpose. Presumably this could be done by ordinary democratic means, and many professed socialists value highly the institutions of parliamentary democracy.

But at this point socialism, particularly in its Marxist form, begins to become highly *un*democratic in practice, despite its spiritual roots in the doctrine of popular sovereignty. If capitalism and socialism represent two irreversible stages in history, as they do in the Marxist scheme, then the movement from the former to the latter represents nothing less than a flight from slavery to emancipation. Once the latter has been achieved definitively, it is inconceivable that a return to bondage can be condoned. Once socialism has been accomplished,

---

[17]Marx and Engels, *Manifesto of the Communist Party* (1847), part 2.

it would hardly be progressive to countenance a return to capitalism, that earlier stage which has now been transcended. The clear implication is that when a socialist party has come to power, even if by normal parliamentary means, it must take measures to keep power in order to complete the transition to the new order. If everyone is not able to see this as clearly as the party's members, then they will almost certainly have to consolidate their own power and act to eliminate other parties from contention. Rule of the people inevitably becomes rule of the proletariat, which further narrows to become rule of a party on behalf of the proletariat. What is touted as communal ownership of property thus in reality becomes monopolization of all property by a self-appointed elite effectively responsible to no one. Ironically then, property becomes more concentrated under socialism than under capitalism and, if the former Soviet Union is at all typical, material equality remains as elusive as ever.

There is no small irony in the pedigree of ideologies that we have just traced. As seen in chapter five, liberalism serves to bring into being an antiliberal democracy, and now it seems that democracy calls forth an antidemocratic socialism. These three ideologies are, of course, based on the same fundamentally religious assumption of human autonomy, yet they coexist uneasily and are in considerable tension with each other, much like quarrelling siblings in the same family. Yet it would be as incorrect to argue that all ideological democrats must become socialists so as to assert that all liberals must eventually profess a belief in popular sovereignty. The spiritual connections are there, to be sure. Yet in the real world flesh-and-blood human beings do not adhere to pure ideological positions, nor are they necessarily willing to buy all the logic thereof. More fundamentally, because we are created by God and are plugged into the same cosmos, even the most ardent of socialists are constrained by the realities of creation, sin and redemption to live out their vision in ways that fall well short of their dreams. On the other hand, there is much in the socialist vision that corresponds to creational possibilities overlooked by others, and we shall look at these in the last section.

Common Ownership and Socialist Ideology

In chapter five we were careful to distinguish between democracy as form of government and democracy as creed. Something similar must be done in this chapter as well. We must make an initial distinction between the empirical phenomenon of communal ownership of property and the ideology of socialism, which in its most significant manifestations claims to be based on the former.

All societies are characterized by common ownership in some measure. Families are probably the most immediately obvious examples. In a family setting, although homeownership may be legally ascribed to one or both of the parents, there is a sense in which the home belongs to the entire family, including the resident children. There may be one or two wage earners in the household, but the fruits of their labors are equitably distributed to all members of the family, all of whom eat at the same table and none of whom are permitted to starve. Dale Vree argues that the family "is uniquely a place where rewards are primarily distributed according to need, not work or merit or luck, and where the harsh judgments of the marketplace can be neutralized by love and forgiveness."[18] As such, he argues, it contains the seeds of a socialist society. Elshtain similarly maintains that the family "helps to keep alive an alternative to the values which dominate the marketplace."[19] If so, then within its context, according to Lesslie Newbigin, no one is free to choose his own company or to pursue unlimited self-interest.[20]

More than two millennia ago, Aristotle noted that there are three possible ways to organize the possession of property in a polis. First, all things might be possessed in common. Second, nothing might be shared by the community and all property owned exclusively by individuals. Third, some property might be communally owned and some individually owned. The second he clearly thought impossible in a community of persons, since the very notion of community implies that something is shared among its members. The first alternative, if not altogether impossible, was at least undesirable because it ignored that phenomenon which has come to be called the tragedy of the commons. The tragedy of the commons means simply that whatever "is common to the greatest number has the least care bestowed upon it."[21] Air, water and soil pollution are vivid examples of this. A particular company will care for its own property and will make continual capital improvements to maintain and even increase its productive capacity. Yet it will not shrink from pouring its waste byproducts into the air and water, even though it thereby poisons the environment common to all human beings. Hence the need for legal regulations enacted by gov-

---

[18]Dale Vree, *From Berkeley to East Berlin and Back* (Nashville: Thomas Nelson, 1985), p. 140.
[19]Jean Bethke Elshtain, "Feminists Against the Family," in *Real Politics at the Center of Everyday Life* (Baltimore, Md.: Johns Hopkins University Press, 1997), p. 150.
[20]Lesslie Newbigin, *Foolishness to the Greeks: The Gospel and Western Culture* (Grand Rapids, Mich.: Eerdmans, 1986), p. 113.
[21]Aristotle *Politics* 1261b.33.

ernment, which is a specific body charged with the care of the commons, among other things.

Aristotle opted for the third alternative, namely, the common ownership of some property and the individual ownership of other property. This is what we today would label a mixed economy. Although Aristotle's insight is fundamentally correct, it requires modification in order to account for actual forms of ownership in virtually every society. To begin with, ownership cannot be reduced to that of *the* individual and *the* community, as if the full complexity of social forms and relationships could be boiled down to these two elements. To be sure, individuals do own property, but other forms of ownership are dependent on specific institutional contexts conditioning the ways this ownership is realized. The subjects of ownership are as diverse as families, schools, corporations, private clubs, libraries, museums, labor unions, and of course political communities or states. Accordingly each of these communities exercises its ownership—or perhaps more properly its stewardship over its share of God's world—in a way appropriate to its specific institutional task. The museum cares for its property in a fundamentally different fashion than does the manufacturing enterprise. The national park treats its property differently than does the timber company.

Moreover, the various forms of ownership properly coexist with each other and ought not attempt to assimilate or abolish each other. The fact that one is an employee of a corporation does not mean that one's personal property belongs to the employer. The fact that one is a citizen does not mean, contra Rousseau and his followers, that one's personal property is enjoyed only at the pleasure of its "real" owner, the state. Even in the family not everything is commonly owned. Children of the household have their own beds, their own clothes, their own toys, their own toothbrushes, their own bicycles, their own books and so forth. As infants and toddlers they quickly develop a strong sense of what belongs to them, although this sense remains immature and is largely captive to a childish egotism that must be tempered by parental training. Clearly then, human societies embody a variety of forms of communal ownership, and any attempt to replace these with a single form carries the risk of totalitarianism.

Here is where we begin to see the development of socialism as an ideology. In and of itself, there is nothing wrong with extending the principle of common ownership of property to, say, a group of families living together voluntarily in an intensive community. The book of Acts twice records that the early Christian believers in Jerusalem lived in such a community. "And all who believed were together and had all things in common; and they sold their possessions and goods and distributed them to all, as any had need" (2:44-45). "There was not a needy person among them, for as many as were possessors of lands or houses sold them, and brought the proceeds of what was sold and laid it at the apostles' feet; and distribution was made to each as any had need" (4:34-35). Once again the kibbutzim of Israel are recent examples of an ongoing attempt to extend a single form of common ownership as far as possible in the interest of economic equality.

Yet at some point all such communities run up against certain undeniable realities placing limits on this common ownership. For example, at the outset of the kibbutz movement, there was a concerted effort to diminish the scope of private (that is, nonkibbutz) ownership to such an extent that even the community's clothing was pooled in a common closet. Each day kibbutz members would be issued garments that had been worn by a similarly sized neighbor only a few days earlier. Thus there would presumably be no pretense attached to specific clothing styles, and apparel-related individuality would be suppressed in the interest of community. Moreover, meals were eaten in a common dining hall. Children were raised among other children by specially trained nurses and teachers. And although workers were generally assigned to the same jobs for long periods of time, the most menial of jobs were rotated to avoid a hardening of the division of labor and the development of an incipient class system.[22]

However, in recent decades the kibbutz movement has modified considerably these practices as privacy has inevitably reasserted itself in a variety of ways. Now families prefer to eat more meals separately. Personal effects are increasingly owned by individuals. Children are being raised by their own parents, and to some degree even a sexual division of labor has reasserted itself, despite deliberate efforts to implement an equality based on identity of tasks between the sexes.[23] Some purists may view such developments as rooted in an apostasy from

---

[22]For a classic account of the history and principles of the kibbutz movement, see Melford E. Spiro, *Kibbutz: Venture in Utopia* (New York: Schocken, 1963). See also H. Darin-Drabkin, *The Other Society* (New York: Harcourt, Brace & World, 1963); Dan Leon, *The Kibbutz: A New Way of Life* (Oxford: Pergamon, 1969), for a positive assessment of the kibbutz movement by an insider; and Henry Rosenfeld, Yehuda Hanegbi and Marc Segal, *The Kibbutz* (Tel Aviv: Sadan, circa 1970), for an obviously partisan apologetic for the movement, replete with photographs.

[23]Ironically, the communal design of the kibbutz, including the collective rearing of the community's children, was the work of men and not of women. Once women began to play a larger role in the actual governing of the kibbutzim, it became clear that they had long experienced this forced separation from their own children as oppressive, and the more normal familial patterns reasserted themselves. Sexual equality had evidently meant one thing to the men and another to the women. See Daniel Gavron, *The Kibbutz: Awakening from Utopia* (New York: Rowman & Littlefield, 2000), pp. 159-88, for a moving account, based on several studies, of how kibbutz women and children negatively experienced this ostensibly liberating separation of parents and offspring.

the original vision. Yet such developments may better be understood as an inevitable reassertion of the different modes of ownership that are intrinsic to human life in community.[24] This latter interpretation is born out by the historical fact that most such communities, if they do not collapse altogether, end up developing in a similar direction over time.[25]

Nevertheless, the larger socialist movement, even where it has been forced to accommodate such realities, still holds to the original egalitarian vision and sees it as the ideal to be sought after. The ideology of socialism, therefore, is based on the assumption that a single form of communal ownership is capable of supplanting all other forms of ownership, both individual and communal. In a small community this places a large amount of decision-making power in the hands of the community's leaders, a concentration mitigated by the voluntary nature of membership in the community. If there is an attempt to implement a single form of common ownership on the scale of a nation-state, and if this effort is pursued with unremitting zeal, the results are likely to be disastrous. Here the voluntary character of the small community is replaced by involuntary coercion on a massive scale. Once again, socialism in practice, even where it is theoretically antistatist, tends to consolidate a dangerous amount of power in the hands of the state apparatus with its coercive capacity. The danger is not simply that government officials will abuse their power, but that they will usurp power properly belonging to other institutions as well as to individual persons.

Thus when socialist parties come to power, they are generally driven to bring as much economic activity as possible under the control of the socialist-dominated government. Outside of the former Soviet Union, the People's Republic of China and other similar states, socialist rule has never entailed the outright extinction of all independent economic enterprise. Yet such governments have generally sought to "nationalize" major corporations, especially those possessing

---

[24]For more recent developments, including those apparently eroding the original principles of the kibbutz, see Gavron once again, and also the published debate concerning the prospects of kibbutzim as they cope with increasing privatizing trends: Jo-Ann Mort and Gary Brenner, "Kibbutzim: Will They Survive the New Israel?" *Dissent* 47 (summer 2000): 64-70; Menachem Rosner, "A 'Third Way' to Save the Kibbutz?" *Dissent* 47 (fall 2000): 89-92 (and the reply by Mort and Brenner, pp. 92-94). Concerning the trend toward greater familial privacy in the kibbutzim, see Karl Zinsmeister, "Actually Villages Are Lousy at Raising Pre-school Children," *The American Enterprise* 7 (May-June 1996): 52-54.

[25]For a survey and analysis of such communities in the twentieth century, see Timothy Miller, *The Quest for Utopia in Twentieth-Century America* (Syracuse, N.Y.: Syracuse University Press, 1998), 1:1900-1960. Although Miller is evidently taken with the persistence of such communal experiments in the United States, his own account demonstrates the equally persistent return to diverse forms of ownership within such communities over the long term.

a natural monopoly in a particular field, such as electricity, telephone communications and mass transportation. If such governments are not precisely hostile to independent enterprises, they nevertheless tend to hold them in suspicion.

The temptation to nationalize is even greater if a sizeable segment of a country's economy is dominated by a transnational corporation based in another country. Yet this strategy is often motivated more by nationalist than by socialist considerations. Indeed a healthy mixed economy is virtually certain to include, in addition to independent enterprises, state enterprises called upon to provide services that cannot be provided profitably by the private sector. Yet such public corporations easily coexist with private corporations, often within the same industrial sectors, provided the former are not granted a legal monopoly.

On the other hand, the mere existence of a substantially nationalized economy does not necessarily make for a society characterized by the principle that each contributes according to ability and each receives according to need. During its seventy years of existence, the Soviet Union never attained such a society and instead, though it may have abolished the old landed gentry, effectively established Milovan Djilas's bureaucratic new class, as noted in chapter one. Those fortunate enough to be ushered into this class were given such privileges as second homes, or *dachas,* in the country, the right to shop at hard-currency stores, and access to the best educational, professional and recreational facilities. The achievement of pure communism, or a fully egalitarian society, was always held out as something that would arrive in the near future, after the economic infrastructure had been sufficiently strengthened and expanded. Of course, this prospect kept receding into the indefinite future, and by the final decades of the Soviet era, massive cynicism had set in, thus contributing to its eventual collapse. The story was little different in other countries following the Soviet model.

Means and Ends: Equality and How to Get There

We have noted, with Bob Goudzwaard, that ideologies are typically motivated to achieve some overarching goal deemed to take precedence over other legitimate human concerns. The ultimate danger, of course, is that followers will come to believe that the end justifies the means and that this goal could demand the sacrifice of millions of human lives. This we saw manifested most flagrantly in the totalitarian ideologies of the twentieth century, especially communism and national socialism, or Nazism. Yet even short of such catastrophe, all ideologies tend to assume that the achievement of some aim—whether it be individual freedom, national liberation or the general will—is sufficient reason to sanction policies that in even modest fashion may end up treating ordinary people unfairly. For socialists this ultimate goal is material equality.

Where socialists differ, however, is in their estimation of the meaning of equality and its relationship to other goals. Socialists usually argue that equality requires at least equal possession of economic resources, but they differ as to what this entails. Democratic socialists are normally content to pursue policies intended to improve the lot of the working class and to redistribute wealth through progressive taxation and other methods. Rather than seeking complete equality, which has inevitably proved incapable of realization even where it has been precisely defined, they try to achieve, somewhat vaguely, a "more egalitarian society" by narrowing the gap between the highest and lowest incomes.

For Marx and his followers, by contrast, attempts to redistribute income are rather beside the point. What is at stake in any society is not so much income as productive power. From the perspective of a revolutionary Marxist, all the efforts of democratic socialists to even out disparities in income leave the basic arrangement of productive power in society untouched. In fact, such programs as U.S. President Franklin Roosevelt's New Deal, William Beveridge's welfare state or John Maynard Keynes's full employment policies are really ways of avoiding more fundamental change and effectively propping up a dying capitalist system. This is because they leave untouched the institution of private property on which capitalism is based. It is not surprising then, that once Marxist parties have come to power, they are driven to nationalize at least the major industries in a country, as indicated earlier.

Still other socialists, following C. A. R. Crosland, argue that collective ownership is at most a means to the achievement of socialism and not equivalent to socialism itself. After all, the policies of nationalization, collectivization and the government-planned economy can be serviceable to a variety of ends, many of which are distinctly inegalitarian. Crosland prefers to identify socialism with five aspirations: (1) the protest against material want engendered by capitalism; (2) a general concern for the needy, the oppressed and the disadvantaged; (3) "belief in equality and the 'classless society'" and a concern for the rights of the worker; (4) a preference for cooperation over competition; and (5) the protest against the deficiencies of capitalism, particularly mass unemployment.[26]

None of these aspirations necessitates a revolutionary redistribution of pro-

---

[26]C. A. R. Crosland, *The Future of Socialism* (New York: Schocken, 1963), p. 67.

ductive power as such. They are quite capable of being implemented gradually through ordinary parliamentary means. In fact, Crosland goes so far as to argue that "traditional capitalism has been reformed and modified almost out of existence" in his native Britain.[27] Clearly Crosland is a democratic socialist for whom the relationship between ends and means is quite different than for a Marxist. Indeed Crosland sees socialism existing not in a particular power arrangement antithetical to capitalism, but in the amelioration of the living and working conditions of the workers generated by the latter.

To complicate matters further, not all socialists can even agree that material equality is a proper end in itself. Ronald Beiner, who is otherwise fairly close to Hannah Arendt's effort to recover a positive account of active citizenship, proposes to implement economic socialism, which he sees as "a large-scale transformation of attitudes, institutions, and relationships in society with a view to the achievement of shared purposes and social justice through the public disposal of collective resources."[28] Yet the achievement of this socialism is not a final goal to which other means—especially political means—are merely serviceable. Material equality is not a good worth pursuing for itself; rather, it is desirable solely for the purpose of facilitating citizenship. After all, only those who have conquered want have sufficient energies and resources to devote themselves to the public business. This very nearly reverses the order of priority of other socialists, for whom politics is ancillary to class interests and political programs of value only insofar as they advance the achievement of material equality. For Beiner socialism is an economic means to a further political end.

Such ambiguities in the socialist vision point to the paradoxes implicit in the larger egalitarian enterprise. Socialism seeks equality above all, but flesh and blood socialists differ over its meaning, precisely what is to be equalized and, as we observed above, who should do the equalizing. They further disagree on whether the final goal of their striving should be equality of income, equality of productive power or even equality in the exercise of citizenship. They can undoubtedly agree that all of the above are in some sense good, but they cannot concur on which good is the highest good and which are simply proximate goods to be used as means to reaching the former. This means that for some socialists, contesting parliamentary elections is a sufficient instrument for the attainment of socialism. For others only a cataclysmic revolution will accomplish

---

[27]Ibid., p. 61.
[28]Ronald Beiner, *What's the Matter with Liberalism?* (Berkeley: University of California Press, 1992), p. 147.

the goal. Since wholesale social transformation does not occur easily and, given its secular underpinnings, will tend to transgress the real limits God has built into his creation, there is a danger that human beings will come to be deemed expendable in the single-minded pursuit of the larger goal, however it be defined.

Here socialism takes on its most destructive potential, as the idol of equality becomes a jealous god, demanding that worshipers go so far as to sacrifice their other, less egalitarian commitments and loyalties on its altar. After all, the very fabric of human life—or perhaps even the creation order itself—demands that specific wives love specific husbands above all other men, that particular parents care for particular children more than others, that employers remunerate their own employees instead of nonemployees. Any ideology that ignores or neglects these specific responsibilities in hope of encouraging an abstract, egalitarian regard for the whole of humanity will quickly find that the latter is far too thin to be an adequate substitute for the existing thick networks of particular commitments and loyalties characterizing the real world of human beings. The followers of such an ideology will thus be tempted to compensate for this thinness with the use of coercive force.

The Marxian Vision and Marxism

Of course, no treatment of socialism would be complete without some discussion of Karl Marx and his followers.[29] Although the category of socialism is, to be sure, much more inclusive than the Marxist alternative, twentieth century manifestations of socialism have been dominated by some variety of Marxism, whether this be the social democratic Marxism of the German Social Democratic Party, the Leninism and Stalinism of the Soviet Union or the Maoist permutation of the People's Republic of China. The popular attraction of Marxism was due in part to the central feature it shares with other forms of socialism, that is, the promise of eradicating want and class-based oppression. Yet Marx did something that other forms of socialist ideology did not do: he articulated an ostensibly scientific philosophy of history that claimed to provide a comprehensive interpretation for a wide variety of social and political phenomena. As is well known, Marx combined Hegel's dialectic, Feuerbach's atheistic materialism and French utopian socialism to produce his own unique theoretical approach, often known as historical materialism or, less accurately, dialectical materialism.

---

[29]I here use the adjective *Marxian* to describe the ideas of Marx himself and *Marxist* to describe the ideas of his followers.

This historical approach offers an extra attraction not necessarily found in other varieties of socialism. Socialism in general holds out the prospect of hard work and struggle to achieve the society based on communal ownership of property and the eradication of want. This grand effort may or may not meet with success, depending on the determination or lack thereof of its followers and on the power of the capitalist opposition. In other words, history is entirely contingent and could go in either direction. By contrast, the Marxian vision promises something that other forms of socialism dare not, that is, that the future belongs, as a matter of certainty, to the dispossessed proletariat. To the convinced Marxist, such a prediction is not a matter of soothsaying or reading tea leaves; it is a matter of empirically discerning the patterns of history and on this (scientific) basis anticipating how they will develop in the future. If it can be shown that throughout history the dispossessed have always triumphed against the ruling propertied class, whatever form the class struggle has assumed, then one can similarly forecast the ultimate victory of the current property-less class—the industrial workers, or the proletariat, over the bourgeoisie.

This then is the primary appeal of the Marxian vision: much as Scripture teaches the ultimate victory of Jesus Christ over his enemies and the reign of the righteous over the new earth in the kingdom of God, so also does Marxism promise an eschatological consummation of human history. This does not, of course, mean that there is not a battle to be waged or work to be done. Indeed there is much of both. But in fighting for the classless society, the proletariat does so fully confident that it is fighting not *against* history but *with* it. Where does this confidence come from? From the conviction that economics holds the key to understanding history.

According to Marx and Engels, we are what we produce. Man is fundamentally *homo economicus* and is motivated in all his activities by economic factors rooted in one's relationship to the means of production, or class. This means that the salient community in which one is embedded is the economic class, loyalty to which inevitably outweighs allegiance to nation, state, family, church and so forth. Marx and Engels open their famous *Manifesto of the Communist Party* with the following remarkable statement, which, for all its deliberate hyperbole, nevertheless draws attention to the singular Marxian focus: "The history of all hitherto existing society is the history of class struggles."[30] The classes are not simply social classes determined somewhat vaguely by income level, as

---

[30]Marx and Engels, *Manifesto*, p. 108.

we tend to think of them now, but groups of people determined by their objective relationship to the means of production. In other words, my status as proletarian is not conditioned by how much or how little I am paid for my labor, but by whether or not I am working for someone else who owns the machinery of production. If I am not in control of the product of my own labor, which is alienated and placed in the hands of the opposing class (the bourgeoisie or capitalists), then I am a proletarian. Because I have effectively sold my labor to someone else who now effectively "owns" this side of me—indeed the most defining feature of who I am—then I am decidedly unfree no matter how much I am paid for my efforts.

In fact, of course, I am probably not paid much at all because the laws of supply and demand, coupled with a glut of potential laborers, drive wages down to subsistence level. During the industrial revolution, at a time when increasing numbers of people were leaving the countryside and pouring into the growing urban areas, class divisions were becoming more pronounced, with factory owners becoming wealthier and workers earning but a pittance in comparison. Moreover, as the large industrial concerns grew even larger through their ability to undercut competition through economies of scale, small shopkeepers were driven out of business only to join the ranks of the growing proletariat. This development convinced Marx that the proletariat would inevitably come to constitute the vast majority of advanced industrialized societies. This is the democratic side of Marx, of which we spoke earlier. If the proletariat is increasingly expanding in size, then it should take very little effort for its members to seize the means of production from the small number of capitalists. After all, production has already effectively been socialized in the factory system; now it remains for ownership to be socialized as well. Once this occurs, all forms of oppression will cease because classes will come to an end.

To be sure, Marx and Engels are not wrong to isolate economic motives in history. This is the considerable truth in their philosophy. One need only think of the sorts of issues generally dominating election campaigns in most Western democracies. Candidates for public office debate what to do about budget deficits and (more recently) surpluses, whether to lower or raise taxes, whether to encourage or discourage greater free trade, and whether a proposed policy will benefit big business, small business or the trade unions. Voters are often said to vote their pocketbooks, which means that they vote for the parties and candidates they believe will pursue policies beneficial to their own particular economically based interest. Even the early architects of the European Union undertook their effort on the assumption that economics drives politics—that increasing economic integration inevitably leads to political unity. Many non-Marxists nevertheless agree with Marx that political events can be traced to underlying economic developments, though not everyone agrees that this will necessarily lead to good.

Marx is obviously a progressive philosopher; he believes that history is being driven in a purposeful direction and that it embodies the continual expansion of human freedom from oppression. Perhaps even more obviously than in the other ideologies we have explored, Marxism is based on an explicit soteriology holding out the possibility of salvation accomplished through the world historical activity of the proletariat. History is moving in a single direction, moved by class struggle, but destined to transcend class struggle after the final eschatological consummation, that is, the revolution, occurs.

This expansion of freedom has little to do with the civil liberties often guaranteed in constitutional documents, for example, freedom of speech, freedom of the press, freedom of religion and the other personal immunities from state control. Rather, freedom is a concrete economic freedom effected by transcending the age-old division of labor, which is the origin of classes and thus of all oppression. If Marxism is a variant of the gnostic heresy, which locates evil in some structural defect in the world, then for Marx the division of labor is precisely this source of evil. For many philosophers, beginning with Plato, it is difficult to imagine human life in community at all without a division of labor of some sort. In fact, a crucial element of Plato's definition of justice is that people do what they are best suited to do and nothing beyond that. By contrast, Marx believes the division of labor inevitably violates and dehumanizes people by artificially restricting them to only one of their productive capacities and by placing control over even this capacity in the hands of others. This is objective oppression, whether or not they are fully conscious of this.

Here we see a clue to the character of the future classless society, on which Marx and Engels are for the most part reluctant to speculate, believing that this is for the proletariat to decide. Because they explicitly repudiate the airy dreams of the utopian socialists and because they are not in the business of setting up cities in speech along Platonic lines, they claim only to be forecasting where history is moving in the most general terms. However, in a very few passages in their writings, they cannot resist indulging in some speculation concerning the socialist future. In one of the more famous of these passages they describe the communist society, where nobody has one exclusive sphere of activity but each can become accomplished in any branch he wishes, society regulates the general production and thus makes it possible for me to do one thing today and another tomorrow, to hunt in the morning, fish in the afternoon, rear cattle in the evening, criticise after dinner, just as I have a mind, without ever becoming hunter, fisherman, shepherd or critic.[31]

In the future society, corresponding to the biblical new heaven and new earth, where God "will wipe away every tear from their eyes, and death shall be no more, neither shall there be mourning nor crying nor pain any more" (Rev 21:4), the division of labor itself shall pass away, leaving human beings liberated to construct a new society altogether lacking the oppressions of the past. Human virtue itself will flourish in this new order, since all the obstacles to virtue will have been abolished. Of course, a principal difference between the Marxian and Christian visions is that, while the latter awaits the ultimate fulfillment of creation in the return of Christ to complete the redemptive process and to make all things new, the former sees this final culmination arising from within history itself.

In the twentieth century two of the most horrific tyrannies, the Soviet Union and the People's Republic of China, claimed to be following a variant of the Marxist vision, as adapted by Vladimir Lenin, Josef Stalin and Mao Zedong. Yet in no respect did any of the countries following the Leninist model achieve the classless society so glowingly extolled by Marx and Engels, despite one of the most concerted transformative efforts in history. It is likely that if Marx had been transported into the year 1955, he would not have recognized these countries as embodying his ideas. Nevertheless, it is worth asking whether these countries were in fact the true spiritual heirs of Marx's legacy or whether they were simply aberrations in an otherwise laudable effort to empower the working class. Many neo-marxists argue for the latter interpretation.

However, I believe that the Marxist enterprise was flawed from the outset because of a serious misreading of human nature. If the diagnosis of the disease is incorrect, then attempts at its healing are likely to go awry as well. A central assumption of Marxism is that a whole host of phenomena are reducible to economically based class struggle. These include political rule, legal systems, marriage, family life, religion, philosophies and national solidarities. All of these fall

---

[31]Marx and Engels, *The German Ideology* (1845), in *Basic Writings on Politics and Philosophy*, ed. Lewis S. Feuer (New York: Anchor/Doubleday, 1959), p. 254.

under the broad category of an ideological superstructure masking the underlying reality of concrete productive relations. Thus government is nothing but
the oppressive rule of the bourgeoisie over the proletariat, the logical implication being that if and when the class struggle ends, so also should government.
Similarly, if national antagonisms simply reflect class struggle, then as the latter
fades away so should the former. Perhaps most notoriously, it was assumed by
Marx and his followers that if religion is the opiate of the people and the sigh
of the oppressed, then bridging class antagonisms and putting an end to oppression should lead, nearly inexorably, to the disappearance of religion.

In the Soviet Union and its client states, the communist party undertook the
herculean task of creating the very type of society Marx and his followers envisioned. But, as noted previously, the New Soviet Man stubbornly refused to
make his appearance. Similarly, national antagonisms refused to go away. Many
Christians, Jews and Muslims continued to worship as before. This failure of
history to move in the direction Marx had forecasted prompted his followers to
give it a push, even if this meant ruthless persecution of those deemed to be
clinging stubbornly to the bourgeois past. Systematic terror was thus necessary
to move society toward what was supposedly inevitable. In the end reality
caught up to the dream and overtook it, finally putting an end to most of the
regimes deliberately constructed on Marxist principles. Unfortunately, many
scores of millions of people paid with their lives, sacrificing themselves or being
sacrificed on the altar of what proved to be a false god.[32]

Marxism may for now be in eclipse, having lost its hold on the spirit of the
age. Yet its method of historical and social analysis is alive and well in other
forms less obviously indebted to Marx. For example, although the various
forms of feminism are rooted in the several ideological visions discussed here,
one radical form owes much to a typical Marxist way of thinking. Much as
Marx reduces society in all its complexity to a class struggle, so also does radical
feminism reduce it to a conflict between males and females, each sex (or *gender*,
the preferred term) corresponding to oppressor and oppressed respectively. Just
as Marx views capitalism as an all-encompassing system stamping its character
on the entire society, so does radical feminism tend to characterize society in
all its complexity as patriarchal. Much as capitalism is something to be tran-

---

[32]Some observers estimate that the total number of victims of communist oppression between 1917 and
1989 ranges between 85 million and 100 million. See Stéphane Courtois et al., *The Black Book of Communism: Crimes, Terror, Repression*, trans. Jonathan Murphy and Mark Kramer (Cambridge, Mass.: Harvard University Press, 1999), pp. 4-5.

scended once for all, because it is *the* source of oppression in the world, so also is radical feminism compelled to work toward the transcending of patriarchy and the establishment of a nonpatriarchal society, on whose precise contours feminists differ. If Marxism effectively locates evil in the division of labor, radical feminists locate it in the sexual division of labor, some going so far as to advocate its abolition even in the biological reproductive process.[33] Feminist jurisprudence thus becomes a general advocacy on behalf of women against men, much as Marxist jurisprudence takes a preferential tack toward the proletariat and against the bourgeoisie. In both cases, justice, rather than carefully and impartially weighing the respective claims of diverse citizens, becomes captive to an ideological agenda. Injustice is the inevitable result, despite the rosy promises of both feminist and socialist visions.

Fair Distribution of Economic Resources

Yet socialism's dark side does not mean that it has no insight at all into the human social condition. Obviously something that has succeeded in obtaining the loyalty of scores of millions of people over the last two centuries must have done something right or seen something more clearly than nonsocialists had. Indeed, insofar as socialism can be seen as a quest for a *fairer* economic arrangement, there is something good to be found in it. Although any attempt to effect absolute economic equality would likely lead to grave injustice, there is clearly something deficient in an economic system that does not *fairly* distribute economic benefits to all participants. One need not be a socialist to recognize that a geographical economic unit characterized by the concentration of productive property in a few hands is not a good place for most people to live. In this respect, there is considerable truth in the characterization of such a system as embodying a structural form of oppression. In other words, although the possessors of productive property may hold legal title to their holdings, the very organization of the system, including the underlying legal framework, may effectively stack the deck against the vast majority of people lacking such property. In such a context, it becomes difficult for ordinary people to feed, clothe and shelter their own families. In short, a certain minimum claim to the fruits

---

[33]See, for example, Shulamith Firestone, *The Dialectic of Sex: The Case for Feminist Revolution* (New York: Bantam, 1971), p. 206. The irony is that Firestone's version of feminism, in its quest to liberate women, does so at the cost of deprecating created female corporeality and implicitly viewing the male body as normative. Furthermore, its effort to "emancipate," like the Marxist-Leninist enterprise, would effectively create a totalitarian state.

of God's creation is needed for his image bearers to fulfill his diverse callings for their lives, which includes functioning as spouses, parents, workers, church-members and so forth. Where they are unable to do so, one rightly speaks of an unjust economic system.

In most circumstances a relatively free operation of the marketplace is able to ensure a just distribution of goods throughout a geographical economic unit. From virtually the dawn of human existence, people have been engaging in exchange of goods and services with each other. Although many socialists typically forget this, it is a structural feature of human life and is therefore not to be rejected. Sometimes this has taken the form of direct bartering, in which, for example, a cobbler exchanges a pair of shoes with a farmer for a bushel of corn. More recently in human history, such exchanges have become indirect, with money serving as an intermediary. The free operation of the market ensures, with a fair degree of accuracy, that the provision of goods corresponds to the actual demand for such goods. It would make little sense, for example, to produce snowmobiles in the island of Jamaica, with its uniformly warm temperatures and its geographical isolation from potential customers in the northern latitudes. The free operation of the market is likely to ensure that snowmobiles are manufactured closer to where they will be used. The market further offers to most people the opportunity for employment and the remuneration that follows from it. The expectation is that widespread employment within a relatively free market should serve to distribute the world's goods fairly.

However, reality does not always keep up with theory. An unfettered market can easily lead to the concentration of economic resources and the concomitant exclusion of many people from the enjoyment of these. As noted in chapter two, despite the market's promise to distribute economic benefits fairly, it was historically unable to prevent the accumulation of productive property in the hands of oligopolies and monopolies, such as Standard Oil and AT&T. After the industrial revolution and the dawn of the factory system, it could do little to enhance the bargaining power of workers vis-à-vis management, especially if there was an oversupply of labor. Workers were forced by circumstances to accept less than fair employment arrangements, although such were entered into legally and "voluntarily." In the nineteenth century and even into the twentieth, the unfettered market facilitated the exploitation of child labor, poverty among the working poor and similar abuses already discussed in the earlier chapter. Those who champion a return to a more libertarian economic policy too highly esteem individual freedom and neglect to take note of the possibilities of its abuse. This is not an argument against freedom or the market as such; it *is* an argument for the recognition of normative limits to the free market, including social and legal limits.

Of course government is itself limited by the divine calling to do justice, which means that it cannot, in totalitarian fashion, do everything people might wish it to. It cannot by itself employ all those lacking work. It cannot eradicate poverty. It cannot in general create the good life for its citizens. It cannot play father or mother to its citizens. But given these limits, justice does require that the government (1) care for those things held in common by the body politic, (2) play at least a minimal redistributive role to temper the potential injustices engendered by the market or to compensate for other deficiencies in its operation, and (3) assume some responsibility for the economically disadvantaged. We shall take these in order.

First, government is obligated to care for what is common to all citizens of the state. This has a number of implications. For example, it must enact laws that protect the physical environment by regulating and, if possible, prohibiting the pollution of air, water and soil. It must also tend that property, including productive property, held in trust for the entire public. National, provincial/ state and municipal parks, public corporations, and historical monuments would all appropriately fall into this category. Even something less tangible, such as public safety, is a "common good" enjoyed, not principally by individuals, but by the community as a whole. Because there is a general tendency for individuals to neglect common property, it is necessary that some person or agency be assigned responsibility for its care. Because of its normative calling to do justice and to play a public integrating role within the political community, the government is almost certainly in the best position to assume this caring responsibility.

Second, government has a minimal responsibility to play a redistributive role within the body politic, recognizing that the market does not always treat every participant fairly. Once again, if government were to try to level out all economic differences, it could do so only at the cost of becoming totalitarian and interfering in minute areas of human life where it does not normatively belong. Justice does not require absolute equality. Nor should government put itself in the position of becoming the principal source of economic well-being for all its citizens. Yet government does bear some responsibility to ensure that citizens and communities have sufficient resources to fulfill their respective callings. It should do so in ways that are appropriate and specific to government, for example, by establishing and maintaining a supportive legal framework. Government may also be called upon to provide services that the private sector could not profitably provide on its own. Postal and rail passenger services are examples of these. Or short of owning postal and rail systems outright, government may instead redistribute resources to private providers. But it must do so in a way that is fair and equitable—consistent with its calling to do justice.

Third, government has a role to play in protecting the economically disadvantaged. The most obvious way of doing this is by vigilantly ensuring that the legal system, including the criminal and civil law courts, is not corrupted by those with greater wealth. It must guarantee access to the legal system to those who might not otherwise be able to afford such access using their own meager resources. However, even beyond this it may be appropriate for government to play a more direct role in alleviating poverty, provided it does not overextend itself by acting beyond its normative competence. Government does indeed bear some responsibility in addressing poverty, but it does not bear sole responsibility. Government may properly share responsibility with a wide variety of private social service agencies undertaking to alleviate poverty in ways appropriate to their own local communities. And of course such responsibility is also shared with the poor themselves.

As for attempts to solve poverty outright, these are fraught with difficulties typically rooted in reductionistic explanations for its persistence. Liberal individualists tend to assume that poverty is a byproduct of personal sloth and indolence. Thus they typically oppose any government policies intended to attack the problem directly. Nationalists often—though not invariably—assume that poverty is caused by oppression by an economically dominant foreign nation from which their own nation needs to be liberated. Socialists, as we have seen, hold that poverty is due to an inadequate economic arrangement rooted in private property known as capitalism. Social scientists working within any of several worldviews may isolate failed marriages, high rates of unwed pregnancies, increased mobility and fragmented communities as possible culprits. None of these approaches is wrong, except insofar as it sees one of these factors as an exhaustive explanation of poverty's continued existence. Any policy approach that views the poor as entirely to blame for their own plight and ignores socioeconomic and political factors risks doing injustice. Similarly any policy approach that portrays the poor as simply victims of external circumstances and deprives them of their status as responsible agents risks dehumanizing the poor and seeing them solely as objects of pity.[34] This too is injustice.

Indeed a plausible and effective solution to poverty is inescapably tied to a society that functions in a healthy way across the full range of human communities and activities. Spouses are faithful to each other. Parents love and care for their children. Schools educate young people. Employers and employees are loyal to each other and treat each other accordingly. Businesses are faithful stewards of their economic resources. Governments do public justice to the variety of people and communities within their respective jurisdictions. If there was a fundamental error in the United States' "war on poverty" in the 1960s, it lay in the assumption that poverty is basically an economic problem capable of being addressed by large-scale government expenditures applied with the intensity and dedication of a military campaign. The "war" metaphor tempted policymakers to ignore the complexities of the issue and to treat it as an easily identifiable enemy capable of being vanquished much as Germany and Japan had been defeated in the Second World War. Of course, the "enemy" turned out to be far more intractable than Johnson administration officials had imagined, primarily because they failed to take into account its full complexity and to appreciate the different levels of responsibility born by both individuals and communities for its perpetuation.

In short, socialism, while correctly noting some of the capacities of the state that were neglected by the other ideologies, is unable to recognize normative limits to the task of the state. Thus, even where socialists are in principle antistatist and antipolitical, the force of their ideological commitments impels them to become heavily statist in practice, despite their intentions. Clearly, the discerning Christian must look elsewhere to find a normative vision of politics and its distinctive place in God's world.

---

[34]The literature of poverty in the 1960s and 1970s, including Michael Harrington, *The Other America: Poverty in the United States*, rev. ed. (New York: Penguin, 1971), and William Ryan, *Blaming the Victim*, rev. ed. (New York: Vintage, 1976), is typical in ascribing the causes of poverty to external circumstances while playing down if not altogether denying cultural and personal factors. While such works properly alert us to the reality of the individual's social embeddedness—something often missing in classical liberal accounts—they risk depriving the poor of responsibility and thus of their humanity. It is not surprising that policies based on notions of universal victimization, with the associated sense of helplessness it breeds in the objects of such policies, have met with less than ringing success. See, e.g., Myron Magnet, *The Dream and the Nightmare: The Sixties' Legacy to the Underclass* (New York: William Morrow, 1993), for a contrasting perspective that emphasizes the impact of changing cultural mores on the persistence of poverty.

7

TRANSCENDING
THE IDEOLOGIES

Affirming Societal Pluriformity

Since virtually the beginning of the Christian era, believers have sought to think through and articulate an approach to the larger culture that is faithful to the imperatives of the gospel, yet recognizes that by God's grace there is much to be learned from that culture. Throughout this time Christians have been conscious of Christ's words that "no one can serve two masters; for either he will hate the one and love the other, or he will be devoted to the one and despise the other" (Mt 6:24). They have also been cognizant of the First Commandment: "You shall have no other gods before me" (Ex 20:3). Similarly and more recently, the Barmen Declaration of 1934, crafted in the early years of Hitler's rule in Germany, rejects "the false doctrine" that there are "areas of our life in which we would not belong to Jesus Christ, but to other lords" (2.2). Yet there is also a widespread recognition that "the heavens are telling the glory of God; and the firmament proclaims his handiwork" (Ps 19:1), and that this glory is potentially accessible to all people, as affirmed by Paul in Romans 1:19-20. Many Christians have recognized that God's truth is available through both general revelation in his creation and special revelation in Christ and in Scripture. Or, as the frequently cited maxim puts it, all truth is God's truth.

Étienne Gilson attempts to address this central dilemma of Christianity's relation to culture by isolating three spiritual families, each of which takes a different approach. The Tertullian/Augustinian family takes a position based on the primacy of faith. Tertullian himself asks, "What indeed has Athens to do with Jerusalem? What concord is there between the Academy and the Church? What between heretics and Christians?"[1] By contrast, the Averroist family approaches the issue on the basis of the primacy of reason, according to which "philosophy itself is absolute truth, as established by the demonstrations of pure reason," while revelation is "nothing but philosophical truth made acceptable to men whose imagination is stronger than their reason."[2] Between these apparent extremes Gilson posits a mediating position that takes seriously both reason and revelation and sees a fundamental harmony between them. Gilson's archetypical figure espousing such an approach is Thomas Aquinas and his scholastic successors.

In a fashion similar to Gilson, H. Richard Niebuhr expands the number of categories from three to five, which represent the typical ways in which Christians have historically related their faith in Christ to culture. "Christ against culture" is a position that includes not only Tertullian but also Tolstoy and the Anabaptists. This is the most antithetical of the positions and sees the believer as engaged in continual conflict with the world. "Christ of culture" represents the views of Abélard, Ritschl and Schleiermacher. This is the most accommodating of positions and indiscriminately sees the kingdom of God in all that is best in human culture—"best" being understood in terms of norms emerging out of the culture itself. In between these extreme positions are three more mediating positions that can be labeled synthesist, dualist and conversionist. These roughly correspond to the traditions of Thomism, Lutheranism and Calvinism respectively. While Gilson opts for a synthesist approach, Niebuhr's favored position is conversionist, based on Christ transforming culture.[3]

A comparable mode of analysis can be taken with respect to the ideologies we have explored thus far. Christians are inclined to take one of several approaches to them. To begin with, many Christians from the outset fail to understand that their faith has anything at all to say to these ideologies. For them politics is an intrinsically secular pursuit from which their religious beliefs can

---

[1] Tertullian, quoted in Étienne Gilson, *Reason and Revelation in the Middle Ages* (New York: Charles Scribner's Sons, 1938), p. 9.

[2] Ibid., pp. 46, 43.

[3] H. Richard Niebuhr, *Christ and Culture* (New York: Harper & Brothers, 1951). The danger of the conversionist model is that if it is divorced from a normative understanding of creation order, it can be harnessed to any of a number of ideological agendas. Simply affirming that Christ transforms culture does not in itself offer an alternative to the ideologies if we lack a sense of the grounding for such transformative activity.

be safely segregated. For many Christians, faith is fundamentally private and consists of their attending church, praying and being honest in their dealings with others. If Christianity touches on politics, it does so only obliquely by making the individual politician more virtuous as a person. This is not to be taken lightly, of course, and we can be grateful if more of our political leaders are upright people. But it does not address politics *as politics*, and it has no real implications for public policy. We shall at this point leave this approach behind, since I am persuaded that it represents a defective understanding of the faith and its all-encompassing claims.

This leaves us with two other basic approaches. The first, following Tertullian once again, takes an antithetical approach to the ideologies of the day, going so far as to recognize nothing good in them. Those taking this approach properly understand that belief in Jesus Christ entails an exclusive loyalty to him that cannot be shared with other such loyalties. The difficulty with this position is that, like the deficient position described immediately above, it often becomes simply apolitical or even antipolitical. It tends to identify politics wholly with Augustine's earthly city, and it too easily accepts Satan's spurious claim to have been given authority over the kingdoms of the world (Lk 4:6). If such antithetical Christians strive to follow Christ alone, to the exclusion of all else, they are in danger of turning over a huge portion of reality to the kingdom of darkness and barricading themselves within the supposedly secure walls of their church institutions. Fearing to be tainted by the likes of socialism or liberalism, they ignore the extent to which many of the policies pursued by socialists and liberals may be very largely good and thus worthy of support. To oppose economic regulatory policies simply because they have socialist roots ignores the fact that the contrary policy of allowing an unregulated market has classical liberal roots. In this context, the only way to avoid socialism and liberalism is to eschew policymaking responsibility altogether. Clearly this is not an acceptable alternative for the discerning Christian.

The opposite approach is to take sides, which even some professedly antithetical Christians may inadvertently end up doing in some fashion. Some Christians try to combine their faith with belief in one or more of the ideologies. Many Afrikaner Christians in South Africa saw themselves as part of a "Christian-national" movement in which the Afrikaner nation became the object of near cultic reverence. The apartheid policy was the destructive fruit of this Christian-nationalist ideology. More recently some Christians in Western Europe, North America and Latin America have freely appropriated for themselves the label "Christian socialist," arguing in their own favor that the scriptural commands to care for the poor and the oppressed require the implementation of a socialist agenda. In the United States, by contrast, many evangelical and fundamentalist Christians have argued just as convincingly that because the Bible supports private property, the most Christian political and economic system is some form of liberal capitalism. And Christians everywhere have styled themselves politically conservative, mostly because they have tended to identify fidelity to the historic faith with loyalty to tradition in general, as we pointed out in chapter three. A central problem with taking sides is that it leaves the body of Christ unnecessarily fragmented, bringing a "scattered voice," as James W. Skillen puts it, to the political arena.[4]

Moreover, and more fundamentally, taking sides is based on a flawed understanding of what the ideologies actually are. Rather than seeing them as intrinsically religious, those Christians choosing this approach prefer to believe that the ideologies are simply neutral accounts of reality, or perhaps systems or structures that can be shown to be more or less reasonable or serviceable to the attainment of laudable goals, and thus worthy of implementation. Hence Christians debating the respective virtues and vices of capitalism and socialism see them as competing economic and political arrangements capable of meeting such criteria as greater efficiency and productivity, more effective protection of human rights, and expanded economic and personal opportunities. None of these things is bad, of course. Each in its place is worth pursuing as a legitimate policy goal. However, a narrow concentration on such goals leads proponents to ignore the spiritual roots of capitalism and socialism, which inevitably impact the way such goals are chosen, articulated and pursued. Even if it could be conclusively proven that socialism is capable of living up to all its promises—particularly to eliminate poverty and to redistribute more equally the abundance of the world's goods–this would in no way vindicate its spiritual underpinnings, based as they are on a belief in human autonomy coupled with a collectivist social ontology. Moreover, because of socialism's false soteriology and distorted way of seeing the world, those promises would certainly be fulfilled at the price of other undoubted social goods, for example, the maintenance of freedom. Similarly, the strong historical connection between liberalism and the protection of human rights and freedoms cannot blind us to the incompatibility of

---

[4]See once again James W. Skillen, *The Scattered Voice: Christians at Odds in the Public Square* (Grand Rapids, Mich.: Zondervan, 1990).

liberalism's religious foundations with those of biblical Christianity.

Believers who fail to understand the dangers of this goal orientation permit themselves to *ontologize* and *instrumentalize* the ideologies. To ontologize means to ignore their spiritual, directional character and to ascribe to them a certain structural, creational status. Thus liberalism and socialism become part of the cosmic landscape and are deemed to be on a par with such phenomena as governments, political parties and legal systems. But there is a fundamental difference between these two sets of phenomena. The latter are institutions rooted in real creational possibilities that perform an important task in the larger human community. As such they are subject, like everything in God's creation, to legitimate use and abuse. There are good and bad governments, helpful and harmful political parties, just and unjust legal systems. By contrast, liberalism and socialism are manifestations of a larger humanistic worldview that attach themselves parasitically to these institutions, attempting both to interpret and to change them in accordance with the central tenets of these doctrines.

To instrumentalize these ideologies entails seeing them as means to any of a number of ends. This is clearly related to Goudzwaard's point, mentioned in chapter one, that ideologies are "goal-oriented" and subordinate principles and means to the achievement of these goals. But the Christian followers of one of these ideologies take this a step further and see the ideology itself as a means to an end. Thus the decision for capitalism or socialism, for liberalism or nationalism, for conservatism or some form of progressivism, is not a choice between alternative, though related, religious accounts of politics and its place in human life; it is a choice between arrangements of institutions and individuals that either are or are not conducive to the attainment of such ends as prosperity, greater equality, greater freedom and defense of the downtrodden. What is missing here is a comprehension of the inescapably religious, and indeed idolatrous, character of the several ideologies. Obviously another approach is needed.

A Biblical Christian Response

The key to approaching properly the ideologies lies in an initial effort to understand their appeal, and hence their legitimate creational underpinnings. It makes no sense to assume that they have got something wrong unless we have first grasped what they have got right. We shall illustrate this by drawing an analogy between the ideologies and a particularly ancient form of idolatry, namely, sun worship. History tells us that a number of ancient peoples worshiped the sun in some form. The Egyptians worshiped the sun god Ra, the Greeks worshiped Helios, and the Aztecs, Tonatiuh. To some extent such worship is comprehensible. The sun is the source of the brightest light accessible to us here on earth. Without it life would be impossible. The yearly cycles of sowing, germination, growth and harvest are dependent on the sun. Earth revolves around the sun, whose gravity keeps it in stable orbit. A decrease in exposure to the sun, that is, the shortening of the days, brings on winter with its frigid temperatures and relative absence of vegetation. People living in northern Canada and Scandinavia are known to suffer from seasonal depression during the long months of winter darkness.

In short, it is difficult to exaggerate the significance of the sun for our very existence. We rightly appreciate the sun and its innumerable benefits. However, *the sun remains a creature, brought into being and sustained by God himself.* In no way ought we to mistake creature for Creator. This is where sun-worshipers fall into error. As the author of the book of Wisdom[5] puts it:

> For all people who were ignorant of God were foolish by nature; and they were unable from the good things that are seen to know the one who exists, nor did they recognize the artisan while paying heed to his works. (Wis 13:1 NRSV)

What is true of the sun is true also of "fire or wind or swift air, or the circle of the stars, or turbulent water, or the luminaries of heaven," many or all of which the ancients assumed to be gods (13:2). For all their attractiveness, these earthly and heavenly phenomena are created by God and are thus subject to his sovereignty, just as we ourselves are. And like us, they have an important but limited place within the overall structure of the cosmos.

In similar fashion, when we are confronted by the ideologies, we must immediately assume that there is a creational good that their followers correctly esteem. Liberals have properly understood that there is a legitimate sphere of individual responsibility in which other individuals and communities ought not to interfere. Historically, liberals have alerted us to the importance of human rights before even Christians were willing to acknowledge this. Conservatives

---

[5]The book of Wisdom is considered canonical Scripture and part of the Old Testament by the Roman Catholic and Orthodox churches. Protestants place this book in the Apocrypha which, according to the Thirty-Nine Articles of Religion, "the Church doth read for example of life and instruction of manners; but yet doth not apply them to establish any doctrine" (article VI). Nevertheless, the passage quoted here unequivocally conforms to the understanding of idolatry found in the undisputed canon of Scripture.

too have rightly called our attention to the significance of tradition and the need to maintain historical continuity when it comes to contemplating and implementing change. Nationalists understand the value of communal solidarity among people sharing common citizenship or ethnicity. Ideological democrats have correctly seen the value of encouraging popular participation in the affairs of government. Socialists have alerted us to the role played by economic class in influencing the way we think and act politically. Moreover, they have also understood the extent to which political authorities are capable of redressing some of the more egregious economic disparities among the citizenry.

However, while they are undoubtedly based on a created good, each of the ideologies goes astray by effectively according it a status of ontological ultimacy and elevating it over the rest of creation. Consequently, whereas individual responsibility, historical continuity, communal solidarity, political participation and economic equity are valid emphases which ought to be mutually compatible, they are in fact driven apart into isolated spiritual corners by the followers of the several ideologies. Liberals, then, have difficulty accounting for legitimate national aspirations and are likely, because of the policy consequences of their individualism, to drive ethnic and other minorities into the arms of nationalist ideology. On the other hand, because many nationalists, once they attain political power, subordinate individual rights to communal aspirations, they inevitably strengthen the arguments of liberals through their abuse of human rights.

Because each of the ideologies is based on a distorted understanding of God's good creation, there are real consequences associated with the living out of such distortions. A deification of community—namely, the party—under Marxism-Leninism led to the horrors of totalitarianism in the Soviet Union and elsewhere. A deification of nation in Afrikaner nationalism led to the injustices of the apartheid policy in South Africa. And a deification of the individual in liberalism has led to the fragmentation of North American societies and the increasing breakdown of marriages, families and other basic communities. The otherwise laudable emphasis on human rights has degenerated in our Western constitutional democracies into what Mary Ann Glendon has perceptively called "rights talk,"[6] which is incapable of placing individual rights in the larger social context and understanding their relationship to mutual responsibilities. Furthermore, the failure of one god tends to lead to the embrace of a seemingly opposite

---

[6]Mary Ann Glendon, *Rights Talk: The Impoverishment of Political Discourse* (New York: Free Press, 1991).

god, which explains why Western polities seem doomed to vacillate between the omnicompetent interventionist state and the autonomous individual.

This distorted nature of the ideologies should indicate to us from the outset why Christians cannot simply join with one or more of these ideologies and champion their agendas. Yet neither can Christianity justifiably make itself into one more ideology. If an ideology is based on a deification of something within God's good creation, then Christians above all should be in a position to discern correctly the difference between idolatry and a more modest estimation of the things being idolized. In short, Christians understand that God is God and that individuals, nations, states, economic classes and so forth are radically dependent on him for their very existence. They are creatures and he is Creator.

A Christian Worldview: Creation, Fall and Redemption

Where then do we start in attempting to articulate a consistently Christian view of the world and of a nonideological understanding of the place of politics within it? Many political theorists, ranging from Plato to Augustine to Hobbes to Arendt, begin their political theories by articulating a philosophical anthropology or view of humanity. Given that politics is a human activity, it would seem to make sense to explore the nature of the human person who undertakes this significant enterprise. Yet the human person is part of a larger context that, the Christian confesses, is nothing less than God's creation. Thus it seems best to begin, not with anthropology but with cosmology or, more properly, basic worldview. This worldview is rooted in the redemptive-historical narrative found in Scripture.

"Our world belongs to God," as a recent publication by a North American church body puts it.[7] Christians believe that God is sovereign, an affirmation particularly emphasized by heirs of the Calvinist Reformation but acknowledged by all other Christians as well. This sovereignty has implications for the whole of our life in the present world. Christianity is certainly a matter of our becoming right with God as individuals. Or, perhaps more accurately, God makes us right with him. This is something the various forms of pietism have correctly emphasized, including those represented by Count Nikolaus von Zinzendorf and the Wesleys. It is also a matter of God calling into being a new, redeemed community of the faithful, as Anabaptists and many free church people have properly noted. But it is more than this. God has re-

---

[7] *Our World Belongs to God: A Contemporary Testimony* (Grand Rapids, Mich.: CRC Publications, 1986).

deemed the whole person, not just her so-called moral and spiritual life. The life of grateful obedience to God's word that follows redemption in Jesus Christ and the renewal of the Holy Spirit is not exhausted by praying daily, reading Scripture or attending church on a weekly basis, though it includes at least these. The cosmic scope of redemption means that the whole of life has been redeemed, including family life, work life, play life, academic life and political life. Since the entire cosmos is the arena for the ongoing battle between the spirits of belief and unbelief, this means we have a God-given responsibility to discern the spirits within each of these realms. That is why understanding the ideologies is so important.

It has often been said that Christians are so heavenly minded as to be of no earthly good. This is a caricature of course, and one to which we should not too easily lend credence. At the same time, it must be conceded that many Christians in a variety of traditions often seem to behave in such a way as to vindicate this charge. Every time a believer says that, say, religion and politics do not mix or that we should concentrate on saving souls and leave the affairs of the world alone, she is implicitly denying the cosmic scope of Christ's redemption and thereby diminishing God's sovereignty. Every time a follower of Jesus Christ forsakes a so-called secular occupation and claims an intention to go into "full-time Christian service," she is in effect relegating a huge portion of the total fabric of human life to something or someone other than the Savior of the world. For the biblically astute Christian, however, there are no "sacred" and "secular" occupations, only obedient and disobedient ones. The obedient farmer or carpenter is as much in full-time Christian service as the pastor or missionary. The same can be said of the civil magistrate, whose calling Calvin esteemed in the highest of terms.[8]

This conviction of the unity of life under God's sovereignty implies a high view of creation and the orderly world it has brought into being. The very first verse of the Bible tells us that God created the heavens and the earth (Gen 1:1). As succeeding verses reveal the progressive unfolding of creation, we are further told that it is good (Gen 1:4, 10, 12, 18, 21, 25, 31). Because God is himself good and the origin of all goodness (Mk 10:18; Lk 18:19), it stands to reason that what he has created is also good. But creation is not limited to the so-called natural world of mountain, soil, sea, plants and animals. In Genesis we read that on the sixth day God created man in his own image (Gen

---

[8]John Calvin *Institutes of the Christian Religion* 4.20.

1:26-27). For centuries Christians and Jews have been debating what this "image" could possibly mean, without coming to any definitive conclusion. At the very least, it seems to imply that man is, of all God's creatures, uniquely capable of responding to his call. God's initial and most basic call is to "Be fruitful and multiply, and fill the earth and subdue it" (Gen 1:28). This is commonly known as the "cultural mandate." Humans are *cultural* beings who, in the normal course of living, *cultivate* or develop the world around them. Normatively speaking, they do so, not haphazardly, but in an orderly way, as intended by God. In other words, humanity's culture-shaping activities are in accordance with God's creative intention. As human beings go about living their lives in God's world, they continually discover the potentialities he has built into his creation. These include not only agriculture and industry, which are most immediately associated with putting bread on the table, but also the various arts and sciences that distinguish humans from the other creatures of the earth. As this human cultural activity progresses, the various fields of activity take on their own unique characters within distinct institutional contexts. This is the foundation for the norm of *societal differentiation*, to be explored further below.[9] Human culture includes politics; hence politics is a part of creation.

Yet if the Bible affirms creation as good, it also acknowledges that it is fallen into sin (Gen 3). Calvinists often speak of this in terms of *total depravity*, a term often subject to misunderstanding. It does not mean that everything we human beings do is entirely sinful, but that all of our activities, however good in their motivations and effects, are tainted by sin's destructive power. The fall, therefore, is cosmic in scope. No part of creation is spared its influence. Individual human beings are fallen, as virtually all Christians recognize. This applies to the whole person including, as the scholastic philosophers would put it, both will and reason. What is less obvious, and indeed is often overlooked by many, is that human cultural activity is fallen too. This includes the visual arts, literature, music, the natural sciences and the entire array of social and political institutions. When human beings rebelled against God in

---

[9]For more on the cultural mandate see Albert M. Wolters, "The Foundational Command: 'Subdue the Earth!'" in *Year of Jubilee, Cultural Mandate, Worldview* (Potchefstroom, South Africa: Institute for Reformational Studies, 1999), pp. 27-34; H. Henry Meeter, *The Basic Ideas of Calvinism*, 6th ed., rev. Paul Marshall (Grand Rapids, Mich.: Baker, 1990), pp. 57-67; Henry R. Van Til, *The Calvinistic Concept of Culture* (Grand Rapids, Mich.: Baker, 2001); and Herman Bavinck, *Our Reasonable Faith: A Survey of Christian Doctrine* (Grand Rapids, Mich.: Baker, 1977), pp. 184-220.

the garden, they took their culture with them, as implied in the biblical account of Cain's descendants (Gen 4:17-24).

But happily, the story does not end with the fall. It ends with redemption in Jesus Christ and the renewal of the Holy Spirit. Just as creation and fall are cosmic in scope, so also is redemption. But not all Christian traditions have been quick to draw out the full implications of this affirmation. The apostle Paul tells us in Romans that "the whole creation has been groaning in travail" (8:22), awaiting redemption in Jesus Christ, and that "the creation itself will be set free from its bondage to decay and obtain the glorious liberty of the children of God" (8:21). This means, in the memorable phrase of Albert M. Wolters, that redemption is nothing less than "creation regained."[10] If the good creation of God was disrupted and distorted by the fall into sin, Christ's redemption restores creation to its original purpose. This implies that not only individual persons can be redeemed, but so, in principle, can the whole range of human cultural activities listed above. Once again, this includes political life.

If we in any way narrow the scope of one of the stages in this redemptive narrative or alter the relationship of one to the other, we come up with something other than biblical Christianity. If, for example, we embrace the currently accepted dichotomy between nature and culture and identify the biblical creation with the former only, we have effectively exempted a huge chunk of human life from the normative patterns implicit in the creation order. This can lead to a kind of antinomianism based on the assumption that culture-shaping activities are in some fashion autonomous. Or in Kantian fashion, we might posit a dichotomy between a deterministic phenomenal world and a noumenal world where the will of the self-governing person is sovereign. If, on the other hand, we narrow the scope of the fall, we may effectively imply that some areas of life are good in themselves and do not stand in need of redemption. It may cause us to assume, for example, that only individual human beings are sinful, but not the social and political structures they have formed.

Alternatively, if we view the fall as having destroyed or canceled altogether the goodness of creation, then we may judge that there is little or nothing in creation worth saving. We may see such things as governments, chambers of commerce, corporations, labor unions and universities as autonomous powers in their own right with which, because they are irremediable, we must at least live in tension

---

[10]Albert M. Wolters, *Creation Regained* (Grand Rapids, Mich.: Eerdmans, 1985).

or perhaps even actively oppose in some sense.[11] Christians taking this approach properly recognize the power of sin and retain a vivid sense of humanity's total depravity. But for them so little of God's good creation shines through that they run the risk of conceding a large portion of life to the opposition. More significantly, they effectively narrow the scope of redemption and fundamentally alter its relationship to both sin and creation. If so, Christians may be left with little else than to try to save as many people as possible out of a doomed cosmos and, while waiting for the end, perhaps to gather true believers into a remnant band and ignore the broader cultural mandate. The irony, of course, is that human beings continue to shape culture, even when they have supposedly withdrawn from it. We are inescapably part of creation, even if we attempt to flee it.

Redemption, then, does not cancel creation or add something essentially different to it. It does not add monastic life and religious orders to everyday life. Nor does it replace or supplement ordinary labor with prayer. It does not append evangelism or the priesthood to carpentry or the dance. Nor does it supplant the cultural mandate with the "Great Commission" (Mt 28:18-20). It does not give "religious" lyrics to secular tunes. Nor does it add the "supernatural" theological virtues (faith, hope and charity) to the ostensibly "natural" cardinal virtues (prudence, justice, courage and temperance). What redemption does do is to bring everyday life, including labor, leisure and liturgy, into conformity with its intended, created purpose, even as it promises a further ultimate fulfillment at Christ's return. A physician brings healing to the body so it may function in a whole, healthy manner. In the gospels Jesus likens himself to a physician (Mt 9:12). Yet this Physician brings healing not to disembodied Platonic souls but to the whole creation. Once again, because political life is part of creation, it too stands under God's redemption in Jesus Christ. We cannot, therefore, be content to consign it either to a neutral, "secular" realm or to the sovereignty of the prince of this world. Rather, we must claim it for Jesus Christ. This is basically what a biblically Christian worldview entails.

---

[11]See, e.g., the argument of John Howard Yoder, *The Politics of Jesus: vicit Agnus noster*, 2nd ed. (Grand Rapids, Mich.: Eerdmans, 1994), pp. 134-61, who derives his interpretation from Hendrikus Berkhof, *Christ and the Powers* (Scottdale, Penn.: Herald, 1962); and ultimately from Karl Barth, "Church and State," in *Community, State, and Church: Three Essays* (Garden City, N.Y.: Doubleday, 1960), pp. 101-48. It has been worked out most systematically by Walter Wink in his "powers" trilogy: *Naming the Powers: The Language of Power in the New Testament* (Philadelphia: Fortress, 1984); *Unmasking the Powers: The Invisible Forces That Determine Human Existence* (Philadelphia: Fortress, 1986); and *Engaging the Powers: Discernment and Resistance in a World of Domination* (Minneapolis: Augsburg Fortress, 1992). Surprisingly, even Lesslie Newbigin picks up this argument in his *The Gospel in a Pluralist Society* (Grand Rapids, Mich.: Eerdmans, 1989), pp. 198-210, drawing on Wink's first two volumes.

In the meantime, of course, we look to a further fulfillment of creation at Christ's return, living in such a way as to recognize that we are in between the times. Christ has come once to inaugurate his kingdom, of which we are citizens and agents. We undertake all of our cultural activities, including politics, confident that God is pleased to use them for his glory and for the larger purposes of his kingdom. But we further confess that Christ will return as promised, not to cancel or supersede his creation, as some might think, but to bring it to its final fulfillment—something to which our own efforts point but cannot themselves bring about.[12]

Creation Order: Misconceptions Dispelled

An emphasis on creation as a normative order is foundational for understanding how we, as God's image bearing creatures, are to live our lives in the world, including our political lives. Because God is faithful to his creation, even in the midst of our *un*faithfulness, he has not left us at sea with respect to his will. The writer of Psalm 119 repeatedly confesses his delight in obeying the law of God: "Your hands have made and fashioned me; give me understanding that I may learn your commandments" (v. 73 NRSV). In so doing, he acknowledges his utter dependence on the God who has made him and who desires him to live accordingly. God's law is not an arbitrary imposition on created human life; it is a reiteration of this created order, a bidding of the responsible creature to live in conformity with its normative contours.

In this written word we are commanded by God to be faithful to our spouses and to keep the sabbath, among other things. Some may deem such precepts the capricious rulings of an omnipotent killjoy, determined to spoil whatever spontaneity or pleasure is to be found in life. Yet life is infinitely richer and more fulfilling when we remain true to our husbands and wives. Failure to do so can only have a deleterious effect on ourselves, our spouses and our children. Similarly, failure to put aside our work and to take regular periods of rest will lead to exhaustion and a probable shortening of our years on earth. In other

---

[12]On the other hand, some Christians have argued that our own efforts do indeed usher in the kingdom and that an ultimate fulfillment worked at Christ's return is an outmoded or unnecessary idea. See, e.g., Walter Rauschenbusch, *A Theology for the Social Gospel* (1917; reprint, Nashville: Abingdon, 1961), which argues inter alia that an "eschatology which is expressed in terms of historic development has no final consummation. Its consummations are always the basis for further development. The Kingdom of God is always coming, but we can never say 'Lo here'" (p. 227). See once again Oliver O'Donovan's critique of historicist approaches to eschatology in *Resurrection and Moral Order: An Outline for Evangelical Ethics* (Grand Rapids, Mich.: Eerdmans, 1986), esp. pp. 53-75.

words, far from being oppressive intrusions on it, the written precepts of Scripture reinforce the created order and thereby make for a better life.

Yet not all Christians are prepared to accept this emphasis on a normative creation order, despite its validity being admitted in some form by the vast majority of Christian philosophers and theologians up until some two centuries ago. There are at least five reasons for this.

First, during the nineteenth century, the influence of historicism alerted many to the variability of human cultures from time to time and from place to place. While it was once assumed by most European Christians that the specific shape of their own social order was God-given, historicism correctly pointed to the dynamic character of society and to the fact of its being conditioned by culturally specific factors. After this discovery it became impossible not to view as misguided the efforts of Christian missionaries to impose the peculiarities of Western clothing on, say, the Pacific islanders. Accordingly, we are no longer likely to speak of "civilization" as if it were a unified phenomenon spreading its assumed virtues around the globe and assimilating local peoples into its project. Instead we now properly speak of "civilizations" in the plural.[13] What historicism failed to understand, however, is that human culture-forming activity is itself subject to norms that cannot be reduced to or derived from the historical process. For our purposes here, for example, a normative conception of politics requires that political authority do justice to everyone under its jurisdiction. Different legal systems legitimately work out this norm in different ways related to the peculiar characteristics of the underlying political culture, but such differences can in no way abrogate the overarching mandate to do justice, which holds for all human beings.

Related to this is a second point. At least some of the misgivings expressed toward a normative creation order are due to the assumption that it is too static and is thus unsupportive of human freedom. An emphasis on law would seem conducive to legalism, that is, to a tendency to compress the legitimate plurality of human communities and individuals into fairly narrow confines into which they are expected to fit. Thus all families everywhere are supposedly bound to conform to the pattern of the mid-twentieth-century North American suburban nuclear family. Or all legal systems must prescribe capital punishment for murder and twenty years imprisonment for larceny. Or all political systems must

---

[13]See, e.g., the argument of Samuel P. Huntington in *The Clash of Civilizations and the Remaking of World Order* (New York: Simon & Schuster, 1996). Huntington's argument is itself by no means historicist, though it is difficult to imagine it being made prior to the rise of historicism.

be representative democracies prescribing a division of powers and an en-
trenched written constitution. But such judgments misconstrue what is meant
by a normative creation order, which is not to be identified with any specific
human attempt to respond to it and to realize it in concrete form. That political
communities are subject to the norm of justice does not necessarily entail the
adoption of a democratic form of government, especially if a people and culture
are ill-suited to it. The working out of forms of government in specific settings
is thus a task for human creativity and freedom coupled with a large measure of
wisdom, discernment and an understanding of context.

Moreover, the very possibility of free human action and innovation is anchored in the normative creation order. The capacity to choose in contingent circumstances presupposes an orderly framework within which such
choices take place. An understanding of creation enables one to draw out its
dynamic possibilities as well as to understand its limits. Our freedom is therefore not infinite freedom, yet *it is genuine freedom* all the same. I can decide
between the options of driving to Toronto and driving to Chicago. But the
possibility of driving to Paris or Prague is not available to me for what should
be obvious reasons. Similarly, I can decide to walk to the corner store or even
to my place of work, provided the weather is warm enough and I give myself
enough time. But I cannot walk to Toronto or Chicago, which lies beyond
my physical capabilities. My choice to marry a particular woman was a free
choice, which nevertheless presupposed a normative framework undergirding and setting conditions on marriage itself, including the lifelong obligation to love and remain faithful to that one woman. I could have chosen not
to marry at all of course, but once I had ruled out that possibility, a third
alternative was not available. Entering marriage is not the same as accepting
employment or taking out citizenship. In short, this choice was exercised
within an orderly, normative context that conditioned my choice and was
ultimately not subject to it.

A third reason for discounting a normative creation order lies in the longstanding propensity to identify creation with nature, as mentioned above. The
natural order, as studied by such disciplines as physics, chemistry and biology, is
subject to laws that operate automatically and involve no human responsibility
for their implementation. The laws of gravity, thermodynamics, nuclear fission
and photosynthesis continue to function quite irrespective of our input or lack
thereof. Nonhuman animals behave according to instinct and do not act responsibly as human beings do. On the other hand, the logical law of noncon-

tradiction is quite capable of being violated, as, for example, when one asserts that the sun shines at night or that the king of Sweden is capable of walking backward and forward at the same time. Similarly, real political communities frequently commit injustices against their own and other countries' citizens. Spouses sometimes fail to live up to the norm of marital fidelity as fully as they ought. And that is the point: the laws of logic, jurisprudence and marriage are precisely *norms* which human subjects are responsible to implement but which are also capable of being violated in numerous, though limited, ways. Creation certainly includes the natural order, but it is much more extensive than this, encompassing human social and cultural life as well.

Quite apart from the influence of historicism, the concern to defend human freedom and the identification of creation with nature, there is a fourth reason why many Christians reject the notion of a normative creation order. This is because it has often been used to maintain support for oppressive social and economic systems or even to justify a totalitarian system. During the apartheid era, many South African Christians justified this policy on the grounds that God had ordained the races to stay apart and thus to refrain from intermingling. Interracial marriage was consequently judged to be a violation of God's law for his creation, which supposedly demanded that distinct peoples remain distinct. That this was a misuse of the notion of creation order is by now admitted by all but a small minority of Afrikaners. Far from facilitating ethnic self-determination, or "plural development" as its proponents euphemistically styled it, apartheid turned out to be a policy of oppression by white South Africans of their nonwhite fellow citizens.

Swiss theologian Karl Barth (1886-1968), arguably the most influential Protestant theologian of the twentieth century, strongly disavowed any notion of a normative creation order. This was in part due to his fear of the resurgence of a scholastic natural theology that might detract from the centrality of Jesus Christ.[14] Even political ethics for Barth must ultimately be christological.[15] Moreover, in contrast to the likes of Emil Brunner (1889-1966), who defends a conception of human life in community based on "the orders,"[16] Barth ar-

---

[14]Karl Barth's major discussion of creation can be found in his *Church Dogmatics* 3, *The Doctrine of Creation,* part 4, ed. G. W. Bromiley and T. F. Torrance (Edinburgh: T & T Clark, 1961).

[15]Barth, "Church and State," pp. 101-48.

[16]See Emil Brunner, *The Divine Imperative,* trans. Olive Wyon (Philadelphia: Westminster Press, 1947), esp. pp. 140-51; and *Justice and the Social Order,* trans. Mary Hottinger (New York: Harper & Brothers, 1945), esp. pp. 85-95; and Barth's response and critique in *Church Dogmatics* 3/4, pp. 19-23.

gues that such reasoning leads inevitably to the distortions characteristic of
Nazism. It is true that in the 1930s many German Lutheran theologians appealed to creation ordinances to support the Nazi regime. As two observers
have recently noted, "Since that time every appeal to ordinances carries a bad
odor."[17] That this misuse of the notion of creation order should prompt such
a reaction is understandable, and Barth's rejection has been carried into various
forms of liberation theology as well as into the radical Anabaptist revival of the
past three decades.[18]

But the fact that something has been abused in the past does not necessarily rule out its legitimate use: *Abusus non tollit usum*, as the old proverb perceptively puts it. Everything God has made is capable of being abused. If we
were to repudiate everything subject to abuse, we should have to flee life itself. Few would wish to abrogate human freedom simply because it often becomes license. The task of the Christian, I would argue, is to try to recover
created good from its fallen condition, understanding once again that redemption in Jesus Christ is cosmic in scope. To rid ourselves of creation order
would be to jettison any possibility of living a coherent, obedient life in accordance with such norms as fidelity, justice, economic stewardship, social
courtesy, logical consistency and so forth, all of which would simply become
either little more than subjective preferences on the part of those claiming to
follow them or the arbitrary precepts of a divine or human will. Furthermore,
we should be prevented from even going so far as to judge whether a particular political or social arrangement is or is not oppressive, *because those very
categories presuppose a normative framework.*

This brings us to the fifth and most formidable objection to the notion of
creation order, which is that, because of sin, we cannot know what it is. As

---

[17]A. van Egmond and C. van der Kooi, "The Appeal to Creation Ordinances: A Changing Tide," in
  God's Order for Creation (Potchefstroom, South Africa: Institute for Reformational Studies, 1994),
  p. 21.
[18]See, for example, Gustavo Gutiérrez, *A Theology of Liberation* (Maryknoll, N.Y.: Orbis, 1973), esp. pp.
  172-73. The works of John Howard Yoder (1927-1997), especially *Politics of Jesus* and *The Original Revolution* (Scottdale, Penn.: Herald, 1971); Jim Wallis, *The Call to Conversion* (New York: Harper & Row,
  1981), and *The Soul of Politics: A Practical and Prophetic Vision for Change* (Maryknoll, N.Y.: Orbis, 1994);
  and Vernard Eller, *Christian Anarchy: Jesus' Primacy over the Powers* (Grand Rapids, Mich.: Eerdmans,
  1987), all reflect the influence of Barth. Yoder was a student of Barth's at University of Basel and has
  in turn been an influence on Wallis, one of the founding leaders of the Sojourners Community in
  Washington, D.C., and one of the editors of *Sojourners* magazine. Barth was also an influence on the
  prolific late social philosopher Jacques Ellul, who was another influence on the Sojourners community.
  See Ellul, *Perspectives on Our Age: Jacques Ellul Speaks on His Life and Work* (New York: Seabury, 1981),
  pp. 17-18.

Yoder puts it, "We have no access to the good creation of God."[19] In Plato's *Republic,* Thrasymachus argues that justice is nothing more than the advantage of the stronger. Thomas Hobbes avers that, because just and unjust are simply names attached to subjective human preferences, a sovereign will is needed to make an authoritative determination of the just. Once this sovereign authority is set in place, justice henceforth consists of obeying its laws, whether or not we as individuals believe they are doing justice to us. Even good and evil are determined by the sovereign, solely because he possesses the power to make this determination stick. We shall explore justice at some length in chapter nine. At this point it is enough to note that, given the disagreements over them, many people doubt the possibility of knowing such universally valid norms as those named above. How indeed is it possible to know the contours of the creation order?

This issue is, of course, complicated by the reality of human sin, which, as we have seen, has affected the whole of creation. If there are norms in creation, how do we distinguish these norms from their sinful realization in our human societies? How, further, can we come to know these norms, given that our own epistemic faculties are tainted by sin? These are not easy questions to answer and we are wise not to come to any quick solutions that turn out not to be solutions at all. At the very least it is inadequate to concoct well-intended slogans or shortcuts that fail to do full justice to the complexities at issue. Though an entire book could be devoted to this question, I shall at this point briefly lay out what I believe to be a possible way out of the dilemma.

To begin with, even when clouds obscure the sun, we can nevertheless distinguish night from day. In other words, despite the undoubted impact of sin, virtually every human society has some intuitive understanding of the norms delineated above, though they may be effected in different ways within each. In North America and many European countries it is customary to shake hands as a friendly gesture upon meeting someone. In some Asian countries people bow to each other. In some Mediterranean countries people embrace and kiss each other on both cheeks. These are simply different ways of giving effect to the creational norm of social courtesy. It may not be appropriate to shake the hands of a Japanese gentleman in his own country, but it is always appropriate to treat another person with respect, whatever particular customs have developed from this norm. In no system of

---

[19]Yoder, *Politics of Jesus,* p. 141. See also Barth *Church Dogmatics* 3/4, p. 20.

social mores is rudeness likely to be a virtue, whether this be among the Fulani of West Africa or among the English aristocracy. Similarly, in no country is murder ever sanctioned, though different legal systems may draw the line between murder and, say, killing in self-defense somewhat differently. On the basis of thoughtful observation of a number of cultures over a long period of time, it is possible, in some manner, to discern the norms underlying their specific usages.

But one must take care because the effects of sin may prevent us from seeing these norms, or they might even prompt us to mistake distortions for the norms themselves. This is where Scripture, coupled with a generous measure of spiritual discernment, plays a crucial role. Because of the obscuring impact of sin, we require a divinely inspired written testimony to creation, or what the psalmist calls "a lamp to my feet and a light to my path" (Ps 119:105). Once more, God has not left us in the dark as to his will for our life in his world. As Calvin puts it, Scripture constitutes the spectacles through which we look to see the world with greater clarity.[20] Other Christians have spoken of general and special revelation, the latter of which illuminates the former. The Belgic Confession speaks of creation and the written Word of God as the two books lying open before us (article 2). Reformed Christians confess that these two revelations reinforce and are continuous with each other. Scripture does not hand down to us arbitrary commands disconnected from creation. Rather, when God tells us in Scripture that we are to "do justice, and to love kindness, and to walk humbly with [our] God" (Mic 6:8), he is asking us to do no more and no less than to live as we are created to live.

How is this relevant to our discussion of ideologies? In one way or another the ideologies deny this normative creation order, tying their transformative agendas to their own subjective dreams and aspirations. For them the cosmos is simply a chaotic mass on which human beings impose their own order autonomously. Furthermore, most in some fashion see something creational as the origin of evil and something else as the source of salvation. The irony is that, unable to see beyond its horizons, the followers of the ideologies condemn themselves both to *fleeing* creation and to *deifying* it. Others properly see creation order, or at least they catch glimpses of it, but they misconstrue its origin, attributing it to something within creation itself. Yet all of the ideologies of necessity have creational underpinnings which condition and limit the ways in

---

[20]John Calvin *Institutes* 1.6.1.

which they live out their basic ideas. These provide an anchor in reality for the ideologies and generally keep them from going too far astray, as we already noted in the first chapter.[21]

Discerning the Spirits: Pluralisms and Pluriformity

In a book such as this there is always the danger of dealing with ideologies as if they were little more than Platonic forms, located in some far-off, unreachable realm in the heavens. At this point one can imagine the frustrated reader asking the author: "What now? How is all this going to help me when it comes time, say, to vote in an election?" To begin with, a Christian approach to politics cannot immediately take the form of a comprehensive program for building a new social order, as disappointing as that might seem to some, although it certainly has profound policy implications, as we shall see. Marx wrote that the philosophers up to his time had merely interpreted the world, while the point for him was to change it.[22] Marx's musings notwithstanding, the desire for change, however appropriate, must be anchored in an initial and foundational interpretation of the world. Otherwise proposals for change become little more than utopian dreams disconnected from a solid understanding of the world *as it is*. To be sure, everyone is dissatisfied with the world in some respects and most would like to make it a better place. Yet without such a proper understanding, would-be transformers of the world are likely to believe that their own recipes for a new social order correspond to the real world without actually troubling themselves to check their own proposals against this reality. Kant famously argued that one cannot simply derive "ought" statements from "is" statements.

---

[21]For those interested in exploring further the issues raised in this section, an excellent discussion of what is meant by creation order can be found in Wolters, *Creation Regained*. See also the articles by Paul G. Schrotenboer, A. Trost, Gordon J. Spykman, Wolters and Craig G. Bartholomew in *God's Order for Creation*. The following passage by Spykman is worth quoting in full:

> Creation . . . was and is and remains God's first and foremost revelation. It is primordial reality. God did not create junk, and being jealous of his handiwork, He does not discard what He creates. The orders of creation are not static, but they are stable. With dynamic constancy, they serve as the normal context and abiding habitat for our life together in God's world. The plan of salvation itself is made to fit the patterns of creation. Redemption *matches* creation. The redirect[ing] power of spiritual renewal is geared to the very structures of creation. It does not bypass the orders of creation, or abandon them, least of all destroy them, but restores them. Thus, the creation order continues to hold for the way we order our lives within the creation. Indeed, its impinging power is so strong that disorder itself is discernible only in relation to the established order. The holding and healing power of this God-given order exerts a corrective pressure even in the most obstinate cases of disorder. (p. 39)

[22]Karl Marx, *Theses on Feuerbach* (1845), in *Basic Writings on Politics and Philosophy*, ed. Lewis S. Feuer (New York: Anchor/Doubleday, 1959), p. 245.

That is, one cannot look at the way things are and argue therefore that this is how things should be. On the other hand, if, like Kant, one accepts too easy a dichotomy between "is" and "ought," between the phenomenal and the noumenal, between fact and value, then one is left with an autonomous ethic disconnected from reality that, like the various ideologies in this study, has tremendous potential for harm. Even Marx, with all his fulminating against the philosophers of the past, nevertheless rooted his revolutionary ideas in a view of the world as fundamentally, and reductively, productive and economic.

So where does a biblically Christian worldview take us? If, as I have been arguing, the various ideologies are rooted in an idolatrous religion, then what does a nonidolatrous approach to society and politics look like? To begin with, it properly and unquestionably acknowledges the sovereignty of God over the whole of life. Like liberalism, it sees a legitimate place for individual rights and freedoms while reminding us that the individual is not sovereign. Like conservatism, it calls us to recognize the proper place of tradition and repudiates those who facilely believe we can do without it. Yet unlike conservatism, it cannot countenance a simple and uncritical deferral to tradition but recognizes that traditions are human formations, subject, like all other human works, to the taint of sin. Like both nationalism and the democratic creed, it recognizes the rightful place of human community, however defined, but rejects all efforts at positing such community as an all-encompassing focus of loyalty from which other loyalties, to the extent they are permitted, are merely derivative. Similarly, a nonidolatrous political perspective recognizes the legitimate though limited capacity of government to effect economic equity, but it eschews socialist expectations of an eschatological consummation engendered by a salvific working class.

This suggests that the one nonidolatrous alternative left is a kind of *pluralism* that spurns the reductive monisms of the ideologies. Indeed, if God is sovereign, then any attempt to locate an earthly sovereign, that is, a person or community invested with final authority in all walks of life, is rooted in nothing less than a false religion. What, then, is meant by *pluralism* as we use it here? To answer this question it is necessary, first, to distinguish among at least three kinds of pluralism, two of which are only tangentially related to our discussion.

First, it is often said that we live in a pluralistic society. This truism is meant to describe the empirical reality of different beliefs and convictions existing within a given territorial (and possibly political) community. We have seen something of this diversity in the present study as we examined the various visions that citizens bring to the political realm. People simply believe different

things about politics, and indeed about life in general. Even apart from the secular religion underpinning the various ideologies, many of our fellow citizens
are Christians, others are Jews, Muslims, agnostics and so forth. Within the
Christian community (taken broadly) we find Roman Catholics, Presbyterians,
Anglicans, Lutherans, Baptists and many others. Richard Mouw and Sander
Griffioen call this pluralism *spiritual* or *directional diversity.*[23] Long gone, we are
told, is the era when it was assumed that political peace depended on internal
religious uniformity within a single polity. In their own ways, the various ideologies have tried to come to grips with this diversity for the sake of enabling
citizens to live together in peace. Ironically, however, their proponents have
succeeded only in adding so many more competing worldviews to the mix,
while claiming for each a certain ultimacy on the unwarranted assumption of
it being best positioned to keep the peace among all the others. Yet directional
diversity now encompasses, not only the competing truth claims of the several
Christian denominations, but also the rival claims of liberals, socialists, nationalists and others in the public square.

Is this directional diversity a good thing? On one level, most people would
have to say that, no, it is not, even if they deem some degree of tolerance politically necessary. As Lesslie Newbigin affirms, if the church must accept plurality as fact, it certainly cannot embrace plural*ism* as creed.[24] Christians in the
mainstream of their tradition believe that salvation is found in Jesus Christ alone
and that God has reconciled the world through the shed blood of his Son on
the cross, his subsequent resurrection and future return. Similarly believing
Jews confess that God has chosen them to be his special people and has given
them the *Torah* (law), the *Nevi'im* (prophets) and the *Kethuvim* (writings) as his
will for their lives, both as individuals and in community. Muslims believe they
are saved by following the five pillars of Islam, including the *shahada* (testimony
of faith), *salat* (five-times-daily prayer), *zakat* (alms-giving), *sawm* (fasting), and
the *Hajj* (pilgrimage to Mecca). Adherents of all three religions believe they
have a duty to testify to outsiders in behalf of revealed truth and even, to some
extent, to bring them into the fold as converts. In this respect, the followers of
all religions believe that a large share of their task on earth is to bring as many
as possible of its inhabitants into a saving knowledge of this truth.

---

[23]Richard J. Mouw and Sander Griffioen, *Pluralisms and Horizons: An Essay in Christian Public Philosophy*
(Grand Rapids, Mich.: Eerdmans, 1993), pp. 87-109.
[24]Lesslie Newbigin, *Foolishness to the Greeks: The Gospel and Western Culture* (Grand Rapids, Mich.: Eerdmans, 1986), p. 115; *Gospel in a Pluralist Society,* p 244.

Lest one think, however, that such proselytizing zeal is peculiar to the traditional religions, in the modern era the followers of the various ideologies, many of whom would explicitly repudiate the supposed intolerance of the traditionally religious, nevertheless believe the world would be a better place if all people were, say, liberals, socialists, conservatives or nationalists. True, conservatives may have to tolerate socialists as parliamentary colleagues, but in their heart of hearts they would prefer them to see the error of their ways and come to their senses. Socialists return the favor by wishing the same on their conservative opponents. Thus even secular ideologues regret directional diversity, even if they are forced to accept it for purposes of peaceful coexistence. But everyone hopes that in the midst of such fundamental disagreements, persuasion will accomplish the task of eliminating or at least diminishing this type of diversity, and everyone, at least nominally, further prefers to avoid the use of coercive means. Where one group, for example, the various pro-Moscow communist parties in the post-Second World War era, refuses to give up on coercion, this creates a political dilemma that may be addressed by stripping it of legitimate political status.

Thus the *political* question is not so much whether directional diversity is a good thing, as how we might go about conciliating that diversity given its empirical reality. This is a question of justice—not of final justice, to be sure, but of a penultimate justice well short of God's complete justice to be realized on the Last Day. Such penultimate justice means that even if we disagree with others on rather basic, ultimate issues concerning the nature of the world, our place within it, and our responsibility to God and to others, we are obligated to protect their freedom to believe and to a large extent, to live out their beliefs in their daily lives. Our desire to protect such religious freedom issues not out of indifference or skepticism toward our own ultimate beliefs but out of a recognition that in the present age, in Newbigin's words, God wills to provide a space and time for people freely to give their allegiance to his kingdom.[25] The state thus refrains from prematurely foreclosing on this divinely permitted freedom. This implies considerable tolerance of religious diversity in between the times.

Yet virtually everyone understands that such tolerance is necessarily a limited tolerance. A religion permitting human sacrifice may be tolerated in its beliefs but certainly not in its actions insofar as they violate legal proscriptions of murder. Similarly, and more controversially, many citizens, including believing

---

[25]Newbigin, *Foolishness to the Greeks*, p. 138.

Christians, observant Jews and even what might be called dissident secularists,[26] believe they are obligated to pursue constitutional and legal protection of the unborn in the face of the abortion license, despite the often-repeated argument that such action breaches the fragile *modus vivendi* holding together a pluralistic society. Yet a political recognition of directional diversity does not mean that all battles come to an end; it does mean that such battles are waged peacefully through proper, constitutionally based procedures. Any premature effort to end political disputes on the supposed basis of a tolerant pluralism risks at least truncating, and perhaps even eliminating, the very diversity it claims to defend.

There is a second way in which one might use the word pluralism—one potentially less controversial than the first. This is *cultural* pluralism, or what Mouw and Griffioen label *contextual diversity*.[27] No one can doubt that the English and the French are different from each other in a variety of ways. At least part of what makes the formation of a European Union such a difficult enterprise is that member states are separated from each other by such factors as language, custom, history and tradition. To be sure, religion may be part of this mix, and much of what fueled the historic enmity between England and France was the divide between Anglicanism and Roman Catholicism. Similarly, the Greek-Turkish cleavage is rooted in historic antagonisms between Orthodox Christianity and Sunni Islam. One could continue in this vein by pointing to India and Pakistan, Serbia and Croatia, and, within Canada, Ontario and Quebec.

Yet for the most part, cultural diversity is rooted in our created finitude: we human beings are limited creatures rooted in specific localities and communities, bounded as they are by geographical, historical, economic and political factors. Two communities separated from each other by distance will inevitably develop different ways of speaking, behaving, engaging in commercial activities and ruling themselves because, in the first place, such matters are contingent matters inevitably of great variety in their accomplishment, and in the second, the communities are not close enough geographically to influence and learn from each other. Linguists tell us that as Indo-Europeans spread out from their aboriginal homeland in eastern Europe, they divided into different linguistic communities that would eventually become the major language groups

---

[26] Nat Hentoff of *The Village Voice* and British journalist Christopher Hitchens have both called into question the dominant pro-choice philosophy among their fellow liberals and socialists. See George McKenna, "On Abortion: A Lincolnian Position," *Atlantic Monthly,* September 1995 <www.theatlantic.com/issues/95sep/abortion/abortion.htm>.

[27] Mouw and Griffioen, *Pluralisms and Horizons,* pp. 130-57.

within this family: Germanic, Celtic, Italic, Balto-Slavic, Hellenic, Illyrian, Armenian, Indo-Iranian, Anatolian and Tocharian. As the Germanic peoples further dispersed across northern Europe, they subdivided into speakers of what would eventually become modern German, Dutch, Frisian, English and the Scandinavian languages. Even the German language, like most other languages, exists in the form of various dialects, many of which are barely mutually intelligible.

Cuisine is another mark of cultural diversity, but once again different cuisines are rooted in large measure in local geographical factors. Bouillabaise, the famous Provençal fish stew, was far more likely to originate in the south of France, with its Mediterranean coastline, than in landlocked Saskatchewan, where such fare is obviously unavailable. Traditional Russian cuisine, with its heavy use of cabbage and root vegetables, is limited not only by what is obtainable in a northerly climate but by what keeps best during the long winters. With vastly improved transportation infrastructures bringing exotic fruits and vegetables to the local supermarket, we tend to forget that our forebears had to rely on whatever foods were ready at hand for nourishment. In the nineteenth and twentieth centuries, immigrants from, say, Greece were able to bring their cuisine with them for the first time in history. Greeks living in Canada or the United States could continue to eat olives, figs, stuffed grapevine leaves and other delectables common to the eastern Mediterranean because it was now easier to import such items, particularly in their fresh forms, from the old country. Because we can now dine at Greek restaurants on Halsted Street in Chicago or Danforth Avenue in Toronto, we have come to think of cuisine as a portable element in the culture of a particular ethnic group, although this portability is, of course, a recent historical development. Prior to the modern era, cuisine was tied to specific geographic regions with their unique climates, soils, and proximity to the sea.

One could further cite the presence or absence of essential building materials in the development of local architectural styles (stucco houses in Minneapolis, brick homes in Toronto, wood structures in New England); climatic differences in the development of sports (hockey in Canada versus surfing in Hawaii); economic differences in the evolution of various modes of transportation (the automobile in the industrial West versus the oxcart in rural southern Asia); and simple geographical distance in the development of different musical styles (the pentatonic scale in China versus the diatonic scale in Europe). Such contextual diversity is not necessarily a matter of better and worse, although one cannot *ipso facto* exclude this possibility.[28] It is rather a matter of different communities separated by geographical, economic, historical and political distances living out their lives and fashioning their cultures in legitimately dissimilar ways with whatever tools are available to them in their immediate environments.

Is contextual diversity a good thing? Ought political authorities to protect cultural diversity just as they protect religious freedom? Indeed, I would argue that such protection is a crucial element in the state's calling to do public justice, which we shall explore further in the next chapter. Recall that the various forms of nationalism, particularly the ethnic variety, believe that the state must either embody the aspirations of a single national community or impose a common culture on a diverse citizenry, as we noted in chapter four. This is perhaps the modern equivalent of the *cuius regio eius religio* of the post-Reformation era: everyone must follow the same cultural patterns or risk being excluded, if only implicitly, from the body politic. It is understandable, of course, that a government would mandate the universal acquisition of a single official or quasi-official language to facilitate shared deliberation within common political institutions. In the former European colonies, particularly of Africa, the post-independence governments have often chosen the language of the mother country as their official languages rather than one of the local vernaculars, perhaps on the theory that learning it would at least minimally inconvenience everyone of whichever ethnic community and thus avoid appearing to privilege one such community over others.

Yet the notion that a government should attempt to stamp out all local customs, traditions and particular ways of life owes more to an ideological attempt to impose uniformity on a citizenry than to the divine calling to do justice to all. The mandate to defend contextual diversity flies in the face of especially nationalism and the democratic creed of popular sovereignty, but to some extent also of liberalism, socialism and even some types of conservatism. If contextual diversity is based on created human finitude, then the attempt to eliminate it is rooted in an overweening effort to deny such finitude and to claim the right to mold people in accordance with a single monistic vision of the world, which is nothing less than idolatrous.

---

[28] According to Newbigin, "The gospel endorses an immensely wide diversity among human cultures, but it does not endorse a total relativism. There is good and bad in every culture and there are developments continually going on in every culture which may be either creative or destructive, either in line with the purpose of God as revealed in Christ for all human beings, or else out of that line" (*Gospel in a Pluralist Society*, p. 197).

Directional and contextual diversity are related to each other insofar as some differences of opinion are rooted not simply in a grasp of the truth versus a failure to grasp the truth, and thus in the dynamics of sin and redemption. Some differences in perspective are rooted precisely in the fact that people are standing in different temporal, physical, ethnic, class, and gender-based locations and are thus seeing the same thing from different angles. This again is rooted in our human finitude, and not in sin as such. One is reminded here of John Godfrey Saxe's famous poem, "The Blind Men and the Elephant," in which six blind men undertake to describe an elephant and each reports that the creature as a whole is either "like a wall" (the animal's side), "round and smooth and sharp" (the tusks), or "very like a snake" (the tail), as he perceives the nature of the one body part he is capable of feeling. Here conflict is rooted not in truth versus error, but in lack of full knowledge. Although Saxe himself confuses directional and contextual diversity in the poem's last verse, it is nevertheless true that different social locations can lead to conflicting expressions of opinion.[29] This is the grain of truth in philosophies ranging from Marxism to deconstructionism, which nevertheless tend unduly to reduce directional to contextual diversity. Where sin enters the picture is precisely where those with limited knowledge of the truth mistake their own partial grasp for the full truth.

A third type of pluralism brings us to the heart of my argument. This is what might be called *structural diversity* or *societal pluriformity*.[30] A recognition of societal pluriformity is based on the understanding that, in Oliver O'Donovan's words, "unity is proper to the creator, complexity to the created world."[31] God is one, but his works are manifold. This multiplicity of creation is obvious with respect to the natural world. Animals and plants are evidently different from each other. As living things, both are different from rocks, soil, air, water and fire. Within the so-called animal kingdom lions, cattle, eagles, snakes and badgers differ from each other irreducibly, despite current evolutionary theories that hold to a fundamental continuity among the various species. Then of course we have human beings, God's image bearers, created with the unique

---

[29]The poem can be found in *Childcraft* (Chicago: Field Enterprises Educational Corporation, 1954), 2:122-23. The final verse runs as follows: "So oft in theologic wars, / The disputants, I ween, / Rail on in utter ignorance / Of what each other mean, / *And prate about an Elephant / Not one of them has seen!*" (emphasis in original).

[30]Mouw and Griffioen refer to this as *associational* diversity, a term I prefer to avoid because of the voluntaristic connotations attached to it. See Mouw and Griffioen, *Pluralisms and Horizons,* pp. 110-29.

[31]Oliver O'Donovan, *The Desire of the Nations: Rediscovering the Roots of Political Theology* (Cambridge: Cambridge University Press, 1997), p. 177.

capacity to respond to his call. Ostensibly scientific opinions to the effect that man is just another species of animal conflict with our common experience of the vast gulf fixed between human beings and even the great apes with which we apparently have so similar a genetic makeup.

We human beings are, once again, culture-forming beings. We inevitably exist in communities of different kinds and associate with each other for various purposes. We are tied to specific locations—homelands, if you will—and develop loyalties to our immediate environment and to the communities nourished by it. We engage in commerce. We marry, have children, rear and educate our young. We work to put bread on the table by, say, tilling the soil, manufacturing goods, providing services or exchanging and applying technical knowledge. We engage in various communal leisure activities, such as team sports and marching bands. We visit art museums and attend orchestral concerts and ballet performances. Or, if we are so gifted, we create the art that finds its way into the museum, compose the music performed in concert or choreograph the dancers on stage. We worship in formal liturgical settings. We pursue education at various levels of schooling. We participate in organizations specially devoted to charitable activities. And, of course, we fulfill our responsibilities as citizens by obeying the law, respecting the rights of others, honoring those in authority, becoming informed on the issues of the day, voting in elections and possibly even standing for public office.

What should impress us immediately about such activities is that they occur within a variety of communal settings, each of which is structured in accordance with its principal task. From the perspective of our common pretheoretical experience we have no difficulty distinguishing between a country club and a marriage, a family and a telephone company, a university and a political party, even if we might not be able to account immediately for these differences theoretically. Furthermore, the roles played by various individuals within these communities are inextricably related to their special communal tasks. Again we have little difficulty distinguishing between a father and a chief executive officer within a corporation, between a husband and a priest, between a sales representative and a ship's captain.

Occasionally, of course, the president of a firm will speak of his employees as a kind of family with the implication that he is their father, but everyone understands—or at least ought to—that this is merely metaphorical. Where the metaphor is taken too literally, however, work relationships take on an unhealthy paternalistic character, whereas in a genuine family the parents raise the children with an eye to their eventually assuming normal adult independence and responsibilities. Richard Sennett recounts the circumstances leading up to the famous Pullman strike of 1894 in Chicago. George Pullman played on the paternal metaphor, going so far as to build a company town around his railway car manufacturing plant on the city's south side. Employees came to expect to be taken care of by this benevolent father figure, and when he could not live up to the expectations he himself had encouraged, relations broke down irreparably and the workers struck.[32] Sennett describes this paternalism as an "authority of false love." This is not to say that an affective bond among the members of a work community is necessarily lacking or improper. But such collegial loyalty ought not to be confused with familial love.

Similarly everyone intuitively understands the difference between marriage and family and the role of husband and father respectively in each. Where the boundary is breached between these two central callings, there is a danger of what we have come to know as child sexual abuse. Where the authority of a king or prime minister is exercised in an improper parental fashion, that is, where citizens are treated as immature biological offspring, such authority becomes abusive. In short, the distinct responsibilities each of us has in God's world are related to the various overlapping communities of which we are part. The authority of parents is precisely related to family life and not to the body politic, as John Locke correctly argued against Sir Robert Filmer's patriarchal political theory.[33] The authority of a conductor extends to the instrumentalists in the orchestra and not to the patrons of a local public library. The authority of a platoon leader extends over the soldiers under her command and not to the spectators lining the streets watching them on parade. And, closer to our purposes here, the authority of a parliament or president extends over people in their capacity as subjects and citizens, but not directly over them in their several capacities as spouses, parents, sons and daughters, church members, employees, students, teachers and café patrons. When a child disobeys her parents, the parents assume responsibility for disciplining her and would never think of calling in the police because they understand intuitively that such a matter lies outside the legitimate sphere of responsibility of the government and its officials.

---

[32]Richard Sennett, *Authority* (New York: Alfred A. Knopf, 1980), pp. 50-83. The Pullman Palace Car Company lowered employee wages by 25 percent in response to the economic downturn of the previous year but maintained rents in the company town at previous levels.

[33]See Sir Robert Filmer, *Patriarcha* (1680) and Locke's less frequently read *First Treatise on Civil Government* for the author's refutation of Filmer's argument therein.

Such statements may seem crushingly obvious, but in one way or another the ideologies we have explored effectively deny the genuine differences among various communities and even between these communities and the individual person. In the absence of a recognition of God's ultimate sovereignty, their followers are forced to locate this sovereignty within his world, as we have continually noted in previous chapters. How does this lead to the sort of monism so typical of the ideologies? Because in one way or another this idolatrous search for earthly sovereignty inevitably breaches O'Donovan's dictum concerning the complexity of creation. God transcends his creation, while the ostensibly sovereign individual, state, race, nation, people or class do not. Thus it is inevitable that any effort to ascribe ontological ultimacy to one of these created elements can only result in the tendency to flatten out and discount the status of everything else.

Thus liberalism, as we have seen above, tends to reduce every community to the aggregating wills of component individuals. If every community, ranging from family to state to church, can be understood reductively in this same way, then the differences among them that we intuit at a pre-theoretical level are inevitably denied. In short, liberalism, while legitimately pointing us to the important place of the individual within communities, cannot fully account for our common experience of the obvious differences among them. As a typical ideology, therefore, liberalism possesses a distorted view of reality. Similarly, the various collectivist ideologies tend inevitably to view individuals and communities in all their variety as mere parts of a larger whole. The school therefore becomes a vehicle to transmit loyalty to the nation, state, proletariat or democratic people. The family becomes a manifestation of this larger whole, with little if any integrity in its own right. Once again diversity is denied in the interest of an idolatrous unity.

But, it might be asked, how does this recognition of societal diversity relate to creation? Are we to assume that God has created states, marriages, business enterprises and schools in the same way as we understand mountains, lakes, forests and meadows to be his creation? After all, we do not read in the first chapter of Genesis that God created the family or the labor union and saw that it was good. We have addressed this issue to some extent above. But the following two points are worth reiterating here. First, human beings are created, once again, to be culture-shapers, as affirmed in Genesis 1:28. The appearance of farms and cities on the landscape does not represent an intrusion of man on a supposedly pristine creation. Farms and cities are *part*

of creation.[34] It is a commonplace that while the Bible places man's beginnings in a garden (Gen 2:8), it associates his final redemption with a city, the
new Jerusalem (Rev 21:2).

This brings us to the second point: God's creation is not a static creation, as
we observed in chapter three. It is filled with dynamic possibilities and is constantly developing under man's stewardship. This is perhaps obvious with respect to the proliferation of new technologies and new medical breakthroughs
in the ongoing fight against disease. But it is also true of the communities that
we form and in which we are unavoidably embedded. No one would sensibly
argue that God called into being the American Automobile Association in the
same way that he called the oceans and dry land into being. Nevertheless, because of man's created capacity for organization, which is part of the cultural
mandate, we are fully justified in speaking of the "Triple A" as part of God's
creation. The state as we now know it is a product of a specific set of historical
circumstances arising in western Europe half a millennium ago. Yet the dawn of
the state conformed to various patterns already implicit in the creation and already partly realized in other contexts as well, for example, in the Davidic monarchy, the Greek polis and the Roman republic.

This dynamic character of God's creation calls attention to the historical process of what might be called *societal differentiation* and what others, somewhat mis-
leadingly, have labeled modernization. In a primitive tribal community a variety
of functions are performed in undifferentiated fashion by a single, all-inclusive
community led by the same leaders whose authority is likely to be passed down
from one generation to the next. The tribal chieftain is at once patriarch of an
extended family, political ruler, cultic religious leader and commander-in-chief
of the military. The biblical Melchizedek, for example, was at once ruler of Salem
(that is, Jerusalem) and priest of the "Most High God" in the Canaanite pan-
theon, whom the author of the biblical account identifies with the one true God
of Abraham (Gen 14:18). The meeting between Melchizedek and Abraham recounted in the Bible obviously reflects the undifferentiated societies of the early
second millennium B.C. in which the priesthood and the kingship had not yet
come to be institutionally distinguished. Furthermore each city in the region had
its own "king" with little political unity beyond this.

Nowhere does Scripture condemn this combination of functions, at least

---

[34]Paul Marshall makes this point in *Heaven Is Not My Home: Learning to Live in God's Creation* (Nashville:
    Word, 1998), pp. 126-31.

prior to the institution of the Levitical priesthood,[35] any more than it condemns the polygamous marriages of the early Hebrew patriarchs. This is where an understanding of the historical process proves to be essential. A professed conservative who believes we can simply turn back the clock to an earlier era and reconstitute the social arrangements proper to that time is misguided. But so also is the progressive who believes that all prior social orders can be judged by the "obviously" more enlightened ones of our own day. Both lack a sense of what is appropriate at a particular historical moment. A similar historical approach can be taken to analyze the centuries-long transition from absolute monarchy to democracy, from Max Weber's traditional authority to legal-rational authority, from slavery to wage labor, and even the changing roles of women, each of which reflects a process of legitimate historical development.

Moreover some Christians regret, along with the secularization of society, its increasing differentiation with a concomitant diminution of the social role of the institutional church. Particularly within Roman Catholic circles, many conservative believers adhere to what some have labeled an integralist approach, which would see a number of societal functions again coming under the auspices of the clergy.[36] This is inadequate insofar as it fails to respect the integrity of nonchurch communities in their own right. At least part of the impetus behind the *Révolution tranquille* in Quebec during the 1960s was not only a lamentable decline in faith, but also the legitimate sense of many Québecois that their society had stagnated under the stifling weight of an overly large and all-pervasive institutional church. Tragically, however, because the institutional church had been so thoroughly identified with the *corpus Christi*, as the former retreated into a more modest role—relinquishing its previous control of schools, hospitals, charitable organiza-

---

[35]After the institution of the levitical priesthood, however, Scripture takes a quite different view of a monarch encroaching on its sphere of authority. See, e.g., 1 Chronicles 26:16-21, which recounts the story of the Judahite king Uzziah's attempt to usurp the priestly function and his subsequent punishment by God.

[36]According to David L. Schindler, "an 'integralist' church seeks a relationship with the world, but does so through coercive means" (*Heart of the World, Center of the Church* [Grand Rapids, Mich.: Eerdmans, 1996], p. 24). To some extent the efforts of the likes of Jacques Maritain, Yves R. Simon and other so-called neo-Thomists represent an attempt to posit an alternative Catholic approach that takes seriously the legitimate structural components of modernity, particularly societal differentiation and the concomitant rise of political democracy, while maintaining fidelity to the church and its traditions. See, e.g., Maritain, *Integral Humanism* (Notre Dame, Ind.: University of Notre Dame Press, 1973), and Simon, *Philosophy of Democratic Government* (Chicago: University of Chicago Press, 1951). On the other hand, see Robert P. Kraynak, *Christian Faith and Modern Democracy: God and Politics in the Fallen World* (Notre Dame, Ind.: University of Notre Dame Press, 2001), in which the author dissents from the apparent Kantian direction of contemporary Roman Catholic approaches to politics, instead reaffirming the Augustinian distinction between the two cities and its predemocratic foundations.

tions, trade unions and so forth—so also did the influence of the community of faith as a whole decrease. In the ensuing institutional and spiritual vacuum, the "state of Quebec," that is, the provincial government, took its place, leaving a statist, nationalist ideology to supplant the once strong Christian religion. Where institutional church and *corpus Christi* are too closely identified, as they were in that province, then normal societal differentiation can only imply secularization. This too manifests an inadequate understanding of the historical process.

Most of the ideologies in some fashion either deny or misconceive the nature of societal differentiation, often misidentifying it with increasing fragmentation and mounting decadence. Conservatism in its several manifestations is often distinctly uncomfortable with it, invoking a nostalgia for an apparently simpler time, when, for example, economic and social life were more closely tied to extended family or a particular church communion was institutionally linked to the state. Nazism tried to recreate a primitive and apparently more robust German *Volk*, headed by a single Führer and freed from what Hitler considered the corrupting influences of modernity. Even communism, claimed by its adherents to be a progressive and emancipatory force, could be seen as a retrograde attempt to reverse the historical process by reenclosing the pluriform structures of society within the bond of an undifferentiated party apparatus— all in the name of an eventual repeal of the age-old division of labor. Well-intended efforts to ameliorate fragmentation can, if wedded to a secular and monistic worldview, lead to an improper suppression of legitimate pluriformity and thus in a totalitarian direction.

8

TOWARD A
NONIDEOLOGICAL
ALTERNATIVE

Two Historic Christian Approaches

The affirmation of structural or societal pluriformity has deep roots within Christianity, though not every Christian tradition has emphasized it to the same degree. The Roman Catholic and Reformed traditions are especially significant. On the Catholic side a renewed interest in the philosophy of Thomas Aquinas in the late nineteenth and early twentieth centuries was strongly associated with a recognition of such pluriformity. The connection with Aristotle is significant here, as Aristotle sought to defend as great a degree of pluriformity as possible within the otherwise totalistic world of the Greek polis. On the Reformed side three figures in the Netherlands proved to be of particular importance: Guillaume Groen van Prinsterer, Abraham Kuyper and Herman Dooyeweerd. On both sides the movement to affirm legitimate pluriformity had its origins within a larger response to the French Revolution and the ideologies it had spawned. In other words, it originally shared considerable common ground with the antirevolutionary restorationism of Maistre and other continental European conservatives.

The Role of Catholic Social Teachings
The groundbreaking work of Pope Leo XIII (1810-1903, pope from 1878) is especially important in understanding what has often been called the neo-

Thomist revival in the Roman Catholic Church. Throughout the nineteenth century, it had become evident to a number of observers that many of the developments in postrevolutionary Europe, such as constitutionalism and democracy, which were initially ascribed to the godless spirit of the Revolution, were more properly seen as legitimate historical manifestations of societal differentiation. In this context Leo issued his famous social encyclicals, which aimed to bring Catholic social and political thought up to date and cautiously affirmed these developments.

Of these encyclicals, three are worth noting briefly here. In his *Immortale Dei* (1885), "on the Christian constitution of states," Leo affirmed the place of both church and state within the order of society as ordained by God. Acknowledging that each has its own area of responsibility, he nevertheless opposed such liberal notions as the separation of church and state, official indifference or antipathy toward religion, freedom of expression (that is, to propagate error), and the general diminution of the church's authority in society as a whole. This would seem to put him squarely within the integralist stream. Yet he also conceded that the particular form of government followed by a given polity was a largely indifferent matter, as long as the common good was being served and the role of the church was not hindered. This is particularly significant in that it manifested a new openness on the part of the church toward democratic institutions, although not, of course, to the democratic creed explored in chapter five.

Perhaps the most famous of the social encyclicals is *Rerum Novarum* (1891), "on the condition of the workers." In this encyclical, Leo sought to undercut the increasing appeal of socialism among the working class by supporting efforts to ameliorate their plight. Reaffirming the legitimacy of private property as rooted in the natural order, he expressed strong disagreement with the socialist position on this matter. To abolish private property, he asserted, would, among other things, harm those whom it was intended to help, namely, the workers, who would still lack the security they sought for themselves and their families. Only Christian teachings could alleviate the injustices inflicted upon the working person by encouraging fraternal feeling between the classes and obligating each class toward the other, particularly capital toward labor. Although the state ought not to absorb particular communities outright, it is still obligated to step in and actively stamp out injustice and to intervene on behalf of the poor.

In his *Graves de Communi Re* (1901), Leo cautiously endorsed the label "Christian democracy" to describe a Christian alternative to social democracy. Whereas social democracy preached class war and reduced the social question to the level of economic causation, a true Christian democracy sought reconciliation among classes, recognized the spiritual and moral aspect of humanity, and looked to the teachings of the church for guidance.[1] During the twentieth century a number of confessional Christian political parties in Europe and Latin America would assume the Christian democratic label.[2]

What emerges out of Leo's social encyclicals is a body of principles on society that revolve around the following teachings: (1) liberalism and socialism alike are to be rejected as providing norms for society and its ills, although Catholic political action can legitimately be conducted within the framework of modern democratic institutions; (2) class conflict ought to be supplanted by reconciliation and cooperation; (3) the state must govern in accordance with the common good; (4) the natural common good of the state is relative to the supernatural good governing the church; (5) the place of the church must therefore be recognized by the state; (6) the state cannot remain passive in the face of social and economic injustices in society, yet at the same time it must not overpower subsidiary communities so as to usurp permanently their legitimate functions; (7) the place of such communities within society must be acknowledged and respected; and, finally and most basically, (8) Catholic social principles find their grounding in a natural law framework as articulated in the writings of Thomas Aquinas.

This doctrine concerning the relation of the state to nonstate communities would come to be known as *subsidiarity,* a term Leo himself did not use. Subsidiarity appears for the first time in the encyclicals of Pius XI, particularly his *Quadragesimo Anno* (1931) on reconstructing the social order, published to commemorate the fortieth anniversary of *Rerum Novarum.* It is in this later encyclical that the classic statement of subsidiarity appears:

> Just as it is gravely wrong to take from individuals what they can accomplish by their own initiative and industry and give it to the community, so

---

[1]For an abridged edition of Leo XIII's social encyclicals, see *The Pope and the People: Select Letters and Addresses on Social Questions,* ed. Charles S. Devas (London: Catholic Truth Society, 1910). The social encyclicals of several popes, from Leo XIII to John Paul II, may be found in Michael Walsh and Brian Davies, eds., *Proclaiming Justice and Peace: Papal Documents from* Rerum Novarum *Through* Centesimus Annus (Mystic, Conn.: Twenty-Third Publications, 1991).

[2]The history of the Christian democratic movements themselves is recounted in a number of works, including Michael P. Fogarty, *Christian Democracy in Western Europe 1820-1953* (Notre Dame, Ind.: University of Notre Dame Press, 1957); R. E. M. Irving, *The Christian Democratic Parties of Western Europe* (London: George Allen & Unwin, 1979); and Stathis Kalyvas, *The Rise of Christian Democracy in Europe* (Ithaca, N.Y.: Cornell University Press, 1996).

also it is an injustice...to assign to a greater and higher association what lesser and subordinate organizations can do. For every social activity ought of its very nature to furnish help to the members of the body [politic] and never destroy and absorb them. The supreme authority of the State ought, therefore, to let subordinate groups handle matters and concerns of lesser importance, which would otherwise dissipate its efforts greatly.[3]

Subsidiarity thus means that wherever possible, tasks are to be fulfilled by the lowest conceivable element in the social hierarchy, and only in the case of a failure in this regard is a higher community, for example, the state, justified in stepping in and offering assistance *(subsidium)*. Once matters are set right, however, the higher community must then withdraw once again and end its intervention. This principle of subsidiarity was deemed important for maintaining a healthy social order in which all parts retain their vitality and initiative over against the threat of an omnicompetent state apparatus.

The Principle of Subsidiarity: Affirming Civil Society

In the twentieth century this principle was picked up and further developed by Jacques Maritain (1882-1973), a French-born convert to Roman Catholicism whose writings range over a number of fields, including politics. Decisive in the development of his thought was the influence of Thomas Aquinas, whose writings he began reading in 1910. In his political theory, Maritain distinguishes between the state as a particular institution and the body politic or political society.[4] The latter is the most perfect of human societies and its end is the common good. The state, on the other hand, is a part of the body politic and ought not to be identified with the latter as a whole. The state is nevertheless the highest part that most directly concerns itself with the maintenance of order and justice within the body politic. The state is superior to other groups in the society in that it orders them to the wider common interest. But if it is the highest part of the body politic, the state is in an important sense inferior to the latter as a whole and must be seen as its servant. In this respect, Maritain rejects the notion of sovereignty to describe the authority of the state, as it has come down from the time of Bodin. Only God possesses sovereignty in the strict sense, and whatever authority the state possesses is given to it by God.[5]

---

[3]Walsh and Davies, *Proclaiming Justice and Peace,* pp. 62-63.
[4]Jacques Maritain, *Man and the State* (Chicago: University of Chicago Press, 1951), pp. 9-10.
[5]Ibid., pp. 49-53.

In opposition to both liberal individualism and totalitarianism, Maritain advocates a societal pluriformity rooted in the principle of subsidiarity, according to which society is made up not merely of the state and the individual citizens who are under it, but also of a variety of smaller communities, groups, associations and particular societies, each of which should be allowed the greatest possible autonomy. Echoing Leo and Pius, Maritain describes what he labels the "pluralist principle" in these words: "everything in the body politic which can be brought about by particular organs of societies inferior in degree to the State and born out of the free initiative of the people *should* be brought about by those particular organs or societies."[6] Only in the pluralist society can the true freedom of persons be respected and extended. Among other things, pluralism implies that spiritual and temporal orders are kept distinct. Although the spiritual order is the higher order, the temporal order does possess a certain autonomy within its own sphere, which is the common good of the earthly society as a whole.

Building on this notion of autonomy, philosopher Yves R. Simon (1903–1961), Maritain's younger compatriot and colleague, posits two complementary principles, authority and autonomy, intended to undergird a free society. According to the former, "Wherever the welfare of a community requires a common action, the unity of that common action must be assured by the higher organs of that community." According to the latter, "Wherever a task can be satisfactorily achieved by the initiative of the individual or that of small social units, the fulfillment of that task must be left to the initiative of the individual or to that of small social units."[7] Although Simon does not refer to subsidiarity as such, both of these principles together constitute what Pius and the larger tradition of Catholic social teaching mean by the term.

It should be noticed that the social ontology presupposed by subsidiarity is definitely hierarchical. If it could be visualized, it would look something like figure 2 (p. 220). Society, and perhaps even the world as a whole, is shaped like a pyramid, with God at the apex and the various social structures ranged below him. Immediately below God is his church, understood as an institution charged with bestowing his supernatural grace on communicants. The church is founded on the revealed will of God in Scripture and tradition. It pronounces on matters of the spirit and attends to the souls of human beings. It

---

[6]Ibid., p. 67.
[7]Yves R. Simon, *The Nature and Functions of Authority* (Milwaukee: Marquette University Press, 1940), p. 45.

points man toward the beatific vision of God, whose full enjoyment awaits the next life. Below the church lies the state, a natural institution rooted in humanity's capacity for reason. The state seeks the common good of its members, understood to mean that which is conducive to a full community of persons and transcends the particular goods both of the various subordinate communities and of the individuals.

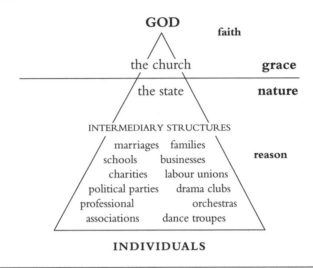

Figure 2. The hierarchical social ontology of subsidiarity

The next level down in the hierarchy is occupied by a variety of subsidiary or subordinate communities that play a multiplicity of roles in the society. This level has attracted much interest in recent years as numerous political theorists have sought to recover something called *civil society*, an expression to which we have already alluded in chapter five. Following Richard John Neuhaus and Peter Berger, others have referred to this plethora of social forms as *mediating structures, intermediary communities* or some combination of these expressions.[8] Particularly following the collapse of communism in Eastern Europe and the former Soviet Union, where the integrity of such structures was impugned or altogether denied, political leaders in these countries are anxious to revitalize the free initiative of the people in a variety of contexts, ranging from business enterprises and educational institutions to independent newspapers and politi-

---

[8]Peter L. Berger and Richard John Neuhaus, *To Empower People: From State to Civil Society*, ed. Michael Novak, 2nd ed. (Washington, D.C.: American Enterprise Institute, 1996). See also Michael Novak, ed., *Democracy and Mediating Structures: A Theological Inquiry* (Washington, D.C.: American Enterprise Institute, 1980).

cal movements, all of which were once subject to the stifling interference of the communist party. Those expressing interest in civil society in their writings and public addresses include, among many others, Elshtain,[9] Don E. Eberly,[10] Ernest Gellner,[11] Adam Seligman[12] and even William Hague, former leader of the British Conservative Party.[13] Yves Simon speaks of a *political* society, that is, one that in its very institutional arrangement embodies a certain resistance to the imperial tendencies of the state.[14] And more than a century earlier, Tocqueville speaks of *civil associations*, as we noted in chapter five.

Below this level, and at the bottom of the hierarchy, we find the individuals. The language of "mediating," "intermediary," and the like indicates that, contrary to those ideologies which would see the individual and the state facing each other directly as the only elements in society, these structures of civil society come between the two, offering foci of loyalty inevitably challenging the potentially overweening claims of the state and serving as buffer between the people and their political authorities. It should, however, be noted immediately that because real, flesh-and-blood human beings are, in Maritain's conception, more than just individuals but full persons capable of communing with other persons in a variety of contexts, we should not look at such people as though they were somehow wholly contained, and thus stranded, at the lowest rung. Insofar as people are parents, brothers and sisters, offspring, employers or employees in a business, members of a labor union, students or instructors in a school, citizens of a state, or clergy or parishioners in a church, they find themselves simultaneously at every level of the social hierarchy, except, of course, for the highest, which is occupied by God himself. Thus the hierarchy must be seen not as a kind of rigid caste structure, but as a hierarchy of overlapping offices and functions embedded in equally overlapping communal structures. To put

---

[9]Jean Bethke Elshtain, "Civil Society Creates Citizens; It Does Not Solve Problems," *The Brookings Review* 15, no. 4 (1997): 13-15; *Democracy on Trial* (Toronto: Anansi, 1993), pp. 5-21; "'In Common Together'" in *Christianity and Democracy in Global Context,* ed. John Witte Jr. (Boulder, Colo.: Westview, 1993), pp. 65-83.

[10]Don E. Eberly, *America's Promise: Civil Society and the Renewal of American Culture* (Lanham, Md.: Rowman & Littlefield, 1998); Eberly, ed., *Building a Community of Citizens: Civil Society in the 21st Century* (Lanham, Md.: University Press of America, 1994).

[11]Ernest Gellner, *Conditions of Liberty: Civil Society and Its Rivals* (Harmondsworth, U.K.: Penguin, 1994).

[12]Adam Seligman, *The Idea of Civil Society* (New York: Free Press, 1992).

[13]William Hague, "Identity and the British Way," speech delivered to Centre for Policy Studies, London, January 19, 1999 <www.conservative-party.org.uk>.

[14]Yves R. Simon, *Philosophy of Democratic Government* (Chicago: University of Chicago Press, 1951), pp. 72-76.

the matter in traditional scholastic language, insofar as human beings are composite beings made up of body and soul, they partake of both nature and grace and find themselves under both temporal and spiritual authorities.

Scholasticism is, of course, historically associated with Thomas Aquinas, and it is in Thomistic, and ultimately Aristotelian, philosophy that subsidiarity finds its roots. Aristotle argues that society is arranged hierarchically, with households at its base.[15] Each household legitimately pursues its own particular good and is governed more or less despotically by the head of the household. Households combine to form villages, each of which in turn pursues its own particular good as well. Although the particular goods are undoubted goods, if left to themselves without overall coordination, they will inevitably come into conflict. This necessitates the formation of another level, the polis, which is uniquely charged with seeking the *common* good of the whole community. For Aristotle and his fellow Greeks of the classical era the polis is the highest imaginable ethical community, beyond which the constitutional governance of free citizens is not possible.

Characteristically, Thomas did not disagree with the substance of Aristotle's approach but deemed it necessary to add another level to complete the social hierarchy. The polis had long passed out of existence, to be replaced by the kingly realms of the late medieval era. The king seeks the common good of all of his subjects and thus replicates the work of the polis at this later period of history. But the Aristotelian common good is only a *natural* common good, oriented solely to the temporal well-being of the subjects. Because human beings are more than temporal beings, however, relating inexorably to the God who has created and redeemed them, another level is needed to point them to their supernatural common good, and this level is occupied by the church. The church itself is a hierarchical organization, ascending from laity through deacons, priests and bishops up to the Pope himself, who came to be styled the vicar of Christ insofar as he was believed to communicate God's grace to those standing below. The term subsidiarity does not occur in Thomas's writings either, but the concept is present in seminal form, insofar as the lower levels in the hierarchy, particularly the natural ones, possess a certain autonomy vis-à-vis the higher.

Before leaving subsidiarity behind, it is worth noting that in its 1992 Maastricht Treaty, the European Union adopted it, not so much as a social doctrine,

---

[15] Aristotle *Politics* 1.

but as an explicitly federal political principle governing relations between the member states and the Union institutions in Brussels, Strasbourg and Luxembourg. Here subsidiarity means that the EU undertakes only those tasks that cannot be feasibly performed by the member states themselves.[16] All other responsibilities are discharged by the latter. It is no accident that the original architects of the Union and its predecessor organizations, such as Jean Monnet and Robert Schuman, were steeped in the tradition of Catholic social teachings.

The Reformation: Calvin and Althusius

A second tradition has affirmed societal pluriformity and this one is rooted in the Reformation of the sixteenth century, particularly that of the Genevan reformer John Calvin (1509-1564). Although Calvin was not primarily a political theorist or philosopher, he nevertheless treated the office of civil magistrate in his writings, especially the *Institutes of the Christian Religion* (4.20). Calvin's political thought was picked up and developed by Johannes Althusius (1557-1638), whose *Politics* shows the influence of both Calvin and Aristotle.[17] The thought of Calvin and Althusius tends in a republican direction toward an understanding of the political community as a *res publica*, or "public thing," actively involving its members or citizens in its common life. It is worth noting that those countries historically influenced by Calvinism, for example, Switzerland, the Netherlands, Scotland, England and the United States, became republics or constitutional monarchies early.

The Reformed tradition of political reflection carried on one side of a late medieval dispute over the relationship between ecclesiastical and political leaders on the one hand, and between both and God on the other. In the high Middle Ages, with the power of such popes as Innocent III (1160-1216, pope from 1198), the church had asserted the right to render God's judgment on political authorities, as earlier seen, for example, in the dramatic submission of Emperor Henry IV to Pope Gregory VII at Canossa in 1077. Granted that the powers that be are ordained by God, as Paul puts it, the question arose how this ordinance was to be bestowed within Christendom: directly by God or indirectly through the mediation of the church. Successive popes asserted the authority to absolve subjects of their allegiance to their temporal rulers if

---

[16]See, e.g., Ernest Wistrich, *The United States of Europe* (London: Routledge, 1994), p. 10.

[17]See Frederick S. Carney, ed., *The Politics of Johannes Althusius* (Boston: Beacon, 1964), for an English translation of Althusius' *Politica methodice digesta* (1603, expanded 1610). For a well-known secondary treatment of Althusius, see Otto von Gierke, *Althusius* (1913).

the latter should, say, apostatize from the faith. Giles of Rome (Aegidius Romanus, c. 1243-1316) supported this broad conception of papal authority with its profound political implications. On the other hand, Dante Alighieri (1265-1321) and John of Paris (c. 1255-1306) believed that spiritual and temporal authorities were coequal and separate, each receiving its position directly from God himself. The Reformers were in some measure heir to the latter tradition and thus conceived the authority of the civil magistrate to stand immediately under God's sovereignty. With a renewed emphasis on a nonhierarchical priesthood of all believers, this translated into a more republican conception in which political authorities could be held accountable to God through the actions of his people rather than through clerical intervention as such.

Because of this republican connection, some scholars have gone so far as to assert that the principal political contribution of Calvinism was to legitimate a general right of popular revolt against tyranny, along the lines of Locke's famous "appeal to heaven."[18] Calvin himself was far from approving any such action, although he did hold out hope for a constitutional solution wherein lower magistrates might be authorized to check the power of a tyrannical chief magistrate. In other words, in contrast to subsidiarity, it would not be a matter of functionaries of the institutional church intervening in an ostensibly "subordinate" institution and setting matters aright from without. The political problem would be addressed precisely *politically*, and its solution would come from within the body politic itself, which was acknowledged to stand directly and immediately under God's sovereignty.

Developments in the Netherlands: Groen and Kuyper

It was in the Netherlands that a distinctively Reformed Christian political theory was developed in the nineteenth and twentieth centuries. Initially it was undertaken as a response to the French Revolution and the ideologies spawned by it. A number of associated events helped to spark this response, including the *Réveil*, a general religious revival sweeping especially the Protestant churches of the European continent; the reestablishment of the Netherlands as a centralized unitary monarchical state after 1815, following almost two centuries as a loose confederal republic; the nationalization of the *Hervormde Kerk* (Reformed

---

[18]See, e.g., George Sabine and Thomas L. Thorson, *A History of Political Theory*, 4th ed. (Hinsdale, Ill.: Dryden, 1973), pp. 339-44, 352-57; and Quentin Skinner, *The Foundations of Modern Political Thought*, vol. 2, *The Age of the Reformation* (Cambridge: Cambridge University Press, 1978), pp. 189-238.

Church) by the new king, Willem I; and the *Afscheiding* (secession) of 1834, which formed a new ecclesiastical body free from state control.

But perhaps more than anything else, the general secularizing trends that had begun during the Enlightenment accelerated as a result of the Revolution and subsequent Napoleonic invasion, and these caused concern to orthodox Christians who saw them sweeping into both their churches and their public life. Initially this Christian response to the Revolution was of one piece with the conservative restorationism we examined in chapter three. A leading figure in what would come to be styled the antirevolutionary or Christian-historical movement was Guillaume Groen van Prinsterer (1801-1876), an archivist to the royal House of Orange.[19] Groen himself came from an aristocratic family, and his own movement was initially in close cooperation with the Conservative Party.

Accordingly the specifics of Groen's political philosophy tended, at least initially, to look back toward feudal patrimonialism—or rather, to the romantic reconstruction of feudalism characterizing the conservatism of this era. Groen taught, among other things, that society is a hierarchy of communities bound together in an organic national unity, that the state is the product of nature and not of human artifice, that the state is the property of a hereditary dynasty, and that the lower communities of society should be accorded a certain amount of autonomy by the state.[20] Thus the early Groen's "Christian-historical" political theory differed little from the romantic historicism of such figures as Karl von Haller and Friedrich Julius Stahl, by whom Groen was influenced. Furthermore, Groen's conception of society was as yet little different from the subsidiarity we explored above.

As Groen's political thought developed further, however, he came to distinguish between the state as a *res publica* (public thing) and the sphere of private law. Having learned from Stahl to differentiate between the two realms of public and private, Groen began to move in a somewhat different direction along the lines of what he called *souvereiniteit in eigen sfeer* (sovereignty in its own sphere). Yet even then this notion was tied to a hierarchical conception of society.[21]

---

[19]See Harry Van Dyke, *Groen van Prinsterer's Lectures on Unbelief and Revolution* (Jordan Station, Ontario: Wedge, 1989), for the best account and analysis of Groen's life and thought in English.

[20]James W. Skillen, "The Development of Calvinistic Political Theory in the Netherlands, with Special Reference to the Thought of Herman Dooyeweerd," Ph.D. dissertation (Duke University, 1974), pp. 217-25.

[21]Herman Dooyeweerd, *The Roots of Western Culture* (Toronto: Wedge, 1979), pp. 51-54.

The broad aim of the antirevolutionary movement was to try to stem the tide of unbelief that had been unleashed by the French Revolution. To this end, Groen wrote his highly polemical *Ongeloof en Revolutie (Unbelief and Revolution)*[22] in 1847, just one year before another wave of revolutions was to sweep the continent. The more immediate goal of the movement was to gain educational freedom, that is, the right of parents to determine how their children would be educated. This was asserted against the centralizing tendency of the Dutch government, which was increasingly coming to assume control of the schools. Yet in opposing centralization along French lines, Groen demanded merely the autonomy of the schools under the supervision of the provinces and municipalities. In short, his approach to this issue was a federal one rather than one of recognizing structural pluriformity as such.

Groen van Prinsterer's successor in the antirevolutionary movement was the remarkable Abraham Kuyper (1837-1920).[23] A pastor, theologian, journalist, scholar, educator and statesman, Kuyper was arguably the most influential figure of his generation in the Netherlands, and his influence continues to be felt to some extent up to the present. Beginning his career as a parish pastor in the Reformed Church, Kuyper went on to assume leadership of Groen's movement, eventually organizing it as the *Anti-Revolutionaire Partij* (Anti-Revolutionary Party or ARP), the first modern Dutch political party and the first Christian democratic party in the world (1879). Kuyper also founded the Free University of Amsterdam (1880), a Reformed Christian university founded on Calvinistic principles; wrote and published prolifically, including the daily *Standaard*; led a second major secession from the state church (1886) and was instrumental in establishing the *Gereformeerde Kerken*

---

[22]Van Dyke's treatment in *Groen van Prinsterer's Lectures* contains an abridged English translation of this work.

[23]There is no definitive English work on the life and thought of Abraham Kuyper. A popular biography with a hagiographic tone exists in Frank VandenBerg, *Abraham Kuyper* (1960; reprint, St. Catharines, Ontario: Paideia, 1978). A good treatment of the highlights of Kuyper's career can be found in McKendree R. Langley, *The Practice of Political Spirituality: Episodes from the Public Career of Abraham Kuyper, 1879-1918* (Jordan Station, Ontario: Paideia, 1984). Perhaps the best treatment of Kuyper's ideas as expressed in his 1898 Stone Lectures at Princeton is Peter S. Heslam, *Creating a Christian Worldview: Abraham Kuyper's Lectures on Calvinism* (Grand Rapids, Mich.: Eerdmans, 1998). Also in English are L. Praamsma, *Let Christ Be King: Reflections on the Life and Times of Abraham Kuyper* (Jordan Station, Ontario: Paideia, 1985) and John Bolt, *A Free Church, a Holy Nation: Abraham Kuyper's American Public Theology* (Grand Rapids, Mich.: Eerdmans, 2001). Dutch language works include P. A. Diepenhorst, *Dr. A. Kuyper* (Haarlem, Netherlands: De Erven F. Bohn, 1931); and P. Kasteel, *Abraham Kuyper* (Kampen, Netherlands: J. H. Kok, 1938), possibly the best biography of Kuyper available to date.

in Nederland (Reformed Churches in the Netherlands, or GKN) by uniting the heirs of the two secessions (1892); and served as prime minister from 1901 to 1905, leading a coalition government comprising one Roman Catholic and two Protestant political parties.

Kuyper's religious worldview was fiercely orthodox. Devoted as he was to the Reformed confessions, he was nevertheless not content to define the Christian faith solely in terms of church and theology, but expanded its scope into an all-inclusive *levens-en wereldbeschouwing* (life-and-world-view or *Weltanschauung*). This is in contrast to developments among Calvinists in North America and elsewhere who were generally preoccupied with theological issues relating to the doctrine of predestination. Among Kuyper's followers in the Netherlands, however, to be Reformed meant to be engaged in developing and living out a consistent and distinctive Christian Weltanschauung, and this was acknowledged to include politics as well as other human cultural and social endeavors.

Kuyper built on the foundations laid by Groen van Prinsterer, yet he sought to pull the ARP away from its initial aristocratic and romantic conservative tendencies. In this he was largely successful, and he was able to combine orthodox Calvinism with a progressive political stance championing the rights of the *kleine luyden* or the "little people" who were still for the most part excluded from active participation in the body politic. It was Kuyper's work for the extension of the franchise that eventually led to the breakoff of the *Christelijk-Historische Unie* (Christian Historical Union, or CHU) under the leadership of Alexander F. de Savornin Lohman. Lohman's followers included the more aristocratic elements within the antirevolutionary movement, who were opposed to Kuyper's attempt to incorporate the lower classes into the Dutch body politic.

It should be noted that during this same period, Roman Catholic Christians were also organized into their own political grouping under Msgr. Herman J. A. M. Schaepman.[24] In the next decades, these three Christian democratic parties would cooperate on specific issues of shared concern and eventually in coalition governments while maintaining their separate organizational identities. In 1976, the three parties came together in a federal unity as the *Christen*

---

[24]This loose grouping was established as a political party in 1926. Originally known as the *Roomsch-Katholieke Staatspartij* (RKSP), it was rechristened the *Katholieke Volkspartij* (KVP) after the Second World War in an attempt to bring its image into line with the progressive orientation of other European Christian democratic parties (Irving, *Christian Democratic Parties,* p. 200).

Democratisch Appel (Christian Democratic Appeal, or CDA) and further cemented their unity as a single organization in 1981.[25]

Kuyper's political ideas did not develop in an ivory tower setting, but in
the course of a life spent both in deep reflection and in the arena of public
affairs. He did not develop a systematic political theory as such, but he did
lay the foundations for such an enterprise. Several characteristic themes can
be seen in Kuyper's thought, and we shall here briefly discuss three of the
most significant.

The first of these is the notion of *antithesis*, which is both a theological
concept and a principle with general societal implications. Although Kuyper
originated this term, the notion that it describes is as old as the Christian tradition itself. Groen van Prinsterer had spoken of the implacable opposition
between belief and unbelief. And of course Augustine had understood history
in terms of the cosmic conflict between the city of God and the city of this
world, each destined to live out its respective spiritual worldview alongside
the other until the final eschatological consummation and the ultimate triumph of the former. Kuyper understood antithesis in the same sense. The antithesis between Christian and nonchristian is of a basic religious character
and cannot be resolved into a higher synthesis; nor can it be eliminated this
side of the eschaton.

What is distinctive in Kuyper's notion is the way it came to be applied within
Dutch society. An emphasis on antithesis developed out of the schools crisis in
which Christians (Reformed and Catholic alike) sought to end the legal monopoly of the state schools over primary education and to gain public recognition and support for all religious schools—Protestant, Catholic and secular—in
an equitable manner. This emphasis led to the proliferation of parallel societies
and institutions organized along confessional lines. Thus, for example, were established separate Reformed, Catholic and secular labor unions, business associations, political parties and so on. The Netherlands therefore came to be
characterized by what is called *verzuiling*, or the vertical division of society into

---

[25]For a concise account of the development of the ARP and the CDA, see D. Th. Kuiper, "Historical and Sociological Development of ARP and CDA," in *Christian Political Options on Education,
Broadcasting, Party Formation, International Partnership, Economic Order, Responsibilities in the Welfare
State,* ed. C. den Hollander (The Hague: AR-Partijstichting, 1979), pp. 10-28. The contents of
this volume were presented at a conference on Christian democracy convened on the occasion of
the ARP's centenary in 1979. See also Irving, *Christian Democratic Parties,* pp. 192-216, for a treatment of Dutch Christian democracy within the context of the Christian democratic movement
as a whole.

various confessional subcultures existing parallel to each other and being largely self-contained.[26]

Second, Kuyper's doctrine of antithesis was complemented by his emphasis on *gemeene gratie* or common grace.[27] Common grace means simply that God in his mercy preserves his creation against the full consequences of sin even amidst the unbelief of mankind. It rains on both the just and the unjust; God's mercies extend to believer and unbeliever alike. Common grace might be seen as a "corrective" to the antithesis insofar as it forced Reformed Christians to acknowledge the good that was accomplished by adherents of *Weltanschauungen* otherwise at odds with them at the religious root level. In fact, however, rather than seeing the antithesis and common grace as dialectically related polarities, it is more accurate to see the former as anchored in the latter insofar as the clash between belief and unbelief occurs not in a shadowy realm of abstract forms, but within the concrete setting of God's creation to which all are subject. Accordingly, as we observed in the previous chapter, Kuyper could even appreciate the good side to the Revolution whose religious worldview he had nevertheless spent his career combating. The recognition of common grace furthermore removed the temptation on the part of Christians to imagine that separate institutions somehow insulated them from the effects of sin and unbelief and that all those outside this institutional network were wholly unaffected by God's preserving and providential grace.

Sovereignty in Its Own Sphere:
A Nonhierarchical Affirmation of Civil Society

A third characteristic theme in Kuyper is *souvereiniteit in eigen kring*, or *sovereignty*

---

[26] See Arend Lijphart, *The Politics of Accommodation: Pluralism and Democracy in the Netherlands* (Berkeley: University of California Press, 1975), esp. pp. 16–58, for an examination of the impact of *verzuiling* on the Dutch political system. See also James W. Skillen and Stanley W. Carlson-Thies, "Religion and Political Development in Nineteenth-Century Holland," *Publius* 12 (summer 1982): 43–64; and H. Daalder, "Parties and Politics in the Netherlands," *Political Studies* 3 (1955): 1–16. Although the configuration of Dutch politics has changed since the 1950s, Daalder's discussion is still important for understanding the historical development of Dutch politics throughout much of the twentieth century. The Netherlands is of interest to comparative political scientists as an example of "consociationalism," a phenomenon explored briefly in chapter five.

[27] In coining this phrase Kuyper deliberately chose the somewhat archaic *gratie* over the more usual *genade* in order to avoid the misunderstanding that common grace means universal saving grace in the specific theological sense (J. Klapwijk, "Calvin and Neo-Calvinism on Non-Christian Philosophy," in *The Idea of a Christian Philosophy* [Toronto: Wedge, 1973], p. 53). Kuyper's theory is set forth in the three volumes of *De Gemeene Gratie* (Kampen, Netherlands: J. H. Kok, 1903-4). For a more recent treatment in English of common grace, see Richard J. Mouw, *He Shines in All That's Fair: Culture and Common Grace* (Grand Rapids, Mich.: Eerdmans, 2001).

in one's own sphere.[28] This crucial motif undergirds neo-Calvinist political theory
and is perhaps its most distinctive doctrine. As we have observed, sovereignty in
one's own sphere, often shortened to simply *sphere-sovereignty,* can be found in
Groen van Prinsterer. Yet like the concepts of antithesis and common grace,
sovereignty in one's own sphere is not original to Calvinism or neo-Calvinism,
having roots in late medieval thought. Perhaps the most important implications
of this doctrine are that (1) ultimate sovereignty belongs to God alone, (2) all
earthly sovereignties are subsidiary to God's sovereignty, and (3) there is no ultimate (or rather, penultimate) locus of sovereignty in this world from which
other sovereignties are derivative. In this respect, sovereignty in one's own
sphere is traceable to Althusius and even to Calvin himself, whose understanding of societal pluriformity was eventually eclipsed by the more unitary theories
of sovereignty associated with Bodin and Hobbes.[29]

Kuyper applied this doctrine not merely to political authorities or to the
church/state question, but to all institutions of society. The family, the school,
business, labor, the arts and so forth, are all sovereign in their respective spheres.
These multiple communities and enterprises possess authority within a specific
sphere whose limits are set by the Creator. These limits may not be transgressed
without doing harm to the structure of society as ordained by God. Thus, for
example, when the state acts in a totalitarian manner and attempts to encroach
upon or subjugate the other societal spheres, sovereignty in one's own sphere
has been transgressed.[30] Kuyper asserted this principle against statist totalitarian
conceptions on the one hand, but also against medieval clericalism, or integral-
ism, which subordinated society to the authority of the church institution on
the other.

---

[28]This doctrine is set forth in Abraham Kuyper, *Souvereiniteit in Eigen Kring* (Kampen, Netherlands: J. H.
Kok, 1930), originally presented in 1880 as the inaugural address on the opening of the Free Univer-
sity. See also Jan D. Dengerink, *Critisch-Historisch Onderzoek naar de Sociologische Ontwikkeling van het
Beginsel der "Souvereiniteit in Eigen Kring" in de 19e en 20e Eeuw* [Critical-Historical Inquiry into the
Sociological Development of the Principle of Sphere-Sovereignty in the Nineteenth and Twentieth
Centuries] (Kampen, Netherlands: J. H. Kok, 1948).

[29]The history of the theory of sphere-sovereignty is briefly traced by Gordon J. Spykman in "Sphere-
Sovereignty in Calvin and the Calvinist Tradition," in *Exploring the Heritage of John Calvin,* ed. David
Holwerda (Grand Rapids, Mich.: Baker, 1976), pp. 163-208.

[30]Kuyper opposed not only the doctrine of state-sovereignty but also that of popular sovereignty as it
was "anti-theistically proclaimed at Paris in 1789" (*Lectures on Calvinism* [Grand Rapids, Mich.: Eerdmans, 1931], p. 85). There is no inconsistency in Kuyper's rejection of popular sovereignty as a political
doctrine and his advocacy of an enlarged franchise. To favor increased popular participation in the affairs of state need not commit one to the belief that the people are the ultimate source of sovereignty.
Similarly, the conviction that a hereditary monarchy is the best form of government need not require
a belief in monarchical absolutism.

It was with the doctrine of sphere-sovereignty in mind that Kuyper deliberately founded the Free University as an institution free from the control of either church or state. As an educational community, its task was distinct from that of either church or state, and it therefore possessed its own sphere of authority to be respected by these other institutions. Similarly the Anti-Revolutionary Party, although a distinctively Christian political party, was not to be subordinated to the authority of an institutional church. Characteristically, although Kuyper's followers have been strong partisans of Christian day school education for their children, the idea of a "parochial school," that is, a school attached to an ecclesiastical parish, has been anathema to them as a violation of sovereignty in one's own sphere.

Of the three implications of sphere-sovereignty mentioned above, the first two are shared with subsidiarity, that is, that ultimate sovereignty is God's alone and that all earthly authorities are subsidiary to this sovereignty. In affirming these two statements, both subsidiarity and sphere-sovereignty stand in implacable opposition to the ideologies I have probed. The will of the individual is not supreme, nor is that of the omnicompetent state. Where the two Christian approaches differ with each other, however, is on the third point: that there is no mediating sovereignty derivative from God's sovereignty and standing between God on the one hand and the individual and various human social formations on the other. We noted above that subsidiarity presupposes a societal hierarchy, ranging from God at the summit down to the individuals at the base. By contrast, sphere-sovereignty views society in a distinctly nonhierarchical manner, as shown in figure 3 (p. 232). The respective authorities of family, state, church, school, business and labor union are conferred by God himself and need no mediating institutions to hand them down.

Obviously this has the most relevance for the place of the institutional church in the larger society, as noted above in our discussion of the successive popes' role in disseminating Catholic social teachings. But it also has implications for the place of the state. In the Catholic account of societal pluriformity it makes sense to speak of *mediating* structures as the aggregate of social formations coming *between* the state and the individual. In the Reformed account this makes much less sense. It is not to say that the heirs of Groen and Kuyper do not value what is often called civil society; it is to say that in speaking of the various spheres of legitimate human activity in God's world, state and individual do not stand apart. Rather, they are simply two more spheres among the rest, standing not so much over and under, as alongside the others.

In Roman Catholic social teaching, because the state is ontologically higher than other social formations, there is need for some measure to prevent it becoming overbearing and absorbing them into its own sphere of competence. Hence subsidiarity.

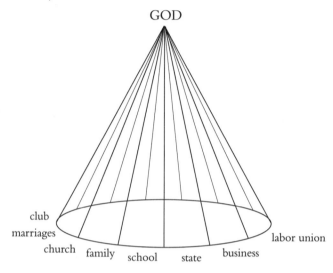

Figure 3. Society according to sphere-sovereignty

But subsidiarity is less a matter of recognizing internal structural differences among these formations than a prudential principle to attenuate the effects of an excessively top-down authority structure, that is, to keep hierarchy from becoming too hierarchical! The fact that subsidiarity is so easily transferred to EU relations with member states already illustrates one of its potential drawbacks. Britons in particular are less than enthusiastic about a fully integrated European federation because they doubt that the principle of subsidiarity will prove adequate to prevent Brussels from accumulating too much political power at the expense of London. Indeed one commentator likens subsidiarity to the tenth amendment to the United States Constitution, which formally allocates residual powers to the several states within the American federal system.[31] Given that this amendment has not kept Washington from what many see as an encroachment on the power of the states over the last century and a half, it is understandable that "Euro-skeptics" would be reluctant to plunge too deeply into a

---

[31]Frank L. Wilson, *European Politics Today: The Democratic Experience*, 3rd ed. (Upper Saddle River, N.J.: Prentice-Hall, 1999), p. 383.

similar arrangement on their side of the Atlantic. At this point I will not weigh in on one side or the other in the ongoing debate over the proper balance of powers in a federal system, except to say that it is almost inevitable that it will shift back and forth as social and economic conditions change over time. However, the same cannot and ought not be said of the relationship between, say, state and family, which are structurally distinct in a way that two levels of government are not.

Here is where sphere-sovereignty offers more potential as an alternative to subsidiarity, but where Kuyper's theoretical defense of this principle begins to find its limitations. Indeed, the problems with sphere-sovereignty are twofold. First, terminologically it is tainted by its association with sovereignty as such, which, at least since Bodin and Hobbes, has come to mean an ultimate authority that no mere human being should be held to possess. This is why some of Kuyper's followers prefer to speak of *differentiated authority* or even *differentiated responsibility*, the latter of which better captures, in addition to the authority of communities, the legitimate freedom of the individual person within the larger social context.[32] Whether one chooses to use sovereignty, authority or responsibility, the central Kuyperian assumption is that society is pluriform and consists of a variety of responsible agents, both communal and individual, whose legitimate range of activity is rooted immediately in God's sovereignty and which exist within normative limits placed on them by God himself.

There is a second and more serious difficulty with Kuyper's defense of sphere-sovereignty: while it is solidly grounded in human experience, it lacks a certain systematic theoretical justification. Why, for example, does the state constitute a sphere distinct from that of, say, the institutional church? Why ought parents to be responsible for disciplining their own children? Why not call in a police officer to do the job? Why, further, should not business enter-

---

[32]The expression "differentiated responsibility" is an English translation of the Dutch *gespreide verantwoordelijkheid*, which has been used in the literature of the Christian Democratic Appeal (CDA) in the Netherlands since the late 1970s as a synonym for both subsidiarity and Kuyper's *soevereiniteit in eigen kring*. See Hans Borstlap, "Differentiated Responsibility: A Christian-Democratic Contribution to the Discussion on Economic Order," in *Christian Political Options on Education, Broadcasting, Party Formation, International Partnership, Economic Order, Responsibilities in the Welfare State*, ed. C. den Hollander (The Hague: AR-Partijstichting, 1979), pp. 206, 209-30. The term has been picked up by Goudzwaard, Skillen and others in their writings. Although the CDA uses this term to cover both sphere-sovereignty and subsidiarity, its specific use for the former is apparently justified by its etymological connection in English with Herman Dooyeweerd's historical norm of differentiation, despite the latter's roots in the Dutch *differentiëring*. See Dooyeweerd, *Vernieuwing en Bezinning: om het reformatorisch grondmotief* (Zutphen, Netherlands: J. B. van den Brink, 1959), esp. pp. 70-76. See my discussion of Dooyeweerd immediately following.

prises and labor unions become arms of the state, as was the case in the former Soviet Union and other countries following its model? To be sure, Kuyper could answer that these spheres normatively remain distinct because of God's creation ordinances. His answer would be correct from a foundational religious standpoint, but in itself it would not take us very far theoretically in our attempts to understand which areas of life are distinct spheres and which are not. Thus Kuyper's work remained to be completed at his death.

Dooyeweerd's Contribution

Kuyper's seminal reflections would come to be fleshed out with greater theoretical sophistication by Herman Dooyeweerd (1894-1977). Having grown up in the Reformed Christian community in the Netherlands, Dooyeweerd studied law at the Free University where he earned his doctorate in 1917. In 1922 he became director of the Kuyper Institute in The Hague. From 1926 until his retirement in 1965, he taught at the Free University. He was a prolific scholar who wrote a large number of publications, culminating in 1935 with his massive three-volume work, *De Wijsbegeerte der Wetsidee*,[33] whose title was thereafter associated with the philosophical movement as a whole.[34] The fact that he wrote largely in the Dutch language initially delayed the wider dissemination of his thought. But some twenty years later his 1935 work was translated into English, revised and given the title *A New Critique of Theoretical Thought*.[35]

As a philosopher, Dooyeweerd has made at least two unique contributions. To begin with, he has developed a systematic philosophy rooted in the conviction that all theoretical thought has pre-theoretical and nonfalsifiable religious underpinnings.[36] Any theory making a pretense to religious neutrality, whether on the grounds of a universal rational faculty within the person or on the basis of the objective nature of so-called facts in the surrounding world, must be seen for what it is: epistemologically naive and unaware of its own dogmatic starting point. It is further rooted in a deficient anthropology that elevates one aspect of the total person and makes this the unifying center of the human self. Yet far

---

[33]Herman Dooyeweerd, *De Wijsbegeerte der Wetsidee* (Amsterdam: H. J. Paris, 1935-1936).

[34]Literally "philosophy of the law-idea," though it is sometimes rendered in English as "philosophy of the cosmonomic idea," the word *cosmonomic* being chosen to emphasize that the *law* at issue is not a positive legal code but the very law by which God upholds the cosmos.

[35]Herman Dooyeweerd, *A New Critique of Theoretical Thought*, 3 vols. (Amsterdam: H. J. Paris; Philadelphia: Presbyterian & Reformed, 1953-1958).

[36]See Herman Dooyeweerd, *In the Twilight of Western Thought: Studies in the Pretended Autonomy of Philosophical Thought* (Nutley, N.J.: Craig, 1960), esp. pp. 1-61.

from being an ostensibly neutral faculty, reason can be understood, according to Dooyeweerd, only as the logical aspect of our total experience. In this respect, faith and reason are not the dialectical polarities that much of the western intellectual tradition, from Averroës and Thomas Aquinas to Hobbes and Marx, has come to think of them. Rather they are two aspects of a much richer and fuller human experience. Any effort to account theoretically for this experience is necessarily dependent on an ultimate religious commitment lying outside of and preceding the theoretical enterprise. Even the behavioral political scientist anchors her endeavor in religious convictions concerning the nature of humanity, of the world we inhabit, and of the place of politics in that world.

In the second place, Dooyeweerd's philosophy eschews all reductionisms. Although this principled antireductionism is by no means peculiar to Dooyeweerd, being found most notably in phenomenology,[37] his own contribution consists in (1) the placement of this insight within the larger understanding that God's creation is not a haphazard product of chance, but an orderly cosmos subject to laws and norms given by his grace; and (2) an effort to spell out those aspects of reality that are themselves irreducible but, if placed in an apostate religious context, nevertheless lend a certain plausibility to the reductionist project. These irreducible aspects of reality are called *modes*, and the mature Dooyeweerd posits fifteen of these, listed here in ascending order: arithmetic (number), spatial, kinematic (extensive movement), physical (energy), biotic (organic life), psychic (feeling, sensation), logical, historical (cultural, formative), lingual (symbolic), social, economic, aesthetic, jural (justice, retribution), ethical (temporal love, loyalty) and pistical (faith). The persistent tendency of nonchristian—or perhaps nontheistic—theoretical thought is, not only to fasten onto one or more of these modal aspects and to read the rest of creation through them, but to assume that doing so provides the key to understanding the world in its totality.[38]

Here is where we see the connection with the various ideologies, which, as we have repeatedly indicated, are fundamentally idolatrous. Idolatry is linked to reductionism, insofar as the one aspect to which everything else is reduced

---

[37]On Dooyeweerd's relationship to Edmund Husserl's phenomenology, see Wolters, "The Intellectual Milieu of Herman Dooyeweerd," in *The Legacy of Herman Dooyeweerd: Reflections on Critical Philosophy in the Christian Tradition,* ed. C. T. McIntire (Lanham, Md.: University Press of America, 1985), esp. pp. 10-16.

[38]There is an interesting analogue to Dooyeweerd's modal analysis in Lesslie Newbigin, *Foolishness to the Greeks: The Gospel and Western Culture* (Grand Rapids, Mich.: Eerdmans, 1986), pp. 65-94, esp. 83ff.

tends inevitably to be imbued with divine qualities. Liberalism commits what may be called a *logical* reduction. It is in the nature of logic to break things down into their components for purposes of analysis. Botanists delve into the workings of photosynthesis, examining the way plants use sunlight to convert water and carbon dioxide into glucose and oxygen, thus enabling them to grow. Philosophers divide their field of endeavor into the various branches of ontology, epistemology, ethics, legal philosophy, aesthetics and so forth. This theoretical division of the object of study does not, however, alter the integral character of reality itself as we experience it at a pretheoretical level. The logical reduction mistakes the analytical enterprise for reality itself, rather than seeing it as enriching our understanding of reality as we experience it. When one succumbs to the temptation to *reduce* phenomena to their constituent parts, then one is guilty of the sort of reductionism Dooyeweerd rejects.

Conservatism tends to fall prey to a *historical* reduction. Reacting against the logical reduction of liberalism, which leads to the overestimation of reason, conservatism tends to emphasize the place of the historical process and the value of that which has emerged within it. Although Dooyeweerd identifies the historical aspect with cultural formation, conservatism by contrast sees traditions emerging in a nearly unconscious manner. Furthermore, in their analysis of society, some conservatives appeal rather too easily to an organic metaphor, thus falling into a *biological* reduction. Organisms grow naturally apart from their own wills. Similarly customs and mores are seen to develop of their own accord, and if one can speak at all of reason it is of a reason transcending that of the mere individual. This higher reason takes on almost divine status.

Socialism, particularly the Marxist variety, tends to fall into an *economic* reduction, as noted in chapter six. Thus reality is fundamentally *economic* reality. Anyone arguing otherwise, for example, that the state is a jural entity normed by the principle of justice, is deluding herself into believing that the world is more complex than it actually is. Similarly the different varieties of nationalism partake of a *biological* reduction, insofar as the national community is viewed as a large family; a *historical* reduction, insofar as the nation is seen to be based in a seminal act of foundation along the lines of the American War of Independence or the subsequent adoption of the Constitution; or perhaps even a *lingual* reduction, as one can see with the focus on language in Quebec nationalism. In reality, as already hinted in chapter four, a nation is a multifaceted phenomenon functioning in all three of these aspects and more.

Ostensibly one might claim that nationalists deify a nation that has not been so reduced. Yet in the real world such a nation would be too vacuous an entity to command the veneration of its members. Furthermore, any creature willfully cut off from the Creator must inevitably be conceived in reduced fashion. If man is not created in God's image, that is, if his relationship with his Creator is not the defining relationship constitutive of his very being, then he is inevitably man the individual, *homo faber, homo economicus* or some such. All reality points to something beyond itself; accordingly, the followers of various secular philosophies and ideologies err in misreading this direction and looking within the immanent horizon of the cosmos for its objective. Hence the tendency to view all communities, whether the supposedly fictive aggregations of liberalism, the national community or the community of the democratic people as "nothing but" a particular facet of human experience through which it is read.

We have suggested that the notion of sphere-sovereignty, or differentiated responsibility (as I shall refer to it from now on), presupposes a nonhierarchical conception of society. But if society is not an *ontological* hierarchy, that is, one based on a chain of being in which God himself can be located, as appears to be the case with subsidiarity, this does not imply an absence of *hierarchies of authority.* Presidents are still presidents. A chief librarian is still chief librarian. Parents are still parents. But such hierarchies are limited by the nature of the authoritative office, which is further limited by institutional context.

For example, in the university classroom the instructor—whom we shall call Theresa—possesses real but limited authority over her students. When she distributes the course syllabus at the beginning of the semester, she is therein informing the students what they are expected to do to pass the course. They must come to class, do the assignments, take the examinations and generally respect the office of the instructor, who is empowered to enforce these expectations in assigning grades. The instructor's authority does not extend, however, to telling the students what they should and should not eat for dinner that evening, whom they should marry or what sort of work they should pursue after graduation. Such decisions properly belong to the individual students themselves, *but not in their capacity as students.* Because the office of student does not exhaust who they are or what their life's responsibilities are, as persons they possess a legitimate sphere of authority in which they are free to make decisions concerning themselves alone.

Furthermore, it may be that one of the students—whom we shall call Norman—is a mature student who also works as a police officer. If Theresa should happen to drive through the intersection Norman is policing, then she would come under the latter's authority *in that context*. While the roles would seem to be reversed, this is not an entirely accurate way to describe the situation. It would be more correct to observe that each person possesses an authoritative office manifesting itself in limited ways in different institutional contexts. Neither Theresa nor Norman is intrinsically subject to the other apart from their respective offices. But Norman the student is subject to Professor Theresa's authority insofar as he is enrolled in her course. And Theresa the automobile driver is subject to Officer Norman's authority on the roads. If Theresa runs a red light, Officer Norman should not refrain from issuing a traffic ticket simply because she is his professor.

Let us say further that Theresa has a grown son, named Thaddeus, who is an alderman in the local city council. As alderman he is responsible, along with his fellow aldermen, for enacting the municipal bylaws to which all citizens, including his mother, are subject. In his capacity as son, Thaddeus owes his mother the proper honor due his mother, but in her capacity as citizen Theresa stands under the authority of Thaddeus in his capacity as alderman. If, out of misplaced honor for his mother, Thaddeus should use his office to seek to exempt her from the provisions of a particular bylaw, we would rightly say that he has abused his office, the abuse at issue being a conflict of interest. Although some political cultures expect that their rulers will, as a matter of course, enrich themselves and their families at public expense, those with greater consciousness of the differentiated responsibilities of various individuals and communities properly understand that conflict of interest entails injustice. An acknowledgment of differentiated responsibility means that Thaddeus will not honor his mother in inappropriate fashion by compromising his public office.[39]

The fact that different authoritative offices reside in different persons in different institutional contexts and at different times indicates the insufficiency of any social theory that would posit a permanent and noninterchangeable hierarchical relationship between any two communities or persons. Here we see, once again, a genuine shortcoming of subsidiarity, as Jonathan Chaplin has

---

[39]In 1973 in a major American city an alderman accused the mayor of nepotism for having appointed the son of another alderman to a city board. "I apologize for nothing," he is reported to have shouted. "What's a father for?" <www.suntimes.com/century/m1973.html>. This unguarded outburst manifests a weak sense of the differentiated responsibility attached to the various authoritative offices in human society.

pointed out.[40] Subsidiarity assumes that if one of the "lower" communities or an individual is unable to function in accordance with its nature, then a "higher" authority steps in and assists the lower until the problem is rectified. This principle justifies, for example, the intervention of the institutional church in the affairs of state through the publication of papal encyclicals and a conference of bishops' pastoral letters. But why might a "lower" community or individual not intervene in a "higher" community to set aright a deficiency in the latter? This is undoubtedly what Martin Luther could be seen to have done with respect to the failings of the Roman Church in nailing his ninety-five theses to the door of the castle church in Wittenberg. Perhaps subsidiarity would not entirely exclude such a possibility, although it does not account for it as well as does the principle of differentiated responsibility.

A recognition of differentiated responsibility would further exclude any conception of society wherein one group of people is permanently subject to another apart from an authoritative office. Obvious examples of this would include various forms of racially based segregation, as in the American South prior to the 1960s and South Africa prior to the 1990s. In both settings the rights and responsibilities of citizenship were apportioned unequally according to skin color. Blacks were seen to be permanently subordinate to whites, the latter of whom were deemed fit to rule simply by virtue of their relative absence of epidermal pigment. Similarly, prior to the late twentieth century many people assumed that women must be permanently subordinate to men simply because of their sex, in a tradition going at least as far back as Aristotle, if not before. To be sure, not all offices can or ought to be allocated irrespective of sex. For example, only a woman can be a mother and a man a father. The office of husband belongs to the man, while that of wife belongs to the woman. Yet one of the genuine contributions of feminism in its various forms is in pointing out the absurdity of arbitrarily excluding women from certain offices for which sex is simply not a relevant characteristic. More than absurd, such exclusion is unjust.

This brings us back to the issue we raised above: how does Dooyeweerd's philosophy help us to distinguish among the various spheres whose differentiated responsibility Kuyper correctly came to understand? He does this through observing that various entities in creation, including societal communal structures, function in all aspects of reality while relating to the individual aspects in

---

[40]Jonathan Chaplin, "Subsidiarity as a Political Norm," in *Political Theory and Christian Vision: Essays in Memory of Bernard Zylstra,* ed. Jonathan Chaplin and Paul Marshall (Lanham, Md.: University Press of America, 1994), pp. 81-100.

different ways relevant to their internal structures. The specifics of Dooyeweerd's modal theory are beyond the scope of the present study and have been
quite adequately treated elsewhere.[41] It will suffice for us to mention a few examples of how it works. To begin with, although an honorary medal and a coin
may be designed by the same artist and although each may be judged individually as splendid works of art, the coin functions as a medium of economic exchange while the medal does not. Both, it is true, possess some economic value,
and thus both can be said to function economically in some sense. But the *economic* aspect is especially crucial to the functioning of the coin in a way that it
is not to the medal. The medal, by contrast, is awarded to someone for some
heroic deed or exemplary accomplishment. One might, of course, argue that
the medal is exchanged economically for something of value performed by the
recipient for the larger society. Yet this is a drastically reduced way of describing
the award, since the recipient did not perform the deed at issue for the express
purpose of acquiring the award. In fact, it would be more accurate to hold that
the *jural* aspect is particularly significant for understanding the nature of the
medal, since the agent bestowing it upon the worthy recipient is in some sense
rendering to her her due, which is the classic definition of justice.

   Thus, for Dooyeweerd, a *modal analysis*, that is, an analysis of something in
terms of the various aspects in which it functions, serves to confirm our pretheoretical experience of the difference between a coin and a medal. In
Dooyeweerd's terminology, the coin is *economically qualified* while the medal is
jurally qualified. Such analysis, to be sure, does not alter our experience, nor is
it absolutely necessary to our experience as such, but it does help to enrich it
and further to distinguish things for which experience as such may lead in ambiguous directions.

   A similar analysis can be undertaken with respect to human communities.
Like the coin and the medal, human communities are historically situated, having been brought into being through the processes of cultural formation. The
coin and the medal are quite evidently products of the artisan's skill, having
been fashioned from preexisting material. Communities, as Aristotle correctly
points out, are less obviously the product of fabrication, nor can they be objects
of ownership, as can the coin and the medal. Yet they too owe their existence
to cultural formation. In Dooyeweerd's language such entities are *historically*

---

[41]In addition to Dooyeweerd's own writings, perhaps the best available secondary treatment of his gen-
    eral philosophy, including his modal theory, is found in Roy Clouser, *The Myth of Religious Neutrality*
    (Notre Dame, Ind.: University of Notre Dame Press, 1992).

founded and thus have this in common with each other. Each has been shaped by cultural formative *power* of some sort, although the type of power may differ vastly from one entity to the next.

With respect to communities Dooyeweerd's modal analysis enables us to differentiate among various kinds. Our second example illustrates this. Both the business enterprise and the state are shaped by formative power, although the nature of that power differs with each. Each is furthermore characterized by an internal authority structure in which persons charged with the appropriate responsible offices exercise a certain limited authority over the other members of the community. In a business enterprise the authoritative hierarchy extends from board members to the chief executive officer to the vice presidents to middle management all the way down to the other employees. The sort of authority that a supervisor exerts over her subordinates may indeed have a mandatory character, but the sorts of sanctions employed to enforce this authority are limited by the nature of the communal setting. If an employee repeatedly fails at his job, he may be transferred elsewhere in the organization or perhaps even removed from the organization entirely. He cannot be spanked, excommunicated from his church, deprived of his right to vote in general elections, imprisoned, have his driver's license revoked, or be put to death, because these types of power lie beyond the competence of an employer.

In the state, by contrast, the hierarchy of authority extends from any of several governmental institutions at the top, including the legislature, the president or prime minister and the court system, down through regional, local and municipal governments to the citizens themselves. In a democratic polity one might indeed place the citizens at the top insofar as political leaders are accountable to them at election time. As Paul puts it in Romans 13, the duly constituted governmental authorities properly have the "power of the sword," that is, the coercive power of life and death over their subjects. Although many jurisdictions, particularly in the West, no longer practice capital punishment, this form of power nevertheless still belongs to government in principle, as part of its mandate to do justice. We shall explore this power more fully in the next chapter. At this point it is enough to observe that such power by no means implies an absolute power over all persons in every aspect of their lives. Government possesses the authority to arrest suspected criminals, lay charges, try, imprison and possibly even execute them if found guilty. It cannot, however, excommunicate them from their ecclesial communions, terminate their employment, suspend their library privileges, dismiss them from their country club or expel them from school. In short, both the business enterprise and the state are founded on a basic organizing power, but the types of power available within each context and how they are exercised are quite different.

But there's another layer of analysis that provides a more profound theoretical insight into the differences among various communities. Once again we point to the business enterprise and the state. A business enterprise exists for an express economic purpose, for example, the manufacture of goods, the provision of a service or the application of technical knowledge. It marshals the various available resources for this pursuit, including capital, labor and raw material. Normatively speaking, a business uses these resources in a stewardly, nonexploitative fashion and enhances these for the greater benefit of others. As it does so, it compensates the various contributors to the enterprise in accordance with the value of their respective contributions. This central task is more than simply an arbitrary goal chosen by the members of the organization; it is, in fact, essential to its structure as a business. Thus, according to Dooyeweerd, a business enterprise is *economically qualified* in a way that, say, a family is not.

The state, on the other hand, is a political community based on a monopolization of the power of the sword over a defined territory. Its citizens are the members of this community, and they are led by governing authorities organized into executive offices, legislatures, courts and bureaucracies. But the mere possession of power is insufficient to distinguish the state from other concentrations of power, especially coercive sword power. As Augustine and many others have repeatedly pointed out, apart from justice a commonwealth is indistinguishable from a band of thieves. Thus the state and its governing authorities are distinguished from other communities by a particular relationship between power and justice. In Dooyeweerd's terms, once again, the state is *historically founded* and *jurally qualified.*

Although some observers, apparently including Augustine himself, believe it possible for justice to be altogether absent from the political community, in fact justice is always present insofar as the state inevitably functions in the jural aspect. The governing authorities within the state are perpetually in the process of balancing various interests both within and without. To be sure, they may get the balance wrong—perhaps gravely so. They may privilege whites at the expense of nonwhites, Castillians at the expense of Catalans, men at the expense of women. Yet the presence of this balancing is an intrinsic part of the state's structure. Thus even the ideologies, rooted as they are in an idolatrous worldview, work with some conception of justice, although it may not be spelled out explicitly. Pursuing a nonideological politic is a matter not of importing justice where it is absent, but of rebalancing the jural task of the state where justice has been perverted, that is, where *injustice* is present. Injustice, after all, is not so much the absence of justice, as is commonly thought, as a distortion in the performance of the state's jural mandate. We now turn in the next chapter to explore this interplay between power and justice in the state's structure.

9

THE STATE
AND ITS TASK

Doing Justice in God's World

There is a perpetual temptation among political theorists to anchor their respective views of politics in either power or justice, as if these were somehow antithetical, or at least dialectically related, principles. Perhaps the most common of these tendencies is the one that would reduce politics to power per se. This is such a ubiquitous tendency that it is impossible to ascribe it to any one school of thought. Nevertheless, the school of political realism is especially prominent, tracing its lineage at least as far back as Augustine. Hans Morgenthau (1904-1980), for example, argues that only power is a specifically political category. Justice is something else entirely and properly belongs in the area of ethics or morality, where the focus of attention is on the individual, and not in the field of politics, whose focus is the larger community.[1] While implicitly disagreeing with Morgenthau's relegation of morality to the purely private realm, Reinhold Niebuhr nevertheless believes that there is a great gulf fixed between the morality of individuals and that of communities. Though individual persons may engage in self-sacrificing acts, communities, including the state, tend to act solely to preserve and enhance their own power.[2] Both Mor-

---

[1]Hans J. Morgenthau, *Politics Among Nations: The Struggle for Power and Peace,* rev. Kenneth W. Thompson, 6th ed. (New York: Alfred A. Knopf, 1985), pp. 3-19.
[2]Reinhold Niebuhr, *Moral Man and Immoral Society* (New York: Scribner's, 1960).

genthau and Niebuhr are recent representatives of political realism, which is based on the premise that power is the primary currency of politics.

Bertrand de Jouvenel's definition of politics also highlights the role of power. According to Jouvenel, politics is "every systematic effort, performed at any place in the social field, to move other men in pursuit of some design cherished by the mover."[3] It is aggregative, insofar as it "builds, consolidates, and keeps in being aggregates of men" for this purpose.[4] If someone is able to bring people together for purposes of action, then that first someone is said to have power. Such power may take the form of brute physical force or at least the implied threat of its use. A man carrying a pistol into a bank has the power to get its personnel to turn their money over to him. A military unit attacking an outpost may have sufficient power to seize it and maintain control of it against the enemy's defenses. Or it may be that the mere threat of an attack by a more powerful army will cause the outpost's current occupiers to abandon it for a more defensible position.

Most of the power we encounter on a day-to-day basis is scarcely identifiable as such—at least at first glance. A favorite teacher or pastor may have a certain influence over us. A friend persuades us to accompany her to a baseball game or a concert. A coworker convinces us of the wisdom of pursuing a certain production or marketing strategy. Or, in a more sinister manifestation, a president selectively submits, or even fabricates, information to the Congress so that it will vote in favor of an unwise military action. All of these are examples of power.

We have indicated earlier that sword power is that power properly belonging exclusively to the state as a political community of citizens and government. But the coercive power of the sword is by no means the only form of power available to political leaders. In fact, where coercive force is too frequently appealed to, a government is likely to be in the process of losing its effective power and thus its capacity to do justice.[5] The police state is a fragile state, where the ubiquitous presence of weapons-bearing soldiers indicates weakness rather than strength. If citizens need to be cowed into submission, they have probably be-

---

[3]Bertrand de Jouvenel, *The Pure Theory of Politics* (New Haven, Conn.: Yale University Press, 1963), p. 30.

[4]Bertrand de Jouvenel, *The Nature of Politics: Selected Essays of Bertrand de Jouvenel*, ed. Dennis Hale and Marc Landy (New Brunswick, N.J.: Transaction, 1992), p. 72. See also de Jouvenal's *On Power: Its Nature and the History of Its Growth* (New York: Viking, 1949).

[5]See Emil Brunner, *Justice and the Social Order*, trans. Mary Hottinger (New York: Harper & Brothers, 1945), p. 213.

gun to doubt the government's *right* to exercise power, that is, its *authority*. And where this has occurred, political community has begun to break down.

Although authority has tended to fall into disrepute in the modern age, particularly in the wake of the French Revolution on the one hand and the Kantian project on the other, it is a phenomenon without which we could hardly live as persons embedded in community. Our very ability to embark on collective endeavors requires some sort of overall coordination by an authoritative agent, whether that agent be manifested personally or institutionally. Authority is, to be sure, subject to abuse, but, as Richard T. De George properly observes, our enemy is not authority as such, but only its abuse.[6] Robert Nisbet argues that despite the evident erosion in respect for authority in the United States, which he traces to the turbulence of the 1960s and early 1970s, there is nevertheless an inexorable drift toward the leviathan state, as bureaucratic institutions attempt to compensate for this erosion within the whole range of nongovernmental institutions.[7] This indicates that, despite widespread skepticism over the need for authority, it inevitably asserts itself in some fashion and not always in healthy ways.

Authority is usually defined as the *right* to exercise power. This would seem to indicate that power and authority are not to be identified as they are in the Hobbesian project. Hannah Arendt is careful to distinguish the two, defining political power as a potentially limitless capacity resident in the people as a whole, and authority as a quasi-religious phenomenon rooted in an initial founding act establishing the body politic and investing it with continuing stability for the future.[8] De George observes that not all authority implies the exercise of a commanding power over subordinates. Performatory authority entails the right to act on someone else's behalf, while epistemic authority denotes the possession of a high level of knowledge over a particular field, for example, mathematics or psychology.[9] To be an authority in one's field is perhaps to possess a certain potential power over others, but not to command obedience as such. Moreover, the mere exercise of commanding power does not always entail its rightful exercise. A bandit and a police officer may both carry a

---

[6]Richard T. De George, *The Nature and Limits of Authority* (Lawrence: University of Kansas Press, 1985), p. 291. This statement is, in fact, the very last sentence of the book and sums up the preceding argument.

[7]Robert Nisbet, *The Twilight of Authority* (New York: Oxford University Press, 1975).

[8]Hannah Arendt, "What Is Authority?" in *Between Past and Future* (Harmondsworth, U.K.: Penguin, 1977), pp. 91-141.

[9]De George, *Nature and Limits of Authority*, pp. 26-92.

weapon. Yet to equate the bandit and the police officer is to gloss over a rather significant difference between the two. Some, especially those of anarchist sentiments, have sought to diminish this difference by speaking of police power as simply organized official violence. On a pretheoretical, experiential level, however, few have difficulty distinguishing between, say, the Royal Canadian Mounted Police and the al-Qaeda terrorist organization. Although both certainly possess coercive power, the former possesses legitimate authority to use this power while the latter does not.

But if power and authority are not identical, there is nevertheless a sense in which *authority is a type of power in itself*, distinct from, though certainly related to, the coercive power of the sword. Moreover, insofar as political authority does justice within the context of the state, the state's power is further enhanced, as Emil Brunner observes.[10] In this respect *political power cannot be reduced to sword power*, but is much more complex and multifaceted. For most people the policeman's authority is felt not by the presence of a gun, but by the wearing of a uniform or badge. It is well known that in Great Britain the police officers, or bobbies, as they are known colloquially, are generally unarmed. Yet crime is no higher there than in countries whose police do carry weapons. In most jurisdictions criminal activity is exceptional rather than typical. For the vast majority of citizens, the very presence of the uniform exerts a subtle power over them that is difficult to account for theoretically but is easily intuited at an experiential level. There is, to be sure, the implied threat of coercive power in the event of disobedience to the law. Yet the uniform connotes much more than this. Most people reflexively honor the uniform and what it stands for: the rule of law, the maintenance of public order and safety, and in general doing justice. They likely do not go through an elaborate process of reasoning, for example, that the social order effected by authority is necessary to human well-being, on every single occasion when they see a uniformed officer of the law. In this respect, whenever authority is encountered—even by mature adults—it is generally not evaluated and tested rationally in the manner extolled by a Kant, Piaget or Kohlberg; it is simply obeyed.[11] At a pretheoretical level it is perceived and experienced as a reality whose very power is intrinsic to its status as authority.

Of course, not everyone is comfortable with this inevitable human ten-

---

[10]Brunner, *Justice and the Social Order*, p. 213.

[11]De George seems to understand this, although he too is influenced by the Kantian notion of moral autonomy. See De George, *Nature and Limits of Authority*, pp. 188-216.

dency to obey authority, and indeed such obedience can have its dark side. Yves R. Simon admits that authority has a bad name in our modern world and that associated with it are fears that it will conflict in some fashion with justice, vitality, truth and order.[12] Richard Sennett argues that authority provokes in those subject to it a fear of domination and dependence, the only answer to which is a periodic disruption in the chain of command through negotiation between authority and subjects that would make the former more visible and legible.[13] Moreover, authority occasionally means that people are made to do things they not only dislike but believe are wrong, as demonstrated by Stanley Milgram's famous Yale University experiments in the early 1960s.[14] Yet, like it or not, people do obey authority and this appears to be part of their very makeup as communal beings.

This tendency to obey can, of course, be observed also with respect to specifically political authority. Political authority is the right possessed by government to exercise power over those subject to it, including citizens and resident noncitizens. To some degree such authority is shared with citizens as members of the state or body politic insofar as they have, in a democracy, the right to vote, to stand for public office and to speak out freely on the issues of the day. Yet this shared authority of citizenship, which might be called secondary political authority, by no means abrogates or diminishes what we might call the primary political authority of government, which continues to exist and to do its job, albeit subject to the periodic assessment of the voters.[15]

---

[12]Yves Simon, *A General Theory of Authority* (Notre Dame, Ind.: University of Notre Dame Press, 1962), pp. 13-22.

[13]Richard Sennett, *Authority* (New York: Alfred A. Knopf, 1980).

[14]Milgram set up a situation in which his subjects believed they were administering successively higher doses of electricity to a "victim" at the urging of a white-coated laboratory supervisor, who assured them that he himself assumed full responsibility for their actions. Milgram himself plays off the tendency to obey against the assumption of personal autonomy in those who broke off the experiment, having become convinced that their continued participation in it was wrong. Yet, contrary to Milgram's analysis, at least two of the subjects claimed to be following a higher authority—God—in opposing the authority of the lab supervisor. Once again, those breaking with the experiment were not morally autonomous in a Kantian sense but were simply obeying what they saw to be an authority superior to that of the lab supervisor. See Stanley Milgram, *Obedience to Authority* (New York: HarperCollins, 1983).

[15]Some might plausibly argue that since a democratic government is ultimately responsible to the voters, the latter bear the primary authority and the former the secondary authority. But this unduly assumes that democracy is intrinsic to government as such, which it is not, as noted in chapter five. Democratic institutions are sometimes very fragile, where a political culture is unsupportive, and often fall prey to military or other autocratic regimes. Yet government as such continues to exist, even as its form may change from time to time. In this respect its authority is primary.

What then is the source of government's authority? To be sure, the Christian would affirm that it comes from God, and this is certainly correct. But this does not mean that every existing form of government and every occupant of every governmental office bears God's stamp of approval, as some might conclude. It does mean that he has ordained an institution with a unique task in his world: to do justice to the diversity of individuals and communities in his world. Thus the authority of government must inevitably be related to its jural task, which is intrinsic to its makeup.

We noted in the previous chapter a certain longstanding tendency to view justice as a substantial entity that is either present in or absent from a given human community. For both Plato and Aristotle justice is a virtue to be cultivated along with other virtues, such as practical wisdom, courage and moderation. Much as one can speak of a person lacking courage, so also can one speak of someone lacking in justice. A disordered person or city is one in which this ordering virtue of justice is not present. Cicero defines a commonwealth as an assembly of people united by a common acknowledgment of right or justice (*ius*, or its Greek equivalent *dikē*). Augustine disputes this definition, apparently on solid empirical grounds. Where a city does not, he argues, pay God the homage that is due him, there can be no justice. Thus pagan cities could not be commonwealths according to Cicero's definition. Augustine famously alters this definition, arguing that a commonwealth is an assembly of reasonable beings held together by shared loves and thereby excluding justice as a criterion.[16] It is this Augustinian approach that has been picked up by the likes of Morgenthau and Niebuhr.

More recently we have come to hear of people working for justice as if it were a distant goal to be accomplished through a variety of possible means. People seek a "just society" as if it were the equivalent of Plato's ideal republic or More's utopia. In other words, it does not exist now and may never come into existence in all its perfection, but it is something we can nevertheless attempt to achieve in part. There is perhaps some irony in the fact that both idealists and political realists subscribe to similar definitions of justice, assuming it is possible for it to be altogether absent from a political community. But this is not true. The classic definition of justice is to render to each person her due *(suum quique)*. This means that justice requires action of some sort. The active character of justice is pointed out by Oliver O'Dono-

---

[16]Augustine *City of God* 9.

van, who observes that the Hebrew word *mishpat*, often translated as "justice," consists not so much of an accomplished state of affairs as of an act of
judgment.[17] While I do not believe acts of judgment can be so easily disconnected from just states of affairs rooted in and produced by them, he is nevertheless correct to note the active nature of justice, which is clearly related
to the jural task of the state.

In other words, justice is a defining aspect of the state and undergirds its
unique political authority. No state is ever altogether bereft of justice in this
sense. Yet under the influence of the various ideologies the state may seriously
misconceive its mandate and perform its jural task in gravely distorted fashion. Among the worst recent examples of this are Nazi Germany and Stalin's
Soviet Union. But even Western democracies routinely pervert justice, albeit
in less overtly destructive ways. If virtually everyone implicitly understands
that, structurally speaking, the state performs its task by rendering to each her
due, there is nevertheless widespread disagreement concerning who is due
what within its jurisdiction. When the followers of the ideologies clash in the
political arena, it is simplistic to assert that one side favors justice while the
other does not. It is more accurate to observe that each party wants to see
justice done but that each conceives of it differently, congruent with its own
ideological presuppositions.

If, for example, there is a dispute between a worker and a labor union over
the issue of the closed shop, the liberal and the socialist will differ as to how
such a dispute should be settled. People seek justice as they understand it,
but each nevertheless comes to a different conclusion as to what justice requires. The consistent liberal will argue that on the basis of the rights of individuals, no person should be required to join a labor union against her
wishes. The socialist, on the other hand, will tend to argue that class solidarity must take priority over individual preferences and that compulsory union
membership is necessary to ensure that workers in general are treated justly
by their employers. Of course, both cannot be right. This difference of opinion is complicated by the fact that governing authorities are required to adjudicate, not only the dispute between the worker and the union, but the
clash between the liberal and the socialist, which is no simple matter, particularly if the government is dominated by a party representing only one of

---

[17]Oliver O'Donovan, *The Desire of the Nations: Rediscovering the Roots of Political Theology* (Cambridge:
Cambridge University Press, 1997), p. 39.

these viewpoints.[18] If government must be evenhanded in its treatment of worker and union, liberal and socialist, it cannot be neutral with respect to which vision of justice will undergird its decision. Yet whatever decision it finally makes, the government will inevitably be exercising its jural task.

Another example will suffice to illustrate the divergent ways liberals and nationalists go about undertaking this jural balancing act animated by their own respective visions of justice. In 1976 the Parti québécois came to power for the first time in the province of Quebec. The following year it enacted Bill 101 into law. This bill, among other things, required that public signs outside of commercial establishments be in the French language only and that, with some exceptions, most parents be required to educate their children in French-language schools. Traditional liberals argued, with some plausibility, that such requirements were unjust because they conflicted with a number of cherished rights of the individual, most notably freedom of speech. But Quebec nationalists argued, to the contrary, that the province's Francophones had historically suffered various forms of discrimination, that the French fact in Canada was in danger of being overwhelmed by the predominant Anglophone culture, and that such a law was thus necessary to protect the Quebec nation. Therefore it was deemed just from a nationalist perspective.

Similar conflicts over justice can be seen with respect to the issues of abortion, affirmative action, aboriginal rights, government economic regulation, the welfare state and so forth. Sometimes the clash is not so much between the followers of different ideologies, as between the followers of the same ideology who draw out different implications—usually related to tensions inherent in the ideology itself—and come to conflicting policy conclusions. For example, classical liberals will tend to argue that affirmative action programs violate the cherished principle of equality before the law and amount to reverse discrimination, while late (that is, fourth- and fifth-stage) liberals may support such policies in the belief that they enhance the freedom of those individuals who have suffered

---

[18]Single-party governments are the rule in most Anglo-Saxon democracies, including Canada and the United States. For example, the Canadian province of Ontario, in the space of a few short years, went from being governed by the democratic socialist policies of Bob Rae's New Democratic Party (1990-1995) to the economic libertarian agenda of Mike Harris's Progressive Conservative Party (1995-2002). In most continental European democracies, by contrast, multiparty coalition governments are the rule, arguably leaving greater scope for compromise among different ideological viewpoints and lessening the possibility of any one of them dominating the political landscape. In this respect, electoral systems based on proportional representation and the coalition governments they usually produce may function to dilute the monolithic power of a single ideological vision.

unjust discrimination in the past on racial or gender-based grounds. Both im-plicitly hold to the sovereignty of individuals and the primacy of their freedom, but each believes that opposing policies will further this freedom. Similarly, dif-ferent liberal approaches champion the right of the unborn child to life or the right of the woman to control her own body. Each seeks a justice consistent with its core beliefs. The irony is that while justice seeks to resolve conflicts, such seeking of justice is itself a cause of conflict if animated by more than one of the ideologies.

Justice and Differentiated Responsibility

No one reading up to this point will expect me to argue in favor of an osten-sibly objective, rational conception of justice as an alternative to the ideolog-ical notions mentioned above. Such does not exist, despite the efforts of some political philosophers to find one. Once again John Rawls assumes the pos-sibility of all rational persons coming to agreement on universally valid prin-ciples of justice to be arrived at through a reasoning process devoid of partic-ularizing commitments.[19] Similarly, Amy Gutmann and Dennis Thompson believe it possible to resolve divisive moral disputes in the political realm through a process of deliberation that accepts certain types of arguments, that is, those rooted in common rationality, while excluding others, for example, those based on a claim of divine revelation.[20] What such approaches ignore is the extent to which all theoretical activity, including theories of justice, is rooted in and conditioned by nonfalsifiable, pretheoretical assumptions of a basic religious character. To transcend the ideologies is not to transcend a par-ticular worldview, which is an impossibility for human beings created in God's image.

This is where the principle of differentiated responsibility (or "sphere-sover-eignty") enters the picture. Creation is, once again, pluriform. Human society is inevitably diverse, and this very diversity necessitates some mechanism for justly interrelating its multiple interests. Justice, in Paul Marshall's words, calls for "giving something its right, its created place in God's world."[21] Brunner af-firms that a Christian view of justice is inescapably tied to God's order of cre-

---

[19] John Rawls, *A Theory of Justice,* 2nd ed. (Cambridge, Mass.: Belknap, 1999), esp. pp. 142-61.
[20] Amy Gutmann and Dennis Thompson in *Democracy and Disagreement* (Cambridge, Mass.: Belknap, 1996), esp. pp. 56-57, 158-59.
[21] Paul Marshall, *God and the Constitution: Christianity and American Politics* (Lanham, Md.: Rowman & Littlefield, 2002), p. 56.

ation, that what is just is that which conforms to God's creative intention.[22] This created place is always a *limited* place. According to Newbigin, because of human sinfulness we have a tendency to claim more than we have a right to, that is, to try to transgress those created limits characterizing not only human persons, but all of God's creatures. This is as true of communities as of individuals, and insofar as it is true the quest for justice takes on a self-destructive character.[23] A healthy society, one characterized by what the Bible calls *shalom*, is one in which the various spheres of human activity develop in balanced, proportionate fashion. Individuals act responsibly within their own recognized sphere of authority. Marriages and families are treated not simply as contractual relationships to be entered and quit at will by sovereign individuals, but as genuine communities building up their members, imposing mutual obligations on them and mandating the proper nurture of their young. Commercial enterprises act so as to fulfill genuine needs and, accordingly, use the earth's resources in stewardly rather than exploitative ways. Churches properly preach the gospel, administer the sacraments and facilitate members in living the Christian life. Schools rightly educate their minor students and prepare them to assume full adult responsibilities. Finally, a wide variety of voluntary associations exist for a multiplicity of purposes as determined by their members.

Of course, in the real world, afflicted as it is by sin, societies tend to develop in lopsided ways, with one or more of these spheres claiming more than they have a right to. Under the influence of various forms of liberalism, the individual may assume too large a place at the expense of other spheres. Communities, including such basic ones as marriage and family, increasingly break down as they are deemed to serve no longer the wants of the aggregating individuals they comprise. The rights of individuals come to take priority over the rights of communities, even of institutional churches making unpopular lifestyle demands on their communicants as a condition for continued membership.

In chapter two we noted the tendency of liberals to exaggerate the place of the market and to extend its validity into areas where it does not properly belong. The principal virtue of the market is that it maximizes personal choice, and to the extent that it forges interpersonal relations, allows participating individuals to decide whether or not to continue these relations insofar as their own needs are adequately served. If a manufacturer has a long-term contract with a supplier who at

---

[22]Brunner, *Justice and the Social Order*, p. 89.
[23]Lesslie Newbigin, *Foolishness to the Greeks: The Gospel and Western Culture* (Grand Rapids, Mich.: Eerdmans, 1986), p. 119.

some point fails to live up to the terms of the contract, the manufacturer can easily abrogate the relationship and look elsewhere for another supplier. Classical liberals properly value the market, where inter-individual relationships are nonhierarchical, voluntary, and based only on mutual benefit. However, these same liberals find it difficult, if not impossible, to resist the temptation to extend this market-driven pattern into other spheres of life where it does not properly belong. Thus much of the rest of life beyond the market proper is caught up in the dynamics of production and consumption, of buying and selling. Political candidates are marketed as "products" intended to appeal to "consumers" at election time. Marriage is viewed as merely a voluntary relationship capable of being redefined at will by the partners as their respective needs change.[24] Wedding vows are routinely rewritten as deemed appropriate by the prospective spouses to express their own expectations of marriage, including its duration and their own level of commitment to each other.[25] More crassly, sex itself comes to be seen as a commodity. Prostitution is, of course, the most ancient example of the commodification of sex. More recently, the invention of the Internet easily brings the basest pornography into nearly anyone's living room or den.

In similar fashion freedom of religion comes to be interpreted not so much as the liberty of religious communities or of ecclesiastical institutions within their own spheres, but as that of the individual to worship as she pleases, possibly irrespective of the expectations of the faith community of which she is part. In such a context the authority of the institutional church, particularly its disciplinary authority, is seriously eroded, as members under threat of discipline can simply pick up and move to another congregation in another denomination with less rigorous standards for membership. Denominationalism, a phenomenon peculiar to the modern age, is at once a product of individualism run rampant and a contributor to its proliferation. That the phone book's yellow pages often carry the slogan "Attend the church of your choice" adjacent their lists of local churches is testimony to the commodification of even the church itself.[26]

In the consumer society it is not surprising that a number of giant, transnational corporations take on the sort of power usually associated with govern-

---

[24]See Gordon Wenham's argument to this effect in "Life and Death and the Consumerist Ethic," in *Christ and Consumerism: A Critical Analysis of the Spirit of the Age,* ed. Craig Bartholomew and Thorsten Moritz (Carlisle, U.K.: Paternoster, 2000), pp. 122-29.

[25]See David Blankenhorn, "I Do?" *First Things* 77 (November 1997): 14-15.

[26]See Nigel Scotland, "Shopping for a Church: Consumerism and the Churches," in *Christ and Consumerism,* ed. Craig Bartholomew and Thorsten Moritz (Carlisle, U.K.: Paternoster, 2000), pp. 135-51.

ments. Indeed the largest of such entities often rival the total resources available to the government of a single African or Asian state. Even in a country of subcontinental proportions such as the United States there is a twofold tendency for (1) the consumer culture to overtake other legitimate areas of life, including politics, and for (2) a small number of corporations to dominate this consumer culture. In such a context it is difficult to speak of a balanced development of society. Like Augustine's earthly city, our Western societies are driven by an inordinate love of self, in which everyone is caught up in the frenzied pursuit of personal happiness—that happiness being defined in largely hedonic, materialist fashion. Given this, it is difficult to persuade people that communal obligations have any place at all, much less those obligations irreducible to their autonomous wills.

There is another way in which society can develop in an unbalanced way. Within the grip of various statist ideologies, such as nationalism and socialism, the state may arrogate to itself more tasks than it ought to. This phenomenon is obvious with respect to totalitarian regimes, where the party-controlled state apparatus acknowledges no limit to its competence and reaches into virtually all areas of life in the interest of implementing the ideology's transformative agenda. Yet even—or perhaps especially—in a democracy there is a great temptation to assume that every problem arising is potentially a *political* problem capable of being resolved politically, that is, by means of direct government action. This temptation is abetted by the candidates for public office, who blame their opponents for doing nothing to solve a particular social problem and promise to do something themselves if elected in their place.

The field of education offers more than one example of this lopsided statism in action. In the United States, education is constitutionally a matter for the individual states, under the reserved powers granted them by the tenth amendment. Accordingly each state maintains a locally administered public school system supported by property taxes. This system is granted a legal monopoly over public funds allocated for education. Within the system parents must send their children to the school in whose district they live and are prohibited from sending them to another school across district boundaries. Moreover, and perhaps more significantly, although parents are legally permitted to send their children to a nonpublic school, that is, one that is structurally external to the public system, they suffer a significant financial penalty for so doing, insofar as they must pay the tuition fees for that school on top of the property taxes to support the government-controlled system. More than one observer has noted

the similarity between the public school systems and the established churches
of England and elsewhere in Europe, where everyone is born and baptized in
a particular parish and is compelled to support the state ecclesiastical establishment through church rates.[27]

To be sure, the government-controlled school was not invented in the
United States. The notion that education is intrinsically a governmental responsibility extends at least as far back as Plato and Aristotle, who argued that the
polis must inculcate in its citizens those civic virtues necessary for its continued
welfare. But for both Plato and even the otherwise more pluralistically inclined
Aristotle, the polis was a totalizing community of citizens with no intrinsic
structural limits, rather than a differentiated community recognizing and protecting its citizens' multiple responsibilities in a variety of overlapping settings.
Many political theorists in the two and a half millennia since then have devoted
at least some of their writings to education, assuming that its treatment is an
essential part of political theorizing.[28] It is not surprising, therefore, that so
many have refused to question the widespread, if not universal, assumption that
education is a primary responsibility of the governing authorities.[29]

Throughout the nineteenth and into the early twentieth centuries, it was
assumed that the American public schools were generically Protestant in orientation. Classes were begun with prayer and Scripture reading, although the
substantive content of the lessons might not be notably affected by an explicitly Christian worldview. This changed in the middle of the twentieth century
as a series of Supreme Court decisions, most notably *Engle* v. *Vitale* (1962) and
Abington School District v. *Schempp* (1963), declared these opening exercises in
violation of the first amendment to the Constitution. Under the impact of
Thomas Jefferson's famous "wall of separation" doctrine, ostensibly sectarian
religious influences were to be excluded, not only from government itself but

---

[27]See, e.g., the argument of Rockne McCarthy, James W. Skillen and William A. Harper, *Disestablishment
a Second Time: Genuine Pluralism for American Schools* (Grand Rapids, Mich.: Christian University Press,
1982).

[28]See, e.g., Locke *Some Thoughts Concerning Education* (1693) and Rousseau *Émile* (1762).

[29]It is particularly unusual to have someone challenge the government's educational monopoly from
within the liberal tradition. Among the few doing so are Richard S. Ruderman and R. Kenneth Godwin, who argue that a regime of school choice better reflects the intentions of early liberals such as
Locke and Mill. See Ruderman and Godwin, "Liberalism and Parental Control of Education," *The Review of Politics* 62, no. 3 (2000): 503-29. More typical is the argument of Amy Gutmann, "What Does
'School Choice' Mean?" *Dissent* 47 (summer 2000): 19-24, in which she argues, from a late liberal
perspective, that choice among nongovernmental schools is incompatible with the *public* character of
education.

also from public education, deemed an arm of government.[30] It should not be surprising that many parents, including those attached to the old unofficial Protestant establishment as well as those with more active Christian commitments, believe that a grave injustice has been perpetuated by successive court decisions that have increasingly excluded their own ultimate beliefs from the public system while making it difficult, if not impossible, for them to send their own children elsewhere.

Again it is evident that the society has developed not in a healthy and balanced manner, but in a lopsided manner in which the state has effectively overstepped its boundaries and assumed the educational role more properly belonging to parents. Some have responded to this imbalance in ways that would curtail the totalizing pretensions of the state but without adequately affirming the unique educational task of the school. Once again from the classical liberal camp one hears calls for parental choice in education, but structured along the lines of the marketplace. According to one such approach, schools would compete for tuition dollars from parents, and eventually government would play no role whatsoever in the educational field, leaving the education of the poor to the vagaries of private philanthropy.[31] But the school is not just another commercial enterprise. Much as the statist approach fails adequately to distinguish structurally the school from government, the classical liberal approach cannot account for the structural difference between the school and the business. Neither approach is adequate to make room for the school *as school.*[32]

Increasing numbers of North Americans are beginning to conclude that the

---

[30]Concerning Jefferson's role, see McCarthy, Skillen and Harper, *Disestablishment a Second Time*, pp. 15-44.

[31]See, e.g., Joe Klesney and Michael B. Barkey, "School Choice: A Prudent Path Toward Liberty," *Acton Commentary* (Acton Institute for the Study of Religion and Liberty), September 17, 2000 <www.acton.org/resources/comment/comment.html>. See also Milton Friedman, *Capitalism and Freedom* (Chicago: University of Chicago Press, 1962), pp. 85-107, for a similar argument that is widely held to have initiated the movement for educational choice based on a voucher system in the United States. Unlike Klesney and Barkey, however, Friedman is still willing to accord government a minimal responsibility in funding education. Yet the emphasis in both arguments remains the betterment of all schools through market competition rather than the primary responsibility of parents for their children's education.

[32]In her *Dissent* article "What Does 'School Choice' Mean?" Gutmann correctly argues against the market model championed by, e.g., Milton Friedman on the grounds that it is unable to account for the obvious difference between private restaurants in postcommunist Prague, which involve no public obligation, and the school's evident public purpose of preparing children "to exercise their rights and fulfill their responsibilities as citizens" (p. 22). Accordingly, she would limit school choice to that among charter schools remaining under public auspices. However, she unduly assumes that public purposes can be assured only under direct government control.

most just approach to education would see an end to the government monopoly and a recognition of the prior rights of parents over the education of their
own children. Some Canadian provinces have already gone some distance in
this direction, the furthest being Alberta, which partially funds independent
schools. Ontario fully funds a complete Roman Catholic school system in addition to the public system, under the terms of the *Constitution Act, 1867,* and
from 2001 it partially funded other confessionally based educational institutions
through tax credits.[33] The Netherlands probably has the most experience with
a system of educational pluralism, and it is seen as a possible model by many
North American proponents. In the United States several jurisdictions have experimented with state funding for independent schools and the formation of
alternative and so-called charter schools within the larger public system. Skillen
has argued that the fairest policy alternative would allocate public moneys to
each school-age child irrespective of which school her parents elect to send her
to. Contrary to a classical liberal, market-oriented approach, government
would still play a role in collecting taxes to ensure that some children are not
unduly privileged at the expense of others. But government would be prohibited from discriminating against a parent-chosen school on the grounds that it
is a "religious" institution.[34]

Justice, once again, gives everything, in Marshall's words, "its right, its created place in God's world." A genuine public justice free from the distortions of
the various ideologies, recognizes the plurality of things in God's world for
what they are. Insofar as it seeks a just state of affairs, it seeks not a static, final
"just society," but a dynamic society which develops in proper differentiated
fashion, where no one entity, be it an individual or community, is permitted to
grow cancerously at the expense of everything else. The state does not claim to
create such entities as marriages and families; it simply *recognizes* them for what

---

[33] For a discussion of issues surrounding religion and education in Canada see Lois Sweet, *God in the Classroom: The Controversial Issue of Religion in Canada's Schools* (Toronto: McClelland & Stewart, 1997). Admitting the injustice of the current system, particularly in Ontario, she would prefer greater open-ness to funding independent schools and an acknowledgment within public schools of the importance of religion. Nevertheless, Sweet brings to her analysis a certain patronizing tone toward the claimed revelatory character of the particular religions themselves. See also Sweet, *The Fourth 'R': Religion in Our Classrooms / En Toute Bonne Foi: l'École et la Religion* (Toronto: Atkinson Charitable Foundation, 1996).

[34] Skillen, "Educational Freedom with Justice," in *The School-Choice Controversy: What Is Constitutional?* ed. James W. Skillen (Grand Rapids, Mich.: Baker, 1993), pp. 67-85. See also Rockne McCarthy, Donald Oppewal, Walfred Peterson and Gordon Spykman, *Society, State, & Schools: A Case for Structural and Confessional Pluralism* (Grand Rapids, Mich.: Eerdmans, 1981).

they are and offers them its legal protection. It refuses to conflate banks and private charities, sporting teams and churches, universities and bowling leagues, art museums and logging companies, labor unions and government agencies. It demands a limited allegiance from its citizens, recognizing that other communities legitimately claim their own share of the person's loyalty. It understands that the person's status as citizen does not exhaust her full identity, with its multiple capacities and responsibilities. She is at once wife, mother, daughter, employee, school board member, consumer in the market (yes, there is a legitimate, limited place for this role), church member and citizen. No single one of these roles exhausts who she is as an image bearer of God. Nor is any one of these roles subordinate to another, overarching role that might take on idolatrous proportions. The state, for example, does not legitimately demand *ultimate* allegiance; only God himself can rightly do this.

What then is the state's proper jural task? How does it do justice in the midst of a society in which the various spheres of human activity tend to overreach their competence, to claim more than they have a right to? According to Marshall, "the governing authority is justly to interrelate the authorities—the areas of responsibility—of others."[35] It properly adjudicates the claims of these authorities and acts so as to ensure that they are granted the opportunity to develop in accordance with their respective callings before God. To be sure, the state cannot enforce these callings as such, nor can it determine their substantive content. This is the responsibility of each of the spheres themselves. But it can serve to protect the legitimate spheres of competence from encroachment by the others and thus remove at least some of the impediments to a healthy, balanced social development. It can protect the interests of consumers without assuming that consumption wholly defines them as persons. It balances the interests of the individuals and the multiplicity of communities found in a complex, differentiated society. It protects individual liberty without assuming that this necessarily trumps all communal interests.

In short, justice is not simply about protecting and advancing rights; it is more often about impartially adjudicating the interests of those making potentially conflicting rights claims. But if this is so, then neither is justice only about finding an acceptable compromise among these interests that would lead to a supposedly stable equilibrium or balance of powers. Otherwise justice comes close to being seen as equivalent to mere legality. To be sure, politics in the real

---

[35]Marshall, *God and the Constitution*, p. 60.

world necessitates a willingness to compromise—of accepting less than we might like—for the sake of civic peace. Yet a balance of powers acceptable only to those able to voice their own interests in the public square would inevitably leave out those whom Scripture calls the widow, the orphan and the stranger or sojourner, that is, those who are most defenseless and vulnerable and lack their own economic resources to fall back on. Furthermore, if government attempts to conciliate the diverse interests of society without a proper prior sense of the principle of differentiated responsibility and of the boundaries of the spheres it must undertake to protect, whatever equilibrium it succeeds in facilitating will indeed be an unstable one—one that simply leads to another form of lopsided social development. This is perhaps the major flaw in Bernard Crick's defense of politics, which otherwise quite sensibly counsels against importing utopian visions into the necessarily imperfect give-and-take negotiations that are part and parcel of an often untidy political process.

Justice and the State

Normatively speaking then, the state is more than the passive referee of classical liberalism, but far from the all-pervasive agent of the statist ideologies. The state is responsible to protect the differentiated responsibilities of the various spheres of society, including those of both individuals and communities. This jural task of the governing authorities is by no means an easy one with quick solutions to difficult problems. In our quest for justice, we should avoid taking sides too quickly without thoughtfully weighing the claims of all parties. We should never assume that individual rights must always take priority over communal obligations. But neither should we assume the inevitable rectitude of communal claims over the individual. Circumstances must be weighed in the balance, and we must be conscious of those principles that would enable us to determine what legitimately falls within the authoritative ranges of the pluriform structures of society, including individuals and the multiple communities in which they participate.

This points to a recognition of the central insight, and not only the fundamental deficiency, of each of the ideological visions we have explored. As liberalism has correctly acknowledged, the just state protects individual rights, but always with the understanding that such rights are not simply the exclusive property of the individual to be exercised absolutely and autonomously. They are, rather, intimately connected with the responsibilities individuals normatively have toward each other and toward the communities in which they are embedded. As conservatism has properly understood, the just state accords history and traditions their proper due, admitting not that they are ultimately normative in a historicistic sense but that they are integral to human life in community. With nationalism, the just state acknowledges the reality that people are inevitably embedded in communities of various sorts, some of which style themselves nations. It treats such nations justly, while refusing to see each as the all-encompassing focus of loyalty envisioned by nationalists. With the democratic creed, it acknowledges the just claims of citizens to the franchise, irrespective of their economic or educational status, but refuses to reduce justice to a simple following of an undifferentiated popular will. Finally, with socialism, the just state recognizes the claims of individuals and communities—some of which style themselves classes—to a fair share of the economic resources of a given body politic, while eschewing the inevitable socialist attempt to assimilate all legitimate forms of ownership into a single monolithic form.

Yet if the state has the divinely appointed task of justly interrelating the pluriform interests of society, including individuals and various communities, this raises the ancient question of *quis custodiet ipsos custodes*, or "who will guard the guardians?" If the state is responsible for ensuring that, say, transnational corporations do not overreach their normative competence, or that marriage be protected as a unique institution distinct from the private contract, who is there to ensure that the state itself remain within its normative boundaries? There is, of course, no supranational political authority capable of enforcing justice on national governments. Over the years the United Nations has issued numerous resolutions on various international and domestic issues that are routinely ignored with impunity by the relevant member states. But even if the UN were an effective supranational government, this would only bump the *quis custodiet* issue up one more level without resolving it in any way. The question remains as to who enforces justice when the government itself violates it.

To some extent we have touched on this question already in the previous chapter, when we examined the Roman Catholic principle of subsidiarity and the Reformed principle of differentiated responsibility, or sphere sovereignty. It is worth taking another look at these approaches, since they offer two distinct ways of addressing the issue. Under the more hierarchical conception of subsidiarity, when something goes awry in one of the institutions of society, a higher organ properly, albeit temporarily, steps in and sets matters straight. Once that institution is able to function normally again, the higher organ withdraws and allows it to do so. Because the institutional church is thought to be higher than the state, when the latter is not doing what it should (acting in the common good), the former is well within its mandate when it intervenes to correct it. In like manner the state is obligated to step in when a subsidiary community becomes unable to function according to its nature.

A Reformed approach offers two basic responses, one internal and the other external, to the *quis custodiet* issue. First of all, Calvin himself offered a *political*, rather than an ecclesiastical, remedy to the threat of tyranny. Accordingly lower magistrates might well be constitutionally authorized to check the power of a would-be tyrant. The American analogy to this is the famous checks and balances written into the United States Constitution. The Canadian counterpart could be seen in the constitutional principle of responsible government, in which the prime minister and cabinet must continue to enjoy the confidence of the House of Commons to continue governing. Virtually all Western countries have written constitutions that limit the power of government in some fashion. Even a country such as Great Britain, with its longstanding unwritten constitution, operates under conventions regulating the activities of parliamentarians and other officials through the force of usage and tradition. Such constitutional mechanisms are not, of course, foolproof, which can hardly be expected of a fallible human instrument. But they are a potent means of ensuring that a government continue to undertake its jural task in normative fashion. Democratic mechanisms also play a role in placing limits on government, although, as we have pointed out, they can work in the opposite direction as well. Nevertheless, where a government has to submit itself to the judgment of the electorate on a regular basis, it is less likely than an autocratic government to pursue policies egregiously detrimental to the common weal.

But there is also an external factor that must be taken into account. If government has a special calling to do justice with respect to adjudicating the interests of the pluriform structures of society, there is also a sense in which *all* of God's image bearers are called to do justice in a variety of individual and communal settings. When the Old Testament prophets instruct the people of Israel and Judah to "let justice roll down like waters" (Amos 5:24), to "do justice, and to love kindness, and to walk humbly with your God" (Mic 6:8), and to "seek justice, correct oppression; defend the fatherless, plead for the widow" (Is 1:17), they are communicating God's word, not simply to the political leaders, but to every member of God's covenant people in every capacity, whether political or nonpolitical.

No one should doubt, for example, that there is an element of justice within the family, even if justice is not its primary raison d'être.[36] Family members normatively treat each other in accordance with their respective offices, that is, their unique places within its structure. If parents treat their underage children as adults before they are ready to be so treated, they treat them unjustly. Brunner affirms that "the child should be respected as [God's] creation in the way befitting its specific mode of being."[37] To treat the child otherwise is to do her an injustice. When the Decalogue instructs children to honor their parents, it is similarly calling on children to do justice to their parents insofar as the latter exercise this divinely appointed parental office within the family. Similarly the prohibition of adultery within the marriage covenant is an expression of justice internal to the marital community itself.[38] Yet despite this mandate to do justice, the family, unlike the state, does not exist primarily for the sake of justice, either for its own members or for others. Employers and employees in a business firm are likewise called to do justice, not only to each other, but to those on the outside to whom they are providing the appropriate goods or services, and even to some extent to the earth itself whose physical bounty they are reaping. If we all understand that the family and the business enterprise are different things with different primary callings in God's world, we nevertheless acknowledge that each is called, as a secondary responsibility, to do justice to the people and things of creation, both within and without that particular institutional context.

This helps to provide at least the beginnings of an answer to the problem of the overextended government acting beyond its normative competence, though it may not solve it outright, especially in the short term. Given that all are called to do justice within the broad range of their life's responsibilities, there is ample cause to address the potential injustice of government from within the other authoritative spheres. The mere fact of people doing and seeking justice in their families, churches, businesses, labor unions, schools, art cooperatives and so forth in itself constitutes a potent limit to the totalizing pretensions of government. Furthermore, where the will to do justice is lacking in these nongovernmental spheres, no amount of government action to the contrary will be an adequate substitute for this lack. In a democratic framework, where the political participation of citizens is permitted and perhaps even encouraged, there is opportunity for them to associate with each other for the express purpose of alerting government to its basic responsibility for doing jus-

---

[36] See, e.g., Brunner's discussion of justice in the family order in *Justice and the Social Order*, pp. 142-47.
[37] Ibid., p. 89.
[38] Ibid., p. 143.

tice and for living within its own normative boundaries. This might be done by establishing a political party working for the deliberate goal of gaining or at least participating in political power, or it might be done by establishing a nonpartisan political action organization with the more modest aim of influencing those exercising such power. As a last resort some form of civil disobedience might be considered where a specific law egregiously violates justice. Whatever strategy is chosen depends largely on the institutional and cultural contexts in which it is pursued. But the mandate to seek justice is itself nonnegotiable, particularly for those claiming to follow Jesus Christ.

EPILOGUE

Toward the Future

Most political movements have sought to rally supporters with concise, catchy slogans that look good on banners and resonate well on the lips of marchers. *"Liberté, égalité, fraternité!"* "Life, liberty and the pursuit of happiness!" "Workers of the world, unite!" "All power to the people!" Such slogans have the virtue of being easily understood and of simplifying complexity for political purposes. However, they have also deluded potential followers into believing that salvation is a simple matter of, say, proclaiming emancipation, granting people their rights, decreeing universal prosperity, or legislating an end to poverty, oppression, homelessness and so forth. Along with this comes a tendency to assume that doing justice calls only for removing the impediments standing in its way, after which will come, almost naturally and effortlessly, the "just society." Perhaps the most famous example of this is Marx's assumption that a brief revolutionary act whereby the proletariat dispossesses the bourgeoisie will usher in the classless society.

We have seen, however, that doing public justice is not so easily summed up in a pithy epigram. Rather, it is a matter of the state fulfilling its divinely appointed jural task, that is, adjudicating the respective claims of the various, multiple spheres of society, weighing these claims carefully and coordinating them in such a way that society develops in balanced, proportionate fashion. A genuine justice will avoid the distorting idolatries of the ideologies that would give the individual or some communal structure—whether state, nation, corporation or economic class—more than its proper due. Moreover, it keeps its feet firmly planted on the ground and refrains from assuming that mere fiat is capable of ameliorating, much less eliminating, various social ills. It respects legitimate diversity and refuses to assimilate this diversity into a single institutional form—into an undifferentiated mass society—for purposes of achieving a supposedly ideal social order.

Given the inevitable complexity surrounding the doing of justice, it should not be surprising that the vision for which I have been arguing here does not lend itself very well to facile sloganeering. A Christian democratic movement—whether in its Catholic or Reformed manifestation—is not easily summed up in an appealing motto capable of inspiring popular enthusiasm for its cause. It is thus at something of a disadvantage relative to the other visions vying for a place in the political realm. Of course, one could conceivably adopt the refrain of the author of the biblical book of Daniel: God's "kingdom is an everlasting kingdom, and his dominion is from generation to generation" (Dan 4:3). Or "if a king judges the poor with equity his throne will be established for ever" (Prov 29:14). Or, once again, "let justice roll down like waters" (Amos 5:24). Yet each of these requires unpacking and fleshing out to derive just policy initiatives. No small amount of theoretical and political legwork is required for this.

On the other hand, what might at first blush seem like a disadvantage for the Christian democratic movement could turn out to be beneficial over the long term. If the ideologies are adept at facile sloganeering, it is precisely because their approaches are deceptively simple—"deceptive" in that they mislead people into believing that the goods they seek are all too readily available if they will only buy into their reductive worldviews. In short, they inevitably make promises they are unable to fulfill, based on a misdiagnosis of the human condition. If the march of communism seemed inevitable in, say, 1950, less than half a century later it had, if not quite breathed its last, at least outlived its historical moment. The old slogans live on in the deteriorating newsreels of the early heady days of the revolution, and many of the statues of Marx and Lenin still stand in the former Soviet heartland of the movement. But they endure solely as mute testimony to the failed promises of the vision they represent.

By contrast, if there are few concise rallying cries to which it can appeal, a Christian approach to politics and justice, *insofar as it avoids ideological thinking*, has the advantage of being more in tune with the world as God's creation, that is, as it really and irreducibly is. Christians must therefore be prepared to approach the political realm with both patience and confidence. It is thus appropriate to end on an eschatological note. Throughout Scripture we are assured that the ultimate victory over evil belongs to the God who has created and redeemed us. God's final triumph is recounted most colorfully in the apocalyptic books, such as Daniel and the Revelation. But we find it also in the Gospels, where Jesus promises, among other things, satisfaction to those who "hunger and thirst to see right *[dikaiosynē* or *justice]* prevail" (Mt 5:6 REB). We find it above all in the death and resurrection of Jesus and in the promise of his return, as recounted and foretold in the Gospels.

Is this cause for triumphalism among Christians? Not in the sense in which this word is usually meant. Many believers are tempted to march as if the battle were already won. Some are enticed into throwing proof texts at social and political problems as if this were sufficient to dispel all the demons of injustice in a single sweep. That "Christ is the answer" is a truth that too easily becomes a truism. Some unduly assume that if enough individual persons accept Christ as Savior, the restoration of social and political structures will follow as a matter of course. Others improperly attempt to use the state apparatus to effect a broader social transformation that can come only with multiple efforts from a variety of directions. Moreover, the crusading mindset risks not only underestimating the opposition, but harnessing Christian faith to one of the very ideological visions we have explored and analyzed.

However, the assurance of God's ultimate victory means, not that we are excused from the hard work of fleshing out the command to do justice in his world, but that we know the end of the story in advance. We do not know quite how the twists and turns in the ongoing plot will contribute to the final chapter, despite the efforts of some Christians to seek such knowledge. We cannot know how soon Christ will return to bring his kingdom to its promised plenitude. It may be tomorrow. It may be a thousand years from now. Nor can we know the extent to which our own fallible labors will contribute to its advance. But we do know that the finale will come and that God sees fit to use these frail efforts of ours for his own purposes and glory. In short, every act of doing justice, whether in the political realm or in any other realm of human activity, is a signpost to the coming of God's final reign of justice over the new heaven and new earth.

Soli Deo gloria! To God alone be the glory!

SELECTED BIBLIOGRAPHY

Listed below are selected works arranged in the following categories: general works, liberalism, conservatism, nationalism, democracy, socialism, Roman Catholicism, and neo-Calvinism and related schools.

General Works

Arendt, Hannah. *The Origins of Totalitarianism*. New York: Harcourt Brace Jovanovich, 1951.

Barth, Karl. *Community, State, and Church: Three Essays*. Garden City, N.Y.: Anchor Books/Doubleday, 1960.

Bell, Daniel. *The End of Ideology: On the Exhaustion of Political Ideas in the Fifties*. New York: Free Press, 1960.

Boxx, T. William, and Gary M. Quinlivan. *Toward the Renewal of Civilization: Political Order and Culture*. Grand Rapids, Mich.: Eerdmans, 1998.

Cochrane, Charles Norris. *Christianity and Classical Culture: A Study of Thought and Action from Augustus to Augustine*. New York: Oxford/Galaxy, 1957.

Colson, Charles, and Nancy Pearcey. *How Now Shall We Live?* Wheaton, Ill.: Tyndale House, 1999.

Crick, Bernard. *In Defence of Politics*. 4th ed. London: Weidenfeld & Nicolson, 1992.

De George, Richard T. *The Nature and Limits of Authority*. Lawrence: University of Kansas Press, 1985.

Ebenstein, Alan O., William Ebenstein and Edwin Fogelman. *Today's ISMS: Socialism, Capitalism, Fascism and Communism*. 10th ed. Englewood Cliffs, N.J.: Prentice-Hall, 1994.

Eberly, Don E. *America's Promise: Civil Society and the Renewal of American Culture*. Lanham, Md.: Rowman & Littlefield, 1998.

————, ed. *Building a Community of Citizens: Civil Society in the 21st Century*. Lanham, Md.: University Press of America, 1994.

Elshtain, Jean Bethke. *Democracy on Trial*. Toronto: House of Anansi Press, 1993.

Fogarty, Michael P. *Christian Democracy in Western Europe 1820-1953*. Notre Dame, Ind.:

University of Notre Dame Press, 1957.

Friedrich, Carl, and Zbigniew Brzezinski. *Totalitarian Dictatorship and Autocracy.* Cambridge, Mass.: Harvard University Press, 1965.

Fukuyama, Francis. *The End of History and the Last Man.* New York: Free Press, 1992.

———. *Trust: The Social Virtues and the Creation of Prosperity.* New York: Free Press, 1996.

Gairdner, William D. *On Higher Ground: Reclaiming a Civil Society.* Toronto: Stoddart, 1997.

Gellner, Ernest. *Conditions of Liberty: Civil Society and Its Rivals.* Harmondsworth, U.K.: Penguin, 1994.

Gibbins, Roger, and Loleen Youngman. *Mindscapes: Political Ideologies Towards the 21st Century.* Toronto: McGraw-Hill Ryerson, 1996.

Gushee, David P., ed. *Christians and Politics Beyond the Culture Wars: An Agenda for Engagement.* Grand Rapids, Mich.: Baker, 2000.

Havel, Václav. *Living in Truth.* London: Faber & Faber, 1986.

Ingersoll, David E., and Richard K. Matthews. *The Philosophic Roots of Modern Ideology: Liberalism, Communism, Fascism.* Englewood Cliffs, N.J.: Prentice-Hall, 1991.

Irving, R. E. M. *The Christian Democratic Parties of Western Europe.* London: George Allen & Unwin, 1979.

Jenkins, Philip. *The Next Christendom: The Coming of Global Christianity.* New York: Oxford University Press, 2002.

Kalyvas, Stathis. *The Rise of Christian Democracy in Europe.* Ithaca, N.Y.: Cornell University Press, 1996.

Kramnick, Isaac, and Frederick M. Watkins. *The Age of Ideology: Political Thought, 1750 to the Present.* Englewood Cliffs, N.J.: Prentice-Hall, 1979.

MacIntyre, Alasdair. *Whose Justice? Which Rationality?* Notre Dame, Ind.: University of Notre Dame Press, 1988.

Macridis, Roy C., and Mark L. Hulliung. *Contemporary Political Ideologies: Movements and Regimes.* 6th ed. New York: HarperCollins, 1996.

Mannheim, Karl. *Ideology and Utopia: An Introduction to the Sociology of Knowledge.* New York: Harcourt, Brace, 1936.

Milgram, Stanley. *Obedience to Authority.* New York: Harper & Row, 1974.

Mott, Stephen Charles. *A Christian Perspective on Political Thought.* New York: Oxford University Press, 1993.

Neuhaus, Richard John. *The Naked Public Square: Religion and Democracy in America.* Grand Rapids, Mich.: Eerdmans, 1984.

Niebuhr, H. Richard. *Christ and Culture.* New York: Harper & Brothers, 1951.

Novak, Michael, ed. *To Empower People: From State to Civil Society.* 2nd ed. Washington, D.C.: American Enterprise Institute, 1996.

O'Donovan, Oliver. *The Desire of the Nations: Rediscovering the Roots of Political Theology.* Cambridge: Cambridge University Press, 1997.

O'Donovan, Oliver, and Joan Lockwood O'Donovan. *From Irenaeus to Grotius: A Sourcebook in Christian Political Thought.* Grand Rapids, Mich.: Eerdmans, 1999.

Putnam, Robert. *Bowling Alone: The Collapse and Revival of American Community*. New York: Simon & Schuster, 2000.

———. *Making Democracy Work: Civic Traditions in Modern Italy*. Princeton, N.J.: Princeton University Press, 1993.

Sabine, George, and Thomas L. Thorson. *A History of Political Theory*, 4th ed. Hinsdale, Ill.: Dryden Press, 1973.

Seligman, Adam. *The Idea of Civil Society*. New York: Free Press, 1992.

Sennett, Richard. *Authority*. New York: Alfred A. Knopf, 1980.

Skidmore, Max J. *Ideologies: Politics in Action*. New York: Harcourt Brace Jovanovich, 1989, 1993.

Strauss, Leo. *What Is Political Philosophy? and Other Studies*. New York: Free Press, 1959.

Strauss, Leo, and Joseph Cropsey, ed. *History of Political Philosophy*. 3rd ed. Chicago: University of Chicago Press, 1987.

Taylor, Charles. *The Ethics of Authenticity*. Cambridge, Mass.: Harvard University Press, 1991. Published in Canada as *The Malaise of Modernity*. Toronto: House of Anansi Press, 1991.

———. *Philosophical Arguments*. Cambridge, Mass.: Harvard University Press, 1995.

Troeltsch, Ernst. *The Social Teaching of the Christian Churches*. 2 vols. London: George Allen & Unwin, 1931.

Voegelin, Eric. *From Enlightenment to Revolution*. Durham, N.C.: Duke University Press, 1975.

———. *The New Science of Politics*. Chicago: University of Chicago Press, 1952.

———. *Science, Politics & Gnosticism*. Chicago: Regnery Gateway, 1968.

Yoder, John Howard. *The Politics of Jesus*. 2nd ed. Grand Rapids, Mich.: Eerdmans, 1994.

Zuckert, Michael P. *The Natural Rights Republic: Studies in the Foundation of the American Political Tradition*. Notre Dame, Ind.: University of Notre Dame Press, 1997.

Liberalism

Beiner, Ronald. *What's the Matter with Liberalism?* Berkeley: University of California Press, 1992.

Berlin, Isaiah. *Four Essays on Liberty*. Oxford: Oxford University Press, 1969.

Bork, Robert H. *Slouching Towards Gomorrah: Modern Liberalism and American Decline*. New York: Regan Books/HarperCollins, 1996.

Boxx, T. William, and Gary M. Quinlivan, eds. *Public Morality, Civic Virtue, and the Problem of Modern Liberalism*. Grand Rapids, Mich.: Eerdmans, 2000.

Gairdner, William D., ed. *After Liberalism: Essays in Search of Freedom, Virtue, and Order*. Toronto: Stoddart, 1998.

Glendon, Mary Ann. *Rights Talk: The Impoverishment of Political Discourse*. New York: Free Press, 1991.

Grant, George Parkin. *English-Speaking Justice*. Sackville, New Brunswick: Mount Allison University Press, 1974.

Hartz, Louis. *The Liberal Tradition in America: An Interpretation of American Political Thought Since the Revolution.* New York: Harcourt Brace Jovanovich, 1955.

Hayek, F. A. von. *The Constitution of Liberty.* London: Routledge & Kegan Paul, 1960.

———. *The Road to Serfdom.* Chicago: University of Chicago Press, 1944.

Hobbes, Thomas. *Leviathan; Or, The Matter, Form, and Power of a Commonwealth Ecclesiastical and Civil.* 1651.

Ignatieff, Michael. *Human Rights as Politics and Idolatry.* Edited by Amy Gutmann. Commentary by K. Anthony Appiah, David A. Hollinger, Thomas W. Laqueur and Diane F. Orentlicher. Princeton, N.J.: Princeton University Press, 2001.

———. *The Rights Revolution.* Toronto: House of Anansi Press, 2000.

Kramer, Hilton, and Roger Kimball, eds. *The Betrayal of Liberalism: How the Disciples of Freedom and Equality Helped Foster the Illiberal Politics of Coercion and Control.* Chicago: Ivan R Dee, 1999.

Kymlicka, Will. *Liberalism, Community, and Culture.* Oxford: Oxford University Press, 1991.

Laxer, James, and Robert Laxer. *The Liberal Idea of Canada: Pierre Trudeau and the Question of Canada's Survival.* Toronto: James Lorimer, 1977.

Locke, John. *Two Treatises on Civil Government.* 1690.

Novak, Michael. *The Spirit of Democratic Capitalism.* New York: Simon & Schuster, 1982.

Nozick, Robert. *Anarchy, State, and Utopia.* New York: Harper Colophon, 1974.

Rawls, John. *Political Liberalism.* New York: Columbia University Press, 1993.

———. *A Theory of Justice.* Cambridge, Mass.: Belknap, 1971, 1999.

Ruggiero, Guido de. *The History of European Liberalism.* Oxford: Oxford University Press, 1927.

Sandel, Michael. *Liberalism and the Limits of Justice.* Cambridge: Cambridge University Press, 1982.

Schindler, David L. *Heart of the World, Center of the Church:* Communio *Ecclesiology, Liberalism, and Liberation.* Grand Rapids, Mich.: Eerdmans, 1996.

Spragens, Thomas A., Jr. *The Irony of Liberal Reason.* Chicago: University of Chicago Press, 1981.

Unger, Roberto Mangabeira. *Knowledge and Politics.* New York: Free Press, 1984.

Conservatism

Burke, Edmund. *Reflexions on the Revolution in France.* 1790.

Genovese, Eugene D. *The Southern Tradition: The Achievement and Limitations of an American Conservatism.* Cambridge, Mass.: Harvard University Press, 1994.

Harbour, William R. *The Foundations of Conservative Thought: An Anglo-American Tradition in Perspective.* Notre Dame, Ind.: University of Notre Dame Press, 1982.

Kirk, Russell. *The Conservative Mind: From Burke to Eliot,* 7th revised ed. Chicago: Regnery, 1986.

———. *The Politics of Prudence.* Bryn Mawr, Penn.: Intercollegiate Studies Institute, 1993.

Mahoney, Daniel J. *Aleksandr Solzhenitsyn: The Ascent from Ideology.* Lanham, Md.: Rowman & Littlefield, 2001.

Maistre, Joseph de. *On God and Society: Essay on the Generative Principle of Political Constitutions and Other Human Institutions.* South Bend, Ind.: Gateway Editions, 1959.

O'Sullivan, Noël. *Conservatism.* London: J. M. Dent & Sons, 1976.

Quinton, Anthony. *The Politics of Imperfection: The Religious and Secular Traditions of Conservative Thought in England from Hooker to Oakeshott.* London: Faber & Faber, 1978.

Rossiter, Clinton. *Conservatism in America.* Cambridge, Mass.: Harvard University Press, 1982.

Solzhenitsyn, Aleksandr. *The Gulag Archipelago.* 3 vols. New York: Harper & Row, 1974–1978.

———. *Letter to the Soviet Leaders.* New York: Harper & Row, 1974.

———. *Rebuilding Russia: Reflections and Tentative Proposals.* New York: Farrar, Straus & Giroux, 1991.

Sowell, Thomas. *The Vision of the Anointed.* New York: BasicBooks, 1996.

Taylor, Charles. *Radical Tories: The Conservative Tradition in Canada.* Toronto: Stoddart, 1982. The author is the late Canadian journalist, not to be confused with the better-known McGill University philosopher of the same name.

Nationalism

Anderson, Benedict. *Imagined Communities: Reflections on the Origin and Spread of Nationalism.* London: Verso, 1983.

Beiner, Ronald, ed. *Theorizing Nationalism.* New York: State University of New York Press, 1999.

Grant, George Parkin. *Lament for a Nation: The Defeat of Canadian Nationalism.* Toronto: McClelland & Stewart, 1965.

Hobsbawm, Eric. *Nations and Nationalism Since 1780: Programme, Myth, Reality.* Cambridge: Cambridge University Press, 1990.

Hutchinson, John. *Modern Nationalism.* London: Fontana, 1994.

Ignatieff, Michael. *Blood and Belonging: Journeys into the New Nationalism.* Toronto: Viking/Penguin, 1993.

Kohn, Hans. *The Idea of Nationalism.* New York: Collier, 1967.

Kupchan, Charles A. *Nationalism and Nationalities in the New Europe.* Ithaca, N.Y.: Cornell University Press, 1995.

Kymlycka, Will. *Politics in the Vernacular: Nationalism, Multiculturalism, and Citizenship.* Oxford: Oxford University Press, 2000.

Lukacs, John. *The End of the Twentieth Century and the End of the Modern Age.* New York: Ticknor & Fields, 1993.

McPherson, James M. *Is Blood Thicker Than Water? Crises of Nationalism in the Modern World.* Toronto: Vintage Canada/Random House of Canada, 1998.

Minogue, K. R. *Nationalism.* Baltimore, Md.: Penguin, 1970.

Moynihan, Daniel Patrick. *Pandaemonium: Ethnicity in International Politics.* Oxford: Oxford University Press, 1993.

Ortega y Gasset, José. *The Revolt of the Masses.* Notre Dame, Ind.: University of Notre Dame Press, 1985.

Pfaff, William. *The Wrath of Nations: Civilization and the Furies of Nationalism.* New York: Touchstone/Simon & Schuster, 1993.

Democracy

Fuller, Graham E. *The Democracy Trap: Perils of the Post-Cold War World.* New York: Dutton, 1991.

Gallup, George, and Saul Forbes Rae. *The Pulse of Democracy: The Public Opinion Poll and How It Works.* New York: Simon & Schuster, 1940.

Gutmann, Amy, and Dennis Thompson. *Democracy and Disagreement.* Cambridge, Mass.: Belknap, 1996.

Hatch, Nathan O. *The Democratization of American Christianity.* New Haven, Conn.: Yale University Press, 1989.

Kennon, Patrick E. *The Twilight of Democracy.* New York: Doubleday, 1995.

Kraynak, Robert P. *Christian Faith and Modern Democracy: God and Politics in the Fallen World.* Notre Dame, Ind.: University of Notre Dame Press, 2001.

Lasch, Christopher. *The Revolt of the Elites and the Betrayal of Democracy.* New York: W. W. Norton, 1995.

Lindbom, Tage. *The Myth of Democracy.* Grand Rapids, Mich.: Eerdmans, 1996.

Lippmann, Walter. *The Public Philosophy.* New York: Little, Brown, 1955.

Niebuhr, Reinhold. *The Children of Light and the Children of Darkness.* New York: Charles Scribner's Sons, 1944, 1960.

Rousseau, Jean-Jacques. *On the Social Contract.* 1762.

Tocqueville, Alexis de. *Democracy in America.* 2 vols. 1835-1840.

Socialism

Berlin, Isaiah. *Karl Marx: His Life and Environment.* Oxford: Oxford University Press, 1963.

Crosland, C. A. R. *The Future of Socialism.* New York: Schocken, 1963.

Djilas, Milovan. *The New Class.* New York: Harcourt Brace Jovanovich, 1957.

Harrington, Michael. *Socialism.* New York: Bantam Books, 1973.

———. *Socialism: Past and Future.* New York: Mentor/Penguin, 1989.

Hoeven, Johan van der. *Karl Marx: The Roots of His Thought.* Toronto: Wedge, 1976.

Lenin, Vladimir. *The Development of Capitalism in Russia.* 1899.

———. *What Is to Be Done?* 1902.

Lerner, Warren. *A History of Socialism and Communism in Modern Times: Theorists, Activists, and Humanists.* 2nd ed. Englewood Cliffs, N.J.: Prentice-Hall, 1994.

Lipset, Seymour Martin. *Agrarian Socialism: The Cooperative Commonwealth Federation. A Study in Political Sociology.* New York: Anchor Books, 1968.

MacIntyre, Alasdair. *Marxism and Christianity.* London: Gerald Duckworth, 1969.

Marks, Gary, and Seymour Martin Lipset. *It Didn't Happen Here: Why Socialism Failed in the United States.* New York: W. W. Norton, 2000.

Marx, Karl. *Das Kapital.* 3 vol. 1867-1895.

Marx, Karl, and Friedrich Engels. *The German Ideology.* 1845.

———. *Manifesto of the Communist Party.* 1848.

Nyerere, Julius. *Ujamaa—Essays on Socialism.* Oxford: Oxford University Press, 1968.

Schumpeter, Joseph. *Capitalism, Socialism, and Democracy.* 2nd ed. New York: Harper & Brothers, 1947.

Roman Catholicism

George, Robert P. *The Clash of Orthodoxies: Law, Religion, and Morality in Crisis.* Wilmington, Del.: ISI Books, 2001.

Gilson, Étienne. *Reason and Revelation in the Middle Ages.* New York: Charles Scribner's Sons, 1938.

John Paul II. *Centesimus Annus (On the Hundredth Anniversary of Rerum Novarum).* 1991.

———. *Evangelium Vitae (The Gospel of Life).* 1995.

———. *Fides et Ratio (Faith and Reason).* 1998.

———. *Solicitudo Rei Socialis (On Social Concern).* 1987.

Kraynak, Robert P. *Christian Faith and Modern Democracy: God and Politics in the Fallen World.* Notre Dame, Ind.: University of Notre Dame Press, 2001.

Leo XIII. *Graves de Communi Re (On Christian Democracy).* 1901.

———. *Immortale Dei (On the Christian Constitution of States).* 1885.

———. *Rerum Novarum (On the Condition of the Workers).* 1891.

Maier, Hans. *Revolution and Church: The Early History of Christian Democracy, 1789-1901.* Notre Dame, Ind.: University of Notre Dame Press, 1969.

Maritain, Jacques. *Integral Humanism: Temporal and Spiritual Problems of a New Christendom.* Notre Dame, Ind.: University of Notre Dame Press, 1973.

———. *An Introduction to Philosophy.* New York: Sheed & Ward, 1937.

———. *Man and the State.* Chicago: University of Chicago Press, 1951.

———. *The Person and the Common Good.* Notre Dame, Ind.: University of Notre Dame Press, 1966.

———. *The Rights of Man and Natural Law.* New York: Scribner's, 1943.

———. *Scholasticism and Politics.* New York: Macmillan, 1941.

Menczer, Béla. *Catholic Political Thought 1789-1848.* Notre Dame, Ind.: University of Notre Dame Press, 1962.

Pius XI. *Quadragesimo Anno (On Reconstructing the Social Order).* 1931.

Simon, Yves R. *Freedom and Community.* Edited by Charles P. O'Donnell. New York: Fordham University Press, 1968.

———. *A General Theory of Authority.* Notre Dame, Ind.: University of Notre Dame Press, 1962.

———. *Nature and Functions of Authority.* Milwaukee: Marquette University Press, 1948.

———. *Philosophy of Democratic Government.* Chicago: University of Chicago Press, 1951.

———. *The Tradition of Natural Law: A Philosopher's Reflections.* Edited by Vukan Kuic. New York: Fordham University Press, 1965.

Neo-Calvinism and Related Schools

Bartholomew, Craig, and Thorsten Moritz, ed. *Christ and Consumerism: A Critical Analysis of the Spirit of the Age.* Carlisle, U.K.: Paternoster, 2000.

Bavinck, Herman. *Our Reasonable Faith: A Survey of Christian Doctrine.* Grand Rapids, Mich.: Baker, 1977.

Bolt, John. *A Free Church, a Holy Nation: Abraham Kuyper's American Public Theology.* Grand Rapids, Mich.: Eerdmans, 2001.

Bratt, James D. *Abraham Kuyper: A Centennial Reader.* Grand Rapids, Mich.: Eerdmans, 1998.

Brunner, Emil. *The Divine Imperative.* Philadelphia: Westminster Press, 1947.

———. *Justice and the Social Order.* New York: Harper & Brothers, 1945.

Clouser, Roy. *The Myth of Religious Neutrality.* Notre Dame, Ind.: University of Notre Dame Press, 1991.

den Hollander, C., ed. *Christian Political Options on Education, Broadcasting, Party Formation, International Partnership, Economic order, Responsibilities in the Welfare State.* The Hague: AR-Partijstichting, 1979.

Dengerink, Jan. *The Idea of Justice in Christian Perspective.* Toronto: Wedge, 1978.

Dooyeweerd, Herman. *The Christian Idea of the State.* Nutley, N.J.: Craig Press, 1968.

———. *Encyclopedia of the Science of Law.* Vol. 1. Edited by Alan M. Cameron, translated by Robert H. Knudsen. Lewiston, N.Y.: Edwin Mellen, 2002.

———. *In the Twilight of Western Thought: Studies in the Pretended Autonomy of Philosophic Thought.* Nutley, N.J.: Craig Press, 1968.

———. *A New Critique of Theoretical Thought.* 3 vols. Philadelphia: Presbyterian & Reformed, 1953-1958. Translation and revision of *De Wijsbegeerte der Wetsidee.*

———. *The Roots of Western Culture.* Toronto: Wedge, 1979.

Goudzwaard, Bob. *Aid for the Overdeveloped West.* Toronto: Wedge, 1975.

———. *Capitalism and Progress: A Diagnosis of Western Society.* Grand Rapids, Mich.: Eerdmans, 1979.

———. *Idols of Our Time.* Downers Grove, Ill.: InterVarsity Press, 1984.

Heslam, Peter S. *Creating a Christian Worldview: Abraham Kuyper's Lectures on Calvinism.* Grand Rapids, Mich.: Eerdmans, 1998.

Kuyper, Abraham. *Lectures on Calvinism.* Grand Rapids, Mich.: Eerdmans, 1931. Originally delivered as the Stone Lectures, Princeton Seminary, 1898.

———. *The Problem of Poverty.* Edited by James W. Skillen. Grand Rapids, Mich.: Baker, 1991. Originally titled *De sociale vraagstuk en de christelijke religie* and delivered to the First Christian Social Congress in the Netherlands, 1891.

Langley, McKendree R. *The Practice of Political Spirituality: Episodes from the Public Career of Abraham Kuyper, 1879-1918.* Jordan Station, Ontario: Paideia, 1984.

Lugo, Luis, ed. *Religion, Pluralism, and Public Life: Abraham Kuyper's Legacy for the Twenty-First Century.* Grand Rapids, Mich.: Eerdmans, 2000.

Marshall, Paul. *God and the Constitution: Christianity and American Politics.* Lanham, Md.: Rowman & Littlefield, 2002.

————. *Thine Is the Kingdom: A Biblical Perspective on the Nature of Government and Politics Today.* Basingstoke, U.K.: Marshall Morgan & Scott, 1984.

Marshall, Paul, with Lela Gilbert, *Heaven Is Not My Home: Learning to Live in the Now of God's Creation.* Nashville: Word, 1998.

McCarthy, Rockne, Donald Oppewal, Walfred Peterson and Gordon Spykman. *Society, State, & Schools: A Case for Structural and Confessional Pluralism.* Grand Rapids, Mich.: Eerdmans, 1981.

McCarthy, Rockne M., James W. Skillen and William A. Harper. *Disestablishment a Second Time: Genuine Pluralism for American Schools.* Grand Rapids, Mich.: Christian University Press, 1982.

McIntire, C. T., ed. *The Legacy of Herman Dooyeweerd: Reflections on Critical Philosophy in the Christian Tradition.* Lanham, Md.: University Press of America, 1985.

Meeter, H. Henry. *The Basic Ideas of Calvinism.* 6th ed. Revised by Paul Marshall. Grand Rapids, Mich.: Baker, 1990.

Mouw, Richard J. *He Shines in All That's Fair: Culture and Common Grace.* Grand Rapids, Mich.: Eerdmans, 2001.

Mouw, Richard J., and Sander Griffioen. *Pluralisms and Horizons: An Essay in Christian Public Philosophy.* Grand Rapids, Mich.: Eerdmans, 1993.

Newbigin, Lesslie. *Foolishness to the Greeks: The Gospel and Western Culture.* Grand Rapids, Mich.: Eerdmans, 1986.

————. *The Gospel in a Pluralist Society.* Grand Rapids, Mich.: Eerdmans, 1989.

Peck, John, and Charles Strohmer. *Uncommon Sense: God's Wisdom for Our Complex and Changing World.* Sevierville, Tenn.: Wise Press, 2000.

Praamsma, Louis. *Let Christ Be King: Reflections on the Life and Times of Abraham Kuyper.* Jordan Station, Ontario: Paideia, 1985.

Runner, H. Evan. *Scriptural Religion and Political Task.* Toronto: Wedge, 1974.

Skillen, James W., ed. *Confessing Christ and Doing Politics.* Washington, D.C.: Association for Public Justice Education Fund, 1982.

————. *Recharging the American Experiment: Principled Pluralism for Genuine Civic Community.* Grand Rapids, Mich.: Baker, 1994.

————. *The Scattered Voice: Christians at Odds in the Public Square.* Grand Rapids, Mich.: Zondervan, 1990.

————, ed. *The School Choice Controversy: What Is Constitutional?* Grand Rapids, Mich.: Baker, 1993.

Storkey, Alan. *A Christian Social Perspective.* Leicester, U.K.: Inter-Varsity Press, 1979.

Van Dyke, Harry. *Groen van Prinsterer's Lectures on Unbelief and Revolution.* Jordan Station, Ontario: Wedge, 1989.

Van Til, Henry. *The Calvinistic Concept of Culture*. Grand Rapids, Mich.: Baker, 1959. Reprinted with a foreword by Richard J. Mouw, 2001.

Walsh, Brian J., and J. Richard Middleton. *The Transforming Vision: Shaping a Christian Worldview*. Downers Grove, Ill.: InterVarsity Press, 1984.

Wolters, Albert M. *Creation Regained: Biblical Basics for a Reformational Worldview*. Grand Rapids, Mich.: Eerdmans, 1985.

———. "Facing the Perplexing History of Philosophy." *Tydskrif vir christelike wetenskap*, 17, no 4 (1981): 1-17.

Wolterstorff, Nicholas. *Until Justice and Peace Embrace*. Grand Rapids, Mich.: Eerdmans, 1983.

Index

Abélard, Peter, 183
abortion, 26, 47, 63, 139, 146, 205, 251
Adler, Mortimer, 74
affirmative action, 251
Ajzenstat, Janet, 79
Althusius, Johannes, 223-24, 230
anarchism, 37-38, 154
Anderson, Benedict, 100-101
apartheid, 14, 184, 188, 197
Arendt, Hannah, 10, 20-22, 111, 127, 136, 170, 189, 246
Aristotle, 17, 48, 61, 79-80, 93, 153, 164-65, 215, 222-23, 239-40, 249, 256
Augustine, 28, 184, 189, 228, 242, 244, 249, 255
Augustine, 28, 30, 184, 189, 228, 242, 249, 255
authoritarianism, 143, 148
autocracy, 148
Babeuf, François-Noël, 161
Bagehot, Walter, 20, 85, 122
Bakunin, Mikhail, 155
Barabanov, Yevgeny, 120
Barth, Karl, 193, 197-98
Bartók, Béla, 116
Bavinck, Herman, 191
Bazarov, 78, 92
Beiner, Ronald, 113, 170
Bell, Daniel, 16
Berger, Peter, 136, 220
Berkhof, Hendrikus, 193
Berkowitz, Peter, 66
Beveridge, William, 169
Bill 101, 251
Blakeslee, Sandra, 63
Blankenhorn, David, 63, 254
Bloom, Allan, 33, 74
Bodin, Jean, 218, 230, 233
Bonald, Louis-Gabriel, Vicomte de, 86
Brunner, Emil, 197-98, 245, 247, 252-53, 263
Bryan, William Jennings, 134
Brzezinski, Zbigniew, 26
Burke, Edmund, 76, 85, 104, 147-48

Calvin, John, 84, 190, 200, 223-24, 230, 262
Calvinism, 183, 191, 223-24, 226, 230
capitalism, 18, 34, 55-56, 68, 82, 91, 100, 156, 158, 162, 169-70, 176, 180, 185-86
Carlson-Thies, Stanley W., 229
Chaplin, Jonathan, 238-39
Chrétien, Jean, 107
Cicero, 249
citizenship, 95, 98, 100, 129, 151, 170, 188, 196, 239, 248
civil religion, 20, 160
civil society, 95, 137-38, 220, 231
class struggle, 18, 156, 172, 174, 176
classical liberalism, 37, 52, 54, 59-60, 95, 260
Clogg, Richard, 112
Clouser, Roy, 10, 240
Cochrane, Charles Norris, 30-31
Cold War, 13, 16, 26, 45, 121, 134
common grace, 69, 229-30
communism, 13, 15-16, 20, 36, 43, 74, 83, 113, 121, 135, 137, 159, 168, 214, 220, 266
    Marxism-Leninism, 16, 31-32, 39, 73, 83, 155, 159
Condillac, Étienne Bonnot de, 17
conflict of interest, 238
Constitution Act, 1867, 107, 258
continentalism, 80
contractarianism, 78, 85
Cortès, Juan Donoso, 86
Courier, Paul Louis, 146
Courtois, Stéphane, 176
Cox, Harvey, 55
Cranmer, Thomas, 84
creation order, 30, 34, 131, 171, 183, 192, 195-96, 198, 200
Crick, Bernard, 10, 16, 20-22, 102, 128, 155, 260
Cropsey, Joseph, 74
Crosland, C. A. R., 169-70
cultural mandate, 93, 191,

193, 212
cyberdemocracy, 144
Cyprus, 106, 112, 136
Daalder, Hans, 135, 229
Dante Alighieri, 224
Darwin, Charles, 57
De George, Richard 148, 246-47
Declaration of Independence, 20, 46, 53, 67, 98, 131
Declaration of the Rights of Man and of the Citizen, 110
Descartes, René, 49
Destutt de Tracy, Antoine, 17-18, 21
differentiated responsibility, 233, 237-38, 252, 260
differentiation, 88, 191, 212, 214, 216, 233
division of labor, 54, 92, 145, 166, 174, 177, 214
Djilas, Milovan, 36, 168
Dooyeweerd, Herman, 101, 117-18, 215, 225, 233, 234-242
Douglas, Tommy, 77
Durham, Lord, 99
Dvořák, Antonín, 116-17
Eberly, Don E., 221
education, 21, 25, 96, 110, 126, 141, 147, 209, 228, 231, 255-56, 258
Eidsmoe, John, 122
Eller, Vernard, 198
Ellul, Jacques, 45, 80, 198
Elshtain, Jean Bethke, 9, 15, 34, 66, 109, 127-28, 137, 164, 221
Engels, Friedrich, 17-18, 57, 134, 145, 156, 158, 161-62, 172-75
Enlightenment, 23, 25, 30, 84, 225
Epicurus, 48-49
Ericson, Edward E., 72
eschatology, 30, 68, 194
European Union, 173, 205, 222
false consciousness, 18, 22
Fanfani, Amintore, 55-56
fascism, 38, 114, 134
federalism, 134, 136
feminism, 38, 176, 239